# VOICES OF
# TERROR

MANIFESTOS, WRITINGS, AND MANUALS
OF AL-QAEDA, HAMAS AND OTHER
TERRORISTS FROM AROUND THE WORLD
AND THROUGHOUT THE AGES

EDITED BY
WALTER LAQUEUR

Reed
PRESS

*This book is dedicated to the memory of*
*Yehoshafat (Fati) Harkabi*

---

## Voices of Terror

Published by Reed Press ™
360 Park Avenue South
New York, NY 10010

www.reedpress.com

Selected material in this volume originally appeared in the following:

*The Terrorism Reader*
published by Penguin in 1987

*The Guerilla Reader*
published by The New American Library, Inc. in 1977

Library of Congress Cataloging-in-Publication Data

Voices of terror : manifestos, writings, and manuals of Al-Qaeda, Hamas, and other
terrorists from around the world and throughout the ages / edited by Walter Laqueur.
        p. cm.
"Part One of the present book is based on the Guerrilla Reader first published in 1977. Part
Two comes from the Terrorism Reader which also appeared in 1977. Part Three, covering
more recent developments, appears for the first time in the present edition"—Pref. Includes
bibliographical references.
    ISBN 1-59429-035-0 (pbk. : alk. paper)
    1. Terrorism —History—Sources. 2. Guerrilla warfare—History—Sources. I. Laqueur,
Walter, 1921— II. Title: Terrorism reader. III. Title: Guerrilla reader.
HV6431.V65 2004
303.6'25 —dc22
2004010571

*Designed and composed by John Reinhardt Book Design*

**Printed in Canada**

10 9 8 7 6 5 4 3 2 1

# ACKNOWLEDGMENTS

Many entries in this Reader were translated into English for the first time. I would like to express my gratitude to the following translators: Anthony Wells (Clausewitz, Ewald, Emmerich, Valentini, Chrzanowski, Hron, Ruestow and others); The late Janet Langmaid (De Grandmaison, De Jeney, Blanqui, Von Decker); Zeev ben Shlomo (Stoltzmann); Hilary Sternberg (Davydov); Marion Rawson (Carlo Bianco); Hana Schlesinger (Romanenko); Robert Shileen (Red Brigades); Daniel Kowalski (ETA); and Odette Boya (Redha Malek).

For having helped me locate source material I am grateful to the directors and staff of the Library of Congress, the British Library, the London Library, the New York Public Library, the Swiss Federal Library (Bern), the Royal United Service Institution (London), the Library of Trinity College (Dublin), the Tel Aviv University Library, the Wiener Library (London), the Widener Library at Harvard, as well as private collections in Copenhagen, Paris, Biel, Berlin, Helsinki and Vienna.

# CONTENTS

# PART 1: THE TERRORISM READER

## SECTION 1: TYRANNICIDE

## SECTION 2: TERRORISM OLD AND NEW

# CONTENTS

## SECTION 3: TERRORISM IN THE TWENTIETH CENTURY

## SECTION 4: INTERPRETATIONS OF TERRORISM

# PART 2: THE GUERRILLA READER

## SECTION 1: THE AGE OF SMALL WAR

# CONTENTS

CONTENTS

## SECTION 5: GUERRILLA DOCTRINE TODAY

# PART 3: THE ORIGINS OF TWENTY-FIRST CENTURY TERRORISM

## SECTION 1: TERRORISM IN THE MUSLIM WORLD

## SECTION 2: TERRORISM—EAST, WEST, AND SOUTH

# CONTENTS

# PREFACE

S INCE SEPTEMBER 11, 2001, the literature on terrorism has grown expo-nentially, much of it one- or two-dimensional at best. It has tried to explain the motivation and describe the spectacular operations of a particular group of terrorists based mainly in the Muslim world. This was a necessary enterprise since these groups had not been the focus of much attention prior to the attacks on the World Trade Center and the Pentagon. But terrorism and guerrilla warfare began long before September 11, 2001, and it is not restricted to one specific part of the globe.

Terrorism and guerrilla warfare have a history dating back many centu-ries, quite possibly one that predates the advent of conventional warfare. The study of this history is not an academic exercise; however, a true understanding of the terrorist phenomenon is impossible without at least some knowledge of what has gone before. To give but two examples: dur-ing the 1970s it was common to regard terrorism as mainly, if not exclu-sively, left wing and revolutionary because the leading terrorist groups at the time in Europe, Latin America, and parts of Middle East, implemented the terminology of the far left.

This focus on one specific trend was based on a profound misjudgment. It assumed that terrorism was an ideology whereas in actual fact it was a strategy used by the extreme right and the far left, by radical nationalist and fanatical religious groups alike. Understanding the history of terror-ism on a worldwide basis would have obviated such a fatal misreading. In a similar way, suicide attacks have struck many observers in recent years as something totally new and unprecedented, though it is an ancient tactic. In fact terrorists attacks predating the twentieth century were almost all suicidal in nature because with daggers, short range pistols and unstable bombs, the attacker's prospects of survival were less than brilliant.

All this is not to say that history provides the key to some magical understanding of terrorism. History shows that terrorism is not a static phenomenon; what is true for a terrorist group in one country at a certain time is not necessarily true with regard to terrorism in another period on another continent. Hence the great difficulties associated with any attempt to generalize about terrorism. Specific political, social and cultural conditions predicate the way in which we will form an understanding of any given situation. What is true with regard to, say, the Irish patriots of the nineteenth century, or the anarchists and the Russian terrorists of the early twentieth century does not necessarily carry through to the Islamist terrorists of today. Again, one example should suffice: The old terrorism was selective in the main, directed against leading figures of the "establishment." The Al-Qaeda-type terrorism, on the other hand, is indiscriminate; the aim is to annihilate a more generalized enemy, not to carry out "propaganda by deed," as the anarchists put it. There were exceptions: few terrorist ideologues such as Karl Heinzen and Johann Most dreamed about weapons of mass destruction one hundred and fifty years ago. At the time, this was merely science fiction, and it was considered splenetic by most terrorists at the time. When an anarchist *litterateur* shouted on a famous occasion in Paris, "There are no innocents," the exhortation was not shocking. It was an absurdity.

The compiler of a historical anthology faces difficulties of another kind given the nature of contemporary terrorism. Nineteenth-century protagonists did not hesitate to talk openly about their aims, beliefs, and strategies. Karl Heinzen entitled his famous essay "Murder," and the ideologues of the Russian Social Revolutionaries (like Morozow and Tarnowski who are represented in the present volume) gave their brochures titles like "The Terrorist Struggle." Boris Savinkov, leader of the left wing insurrection in Russia, called his autobiography (a most interesting book still in print) *Memoirs of a Terrorist*. Needless to say, such titles would not pass muster in today's political climate.

It is interesting, though not perhaps altogether surprising, that in the measure terrorism became more indiscriminate it became more reticent in openly stating its aims. No one wants to admit openly that the murder of children is morally acceptable, that it might even be a useful weapon in the terrorist struggle, insofar as it weakens the spirit of the enemy. Public relations and projecting the right image matter even today and for this reason there has been a widening cleavage between terrorist propaganda and terrorist practice. Or, to put it in a different way, the true aims of terrorist groups are often stated in veiled terms or implication, and sometimes they are not stated at all.

Recent terrorists groups have given a bad name to terrorism. Once upon a time, the term signified a "value free" strategy that could be used for all kinds of causes by radical groups from all parts of the entire political spectrum—the extreme left and right, fanatical nationalists and religious zealots. In the view of much of today's media "terrorism" has become a dirty word. And while "terrorism" has been used indiscriminately in the media, the desperate chase for synonyms has only further confused a complicated situation. Having said this, I can find no compelling reason to rename this volume the Activist, or the Militant Reader. Part One of the present book is based on the *Guerrilla Reader*, first published in 1977. Part Two comes from the *Terrorism Reader* which also appeared in 1977. Part Three, covering more recent developments, appears for the first time, in the present edition.

I would like to express my gratitude to Marek Michalewski who helped me all along to prepare this volume.

Walter Laqueur, Washington, D.C., May 2004

# PART ONE
# THE TERRORISM READER

# SECTION 1
# Tyrannicide

# INTRODUCTORY NOTE

"T ERRORISM" HAS CROPPED UP since time immemorial, sometimes as a manifestation of religious protest, at still other times in the wake of political revolt and social uprisings. One of the earliest recorded examples came by way of the *sicarii,* a highly organized religious sect consisting of "men of lower orders" in the Zealot struggle in Palestine (66—73 A.D.). Messianic hope and political terrorism were prominent features, too, of a much better known sect, the Assassins, who appeared in Persia and Syria during the eleventh century and were later suppressed by the Mongols in the thirteenth century. Contempories of the Assassins described them as an order of almost ascetic discipline, who courted death and martyrdom and were avid millenarians. However, the origins of the doctrine of terrorism can be traced back much further; resistance to despotism was frequently justified in the writings of ancient Greek and Roman authors. Plato and Aristotle regarded tyranny as a perversion, and the worst possible form of government. The acts of the tyrannicides, from Harmodios and Aristogeiton onward, were glorified in the works of poets, playwrights, sculptors, and bards. It was quite immaterial to them that some of these liberators were selfishly motivated. Cicero noted in *De officiis* that tyrants always came to a violent end, and that the Romans usually acclaimed those who killed them. The civil virtues of Brutus and Cassius were praised by their fellow Romans—though not by all of them. Seneca was reputed to have said that no offering was more agreeable to the gods than the blood of a tyrant.

Medieval writers on tyrannicide generally chose well-known examples from the Bible as well as episodes from Greek and Roman history to demonstrate that usurpers should not be obeyed. The power of the king, as these writers saw it, was based on a contract with the people; if the king did not keep his part of the bargain, he could, and should, be removed. This, then, was the beginning of the concept of popular sovereignty, a concept discussed by both Protestant and Catholic authors.

In his *Republic* (Book IX), Plato (ca. 429–347 B.C.) dealt with the character of a tyrant whose supreme misery was that "he has to be master of others when he is not master of himself." But the question of tyrannicide was more fully discussed in the *Politics of Aristotle* (384–322 B.C.). (It should be noted that although the ancient Greeks regarded tyranny as the worst form of government, they thought little better of democracy.) The motif of tyrannicide also appears in the writings of ancient poets and playwrights. *The True History* of Lucian of Samosata (120 A.D.) relates how a man forced his way into the stronghold of a tyrant with the intention of killing him. Unable to find the tyrant, he kills his son, leaving the sword in his body. The tyrant finds his dead son and slays himself with the same sword. The assailant now claims that the killing of the son entitles him to the reward of tyrannicide.

The story of Marcus Junius Brutus (like those of Wilhelm Tell and Charlotte Corday, the slayer of Jean Paul Marat) has frequently been treated in world literature. Although Dante relegated the murderers of Caesar to the depths of hell, the Renaissance rescued them, and, in the eighteenth century, Brutus became something of a cult figure. The story of Brutus was told by Appian and Dio Cassius, but the classic account is by Plutarch, which served as the inspiration for would-be tyrannicides until the early nineteenth century. Plutarch's *Lives* appeared in 105–115 A.D., a century and a half after the slaying of Caesar. Marcus Tullius Cicero, on the other hand, was a contemporary of Brutus (Ciscero's son served in the Roman army under Brutus). Although he justified tyrannicide in his *De officiis,* Cicero was not personally involved in the plot leading to Caesar's murder.

A commentary on Thomas Aquinas (1225–1274) has been included in the present selection of texts in view of the enormous influence exerted by the writings of Doctor Angelicus on Catholic writers of subsequent generations. It deals not with Aquinas's main work, the *Summa Theologica,* but with his *Scriptum in secundum librum Sententiarum.* Max Lossen's *Die Lehre vom Tyrannenmord in der Christlichen Zeit,* from which the commentary on Aquinas is excerpted, was published in Munich in 1894.

Even earlier, tyrannicide was discussed by John of Salisbury (ca. 1120–1180), Thomas á Becket's secretary who was exiled to France where he served as Bishop of Chartres. In *Poycraticus,* his main work, tyranny per se is by no means condemned. Yet he contends that it is not only lawful but glorious to slay a tyrant if he sins against divine law, provided only that the killer is neither bound to the tyrant nor sacrifices honor and justice. *Poycraticus* retained its influence until the sixteenth century when the question of tyrannicide became a central issue in a school of mainly French Protestant writers known as the Monarchomachs. Perhaps the most influential of their pamphlets was *Vindiciae contra tyrannos,* published in 1579 under the pen name Junius Brutus. The authorship is in dispute, but most historians believe that it was written by Duplessis Mornay (1549–1623), who was political adviser to the king of Navarre. In this pamphlet, the author asks whether it is lawful to resist a prince who infringes the law of God, but he also raises other questions such as whether one should resist a prince who merely ruins the temporal state, and into whose hands the organization of resistance should be entrusted. Among Catholic writers dealing with the topic, Juan de Mariana (1536–1624) is the most outstanding. Mariana was a Jesuit professor who taught in Paris, Rome, and Toledo, where his main work, *De rege et regis institutione,* was published. Like his contemporaries, Mariana got sidetracked by questions such as the use of poison, which were hardly of paramount importance once the principle of tyrannicide had been accepted.

The most famous British works on tyrannicide are George Buchanan's *De jure regni apud Scotos,* published in London in 1579, and Colonel Edward Saxby's *Killing No Murder* which appeared in 1657. Buchanan (1506–1582) was a great Scottish humanist whose book created a scandal and which was ordered burned by an act of Parliament. *Killing No Murder* appeared in Holland under Saxby's pen name, William Allen. Saxby, a leveler and enemy of Cromwell, was executed after his return to England in 1658. His pamphlet was frequently reprinted and was given a new lease on life between 1793 and 1804 in a French edition. Vittorio Alfieri's *Delia Tirannide* influenced a whole generation of militants of the Risorgimento, including Giuseppe Mazzini, because it lent strength to their belief that it was their sacred duty to remove those princes and princelings who stood in the way of Italy's unification. Alfieri (1749–1803) is better known as the greatest Italian poet of this period. *Della Tirannide,* written in the early 1780s, was first published only after the French Revolution.*

---

* The most comprehensive study available is Mario Turchetti, *Tyrannie at tyrannicide de l'Antiquité à nos jours.* PUF, Paris, 2001.

ARISTOTLE

# THE ORIGIN OF TYRANNY

T HAT TYRANNY HAS ALL THE VICES both of democracy and oligarchy is evident. As of oligarchy so of tyranny, the end is wealth (for by wealth only can the tyrant maintain either his guard or his luxury). Both mistrust the people, and therefore deprive them of their arms. Both agree, too, in injuring the people and driving them out of the city and dispersing them. From democracy tyrants have borrowed the art of making war upon the notables and destroying them secretly or openly, or of exiling them because they are rivals and stand in the way of their power; and also because plots against them are contrived by men of this class, who either want to rule or escape subjection. Hence Periander advised Thrasybulus to cut off the tops of the tallest ears of corn, meaning that he must always put out of the way the citizens who overtop the rest. And so, as I have already intimated, the beginnings of change are the same in monarchies as in other forms of government: subjects attack their sovereigns out of fear or contempt, or because they have been unjustly treated by them. And of injustice, the most common form is insult, another is confiscation of property.

The ends sought by conspiracies against monarchies, whether tyrannies or royalties, are the same as the ends sought by conspiracies against other forms of government. Monarchs have great wealth and honor which are objects of desire to all mankind. The attacks are made sometimes against their lives, sometimes against the office, and where the sense of insult is the motive, against their lives. Any sort of insult (and there are many) may stir up anger, and when men are angry, they commonly act out of revenge, and not from ambition. For example, the attempt made upon the Peisistratidae arose out of the public dishonor offered to the sister of Harmodios and the insult to himself. He attacked the tyrant for his sister's sake, and Aristogeiton joined in the attack for the sake of Har-

11

modios. A conspiracy was also formed against Periander, the tyrant of Ambracia, because, when drinking with a favorite youth, he asked him whether by this time he was not with child by him. Philip, too, was attacked by Pausanias because he permitted him to be insulted by Attalus and his friends, and Amyntas the little, by Derdas, because he boasted of having enjoyed his youth. Evagoras of Cyprus, again, was slain by the eunuch to revenge an insult, for his wife had been carried off by Evagoras' son.

Many conspiracies have originated in shameful attempts made by sovereigns on the persons of their subjects. Such was the attack of Crataeus upon Archelaus. Crataeus had always hated his connection with Archelaus, and when Archelaus, having promised Crataeus one of his two daughters in marriage, did not give either of them to him, but broke his word and married the eldest daughter to the king of Elymaea when he was hard-pressed in a war against Sirrhas and Arrhibaeus, and then married the younger to his own son Amyntas, with the idea that he would then be less likely to quarrel with the son of Cleopatra. Crataeus took this slight as a pretext for attacking Archelaus, though even a lesser reason would have sufficed, for the real cause of the estrangement was his disgust of the king. And from a like motive Hellanocrates of Larissa conspired with him; for when Archelaus, who was his lover, did not fulfill his promise of restoring him to his country, he thought that the connection between them had originated, not in affection, but in the wantonness of power. Parrhon, too, and Heracleides of Aenos, slew Cotys in order to avenge their father, and Adamas revolted from Cotys in revenge for the wanton outrage which he had committed in mutilating him when a child.

Many, too, irritated at blows inflicted on the person which they deemed an insult, have either killed or attempted to kill officers of state and royal princes by whom they have been injured. Thus, at Mitylene, Megacles and his friends attacked and slew the Penthalidae, as they were going about and striking people with clubs. At a later date Smerdis, who had been beaten and torn away from his wife by Penthilus, slew him. In the conspiracy against Archelaus, Decamnichus stimulated the fury of the assassins and led the attack; he was enraged because Archelaus had delivered him to Euripides to be scourged, for the poet had been irritated at some remark made by Decamnichus on the foulness of his breath. Many other examples might be cited of murders and conspiracies which have arisen from similar causes.

Fear is another motive which has caused conspiracies in monarchies as well as in more popular forms of government. Thus, Artapanes conspired against Xerxes and slew him, fearing that he would be accused of hanging Darius against his orders—he being under the impression that Xerxes would forget what he had said in the middle of a meal, and that the offense would be forgiven.

Another motive for tyrannicides is contempt, as in the case of Sardanapulus, whom someone saw carding wool with his women, if the storytellers say truly; and the tale may be true, if not of him, of someone else. Dion attacked the younger Dionysius because he despised him, and saw that he was equally despised by his own subjects, and that he was always drunk. Even the friends of a tyrant will sometimes attack him out of contempt; for the confidence which he reposes in them breeds contempt, and they think that they will not be found out. The expectation of success is likewise a sort of contempt. The assailants are ready to strike and think nothing of the danger because they seem to have the power in their hands. Thus generals of armies attack monarchs. For example, Cyrus attacked Astyages, despising the effeminacy of his life, and believing that his power was worn out. Thus, again, Seuthes the Thracian conspired against Amadocus, whose general he was.

And sometimes men are actuated by more than one motive, like Mithridates, who conspired against Ariobarzanes, partly out of contempt and partly from the love of gain.

Bold natures, placed by their sovereigns in a high military position, are most likely to make the attempt in the expectation of success, for courage is emboldened by power, and the union of the two inspires them with the hope of an easy victory. Attempts in which the motive is ambition arise from other causes. There are men who will not risk their lives in the hope of gains and rewards however great, but who nevertheless regard the killing of a tyrant simply as an extraordinary action, which will make them famous and honorable in the world. They wish to acquire, not a kingdom, but a name. It is rare, however, to find such men; he who would kill a tyrant must be prepared to lose his life if he fails. He must have the resolution of Dion, who, when he made war upon Dionysius, took with him very few troops, saying that whatever measure of success he might attain would be enough for him. Even if he were to die the moment he landed, such a death would be welcome to him. But this is a temper to which few can attain.

There are two chief motives which induce men to attack tyrannies: hatred and contempt. Hatred of tyrants is inevitable, and contempt is also a frequent cause of their destruction. Thus we see that most of those who have acquired power have retained, but those who have inherited, have lost it, almost at once, for living in luxurious ease, they have become contemptible and offer many opportunities to their assailants. Anger, too, must be included under hatred and produces the same effects. Oftentimes the angry are more impetuous in making an attack, for they do not listen to reason. And men are very apt to give way to their passions when they are insulted. To this cause is to be attributed the fall of the Peisistratidae and of many others. Hatred is more reasonable, but anger is accompanied by pain, which is an impediment to reason, whereas hatred is painless.

In a word, all the causes which I have mentioned as destroying the last and most unmixed form of oligarchy, and the extreme form of democracy, may be assumed to affect tyranny; indeed the extreme forms of both are only tyrannies distributed among several persons.

---

Aristotle, *Politics* Book V

# THE TYRANNICIDE

TWO TYRANTS—a father advanced in years, a son in the prime of life, waiting only to step into his nefarious heritage—have fallen by my hand on a single day: I come before this court, claiming but one reward for my twofold service. My case is unique. With one blow I have rid you of two monsters. With my sword I slew the son; grief for the son slew the father. The misdeeds of the tyrant are sufficiently punished: he has lived to see his son perish untimely; and—wondrous sequel!—the tyrant's own hand has freed us from tyranny. I slew the son and used his death to slay another: in his life he shared the iniquities of his father; in his death, so far as in him lay, he was a parricide. Mine is the hand that freed you, mine the sword that accomplished all: as to the order and manner of procedure, there, indeed, I have deviated from the common practice of tyrannicides: I slew the son, who had strength to resist me, and left my sword to deal with the aged father. In acting thus, I had thought to increase your obligation to me; a twofold deliverance, I had supposed, would entitle me to a twofold reward, for I have freed you not from tyranny alone, but from the fear of tyranny, and by removing the heir of iniquity, I have made your salvation sure. And now it seems that my services are to go for nothing; I, the preserver of the constitution, am to forego the recompense prescribed by its laws. It is surely from no patriotic motive, as my adversary asserts, that he disputes my claim; rather it is from grief at the loss of the tyrants, and a desire to avenge their death.

Bear with me, gentlemen, for a little, while I dwell in some detail upon those evils of tyranny with which you are only too familiar. I shall thus enable you to realize the extent of my services, and to enjoy the contemplation of sufferings from which you have escaped. Ours was not the common experience: we had not one tyranny, one servitude to endure, we were not subjected to the caprice of a single master. Other cities have had their tyrant, but it was reserved for us to have two tyrants at once, to groan beneath a double oppression. That of the old man was light by comparison, his anger mildness, his resentment long-suffering; age had blunted his passions, checked their headlong impetus, and curbed the lust of pleasure. His crimes, so it is said, were involuntary, resulting from no tyrannical disposition in himself, but from the instigations of his son. For in him paternal affection had too clearly become a mania; his son was all in all to him; he did his bidding, committed every crime at his son's pleasure, dealt out punishment at his command, was subservient to him in all things; the minister of a tyrant's caprice, and that tyrant his son. The young man left him in possession of the name and semblance of rule; so much he conceded to his years. But in all essentials the son was the real tyrant. By him the power of the tyrant was upheld; by him and by him alone the fruits of tyranny were gathered. He it was who maintained the garrison, intimidated the victims of oppression, and butchered those who meditated resistance. It was he who laid violent hands on boys and maidens and trampled on the sanctity of marriage. Murder, banishment, confiscation, torture, and brutality—all bespeak the wantonness of youth. The father followed his son's lead, and had no word of blame for the crimes in which he participated. Our situation became unbearable: for when the promptings of passion draw support from the authority of rule, then iniquity knows no further bounds.

We knew moreover (and here was the bitterest thought of all) that our servitude must endure—ay, endure forever; that our city was doomed to pass in unending succession from master to master, to be the heritage of the oppressor. To others it is no small consolation that they may count the days, and say in their hearts, "The end will be soon; he will die, and we shall be free." We had no such hope: There stood the heir of tyranny before our eyes. There were others—men of spirit—who cherished like designs with myself, yet all lacked resolution to strike the blow. Freedom was despaired of; to contend against a succession of tyrants seemed a hopeless task.

Yet I was not deterred. I had reckoned the difficulties of my undertaking and shrank not back, but faced the danger. Alone, I issued forth to cope with tyranny in all its might. Alone, did I say? Nay, not alone; I had my sword for company, my ally and partner in tyrannicide. I saw what the end was like to be and, seeing it, resolved to purchase your freedom with my blood. I grappled with the outer watch, with difficulty routed the guards, slew all I met, broke down all resistance—and so to the fountainhead, the wellspring of tyranny, the source of all our calamities. Within his stronghold I found him, and there slew him with many wounds, he fighting valiantly for his life.

From that moment, my end was gained. Tyranny was destroyed; we were free men. There remained the aged father, alone, unarmed, desolate. His guards scattered, his strong protector slain; no adversary this for a brave man. And now I debated within myself: "My work is done, my aim achieved, all is as I would have it. And how shall this remnant of tyranny be punished? He is unworthy of the hand that shed that other blood: the glory of a noble enterprise shall not be so defiled. No, let some other executioner be found. It were too much happiness for him to die and never know the worst; let him see all, for his punishment, and let the sword be ready to his hand. To that sword I leave the rest." In this design I withdrew; and the sword—as I had foreseen—did its office, slew the tyrant, and put the finishing touch to my work.

And now I come to you, bringing democracy with me, and call upon all men to take heart and hear the glad tidings of liberty. Enjoy the work of my hands! You see the citadel cleared of the oppressors. You are under no man's orders, and the law holds its course; honors are awarded, judgments given, pleadings heard. And all springs from one bold stroke, from the slaying of that son whom his father might not survive. I claim from you the recompense that is my due, and that in no paltry, grasping spirit. It was not for a wage's sake that I sought to serve my country, but I would have my deed confirmed by your award. I would not be disparaged by slanderous tongues, as one who attempted and failed, and was deemed unworthy of honor.

---

*The Works of Lucian of Samosata*, Vol. 2
Leipzig, 1906.

# NO FELLOWSHIP WITH TYRANTS

For in exceptional circumstances that which is commonly held to be wrong is found on reflection not to be wrong. I shall illustrate my meaning by a special case which, however, has a general bearing. There is no greater crime than to murder a fellow man, especially a friend. Still, who would say that he commits a crime who assassinates a tyrant, however close a friend? The people of Rome, I tell you, think it no crime, but the noblest of all noble deeds. Did expediency here triumph over virtue? No, virtue followed in the train of expediency....

There can be no such thing as fellowship with tyrants, nothing but bitter feud is possible. And it is not repugnant to nature to despoil, if you can, those whom it is a virtue to kill; nay, this pestilent and godless brood should be utterly banished from human society. For, as we amputate a limb in which the blood and the vital spirit have ceased to circulate, because it injures the rest of the body, so monsters, who, under human guise, conceal the cruelty and ferocity of a wild beast, should be severed from the common body of humanity.

---

Cicero, *De officiis*

# BRUTUS

A ND NOW WORD WAS BROUGHT that Caesar was coming, borne on a litter. For in consequence of the dejection caused by his omens, he had determined not to sanction any important business at that time, but to postpone it, under pretext of indisposition. As he descended from his litter, Popilius Laenas, who, a little while before, had wished Brutus success in his enterprise, hurried up to him and conversed with him for some time, and Caesar stood and listened to him. The conspirators (for so they shall be called) could not hear what he said, but judging from their suspicions that what he told Caesar was a revelation of their plot, they were disconcerted in their plans, and mutually agreed by looks which passed between them that they must not await arrest, but at once dispatch themselves. Cassius and some others, indeed, had already grasped the handles of the daggers beneath their robes and were about to draw them, when Brutus observed from the mien of Laenas that he was asking eagerly for something and not denouncing anyone. Brutus said nothing, because many were about him who were not in the plot, but by the cheerfulness of his countenance gave courage to Cassius and his friends. And after a little while Laenas kissed Caesar's hand and withdrew. He had made it clear that it was in his own behalf and on something which closely concerned himself that he had consulted Caesar.

When the senate had preceded Caesar into the session room, the rest of the conspirators stationed themselves about Caesar's chair, as if they intended to have some conference with him, and Cassius is said to have turned his face toward the statue of Pompei and to have invoked it, as if it had understanding; but Trebonius drew Antony into conversation at the door and kept him outside. As Caesar entered, the senate rose in his honor, but as soon as he was seated the conspirators surrounded him in a body, putting forward Tullius Cimber of their number with a plea in behalf of his brother, who was in exile. The others all joined in his plea, and clasping Caesar's hands, kissed his breast and his head. At first, Caesar merely rejected their pleas, and then, when they would not desist, tried to free himself from them by force. At this, Tullius tore Caesar's robe from his shoulders with both hands, and Casca, who stood behind him, drew his dagger and gave him the first stab, not a deep one, near the shoulder. Caesar caught the handle of the dagger and cried out loudly in Latin, "Impious Casca, what doest thou?" Then Casca, addressing his brother in Greek, bade him come to his aid. And now Caesar had received many blows and was looking about and seeking to force his way through his assailants, when he saw Brutus setting upon him with drawn dagger. At this, he dropped the hand of Casca which he had seized, covered his head with his robe, and resigned himself to the dagger strokes. The conspirators, crowding eagerly about the body, and plying their many daggers, wounded one another, so that Brutus also got a wound in the hand as he sought to take part in the murder, and all were covered with blood.

Caesar thus slain, Brutus went out into the middle of the session room and tried to speak, and would have detained the senators there with encouraging words; but they fled in terror and confusion, and there was a tumultuous crowding at the door, although no one pressed upon them in pursuit. For it had been firmly decided not to kill anyone else, but to summon all to the enjoyment of liberty. All the rest of the conspirators, indeed, when they were discussing their enterprise, had been minded to kill Antony as well as Caesar, since he was a lawless man and in favor of a monarchy, and had acquired strength by familiar association with the soldiery and particularly because to his natural arrogance and ambition he had added the dignity of the consulship, and was at that time a colleague of Caesar. But Brutus opposed the plan, insisting in the first place on a just course, and besides, holding out a hope of a change of heart in Antony. For he would not give up the belief that Antony, who was a man of good parts, ambitious, and a lover of fame, if once Caesar were out of the way, would assist his country in attaining her liberty, when their example had induced him to follow emulously the nobler course. Thus Antony's life was saved by Brutus; but in the fear which then reigned, he put on a plebeian dress and took to flight.

And now Brutus and his associates went up to the Capitol, their hands smeared with blood, and displaying their naked daggers they exhorted the citizens to assert their liberty. At first, then, there were cries of terror, and the tumult was increased by wild hurryings to and fro which succeeded the disaster; but since there were no further murders and no plundering of property, the senators and many of the common people took heart and went up to the men on the Capitol. When the multitude was assembled there, Brutus made a speech calculated to win the people and befitting the occasion. The audience applauding his words and crying out to him to come down from the Capitol, the conspirators took heart and went down into the forum. The rest of them followed along in one another's company, but Brutus was surrounded by many eminent citizens, escorted with great honor down from the citadel, and placed on the rostra. At sight of him, the multitude, although it was a mixed rabble and prepared to raise a disturbance, was struck with awe, and awaited the issue in decorous silence. Also when he came forward to speak, all paid quiet attention to his words; but that all were not pleased with what had been done was made manifest when Cinna began to speak and to denounce Caesar. The multitude broke into a rage and reviled Cinna so bitterly that the conspirators withdrew again to the Capitol. There Brutus, who feared that they would be besieged, sent away the most eminent of those who had come up with them, not deeming it right that they should incur the danger too, since they had no share in the guilt.

---

Plutarch, *Lives VI*. With kind permission
of Loeb Classical Library (Harvard University Press:
William Heinemann)

# JOHN OF SALISBURY

# ON SLAYING PUBLIC TYRANTS

THE WELL-KNOWN BIBLICAL NARRATIVE of the Books of Kings and Chronicles shows, according to the authority of Jerome, that Israel was oppressed by tyrants from the beginning and that Judah had none but wicked kings save only David, Josiah, and Ezechiah. Yet I can easily believe that Solomon and perhaps some of the others in Judah recovered when God recalled them to the true way. And I will be readily persuaded that tyrants instead of legitimate princes were rightly deserved by a stiffnecked and stubborn people who always resisted the Holy Spirit, and by their gentile abominations provoked to wrath not Moyses only, the servant of the law, but God Himself, the Lord of the law. For tyrants are demanded, introduced, and raised to power by sin, and are excluded, blotted out, and destroyed by repentance. And even before the time of their kings, as the Book of Judges relates, the children of Israel were time without number in bondage to tyrants, being visited with affliction on many different occasions in accordance with the dispensation of God, and then often, when they cried aloud to the Lord, they were delivered. And when the allotted time of their punishment was fulfilled, they were allowed to cast off the yoke from their necks by the slaughter of their tyrants; nor is blame attached to any of those by whose valor a penitent and humbled people was thus set free, but their memory is preserved in affection by posterity as servants of the Lord. This is clear from the subjoined examples.

"The people of Israel were in bondage to Eglon, the king of Moab for eighteen years; and then they cried aloud to God, who raised up for them a saviour called Aoth, the famous son of Iera, the son of Gemini, who used both hands with the same skill as the right hand. And the children of Israel sent presents to Eglon, the king of Moab, by Aoth, who had made for himself

22

a two-edged sword having in the midst a haft of the length of the palm of the hand, and girded himself therewith beneath his cloak on his right thigh, and presented the gifts to Eglon. Now Eglon was exceeding fat, and when Aoth had made an end of presenting the gifts, he went away after his companions who had come with him. But he himself turned back from Gilgal where the idols were, and said to the king, 'I have a secret word for thy ear, O king.' And the king commanded silence. And all that were about him having gone forth, Aoth came unto him. And he was sitting alone in a cool upper room. And Aoth said, 'I have a word from God unto thee.' And the king forthwith rose up from his throne. And Aoth put forth his left hand and took the dagger from his right thigh, and thrust it into his belly with such force that the haft also went into the wound after the blade, and the fat closed over it. And he did not draw out the sword, but left it in the body where it had entered. And straightway by nature's secret passages, the excrements of Eglon's belly burst forth. But Aoth closed the doors carefully, and fastened them with the bolt and departed by a postern."

And elsewhere, "Sisara, fleeing, came to the tent of Jael the wife of Abner Cinei. For there was peace between Jabin, the king of Asor, and the house of Abner Cinei. Therefore, Jael went forth to meet Sisara and said to him, 'Come in to me, my lord; come in and fear not.' And he, having entered Jael's tent and been covered by her with a cloak, said to her, 'Give me, I pray thee, a little water because I thirst greatly.' And she opened a skin of milk, and gave him to drink, and covered him. And Sisara said to her, 'Stand before the door of the tent and when any shall come inquiring of thee and shall say, "Is there any man here?" thou shalt say, "No, there is none."' Then Jael, the wife of Abner, took a nail of the tent, and took likewise a hammer. And entering softly and silently, she put the nail upon the temple of his head, and striking it with the hammer, drove it through his brain fast into the ground. And thus passing from sleep into death he fainted away, and died."

Did she thereby win the praise or the censure of posterity? "Blessed among women shall be Jael the wife of Abner Cinei," says the scripture, "and blessed shall she be in her tent. He asked for water, and she gave him milk and offered him butter in a princely dish. She put her left hand to the nail, and her right hand to the workman's hammer, and she smote Sisara, seeking in his head a place for a wound, and piercing his temple forcefully."

Let me prove by another story that it is just for public tyrants to be killed and the people thus set free for the service of God. This story shows that even priests of God repute the killing of tyrants as a pious act, and if it appears to wear the semblance of treachery, they say that it is consecrated to the Lord by a holy mystery. Thus Holofernes fell a victim not to the valor of the enemy but to his own vices by means of a sword in the hands of a woman; and he who had been terrible to strong men was vanquished by luxury and drink, and slain by a woman. Nor would the woman have gained access to the tyrant had she not piously dissimulated her hostile intention. For that is not treachery which serves the cause of the faith and fights in behalf of charity. For verily it was due to the woman's faith that she upbraided the priests because they had set a time limit upon the divine mercy by agreeing with the enemy that they would surrender themselves and deliver up the city if the Lord should not come to their aid within five days. Likewise it was because of her charity that she shrank from no perils so long as she might deliver her brethren and the people of the Lord from the enemy. For this is shown by her words as she went forth to save them: "Bring to pass, Lord," she prayed, "that by his own sword his pride may be cut off, and that he may be caught in the net of his own eyes turned upon me, and do Thou destroy him, through the lips of my charity. Grant to me constancy of soul that I may despise him, and fortitude that I may destroy him. For it will be a glorious monument of Thy name when the hand of a woman shall strike him down."

"Then she called her maid, and, going down into her house, she took off her hair-cloth from her, and put away the garments of her widowhood, and bathed her body and anointed herself with the finest myrrh, and parted the hair of her head, and placed a mitre upon her head, and clothed herself with garments of gladness, binding sandals upon her feet, and donned her bracelets and lilies and earrings and finger-rings, and adorned herself with all her ornaments. And the Lord gave her more beauty because all this toilet was for the sake of virtue and not of lust. And therefore the Lord increased her beauty so that she appeared to the eyes of all men lovely beyond compare." And thus arriving at her destination, and captivating the public enemy, "Judith spake unto Holofernes, saying, 'Receive the words of thy handmaid, for if thou wilt follow them, God will do a perfected work with thee. For Nebugodonosor, the king of the earth, liveth; and thy virtue liveth, which is in thee for the correction of all erring souls, since not men alone, but also the beasts of the field serve him through thee, and obey him. For the strength and industry of thy mind is heralded abroad to all nations, and it has been told to the whole age that thou alone art mighty and good in all his kingdom, and thy discipline is preached to all nations.'" And in addition she said, "I will come and tell all things to thee, so that I may bring thee through the midst of Jerusalem, and thou shalt have all the people of Israel as sheep that have no shepherd; and not a single dog shall bark against thee, because these things are told to me by the providence of God." What more insidious scheme, I ask you, could have been devised, what could have been said that would have been more seductive than this bestowal of mystic counsel? And so Holofernes said: "There is not another such woman upon the earth in look, in beauty, or in the sense of her words." For his heart was sorely smitten and burned with desire of her. Then he said, "Drink now and lay thee down for jollity since thou hast found favor in my sight." But she who had not come to wanton, used a borrowed wantonness as the instrument of her devotion and courage. And his cruelty she first lulled asleep by her blandishments, and then with the weapons of affection she slew him to deliver her people. Therefore, she struck Holofernes upon the neck, and cut off his head, and handed it to her maid that it might be placed in a wallet to be carried back into the city, which had been saved by the hand of a woman.

The histories teach, however, that none should undertake the death of a tyrant who is bound to him by an oath or by the obligation of fealty. For we read that Sedechias, because he disregarded the sacred obligation of fealty, was led into captivity. In the case of another of the kings of Judah (whose name escapes my memory), his eyes were plucked out because, falling into faithlessness, he did not keep before his sight God, to whom the oath is taken; since sureties for good behavior are justly given even to a tyrant.

But as for the use of poison, although I see it sometimes wrongfully adopted by infidels, I do not read that it is ever permitted by any law. Not that I do not believe that tyrants ought to be removed from our midst, but it should be done without loss of religion and honor. For David, the best of all kings that I have read of, and who, save in the incident of Urias Etheus, walked blamelessly in all things, although he had to endure the most grievous tyrant, and although he often had an opportunity of destroying him, yet preferred to spare him, trusting in the mercy of God, within whose power it was to set him free without sin. He therefore determined to abide in patience until the tyrant should either suffer a change of heart and be visited by God with return of charity, or else should fall in battle, or otherwise meet his end by the just judgment of God. How great was his patience can be discerned from the fact that when he had cut off the edge of Saul's robe in the cave, and again when, having entered the camp by night, he rebuked the negligence of the sentinels, in both cases he compelled the king to confess that David was acting the juster part. And surely the method of destroying tyrants which is the most useful and the safest, is for those who are oppressed to take refuge humbly in the protection of God's mercy, and lifting up undefiled hands to the Lord, to pray devoutly that the scourge wherewith they are afflicted may be turned aside from them. For the sins of transgressors are the strength of tyrants. Wherefore Achior, the captain of all the children of Amon, gives this most wholesome counsel to Holofernes: "Inquire diligently, my lord," said he, "whether there be any iniquity of the people in the sight of their God, and then let us go up to them, because their God will abandon them and deliver them to thee, and they shall be subdued beneath the yoke of thy power. But if there be no offense of this people in the sight of their God, we shall not be able to withstand them, because their God will defend them, and we shall be exposed to the reproach and scorn of all the earth."

---

John Dickinson, translator. *The Statesman's Book of John of Salisbury,* © 1963, pp. 368–371. Reprinted by permission of Prentice-Hall, Inc., Englewood Cliffs, New Jersey.

MAX LOSSEN

# THOMAS AQUINAS AND THE QUESTION OF TYRANNICIDE

I N HIS CHIEF THEOLOGICAL WORK, the *Summa Theologica,* St. Thomas touches on the question of tyrannicide only fleetingly, in the course of a discussion of other ethical problems. The question of whether rebellion is a separate mortal sin is here answered in the affirmative and the contention that—according to the philosopher's teaching—the liberation of a people from tyranny is to be considered a laudable act met by the assertion that the shaking off of the yoke of tyranny is only to be counted an act of rebellion if it has rebellion as a consequence. Otherwise, it is rather the tyrant than the people who is to be considered the rebel. The killing of tyrants is nowhere explicitly discussed in the work; however, we find an indication of St. Thomas's views in those passages of the *Summa* where he deals with the right of self-defense and its limits. Here, following St. Augustine, he restricts the right to kill another human being to those cases where it is done by public authority and in the best interests of the commonweal. Self-defense on the part of an individual is permitted only insofar as it is an act of justifiable self-preservation—*cum moderamine inculpatae tutelae*—a proviso which has since provided welcome ground for sophistic interpretation, but which St. Thomas himself narrowed down even further by saying that the killing of an assailant was permitted only when it happened unintentionally and accidentally—*praeter intentionem et per accidens.*

A thorough treatment of the concept of the tyrant, and one which is very largely a continuation of the arguments in Aristotle's *Politics,* can be found in the first book on "The Rule of Princes," a work which can without doubt be attributed to him and which he wrote during the last years of his life. For him, too, just as monarchy is the best form of government, so tyranny, the corruption of monarchy, is the worst. In exactly the same way as the ancients, St. Thomas depicts the tyrant as a violent ruler, more comparable to a wild animal than a human being, who panders entirely to his own passions, sows discord among his subjects, drives them into poverty and degradation, and in short reduces them to the level of slaves. St. Thomas gives three means of either preventing or removing such tyrants: the first is to constitute the monarchy in such a way that the people (*multitudo*) retains the right of deposition—expressed in modern terminology, the establishment of popular sovereignty. The second means is appeal to a higher authority. St. Thomas does not state explicitly who this authority might be for his own age, but from what he says later we can unhesitatingly conclude that he is thinking in the first instance of the Roman Pope, for whom he arrogates the right to depose a tyrannical and, more especially, a stubbornly heretical prince and even to sentence him to death. For the Middle Ages, however, the responsibility for carrying out this sentence would hardly lie with the Church but, very probably, with the prince of a neighboring territory. He rejects the example of Aoth adduced by John of Salisbury, firstly on the grounds that the murdered Eglon was not a legitimate prince acting in a tyrannical way but an open enemy and secondly, and more emphatically, by setting the teaching of the apostles and the example of the Christian martyrs against the examples of the Old Testament.

Finally, as his third remedy against unbearable tyranny, St. Thomas recommends prayer to the King of Kings, to God. God, who can move the king's heart howsoever he pleases and convert him from sinfulness; for tyrannical kings are a punishment sent by God, who allows a hypocrite to reign because of the sins of the people.

St. Thomas expounds very similar ideas in his commentary on Aristotle's *Politics*. By contrast, there is one passage in his writings in which he appears to be putting forward a different viewpoint and it is this passage which has often been used to justify the claim that the teachings of later scholars in general, and of the Jesuits in particular, in no way differed from those of the "Angel" of the school. The passage in question is the famous one from the commentary on the *Magister Sententiarum* where the question of in which cases a potentate is not from God is discussed scholastically. One of the reasons advanced for why no one need obey an unlawful usurper is that Tullius praises Caesar's murderers as tyrannicides. St. Thomas tries to qualify this argument by maintaining that Tullius is in this case speaking of a violent usurper against whom no appeal to a higher judge was possible. "In this case," he concludes, "he who kills the tyrant in order to liberate his country is praised and rewarded."

St. Thomas's apologists have been right to point out that undue weight should not be placed on this single, ambiguous passage from a youthful work, at the expense of those others where he declares himself to be firmly opposed to tyrannicide. They have, however, been wrong to dispute that the passage does indeed contain a qualified justification of tyrannicide—the murdering of a *tyrannus in titulo*. A less partisan observer would have to concede that in this case the great theologian allowed himself to be directed more by his heathen authorities than by the prescriptions of the Gospels.

---

Max Lossen, *Die Lehre vom Tyrannenmord in der Christlichen Zeit* (Munich, 1894).

# JUNIUS BRUTUS
## (DUPLESSIS MORNAY)

# IN DEFENSE OF LIBERTY

I T IS THEN LAWFUL for Israel to resist the king, who would overthrow the law of God and abolish His church; and not only so, but also they ought to know that in neglecting to perform this duty, they make themselves culpable of the same crime, and shall bear the like punishment with their king.

If their assaults be verbal, their defense must be likewise verbal; if the sword be drawn against them, they may also take arms and fight either with tongue or hand, as occasion is. Yea, if they be assailed by surprisals, they may make use both of ambuscades and countermines, there being no rule in lawful war that directs them for the manner, whether it be by open assailing their enemy, or by close surprising; provided always that they carefully distinguish between advantageous stratagems and perfidious treason, which is always unlawful.

But I see well, here will be an objection made. What will you say? That a whole people, that beast of many heads, must they run in a mutinous disorder, to order the business of the commonwealth? What address or direction is there in an unruly and unbridled multitude? What counsel or wisdom to manage the affairs of state?

When we speak of all the people, we understand by that, only those who hold their authority from the people—to wit, the magistrates, who are inferior to the king, and whom the people have substituted, or established, as it were, consorts in the empire, and with a kind of tribunitial authority, to restrain the encroachments of sovereignty—and to represent the whole body of the people. We understand also the assembly of the estates, which is nothing else but an epitome, or brief collection of the kingdom, to whom all public affairs have special and absolute reference; such were the seventy ancients in

30

the kingdom of Israel, amongst whom the high priest was, as it were, president, and they judged all matters of greatest importance, those seventy being first chosen by six out of each tribe, which came out of the land of Egypt, then the heads or governors of provinces. In like manner the judges and provosts of towns, the captains of thousands, the centurions and others who commanded over families, the most valiant, noble, and otherwise notable personages, of whom was composed the body of the states, assembled divers times as it plainly appears by the word of the holy scriptures. At the election of the first king, who was Saul, all the ancients of Israel assembled together at Kama. In like manner all Israel was assembled, or all Judah and Benjamin, etc. Now, it is no way probable that all the people, one by one, met together there. Of this rank there are in every well-governed kingdom the princes, the officers of the crown, the peers, the greatest and most notable lords, the deputies of provinces, of whom the ordinary body of the estate is composed, or the parliament or the diet, or other assembly, according to the different names used in divers countries of the world; in which assemblies, the principal care is had both for the preventing and reforming either of disorder or detriment in church or commonwealth.

For as the councils of Basil and Constance have decreed (and well decreed) that the universal council is in authority above the Bishop of Rome, so in like manner, the whole chapter may overrule the bishop, the university, the rector, the court and the president. Briefly, he, whosoever he is, who has received authority from a company, is inferior to that whole company, although he be superior to any of the particular members of it. Also it is without any scruple or doubt that Israel, who demanded and established a king as governor of the public, must needs be above Saul, established at their request and for Israel's sake, as it shall be more fully proved hereafter. And for so much as an orderly proceeding is necessarily required in all affairs discreetly addressed, and that it is not so probably hopeful that order shall be observed amongst so great a number of people; yea, and that there oftentimes occur occasions which may not be communicated to a multitude, without manifest danger of the commonwealth. We say that all that which has been spoken of privileges granted, and right committed to the people, ought to be referred to the officers and deputies of the kingdom, and all that which has been said of Israel is to be understood of the princes and elders of Israel, to whom these things were granted and committed as the practice also has verified.

Queen Athalia, after the death of her son Ahazia, king of Judah, put to death all those of the royal blood, except little Joas, who, being yet in the cradle, was preserved by the piety and wisdom of his aunt Jehoshabeah. Athalia possessed herself of the government and reigned six years over

Judah. It may well be the people murmured between their teeth, and dare not by reason of danger express what they thought in their minds.

Finally, Jehoiada, the high priest, the husband of Jehoshabeah, having secretly made a league and combination with the chief men of the kingdom, did anoint and crown king his nephew Joas, being but seven years old. And he did not content himself to drive the queen mother from the royal throne, but he also put her to death, and presently overthrew the idolatry of Baal. This deed of Jehoiada is approved, and by good reason, for he took on him the defense of a good cause, for he assailed the tyranny and not the kingdom. The tyranny (I say) had no title, as our modern civilians speak. For by no law were women admitted to the government of the kingdom of Judah. Furthermore, that tyranny was in vigor and practice. For Athalia had with unbounded mischief and cruelty invaded the realm of her nephews, and in the administration of that government committed infinite wickedness. What was the worst of all, she had cast off the service of the living God to adore and compel others with her to worship the idol of Baal. Therefore then was she justly punished, and by him who had a lawful calling and authority to do it. For Jehoiada was not a private and particular person, but the high priest, to whom the knowledge of civil causes did then belong. Being himself the king's kinsman and ally he had for his associates the principal men of the kingdom, the Levites. Now for so much as he assembled not the estates at Mizpah, according to the accustomed manner, he is not reproved for it, neither for that he consulted and contrived the matter secretly, for that if he had held any other manner of proceeding, the business most probably would have failed in the execution and success.

A combination or conjuration is good or ill, according as the end whereunto it is addressed is good or ill; and perhaps also according as they are affected who are the managers of it. We say, then, that the princes of Judah have done well, and that in following any other course they had failed of the right way. For even as the guardian ought to take charge and care that the goods of his pupil fall not into loss and detriment (and if he omit his duty therein, he may be compelled to give an account thereof) in like manner, those to whose custody and tuition the people have committed themselves, and whom they have constituted their tutors and defenders, ought to maintain them safe and entire in all their rights and privileges. To be short, as it is lawful for a whole people to resist and oppose tyranny, so likewise the principal persons of the kingdom may as heads, and for the good of the whole body, confederate and associate themselves together. And as in a public state, that which is done by the greatest part is esteemed and taken as the act of all, so in like manner must it be said to be done, which the better part of the most principal have acted, briefly, that all the people had their hand in it. ...

Now, seeing that the people choose and establish their kings, it follows that the whole body of the people is above the king; for it is a thing most evident that he who is established by another is accounted under him who has established him, and he who receives his authority from another is less than he from whom he derives his power. Potiphar the Egyptian sets Joseph over all his house; Nebuchadnezar, Daniel over the province of Babylon; Darius the six-score governors over the kingdom. It is commonly said that masters establish their servants, kings their officers. In like manner, also, the people establish the king as administrator of the commonwealth. Good kings have not disdained this title; yea, the bad ones themselves have affected it. Insomuch as for the space of divers ages, no Roman emperor (if it were not some absolute tyrant, as Nero, Domitian or Caligula) would suffer himself to be called lord. Furthermore, it must necessarily be that kings were instituted for the people's sake. Neither can it be that for the pleasure of some hundreds of men, and without doubt more foolish and worse than many of the other, all the rest were made; but much rather that these hundred were made for the use and service of all the other, and reason requires that he be preferred above the other, who was made only to and for his occasion: so it is that for the ship's sail the owner appoints a pilot over her, who sits at the helm and looks that she keep her course, nor run not upon any dangerous shelf. The pilot doing his duty is obeyed by the mariners; yea, and of himself who is owner of the vessel, notwithstanding, the pilot is a servant as well as the least in the ship, from whom he only differs in this, that he serves in a better place than they do.

In a commonwealth, commonly compared to a ship, the king holds the place of pilot. The people in general are owners of the vessel, obeying the pilot, whilst he is careful of the public good. This pilot neither is nor ought to be esteemed other than servant to the public—as a judge or general in war differs little from other officers, but that he is bound to bear greater burdens and expose himself to more dangers. By the same reason also which the king gains by acquisition of arms, be it that he possesses himself of frontier places in warring on the enemy, or that which he gets by escheats or confiscations, he gets it to the kingdom and not to himself, to wit, to the people, of whom the kingdom is composed, no more nor less than the servant does for his master. Neither may one contract or oblige themselves to him, but by and with reference to the authority derived from the people. Furthermore, there is an infinite sort of people who live without a king, but we cannot imagine a king without people.

---

Junius Brutus, *Vindiciae contra Tyrannos* (n.p., 1579).

JUAN DE MARIANA

# WHETHER IT IS RIGHT TO DESTROY A TYRANT

W E REFLECT, in all history that whoever took the lead in killing tyrants was held in great honor. What indeed carried the name of Thrasybulus in glory to the heavens unless it was the fact that he freed his country from the oppressive domination of the Thirty Tyrants? Why should I mention Harmodios Aristogeiton? Why the two Brutuses, whose praise is most gratefully enshrined in the memory of posterity and is born witness to with the peoples' approval? Many conspired against Domitius Nero with luckless result, and yet without censure, but rather with the praise of all ages. Thus Caius, a grievous and sinful monster, was killed by the conspiracy of Charea; Domitian fell by the sword of Stephen; and Caracalla, by Martial's. The Praetorians slew Elagabalus, a monstrosity and disgrace of the empire—his sin atoned for by his own blood.

Whoever criticized the boldness of these men, and not rather considered it worthy of the highest commendations? Also, common sense, like the voice of nature, has been put into our minds, a law sounding in our ears, by which we distinguish the honest from the base.

You may add that a tyrant is like a beast, wild and monstrous, that throws himself in every possible direction, lays everything waste, seizes, burns, and spreads carnage and grief with tooth, nail, and horn.

Would you be of the opinion that anyone who delivered the state safely at the peril of his own life ought to be ignored, or rather would you not honor him? Would you determine that all must make an armed fight against something resembling a cruel monster that is burdening the earth? And that an end to butchery would not be reached so long as he lived? If you should see your most dear mother or your wife misused in your presence, and not aid if you were able, you would be cruel and you incur the

34

opprobrium of worthlessness and impiety. Would you leave to the tyrant your native land, to which you owe more than to your parents, to be harassed and disturbed at his pleasure? Out with such iniquity and depravity! Even if life, safety, fortune are imperiled, we will save our country free from danger, we will save our country from destruction.

These are the arguments of both sides; and after we have considered them carefully, it will not be difficult to set forth what must be decided about the main point under discussion. Indeed, in this I see that both the philosophers and theologians agree, that the prince who seizes the state with force and arms, and with no legal right, no public, civic approval, may be killed by anyone and deprived of his life and position. Since he is a public enemy and afflicts his fatherland with every evil, since truly and in a proper sense he is clothed with the title and character of tyrant, he may be removed by any means and gotten rid of by as much violence as he used in seizing his power.

Thus meritoriously did Ehud, having worked himself by gifts into the favor of Eglon, king of the Moabites, stab him in the belly with a poniard and slay him; he snatched his own people from a hard slavery, by which they had been oppressed for then eighteen years.

It is true that if the prince holds the power with the consent of the people or by hereditary right, his vices and licentiousness must be tolerated up to the point when he goes beyond those laws of honor and decency by which he is bound. Rulers, really, should not be lightly changed, lest we run into greater evils, and serious disturbances arise, as was set forth at the beginning of this discussion.

But if he is destroying the state, considers public and private fortunes as his prey, is holding the laws of the land and our holy religion in contempt, if he makes a virtue out of haughtiness, audacity, and irreverence against heaven, one must not ignore it.

Nevertheless, careful consideration must be given to what measures should be adopted to get rid of the ruler, lest evil pile on evil, and crime is avenged with crime.

In this the procedure should be by the following steps: first, the prince must be warned and invited to come to his senses. If he complies, if he satisfies the commonwealth, and corrects the error of his way, I think that it must stop there, and sharper remedies must not be attempted. Second, if he refuses to mend his ways, and if no hope of a safe course remains, after the resolution has been announced, it will be permissible for the commonwealth to rescind his first grant of power. And, third, since war will necessarily be stirred up, it will be in order to arrange the plans for driving him out, for providing arms, for imposing levies on the people for the expenses of the war. Fourth, if circumstances require, and the commonwealth is not able otherwise to protect itself, it is right, by the same law of defense and even by an authority more potent and explicit, to declare the prince a public enemy and put him to the sword.

Let the same means be available to any individual, who, having given up the hope of escaping punishment and with disregard for his personal safety, wishes to make the attempt to aid the commonwealth.

You would ask what must be done, if the practicability of public assembly is taken away, as can often happen. There will be, truly, in my opinion at least, no change in the decision, since, when the state is crushed by the tyranny of the ruler and facility for assembly is taken away from the citizens, there would be no lack of desire to destroy the tyrant, to avenge the crimes of the ruler—now plainly seen and intolerable—and to crush his destructive attempts. And so, if the sacred fatherland is falling in ruins and its fall is attracting the public enemies into the province, I think that he who bows to the public's prayers and tries to kill the tyrant will have acted in no wise unjustly. And this is strengthened enough by those arguments against the tyrant which are put at a later place in this discussion.

So the question of fact remains, who justly may be held to be a tyrant, for the question of law is plain that it is right to kill one.

Now there is no danger that many, because of this theory, will make mad attempts against the lives of the princes on the pretext that they are tyrants. For we do not leave this to the decision of any individual, or even to the judgment of many, unless the voice of the people publicly takes part, and learned and serious men are associated in the deliberation.

Human affairs would be very admirably carried on, if many men of brave heart were found in defense of the liberty of the fatherland, contemptuous of life and safety; but the desire for self-preservation, often not disposed to attempt big things, will hold back very many people.

Finally, we are of the opinion that upheavals in the commonwealth must be avoided. Precaution must be taken lest joy run wild briefly on account of the deposition of a tyrant and then turn out sterile. On the other hand, every remedy must be tried to bring the ruler to right views before that extreme and most serious course is reached. But if every hope is gone, if the public safety and the sanctity of religion are put in danger, who will be so unintelligent as not to admit that it is permissible to take arms and kill the tyrant, justly and according to the statutes? Would one, perhaps, be influenced unduly that the proposition was disapproved by the Fathers in the fifteenth session of the Council of Constance, that "a tyrant may and ought to be killed by any subject, not only openly with violence but also through conspiracy and plots"? But this decision I do not find approved by the Roman Pontiff, Martin V, nor by Eugenius or his successors, by whose consent the legality of the proceedings of ecclesiastical councils is confirmed; this council's decrees especially needed approval, since we know that it was held not without disturbance of the Church on account of the three-way disagreement of claimants struggling for the supreme pontificate.

So it is generally known that it is legal to kill a tyrant openly by force of arms, either by breaking into his palace or by starting a civil disturbance.

But it has been undertaken also by guile and treachery. This Ehud did; by bringing gifts and feigning a message from above he got close enough, and when the witnesses had left he killed Eglon, king of the Moabites.

It is, indeed, more manly and spirited to show your hate openly, to rush upon the enemy of the state in public; but it is not less prudent to seize the opportunity for guileful stratagems, which may be carried out without commotion and surely with less public and individual danger.

So, I praise the custom of the Lacedaemonians in their sacrificing to Mars, the protector in battle (as deluded antiquity thought), with a white cock, when the victory had been gained in battle. When, however, the enemy were overcome by ambushes and cunning, they sacrificed a fat bull, as if it is more outstanding to conquer the enemy and keep the army intact by prudence and reasoning power, which distinguish us as men, than by main strength and robustness, in which we are surpassed by the beasts. Besides, there is the point of great loss on one's side.

Yet there is a question whether there is equal virtue in killing a public enemy and tyrant (indeed, they are considered the same) by poison and lethal herbs. A certain prince asked me this years ago in Sicily, when I was teaching theology in that island. We know that it has often been done. We do not think that there will be anyone, bent on killing, who, because of the opinion of the theologians, will neglect and pass up the offered opportunity of inflicting this kind of death and prefer to make the assault with the sword, especially in view of the lesser danger and the greater hope of escape. By this method the public joy is not less, when the enemy is destroyed, but the author and architect of the public safety and liberty is saved.

However, we regard not what men are likely to do but what is permitted by natural law. From a rational standpoint, what difference does it make whether you kill by steel or poison, especially since the means of acting by fraud and deceit are conceded? Now, there are many examples in ancient and modern history of enemies killed in this manner. It is, of course, hard to poison a prince, surrounded as he is by his ministers of the court; besides, he is in the habit of having his food tried by a taster. It is difficult to break through the massive citadel of the regal mode of life.

But if an opportune occasion would be offered, who will have such an acute intellect, be so keen in discrimination as to strive to distinguish between the two kinds of death? At least, I will not deny that great force inheres in these arguments; that there will be those that are led on by these reasons and will approve this type of death, as in consonance with justice and equity and in agreement with what has been said—namely, that a tyrant or public enemy is killed justly by using not only an assassin but also a poisoner.

Nevertheless we see that it is not in accordance with our customs to do what was done at Athens and Rome frequently in the olden time, in that those convicted of capital crimes were gotten rid of by poison. Truly, we think it cruel, and also foreign to Christian principles to drive a man, though covered with infamy, to the point that he commit suicide by plunging a dagger into his abdomen, or by taking deadly poison which has been put into his food or drink. It is equally contrary to the laws of humanity and the natural law, since it is forbidden that anyone take his own life.

We deny, therefore, that the enemy, whom we admit it is lawful to kill by treachery, may be made away with by poison.

---

Juan de Mariana, *The King and the Education of the King.*
(First published Toledo, 1598)

# WAR WITH THE ENEMY OF ALL MANKIND

B: Now if a king do those things which are directly for the dissolution of society, for the continuance whereof he was created, how do we call him?

M: A tyrant, I suppose.

B: Now a tyrant hath not only no just authority over a people but is also their enemy.

M: He is indeed an enemy.

B: Is there not a just and lawful war with an enemy for grievous and intolerable injuries?

M: It is, forsooth, a just war.

B: What war is that which is carried on with him who is the enemy of all mankind, that is, a tyrant?

M: A most just war.

B: Now a lawful war being once undertaken with an enemy, and for a just cause, it is lawful not only for the whole people to kill that enemy, but for every one of them.

M: I confess that.

B: May not everyone out of the whole multitude of mankind assault, with all the calamities of war, a tyrant who is a public enemy, with whom all good men have a perpetual warfare?

M: I perceive all nations almost to have been of that opinion. For Thebe is usually commended for killing her husband, Timoleon for killing his brother, and Cassius for killing his son; and Fulvius for killing his own son going to Catiline, and Brutus for killing his own sons and kinsmen, having understood they had conspired to introduce tyranny again.Public rewards were appointed to be given, and honors appointed by several cities of Greece to those that should kill tyrants. So that (as is before said) they thought there was no bond of humanity to be kept with tyrants. But why do I collect the assent of some single persons, since I can produce the testimony almost of the whole world? For who doth not sharply rebuke Domitius Corbulo for neglecting the safety of mankind, who did not thrust Nero out of his empire, when he might very easily have done it? And not only was he by the Romans reprehended, but by Tyridates the Persian king, being not at all afraid, lest it should afterward befall an example unto himself. But the minds of most wicked men enraged with cruelty are not so void of this public hatred against tyrants but that sometimes it breaketh out in them against their will and forceth them to stand amazed with terror at the sight of such a just and lawful deed. When the Ministers of Caius Caligula, a most cruel tyrant, were with the like cruelty tumultuating, for the slaughter of their lord and master, and required those that had killed him to be punished, now and then crying aloud, "Who had killed the emperor?" one of the senators standing in an eminent high place from whence he might be heard, cried out loud, "I wish I had killed him." At which word these tumultuary persons void of all humanity stood as it were astonished, and so forebore anymore to cry out tumultuously. For there is so great force in an honest deed that the very lightest show thereof, being presented to the minds of men, allays the most violent assaults. Fierce fury doth languish, and madness nill it, will it, doth acknowledge the sovereignty of reason. Neither are they of another judgment who with their loud cries mix heaven and earth together. Now this we do easily understand either from hence, that they do reprehend what now is done, but do commend and approve the same seemingly more atrocious, when they are recorded in an old history—and thereby do evidently demonstrate that they are more obsequious to their own particular affections than moved by any public damage. But why do we seek a more certain witness what tyrants do deserve than their own conscience? Thence is that perpetual fear from all, and chiefly from good men, and they do constantly see hanging above their own necks the sword which they hold still drawn against others and by their own hatred against others they measure other men's minds against them. But contrariwise, good men, by fearing no man, do often procure their own hazard, whilst they weigh the goodwill of others toward them, not from the vicious nature of men, but from their own desert toward others.

B: You do then judge that to be true, that tyrants are to be reckoned in the number of the most cruel brute beasts; and that tyrannical violence is more unnatural than poverty, sickness, death, and other miseries which may befall men naturally.

M: Indeed, when I do ponder the weight of your reasons, I cannot deny but these things are true. But whilst hazards and inconveniences do occur, which follow on the back of this opinion, my mind, as it were tied up with a bridle, doth instantly, I know not how, fail me, and bendeth from that too stoical and severe right way toward utility, and almost falleth away. For if it shall be lawful for any man to kill a tyrant, see how great a gape you do open for wicked men to commit any mischief, and how great hazard you create to good men: to wicked men you permit licentiousness, and lets out upon all the perturbation of all things. For he that shall kill a good king, or at least none of the worst, may he not pretend by his wicked deed some show of honest and lawful duty? Or if any good subject shall in vain attempt to kill a prince worthy of all punishment, or accomplish what he intended to do, how great a confusion of all things do you suppose must needs follow thereupon? Whilst the wicked do tumultuate, raging that their head and leader is taken away from them, neither will all good men approve the deed, nor will all those who do approve the deed defend the doer and author of their liberty against a wicked crew.

---

George Buchanan, *De Jure Regni apud Scotos*
(London, 1680)

EDWARD SAXBY

# KILLING NO MURDER

To US PARTICULARLY it belongs to bring this monster to justice, whom he hath made the instruments of his villany, and sharers in the curse and detestation that is due to himself from all good men. Others only have their liberty to vindicate, we our liberty and our honor. We engaged to the people with him, and to the people for him, and from our hands they may justly expect a satisfaction of punishment, being they cannot have that of performance. What the people at present endure, and posterity shall suffer, will be all laid at our doors; for only we under God have the power to pull down this dragon which we have set up. And if we do it not, all mankind will repute us approvers of all the villanies he hath done, and authors of all to come. Shall we that would not endure a king attempting tyranny suffer a professed tyrant? We that resisted the lion assailing us, shall we submit to the wolf tearing us? If there be no remedy to be found we have great reason to exclaim, *"Utinam te potius (Carole) retinuissemus quam hunc habuissemus, non quod ulla sit optanda servitus, sed quod ex dignitate Domini minus turpis est conditio servi."* (We wish we had rather endured thee [O Charles] than have been condemned to this mean tyrant; not that we desire any kind of slavery, but that the quality of the master something graces the condition of the slave.)

But if we consider it rightly what our duty, our engagements, and our honor exact from us, both our safety and our interest oblige us to, and it is as unanswerable in us to discretion, as it is to virtue, to let this viper live. For first, he knows very well it is only we that have the power to hurt him, and therefore of us he will take any course to secure himself. He is conscious to himself how falsely and perfidiously he hath dealt with us, and therefore he will always fear that from our revenge, which he knows he hath so well deserved.

Lastly, he knows our principles, how directly contrary they are to that arbitrary power he must govern by. Therefore, he may reasonably suspect that we that have already ventured our lives against tyranny and will always have the will, when we have the opportunity, to do the same again.

These considerations will easily persuade him to secure himself of us, if we prevent him not, and secure ourselves of him. He reads in his practice of piety, *"chid diviene patron,"* etc. "He that makes himself master of a city that hath been accustomed to liberty, if he destroys it not he must expect to be destroyed by it." And we may read, too, in the same author, and believe him, that those that are the occasion that one becomes powerful, he always ruins them if they want the wit and courage to secure themselves.

Now as to our interest, we must never expect that he will ever trust those that he hath provoked and feared; he will be sure to keep us down, lest we should pluck down him. It is the rule that tyrants observe when they are in power, never to make much use of those that helped them to it; and indeed it is in their interest and security not to do it, for those that have been the authors of their greatness, being conscious of their own merit, are bold with the tyrant, and less industrious to please him. They think all he can do for them is their due, and still they expect more. And when they fail in their expectations—as it is impossible to satisfy them—their disappointment makes them discontented, and their discontent is dangerous. Therefore, all tyrants follow the example of Dionysius, who was said to use his friends as he did his bottles: when he had use for them he kept them by him, and when he had none, that they should not trouble him and lie in his way, he hung them up.

But, to conclude this already over-long paper: let every man to whom God hath given the spirit of wisdom and courage be persuaded by his honor, his safety, his own good, and his country's, and indeed the duty he owes to his generation and to mankind, to endeavor by all rational means to free the world of this pest. Let not other nations have the occasion to think so meanly of us as if we resolved to sit still and have our ears bored, or that any discouragement or disappointments can ever make us desist from attempting our liberty, till we have purchased it, either by this monster's death or by our own. Our nation is not yet so barren of virtue that we want noble examples to follow amongst ourselves. The brave Sindercombe hath shown as great a mind as any old Rome could boast of; and had he lived there his name had been registered with Brutus and Cato, and he had had his statues as well as they.

But I will not have so sinister an opinion of ourselves, as little generosity as slavery hath left us, as to think so great a virtue can want its monuments even amongst us. Certainly in every virtuous mind there are statues reared to Sindercombe. Whenever we read the elegies of those that have died for their country; when we admire those great examples of magnanimity that have tried tyrants' cruelties, when we extol their constancies, whom neither bribes nor terrors could make betray their friends, it is then we erect Sindercombe's statues, and 'grave him monuments, where all that can be said of a great and noble mind we justly make an epitaph for him. And though the tyrant caused him to be smothered, lest the people should hinder an open murder, yet he will never be able either to smother his memory or his own villany. His poison was but a poor and common device to impose only on those that understood not tyrants' practices and are unacquainted, if any be, with his cruelties and falsehoods. He may therefore if he please take away the stake from Sindercombe's grave, and if he have a mind it should be known how he died, let him send thither the pillows and feather beds with which Barkstead and his hangman smothered him. But, to conclude: let not this monster think himself the more secure that he hath suppressed one great spirit; he may be confident that *longus post ilium sequitur ordo idem petentium decus.*

There is a great roll behind, even of those that are in his own muster rolls, that are ambitious of the name of the deliverers of their country; and they know what the action is that will purchase it. His bed, his table, is not secure; and he stands in need of other guards to defend him against his own. Death and destruction pursue him wheresoever he goes. They follow him everywhere, like his fellow travelers, and at last they will come upon him like armed men. Darkness is hid in his secret places, a fire not blown shall consume him. It shall go ill with him that is left in his tabernacle. He shall flee from the iron weapon, and a bow of steel shall strike him through, because he hath oppressed and forsaken the poor, because he hath violently taken away a house which he builded not. We may be confident, and so may he, that ere long all this will be accomplished. For the triumphing of the wicked is but short, and the joy of the hypocrite but for a moment. Though his excellency mount up to the heavens, and his head reacheth unto the clouds, yet he shall perish forever like his own dung. They that have seen him shall say, "Where is he?"

---

*Killing No Murder* (originally published as an
anonymous pamphlet).

## VITTORIO ALFIERI

# ON TYRANNY

TYRANNICAL RULE CAN ONLY BE MAINTAINED by the will of all, or of the majority of a people; and only the will of all, or of the majority, can really destroy it. But since, under our tyrannies, the mass of the people have no notion of any other government, how can this new idea of liberty be instilled into them? To my grief I have to reply that no one has any means of producing, in a short space of time, such an effect; and that in the countries where tyranny has been rooted for many generations it will take many more before public opinion slowly lays it bare.

Thus I perceive that owing to this fatal truth the European tyrants pardon me for all that until now I have argued against them. But in order somewhat to moderate this no less stupid than inhuman pleasure of theirs, I must observe that although there are no prompt and efficacious remedies against tyrannical government, there are, however, many, and one above all, rapid in the extreme and infallible, against tyrants.

Remedies against a tyrant lie within the reach of any and all private individuals, however obscure. But the most sure, efficacious, and swift measures against tyrannic rule lie in the hands, strange as it may seem, of the tyrant himself, as I will explain. A man of fierce and freedom-loving spirit, when outraged as a private person or when deeply shocked by outrages against a whole people, can be certain of acting effectively against the tyrant by himself, and at once, with cold steel. And if many of such a bold spirit were to unite under tyrannies, very soon the mass of the people themselves would change its attitude of mind and at the same time bring about the end of despotic rule. But since men of such resolute character are rare, especially under these evil rulers, and since the elimination of the tyrant alone usually has no other effect than that of increasing the tyranny, I shudder to have to express here a very hard truth, which is that cruelty

45

itself, constant injustice, plundering and atrocious corrupt practice on the part of the tyrant form the surest and most speedy remedy against tyrannic government. The more guilty and villainous the ruler is and the further he goes in open abuse of his unlimited wrongful authority, the more will he leave room for hope that the people will at last resent it, will listen and understand, and becoming inflamed with a passion for the truth, will solemnly put an end forever to so violent and irrational a form of government. It must be borne in mind that the mass of the people very rarely is persuaded of the possibility of an evil that it has not itself experienced, and experienced at length. Therefore, the common herd does not regard despotism as a monstrous form of government until one or more successive monsters ruling over them have given grievous and undeniable proof of unheard-of monstrous excesses.

If it should ever happen that a good citizen were able to become the minister of a tyrant and were to have determined to carry out the sublime resolve to sacrifice his own life and even his own reputation in order effectively and speedily to rid the state of despotism, he would have no better nor more certain means to use than to let the tyrant continue his evil ways and to advise him in this sense, even instigating him to indulge his violent nature to the full, so that in abandoning him to the most atrocious excesses he renders his person and his authority hateful and intolerable to everyone. And I expressly use these particular phrases ("his person," "his authority," and "to everyone") because every private outrage by the tyrant will injure only himself, but all public excesses, added to the private ones, will bring both tyrannic rule and the tyrant equally into disrepute and, by enraging the people as a whole and individually will equally injure both tyrannic government and the tyrant, and therefore could be able to destroy both at the same time. These infamous and atrocious means employed by the ministers (as I readily acknowledge them to be) are undoubtedly and always have been the only speedy and efficacious means of accomplishing so important and difficult an undertaking. It horrifies me to say so, but it is yet more horrifying to think of what these governments are, in which if a good man were to wish to achieve with the greatest certainty and speed the supreme good of all, he would find himself forced first into wrongdoing and infamy, or else into giving up an undertaking otherwise impossible to carry out. Such a man, therefore, can never be found, and the rapid effect of the abuse of tyrannical rule can only be expected through a truly wicked minister. But the latter, not wishing to lose more than his reputation (of which he generally has had none) and determined to retain to the full his usurped authority, his booty and his life, will prefer to allow the tyrant to become cruel and evil only insofar as to render his subjects wretched, but never to such a pitch as to rouse them to fury and vengeance.

From this it comes about that in this much milder century the art of ruling despotically has become more subtle and (as I have shown in Book I) is based on not only well-concealed and varied but firm foundations, that so long as the tyrant does not commit excesses, or very rarely, against the mass of the people and almost never against individuals except under the guise of some appearance of legality, tyranny seems assured of lasting forever.

But now I hear voices about me exclaiming, "How is it, then, that if these tyrannies are moderate and possible to endure, you expose and persecute them with such heat and rancor?" Because it is not always the crudest of injuries that offend most cruelly: because injuries should be measured by their greatness and their effects rather than their force; because, in short, the man who takes from you a few ounces of blood every day kills you in the end no less inevitably than he whose sudden violence causes you at once to bleed to death, but makes you suffer much more. To feel all one's spiritual qualities numbed, all man's rights reduced or taken away, every magnanimous impulse curbed or distorted, and to have to suffer a thousand other offenses which, were I to enumerate them here one by one would make me appear too tedious and self-important an accuser: when a man's true life is in the spirit and the intellect, is not living in such fear a continual dying? Of what importance is it to a man, who feels himself born to act and think nobly, to preserve in trepidation the life in his body, his possessions and the rest of what he cares for (though without any security) when he must lose, without hope of ever regaining them, all—absolutely all—the truest and most noble gifts of the spirit?

---

Vittorio Alfieri, *Della Tirannide*, Vol. II, Chap. 7.
(new edition, Torino, 1943)

# Terrorism
# Old and New

# INTRODUCTORY NOTE

CONSPIRACY WAS IN THE AIR as secret societies multiplied during the first third of the nineteenth century. The most influential plotter was Philippe Buonarroti (who had assisted François-Noël Baboeuf in 1795); his best-known heir was Auguste Blanqui (1805–1881). But neither preached terrorism. Their central idea was one of a conspiracy leading to a sudden coup, barricades, and street fighting which would result in the overthrow of the old order. (Excerpts from Blanqui's "Instructions for an Insurrection" are reprinted in *The Guerrilla Reader* [New York: New American Library, 1977].) Terrorist practice was more frequent in the Italian secret societies (better known as Carbonari). A somewhat sensational but basically correct account was provided by Bertoldi, a Prussian diplomat in Italy in his *Memoirs of the Secret Societies of the South of Italy* (London, 1821). Little is known about Bertoldi, who in fact might have been J.S. Bartholdy (1774–1825), Prussian consul general in Rome from 1815 and an uncle of the famed composer Felix Mendelssohn Bartholdy.

The idea of mobilizing the criminal underworld in a revolutionary struggle appeared first in the writings of the early German socialist Wilhelm Weitling (1808–1871) who, in turn, influenced Mikhail Bakunin. Weitling's ideas on the subject appear in his *Garantien der Harmonie und Freiheit* and more openly in letters to friends that were apparently intercepted and edited on behalf of the Swiss government by J. C. Bluntschli, *Die Kommunisten in der Schweiz* (Zurich, 1843). Bluntschli was one of the most important nineteenth-century theorists of international law. Karl Heinzen's *Der Mord* (Murder) is the most important ideological statement of early terrorism. Published in early 1849, it was reprinted and quoted innumerable times among the advocates of "direct action." It first appeared in 1849 in a journal edited by German political refugees in Biel, Switzerland. The original title, *Die Revolution,* was unacceptable to the authorities, but after the editor decided to drop the "R," the paper was passed. Heinzen's extremist ideas were opposed and sometimes ridiculed by many of his radical contemporaries, including

Marx and Engels, who singled him out for attack because, for all his radicalism, he was not a socialist. Like Weitling, Heinzen emigrated to America after the revolution of 1848–1849, where he edited various German language newspapers. He died in Boston ("the only civilized place in America") in 1880.

The concept of systematic terrorism and its use in revolutionary strategy first appeared between 1869 and 1881 in the writings of the Russian revolutionaries. Whether the famous "Catechism of a Revolutionary" was written by Sergey Nechaev or Bakunin has remained a bone of contention among historians, but most experts now believe that the former was its author. The background to the Nechaev affair, which preoccupied the Russian revolutionary movement for years, has been described in various books, most recently and most authoritatively in Michael Confino's *Violence dans le Violence* (Paris, 1973). Bakunin's influence was greatest on both the Russian revolutionary movement and on anarchism, especially in southern Europe.

The two most prominent advocates of terrorist action were Nikolai Morozov and G. Tarnovski (aka G. Romanenko), whose pamphlets appeared in Geneva in 1880. Both were members of the *Narodnaya Volya (People's Will)* which plotted and ultimately succeeded in killing the tsar in 1881. Morozov was arrested and sentenced to a long prison sentence. He studied physics, chemistry and astronomy and eventually became an honorary member of the Soviet Academy of Sciences. Though not a Marxist, he decided to stay in Russia after the Bolsheviks came to power and died after the Second World War at the ripe old age of ninety-two. While Morozov had sympathized with the liberal constitutionalists after his release from prison, Tarnovski-Romanenko moved to the extreme right and became one of the ideologists of the anti-Semitic Black Hundred. Serge Stepniak-Kravchinski's *Underground Russia* is a sympathetic and, on the whole, accurate account of the main figures of the Russian revolutionary movement of the 1870s. First published in Italian, it was translated into many languages and is widely read to this day. Kravchinski (1851–1895) was actively involved in terrorist operations; he escaped to London, where he died in a traffic accident.

The other main focus of terrorist thought was early anarchism. The role that a few courageous men, dissatisfied with words, might play was forcefully revealed in Prince Pyotr Kropotkin's (1842–1921) *The Spirit of Revolt,* first published in *Le Revolte* (Geneva, 1880). Instructions on how to play such a role were provided in many newspaper articles appearing in John Most's *Freiheit,* the leading German language newspaper advocating terrorist action. *Freiheit* was first published in London (1879–1881) and later in New York. Most had been a Social Democratic deputy to the

Reichstag, and who, like many others, had to leave Germany following Bismarck's anti-socialist emergency laws. His writings influenced the radical wing of the American labor movement, as evidenced by speeches of the main defendants in the Haymarket Trial. In France the *ère des attentats* had tremendous repercussions as far as the press and public opinion were concerned, but their political impact was nil for, unlike in Russia, these were actions of individuals rather than of organized groups.

Lastly, there was Irish terrorism as advocated by Jeremiah O'Donovan Rossa (1831–1915) and others in the United States. A "skirmishing fund" was established in the 1870s to help the dynamiters. But the results were disappointing with only a few Irish patriots supporting Rossa. Moreover, the Irish underground was riddled with informers. As an Irish-American humorist remarked in the understatement of a decade: "Irish-American terrorists were always unlucky, maybe they were indiscreet. Perhaps they dropped a hint of their intentions." (Desmond Ryan, *The Phoenix Flame,* London, 1937, page 215.) William Mackey Lomasney (1841–1884) was one of the most remarkable Fenian dynamiters. He lost his life in an attempt to bomb London Bridge. His personality is described in John Devoy's *Recollections of an Irish Rebel,* one of the most important accounts of the Irish nationalist movement. Devoy (1842–1928) won fame as a Fenian organizer and was later one of the leaders of the "physical force" party among Irish-Americans, even though he had dissociated himself from Rossa's terrorist projects.

# DAGGER AND POISON

URING THE LAST WINTER AND SPRING of 1817, fires which were reported to have succeeded each other rapidly, took place, coinciding with the escape of convicts and prisoners in various places from Bologna to Spoleto—where the sectaries particularly abounded. These fires were discovered to be generally suppositious, although some were really accidental. The escape of prisoners could only have been effected by cooperation from without. This, with the support of other arguments, warranted the conclusion that all was owing to the sectaries, whose object was to unsettle the people of those provinces, to promote brigandage, to call the attention of the government forces against robbers and to divert them from their stations, by which means the intended revolt would have been easily and securely effected.

The sentiments were echoed by the speeches of the members in language equally specific, and corresponding with the object of the revolt. Such, too, were the discourses held by the chief orators and sectaries in various meetings, both before and after the date of Papis's letter. In one of these meetings held at San Elpidio, the sacred purple was strongly inveighed against, and it was announced that the day would come when it would be changed into a mantle of blood. In another, held subsequently in the same place, the necessity of destroying monarchy, and especially the holy authority of the Pope, was set forth; and the sectaries were exhorted to undertake any project, however difficult, for the purpose of regaining liberty. In another, held at San Ginnesio, it was recommended to the members to provide themselves with arms and ammunition to serve as occasion offered; for, they were told, liberty and independence would soon be attained. In another, held at Macerata, in inculcating the necessity of rigid attention to secrecy with respect to the operations of the Society, a threat of death by the poignard was expressed against those who should attempt to violate their oath, and it was hinted that the same means would be necessary, ere the happy moment would arrive, when liberty would be regained, and the yoke of the present government thrown off. At Loreto, on the establishment of the Guelph Council, a discussion was held on the revolution which was shortly to take place, and on the satisfactory accounts of preparations for it, in consequence of which all the sectaries evinced a determination to follow it up. At Monte Lupone the same subject was discussed, and the members animated each other to action, declaring themselves eager for the crisis, and exulting in the prospect of establishing an independent republic.

Again, at Montolmo, in another assembly, the members were assured that liberty and independence would be soon regained. In another, at Monte Lupone, held on the fifth of June, one of the sectaries, grasping a dagger in his hand, caused his companions to renew their oath of secrecy, and declared that whoever betrayed it should perish by the weapon he held. After this preface he showed the advantages that would be obtained by taking the reins of power out of the hands of the actual government, and by erecting an independent republic. Another member recommended the imitation of Brutus, by dethroning tyrants and destroying monarchy, and by erecting upon their ruins an independent republic—and concluded that in a short time the yoke of the present government would be thrown off, exhorting his associates to provide themselves for this object, even with poisoned weapons *(arme anche avvelenate)* and with ammunition, in order to be ready on the first opportunity.

The plan for the execution of the revolt was the most terrible and sanguinary. An incendiary proclamation was to have been circulated in the Marches and other provinces of the state, immediately on the breaking out of the conspiracy in Macerata, to excite the people to join it. To that place the various Vendite of the Carbonari and Councils of the Guelphs, expressly informed of the event, were to have sent, in the same night, a number of armed rebels of their order. These were to have been admitted into the city, in which part of the sectaries were to have been ready to act. The watchword for the rebel bands in answer to the challenge, *"Chi evviva?"* was to have been, *"San Teobaldo"* (whom the Carbonari consider the protector of the order). The other secret word among the leaders was *"Vendetta al Popolo."* Having insinuated themselves by stratagem into the places where the government troops are stationed, they would have overpowered them and deprived them of their arms, confining such as were unwilling to take a part in their operations. In the same manner, entering the public prisons, they would have confined the keepers, and released the prisoners, selecting from the latter those who are fit to bear arms.

Afterwards dividing the number of the rebels into patrols of twelve men, some were to have attacked the public treasuries, others the habitations of rich private individuals whose property was to have been plundered. And some, known to be hostile to the sect, were to have been seized and conducted to the deep subterraneous cells of the monastery of Santa Chiara, which was fixed upon as a rebel station—there they were to be destroyed by fire or poison, their relations being made to believe that they were sent as hostages elsewhere. The plunder, under the faith and responsibility of the appointed heads of the patrols, was to have been deposited in the convent "dei Bernabiti," where others would have registered it, to be afterwards employed in the necessary expenses. The principal civil and ecclesiastical authorities would not have been exempted from seizure and imprisonment. ...

In the midst of these insidious proceedings, they did not omit to impose, by means of crime, on the sectaries themselves, as well as on the uninitiated, called by them pagans, to remove every possible obstacle to the free prosecution of their labors, as well as to confirm the former in the obligations they had contracted, and to convince both of the formidable power of the society. Several individuals, who were adverse to their maxims, were destined to the poignard, and were actually wounded in a sudden attack, one of them mortally. These victims were (in addition to their colleague Priola, of San Elpidio, accused of perjury) Feliziani of Ascoli; the advocate Martini, judge in the tribunal at Fermo; the commissary of police, Ricci; the legal vicar of Petritoli, D. Ignazio Scarsini; Valeriani of Montelpare; and the brigadier of Carabiniers, Pastori, who, after repeated threats of death (conveyed in public notices—although he escaped a pistol shot) was afterwards poisoned, etc. Such aggressions and homicide (without reckoning that of Pastori) having been committed without any *immediate* cause, in the *night*, by persons *unknown*, and in *disguise*.

In fact, it is a system universally observed by the Carbonari, that every one of them should be armed with a poignard, as the hand grasping a dagger upon the seals of the order denotes; nor do they deny this.

When a new member is admitted to their society, they brandish these weapons before the novice, intimating that they will be always ready in his defense if he is faithful to the Society and that they will shed his blood if he violates his oath.

It is on this account that all the accused, in whatever manner they have confessed, tremble lest they should fall beneath the stilettoes of their colleagues, which would infallibly happen if their confessions were made public. It is on this account they entreat secrecy. The expressions employed by Massone, president of the Supreme Vendita of the Carbonari, and of the Guelph Council at Ancona, on this subject, are very remarkable. "Giacomo Papis fears the vengeance of the sect much more than the decision of justice in the present cause." This terror, unlike other circumstances of which this is not the place to treat, accounts of itself for the aforementioned crimes. Poison was at last called in to aid the poignard, as fitter to destroy in some circumstances, by placing the assassin in less danger. This atrocious system, notwithstanding the restriction of the chief sectaries, is at this moment followed up by the most abandoned of the order, who are not easily shaken in their resolutions. But their audacity went still farther, although the vigilance of government, toward the end of 1816, was enabled to check the course of these proceedings, by the arrest of some individuals at Ascoli. The sectaries did not desist from the practices above alluded to, but, more insolent than ever, dared to conspire against the sovereign and his throne.

---

Bartoldi, *Memoirs of the Secret Societies of the South of Italy* (London, 1821)

KARL HEINZEN

# MURDER

W
E MUST CALL A SPADE A SPADE. The truth must out, whether it seems amiable or terrible, whether it is dressed in the white of peace or the red of war. Let us then be frank and honest, let us tear away the veil and spell out in plain speech what the lesson is which is now being illustrated every day before our eyes in the form of actions and threats, blood and torture, cannons and gallows by both princes and freedom fighters, Croats and democrats; to wit, that murder is the principal agent of historical progress.

The egoists begin the murdering, and the men of ideas reply in kind. Twist and turn as they may, neither party can escape either murdering or being murdered, and the "ultima ratio" of both is quite simply the obliteration of their enemies. *both sides partake in violence*

A wide variety of names have been coined for the art of obliterating one's enemy. In one country they have him put to death "legally" by an executioner and call it the death penalty. In another, they lie in wait with stiletto blades behind hedges and call it assassination. In another they organize obliteration on a grand scale and call it war. Examined in the clear light of day, these various appellations appear for what they are, entirely superfluous, being all expressions of what is fundamentally one and the same thing, and whether I am executed or assassinated or torn to pieces, the end effect is the same. I am dispatched to the other world and this dispatching to the other world was the purpose of my enemy. No clear-thinking, rational person can accept the hair-splitting distinctions by which certain methods of obliterating the enemy are justified and others condoned. Such distinctions rest on theological and legal fictions and do not in any way alter the facts of the matter, which are that in each case it is purely and simply a question of obliterating one's enemy.

We maintain, in conformity with the fundamental principles of humanity and justice, that any voluntary killing of another human being is a crime against humanity, that no one under any pretext whatsoever has the right to destroy another's life and that anyone who does kill another or has him killed is quite simply a murderer. But against our enemies, with their executioners and soldiers, their laws of "high treason" and their inquisitions, their cannons and needle-guns, their shrapnel and Congreves, we are able to achieve precious little with our humanity and our ideas of justice, and merely to claim in some places that an inquisitor or a general is as much a murderer as any bandit or partisan would only serve to convince ourselves that we may quite "legitimately" be done away with.

Let us, then, be practical. Let us call ourselves murderers as our enemies do, let us take the moral horror out of this great historical tool and just examine closely whether perchance our enemies may claim a special privilege in the matter of murder. If to kill is always a crime, then it is forbidden equally to all; if it is not crime, then it is permitted equally to all. Once one has overcome the objection that murder per se is a crime, all that remains is to believe one is in the right against one's enemy and to possess the power to obliterate him. Simple logic as much as the facts of history compels this conclusion. We do not desire *any* killing, *any* murder, but if our enemies are not of the same mind, if they can justify murder, even going so far as to claim a special privilege in the matter, then necessity compels us to challenge this privilege. And it is no great step from this necessity to becoming Robespierre and to the adoption of Robespierre's role, condemning hundreds of thousands to the scaffold in the interests of humanity.

We take as our fundamental principle, taught us by our enemies, that murder, both of individuals and masses, is still a necessity, an unavoidable instrument in the achievement of historical ends. Let us now consider various attitudes to the question, in order to illustrate when the use of this bloody instrument is justified and when not.

As schoolchildren, we were excited and thrilled by the story of those two youthful heroes Harmodios and Aristogeiton, who murdered the tyrant Hipparchos. Those who told us the story, who presented this murder to us as a glorious deed, were "the king's" teachers, men who oozed morality, loyalty, and the fear of God from every pore. We never heard them say that Harmodios and Aristogeiton were "heinous murderers," "anarchists," "agitators," etc., nor that the victim Hipparchos was a "legitimate ruler," a "sacred person," etc., nor that, instead of opting to murder him they should have attempted to remove him "by constitutional means." Now what conclusion are we to draw from this?

Pupils in every school in the land are made to recite a poem composed by the highly moral Schiller, who at the very beginning has an "assassin" "creep up on a tyrant" with a "dagger concealed in his cloak," and then subsequently makes the tyrant a friend of the murderer's. What are we to conclude from this?

Mucius Scaevola slipped into Porsenna's camp with the intention of murdering an enemy dangerous to his fatherland. By mistake he killed Porsenna's scribe. Later he told Porsenna that three hundred other Romans besides himself had sworn to kill him. In all the history books and schools, Mucius Scaevola is praised to the skies as a hero, and it would never occur to anyone to be scandalized by the fact that there were three hundred other Romans ready to take his place. What are we to conclude from this?

One of the chief enemies of the great Caesar, and one of his assassins, was Junius Brutus, the favorite Caesar loved so tenderly and who may even have been his own dear son. No one has yet been roused to indignation by the fact that this republican suppressed all human feeling and gratitude in order to become a murderer, perhaps even a parricide. On the contrary, royalists, moralists, republicans, and "anarchists" all still consider him to be one of the greatest men in history and "the last Roman." What are we to conclude from this?

In heathen antiquity, the murder of a tyrant was right, honorable, and one's duty, and no "king's" teacher or professor in our Christian era would ever dream of trying to correct them on this score. What are we to conclude from this?

Let us take a few examples from more recent history.

Sand murdered the traitor Kotzebue with a dagger instead of killing him with a stroke of the pen.

The reactionaries denounced him, while the liberals expressed regret that he had risked his life in killing a man whose position and person did not warrant such action. What are we to conclude from this?

A young man from Germany by the name of Statz tried to murder Napoleon but was caught and disarmed. This young man Statz was lauded for his attempt and his name would doubtless have become one of the most celebrated among the moral Germans if he had succeeded in carrying out his deed, if he had plunged a dagger into the body of the most powerful man in history. What are we to conclude from this?

In Frankfurt am Main two deputies, Lichnowski and Auerswald, were murdered. The entire reactionary and constitutional parties boiled over with indignation, and the central authorities mobilized half the continent to try and catch the murderers. In Vienna, another deputy, Robert Blum, was murdered by Windischgratz's executioners and in his honor the central authorities made a few preliminary inquiries from which nothing followed. If R. Blum had been a German prince rather than a German deputy, the "National Parliament" would have instructed the central authorities to declare war on Austria. What are we to conclude from this?

In Frankfurt, it was Prince Lichnowski and Count Auerswald who were murdered. In Vienna, it was simply Robert Blum, man of the people, who was murdered. On the occasion of this first murder, the reactionary party raised an unending hue and cry against the "anarchists." When, however, a collection was taken for Mr. Auerswald's descendants, the token of sympathy raised by this rich party proved to be a very paltry sum. The second murder caused such sorrow within the dead man's party that memorial services were held in hundreds of churches and his family very rapidly became rich. What are we to conclude from this?

Here are a few conclusions which follow irrefutably from these facts:

1. It seems that what is decisive in the way history judges a murder is the motive. History does not appear to condemn murder itself.
2. It seems that moral reactions to a murder are closely linked to the self-interest of those reacting, for that which is esteemed a virtue among the ancients would be considered a crime in our age of police rule. None of the teachers who so enthusiastically translate accounts of murderous deeds from the Greek tongue into the German would dare recommend a "translation" of the deeds themselves.
3. The courageous bearing of the murderer seems to be of equal weight in the scales of judgment as the success of the attempt.
4. It seems that murder is only justified when it selects a victim whose elimination also signifies the removal of a representative or upholder of a pernicious principle.
5. It seems that it is not just the "petty thieves" but also the petty murderers who are "hanged," while the "big" ones get off scot-free.
6. It seems that only the party of freedom has martyrs, the reactionary party having nothing but tools.

We are driven to similar conclusions when we consider mass murder and organized murder, or war, as it is called. In the past it is the most just who are in the right; in the present, it is the most strong. In the past, motive is the determining factor, in the present, self-interest. In the past, justice is the judge; in the present, the party. In the past, it is the idea which is decisive; in the present, it is expediency. Organized murder, war, is accepted as a necessity per se. It is a tool, like a knife, and the only question of any relevance is whether it is used to this or that end and, further, whether it succeeds or fails in achieving it.

Thus we see that in practice, once killing has been accepted, the moral stance is seen to have no foundation, the legal is seen to be ineffectual, and the political is alone of any significance. Is the end achieved? This is the only question which you cultivators and organizers of murder permit us to ask ourselves, by forcing us to adopt your theory of murder.

It is possible that murder is not only a historical but also a physical necessity. It is possible that the atmosphere or the earth's crust requires a certain quantity of human blood to satisfy its chemical or other interests. However, even should such a requirement on nature's part exist, no one is ever going to manage to persuade us that the blood of aristocrats is less suitable than the blood of democrats. There is as yet no law of physics stating that it is only those who champion the rights of man who must give their quota to satisfy history's or nature's need for blood. We shall therefore have to ask ourselves whether the time has not yet come—or is not coming—and whether we will not very soon be sufficiently strong to make some claims on our enemies. It would appear that it is in the nature of the democratic party all at once to make huge demands in settlement of the debts which the other party has gradually accumulated with it. The French Revolution of the last century was an example of just such a settlement of an outstanding murder account, and, if we are to believe the signs, there will presently be a repeat of the French Revolution on a European scale. The reactionary party has never had any reservations about murdering others and has fewer than ever at the present time. "Have I the means to carry out the murder and will it achieve its purpose?" This is the only question the Reactionary Party has ever asked itself.

What answer do we get when we ask ourselves this question? Being the conscientious Germans we are, we first inquire of our teachers whether we would have been committing more of a crime than Harmodios, Mucius or Brutus were we to have done away with a Metternich, a Nicholas, a Windischgratz or a Ferdinand of Naples—in other words, were we to have dispatched to the other world several individuals who have been responsible for torturing and murdering millions. If our teachers speak the language of the Greeks and Romans, they will have to answer: ask your own capacity for self-sacrifice and your courage. If, however, they speak German, they will call for the police. How are we to escape from this dilemma?

Our enemies will come to our aid. With homicidal violence, our enemies are at present urging upon us the lesson that murder is the chief instrument of historical progress and that the most valuable art to be versed in in our time is that of destroying human life, Ferdinand bombards Naples, Radetsky murders the Lombards, Windischgratz mounts an attack on Vienna, Jellachich allows his Croats to roll about in the entrails of their victims, "Olim der Grosse" keeps all his murderers at their posts, and in the background stands the czar with hundreds of thousands of bloodthirsty comrades. None of these men thinks twice about destroying whole towns, ruining whole countries, having the most honorable men shot, the most innocent murdered, women abused, children impaled—in short, about reviving all the bestiality and barbarity of former times, in order to save a few crowns and keep the rights of man at bay. And we?

Invention tends to go hand in hand with developments in other spheres. Our enemies, with their means of mass destruction, will stimulate inventions which vie with the present armies as agents of destruction. The greatest benefactor of mankind will be he who makes it possible for a few men to wipe out thousands. So when we hear that trainloads of murderers' accomplices have been hurled from the track by a thimbelful of fulminating silver placed under the rails; or that bombs, filled to the brim and complete with detonator, have been placed beneath paving stones in order to tear apart whole companies of invading barbarians as soon as they arrive; or that, perhaps, containers filled with poison, which burst in the air, can rain down ruin on entire regiments; or that underground rooms full of fulminating silver can blow whole towns into the air, complete with their one hundred thousand murderous slaves, then in such methods we shall perceive only to what desperate measures the party of freedom has been driven by the mass party of the barbarians. To have a conscience with regard to the murdering of reactionaries is to be totally unprincipled. They wreak destruction, in any way they can, thereby obliging us to respond in kind as defenders of justice and humanity. Kossuth was a man of great energy, but Kossuth did not show sufficient interest in inventions and Kossuth overlooked the possibilities of fulminating silver.

Even if we have to blow up half a continent or spill a sea of blood, in order to finish off the barbarian party, we should have no scruples about doing it. The man who would not joyfully give up his own life for the satisfaction of putting a million barbarians into their coffins carries no republican heart within his breast.

In my last article, I said that the greatest benefactor of mankind will be he who makes it possible for a few men to wipe out thousands.

The entire democratic party should make it its business to bring about this state of affairs. We are surely now agreed that murder, in both its passive and active forms, is something we cannot avoid. And if the only choice *trying to justify murder terrorism.*

we have is either to be murdered for freedom's sake or to murder for it, it is difficult to imagine any democrat having such humane feelings toward the barbarians that he would obediently place his own head on the chopping block. So there can really be no doubt about which alternative to choose, and all that we have to concern ourselves with is gaining the upper hand in the mortal struggle which is about to erupt—or has already erupted—with the Barbarian Party. Hitherto, the barbarian party has been far superior to us in the matter of murder. Murder has for centuries been their chief study; they have trained and organized hundreds of thousands of murderous lackeys. They have on their side such hoards of instruments of murder and means of destruction that one could without being an Archimedes— providing the *da mihi punctum* has been satisfied—deprive astronomy of several exquisite planets and stars. All that nature, science, art, industry, zeal, avarice, and bloodthirstiness have been able to produce or invent is at the disposal of the barbarians' party in its efforts to destroy, to murder the humane party, the party of freedom. Blood is their alpha, blood their omega, blood their end, blood their means, blood their delight, blood their life, blood their dream, blood their endeavor, blood their first principle, and blood their last. So be it, then: blood for blood, murder for murder, destruction for destruction. The spirit of freedom must raise itself up to its full height, show its true vigor, and if it goes under, it must turn destroyer.

People have said so often that the freedom party has no need to concern itself with numbers, that its principle alone is sufficient assurance of victory, that ultimately it will overcome any enemy no matter how powerful, etc. They cite the cases of the Greeks, and the Swiss, and the Dutch. For centuries now they have been regurgitating the same few examples to give us consolation and bolster our hopes. In my opinion, these few crumbs of comfort only feed our indecision and our superstition. Of course, it is as certain that progress will finally overcome reaction as it is certain that spring will finally overcome winter; but the general truth of this statement does not rule out the myriad variables of Where? How? and How Long?—variables which can be so important, so crucial, that for entire peoples and for entire centuries the law of progress may shrivel up into nothing, whereas with the aid of a few pistol shots, a few cannons or a few pounds of fulminating silver, the same law might be made reality for those same peoples and centuries.

Hence, this mere, vague belief in the moral force and ultimate victory of the party of freedom over that of the barbarians is merely a soporific, an instrument of self-destruction. Simple common sense refuses to accept a "law" which forbids one to defend oneself against certain attack until the murderer's knife is at one's throat; as it would refuse to accept a law

63

instructing fathers to permit themselves to be killed in order that their sons might learn to defend themselves; as it would refuse to accept a law forbidding one to fire no more than one shot at the enemy for every ten he fires; as it would refuse to accept a law instructing one to use water sprinklers against an enemy who fights with poison and fire; as it would refuse to accept a law instructing one to trust in future reconciliation with an enemy whose very nature is rebarbative to peacemaking and the very principle of whose being is that he will never get any better. Therefore, once again, I say we must answer blood with blood, murder with murder, and destruction with destruction.

Those who point to the progressive minority's qualitative superiority over the reactionary majority have in most cases failed to perceive how the conditions and circumstances of the struggle have changed. One gun has more courage than a thousand freedom fighters, and it is a matter of the purest indifference to caseshot and shrapnel whether they are to decimate a troop of Spartans or Thebans, a corps of confederates, or a corps of Hungarians. In earlier times, before the present system of standing armies arose, before courage and physical strength were replaced by mere instruments of murder, before it became possible for cowards to wreak destruction from a great distance away, before the business of equipping an army began to cost the people as much as half their entire wealth, before the possession of and training in arms had reached the inequality we see today and when it was possible to fight man to man, "eyeball-to-eyeball"—then, admittedly, it was possible for a small band of men inspired by the spirit of freedom and by a courage born of desperation to defeat with ease a superior force of murderous lackeys, who were simply acting on some despot's orders. In modern times, however, circumstances have changed. Certainly, the spiritual force driving the combatants is still of importance, and, where there is equality of instruments of destruction, a corps of freedom fighters will rout any troop of despot's mercenaries of the same size. But the barbarian party's superiority in organization, training, numbers, means of destruction has, as we see from almost all the battles of recent times, grown so great that it is simply ridiculous to claim this superiority can be counterbalanced by the freedom fighter's spirit and his knowledge of the rightness of his cause.

We must become more practical than we are, we must become more resolved, we must become more energetic, we must become more reckless. The "spirit of freedom" will have to familiarize itself with daggers and poison, and "the good cause" will have to study the mysteries of powder and fulminating silver.

The aim of our study must be to eliminate the superiority of the barbarian party through the invention of new methods of killing, so as to nullify the numerical advantage of the organized masses by means of instruments of destruction which can: *drones.*

1.  be operated by a small number of people, and
2.  do greater damage, the greater the mass of those against whom they are used.

The barbarian party has gun foundries in which to produce guns, powder mills in which to manufacture powder, and it has complete freedom to mount its guns and pour in the powder. We have none of these things. We have no money to buy guns with, and even had we the guns, we should never be able to bring them out into the open; a few policemen would immediately relieve us of them. The first question is thus whether it is not possible to invent instruments which can be made without being seen, be transported without attracting notice, be operated without any great effort, and which are, in sum, no less effective than big guns?

The barbarian party possesses shrapnel, Congreve missiles, etc. Such instruments are only of use, or practical, when one wishes to wipe out masses of people. A Congreve hurled into the middle of a group of a few hundred can scatter or kill, a few hundred. Thrown at one single man, it may fail to hit even this individual and even if it does achieve its object, it kills only this one individual, for all its destructive power. Would it not be possible, then, to devise some sort of missile which one man can throw into a group of a few hundred, killing them all? We need instruments of destruction which are of little use to the great masses of the barbarians when they are fighting a few lone individuals but which give a few lone individuals the terrifying power to threaten the safety of whole masses of barbarians. Our powers of invention will thus have to be directed toward the concentration, the homeopathic—as it were—preparation of those substances whose destructive powers physics and chemistry have brought to light, and toward solving the problem of how these substances can be used in a way which minimizes their cost, makes them easy to transport, and diminishes the effort required to propel them. For instance, were it possible with no more than a shotgun to fire into the massed ranks of an army a capsule equal in effect, on contact, to a shrapnel shell or a case shot, then a dozen democratic partisans would be able to do more damage than an entire battery of barbarian artillery and the large-scale organization and huge accumulation of instruments of death to which the barbarian party owes its superiority would in a short space be rendered useless.

Being myself neither a chemist, nor a sergeant-artificer, nor a gunner, I am in no position to judge whether the problems an invention along these lines would pose are, in fact, insuperable; however, from what man's powers of invention have achieved so far, I take it they are not. These revolutionaries who, like the Italians, Poles, and Hungarians, have no shortage of funds, should put up the prize money for an open competition—it would not be long before success was achieved.

As much as new inventions, however, we desperately need firmness of purpose, that revolutionary firmness of purpose which is prepared to oppose the barbarians' system of murder and violence with any means which help to fulfill the aim of destroying them. When at the start of the Hungarian war, the Hungarians began using chain-shot and the humane Windischgratz protested against this inhuman violation of the conventions of war, the Hungarians declared they would lay their inhuman chain shots aside if Herr Windischgratz would hand over to them a few humane batteries of Congreves. It is exceedingly naive of professional barbarians who take the greatest delight and derive their greatest honor from murdering men in their thousands, to appeal in the name of humanity to the conventions of war when their weaker enemy attempts to reduce his superiority by newer, more effective weapons. It is not contrary to the dictates of "humanity" for Herr Windischgratz, as a myrmidon of despotism, to set Vienna in flames and order the Hungarians to be mown down. But it is contrary to the "conventions of war" for the Hungarians, defending what it is their right to defend, to use chain-shot in attempting to stop bands of Croatian murderers invading their territory. What a fuss did Herr Windischgratz make when the Hungarians poisoned all the meat before they retreated from Raab! To be frank, the only regret I have about the whole affair is that a few thousand of those wild animals who call themselves Croats and saviors of Austrian despotism did not eat sufficiently large quantities of that poisoned meat to snuff it. In my view, it is "more shameful" and "more immoral" to poison a few thousand rats than a few thousand of those Croats. If the Croats and their masters do not wish to be poisoned and shot at with chain-shot in Hungary, there is one very simple way of ensuring they are not: to wit, to leave the Hungarian people in peace and their rights unchallenged. Once, however, they violate those rights, once they close in on the Hungarians as murderers, the Hungarians have the authority and the duty to use any means whatever to achieve their end, which is the destruction of an enemy superior to them in numbers, organization, or instruments of death. The Hungarians would now be a lot better off had they been a little more inhuman and more consistently violated the "conventions of war." The same is true of the Italians. The revolutionaries must try to *psychological terror.*

bring about a situation where the barbarians are afraid for their lives every hour of the day or night. They must think that every drink of water, every mouthful of food, every bed, every bush, every paving stone, every path and footpath, every hole in a wall, every slate, every bundle of straw, every pipe bowl, every stick, every pin may be a killer. For them, as for us, may fear be the herald and murder the executor. Murder is their motto, so let murder be their answer. Murder is their need, so let murder be their payment. Murder is their argument, so let murder be their refutation.

The European barbarian party has left us no other choice than to devote ourselves to the study of murder and refine the art of killing to the highest possible degree. Recently the Austrians have been rather overdoing a public boast that they have invented balloons of death which they intend to use to set fire to Venice. It has not occurred to anybody to appeal to Humanity and Morality about this. The entire "humane" and "moral" world will, in all likelihood, get convulsions when a revolutionary insists that the Freedom Party must meet the murdering of the barbarian party with murder themselves.

The path to Humanity will pass through the zenith of Barbarity. Our enemies have made this principle a law of politics and we shall either have to observe this "law," follow this "constitutional path," or be buried, and our freedom with us.

---

*Die Evolution* (Biel, February-March, 1849)

MIKHAIL BAKUNIN

# REVOLUTION, TERRORISM, BANDITRY

BANDITRY IS ONE OF THE MOST HONORABLE WAYS of life within the Russian state. Since the establishment of the Muscovite state, it has represented a desperate protest by the people against the infamous social order, perfected on the western pattern and still further consolidated by Peter's reforms and the benign Alexander's grants of freedom. The bandit is the people's hero, defender, and savior. He is the implacable enemy of the state and the whole social and civil order set up by the state. He is a fighter to the death against the entire civilization of the aristocratic *chinovniks* and governmental priesthood.

Without understanding the essential nature of the bandit, no man will ever understand the history of the Russian people. Without sympathy for that nature, he cannot sympathize with the life of the Russian people. He has no heart for the people's age-old immeasurable suffering, for he has thrown in his lot with their enemies, the supporters of state supremacy.

The nature of Russian banditry is cruel and ruthless; yet no less cruel and ruthless is that governmental might which has brought this kind of bandit into being by its wanton acts. Governmental cruelty has engendered the cruelty of the people and made it into something necessary and natural. But between these two cruelties, there still remains a vast difference. The first strives for the complete annihilation of the people, the other endeavors to set them free.

Since the Muscovite state was founded, there has been no break in the Russian organization of banditry. In it the memory of the people's humiliation is preserved, and in itself alone it is proof of the passion, vitality, and strength of the people. Should banditry cease in Russia, it would mean that either final extinction or complete freedom had come to the people.

In Russia, the bandit is the only true revolutionary—a revolutionary without fine phrases or book-learned rhetoric—an implacable, tireless, indomi-

68

table, practical revolutionary, a social revolutionary sprung from the people, though with no politics and no social status.... In the difficult intervals when the whole world of working peasants sleep what seems to be a sleep with no awakening, crushed by the whole burden of the state, the world of bandits in the forests carries on its desperate fight and battles on until at last the Russian villages awake. And should these two kinds of rebellion, that of the bandit and that of the peasant, ever unite, then the people's revolution will come about. The movements of Stenka Rasin and Pugachev were, in fact, just this.

And now the underground river of banditry flows unbroken from Petersburg to Moscow, from Moscow to Kasan, from Kasan to Tobolsk, to the mines of the Altai, to Irkutsk and Nerchinsk. The robbers, dispersed throughout Russia, in the forests, the towns and villages, and the captives in the innumerable prisons of the empire—they all make up one inseparable, tightly knit world, the world of the Russian revolution. Here and only here has there long been a genuine revolutionary conspiracy. And so, whoever truly wants to conspire in Russia, whoever desires the people's revolution should find his way into this world. The time of general revolt approaches. The villages are not asleep. No! They are in rebellion. From all ends of the empire groans, plaints, and threats resound. In the north, in the east, in the Baltic provinces, significant popular risings have already occurred. Beneath the soldiers' bayonets, the blood of the people has begun to flow more strongly than ever before. Yet the measure of the people's patience is exhausted. Death by starvation is no easier than death by bayonet or bullet. Now the people will no longer fall asleep, and the number of isolated risings will grow ever greater. The tally of those who flee into the forest also grows ever greater; the world of banditry is awake and alert once more. The anniversaries of Stenka Rasin and Pugachev draw near, when the memory of the people's champions must be honored. All must arm themselves for that celebration....

What, in truth, is now our task?

We must take the path at present shown to us by the government, which drives us out of academies, universities, and schools. Let us then, brothers, as one man fling ourselves among the people, the popular movement, the bandit and peasant revolts, and, while maintaining our true, firm friendship, we will unite the isolated peasant outbursts into a well-planned yet relentless revolution....

Even if we recognized no activity other than the cause of destruction, we should still be of the opinion that the forms which that activity might take could be multiplied to an extraordinary degree. Poison, dagger, noose, and the like! ... Everything in this fight is equally sanctified by the revolution. So the field is open! ... The victims are marked out by the unconcealed indignation of the people! And so may all honest and fresh minds, after centuries of degradation, pluck up courage for a renewal of life! Dismal be the last days of the leech upon the body politic! Lamentations of fear and remorse will re-echo throughout society. Beggarly writers will strike lyric notes. Shall we pay heed to them? ... By no means! We must remain impassive in the face of all this howling and not enter into any compromises with those destined to perish. They will call it terrorism! They will give it some resounding nickname! All right, it's all the same to us. We don't care for their opinion. We know that in all Europe not a single person leads a quiet bourgeois life or can with honor reproach us without being forced into hypocrisy. From contemporary literature, made up of nothing but denunciation and flattery, from venal literature nothing but beastliness and tittle-tattle can be expected. The interests of applied science today are the interests of the tsar and of capital, which it exclusively serves—exclusively because up to now not a single discovery has been utilized for the good of the people. All discoveries are either exploited by fine gentlemen, dilettantes or moneymakers, or else used to increase military power. None of the inventive talent of academics is directed toward the needs of the people. Therefore, the interests of this applied science are not ours, either. Need we, then, even speak of social science? Who does not know the names of dozens of dear ones who have been exiled to Siberia or elsewhere because they wished to restore the rights of man with the sincere words of a warm conviction. Their ardent speeches, breathing faith and love, were stifled by brute force.

The present generation must in its turn produce an inexorable brute force and relentlessly tread the path of destruction. The healthy, uncorrupted mind of youth must grasp the fact that it is considerably more humane to stab and strangle dozens, nay hundreds, of hated beings than to join with them to share in systematic *legal* acts of murder, in the torture and martyrdom of millions of peasants. These are the acts that our *chinovniks,* our scholars, priests, and traders share in, in a word by all the people of standing who, directly or indirectly, oppress those who have no standing! ... So may all healthy young minds forthwith set themselves to the *sacred cause* of rooting out evil, purifying and clearing Russia's soil by fire and sword, and join fraternally with those who will do likewise throughout Europe.

---

Mikhail Bakunin, *Neskolko slov k molodym bratyam v Rosii* (Geneva, 1869), reprinted in M.P. Dragomanov's edition of the exchange of letters between Bakunin and Herzen and Ogarev.

SERGEY NECHAEV

# CATECHISM OF THE REVOLUTIONIST (1869)

Principles by Which the Revolutionary Must Be Guided:

1. The revolutionary is a doomed man. He has no interests of his own, no affairs, no feelings, no attachments, no belongings, not even a name. Everything in him is absorbed by a single exclusive interest, a single thought, a single passion—the revolution.
2. In the very depths of his being, not only in words but also in deeds, he has broken every tie with the civil order and the entire cultured world, with all its laws, proprieties, social conventions, and its ethical rules. He is an implacable enemy of this world, and if he continues to live in it, that is only to destroy it more effectively.
3. The revolutionary despises all doctrinairism and has rejected the mundane sciences, leaving them to future generations. He knows of only one science, the science of destruction. To this end, and this end alone, he will study mechanics, physics, chemistry, and perhaps medicine. To this end he will study day and night the living science: people, their characters and circumstances and all the features of the present social order at all possible levels. His sole and constant object is the immediate destruction of this vile order.
4. He despises public opinion. He despises and abhors the existing social ethic in all its manifestations and expressions. For him, every thing is moral which assists the triumph of revolution. Immoral and criminal is everything which stands in its way.
5. The revolutionary is a dedicated man, merciless toward the state and toward the whole of educated and privileged society in general; and he must expect no mercy from them either. Between him and

them there exists, declared or undeclared, an unceasing and irreconcilable war for life and death. He must discipline himself to endure torture.

6. Hard toward himself, he must be hard toward others also. All the tender and effeminate emotions of kinship, friendship, love, gratitude, and even honor must be stifled in him by a cold and single-minded passion for the revolutionary cause. There exists for him only one delight, one consolation, one reward and one gratification—the success of the revolution. Night and day he must have but one thought, one aim—merciless destruction. In cold-blooded and tireless pursuit of this aim, he must be prepared both to die himself and to destroy with his own hands everything that stands in the way of its achievement.

7. The nature of the true revolutionary has no place for any romanticism, any sentimentality, rapture, or enthusiasm. It has no place either for personal hatred or vengeance. The revolutionary passion, which in him becomes a habitual state of mind, must at every moment be combined with cold calculation. Always and everywhere he must be not what the promptings of his personal inclinations would have him be, but what the general interest of the revolution prescribes.

8. The revolutionary considers his friend and holds dear only a person who has shown himself in practice to be as much a revolutionary as he himself. The extent of his friendship, devotion, and other obligations towards his comrade is determined only by their degree of usefulness in the practical work of total revolutionary destruction.

9. The need for solidarity among revolutionaries is self-evident. In it lies the whole strength of revolutionary work. Revolutionary comrades who possess the same degree of revolutionary understanding and passion should, as far as possible, discuss all important matters together and come to unanimous decisions. But in implementing a plan decided upon in this manner, each man should as far as possible rely on himself. In performing a series of destructive actions each man must act for himself and have recourse to the advice and help of his comrades only if this is necessary for the success (of the plan).

10. Each comrade should have under him several revolutionaries of the second or third category, that is, comrades who are not completely initiated. He should regard them as portions of a common fund of revolutionary capital, placed at his disposal. He should expend

his portion of the capital economically, always attempting to derive the utmost possible benefit from it. Himself he should regard as capital consecrated to the triumph of the revolutionary cause; but as capital which he may not dispose of independently without the consent of the entire company of the fully initiated comrades.

11. When a comrade gets into trouble, the revolutionary, in deciding whether he should be rescued or not, must think not in terms of his personal feelings but only of the good of the revolutionary cause. Therefore he must balance, on the one hand, the usefulness of the comrade, and on the other, the amount of revolutionary energy that would necessarily be expended on his deliverance, and must settle for whichever is the weightier consideration.

12. The admission of a new member, who has proved himself not by words but by deeds, may be decided upon only by unanimous agreement.

13. The revolutionary enters into the world of the state, of class, and of so-called culture, and lives in it only because he has faith in its speedy and total destruction. He is not a revolutionary if he feels pity for anything in this world. If he is able to, he must face the annihilation of a situation, of a relationship, or of any person who is a part of this world—everything and everyone must be equally odious to him.

   All the worse for him if he has family, friends, and loved ones in this world; he is no revolutionary if they can stay his hand.

14. Aiming at merciless destruction the revolutionary can and sometimes even must live within society while pretending to be quite other than what he is. The revolutionary must penetrate everywhere, among all the lowest and the middle classes, into the houses of commerce, the church, the mansions of the rich, the world of the bureaucracy, the military, and of literature, the Third Section [the secret police], and even the Winter Palace.

15. All of this foul society must be split up into several categories: the first category comprises those to be condemned immediately to death. The society should compile a list of these condemned persons in order of the relative harm they may do to the successful progress of the revolutionary cause, and thus in order of their removal.

16. In compiling these lists and deciding the order referred to above, the guiding principle must not be the individual acts of villainy committed by the person, nor even by the hatred he provokes

among the society or the people. This villainy and hatred, however, may to a certain extent be useful, since they help to incite popular rebellion. The guiding principle must be the measure of service the person's death will necessarily render to the revolutionary cause. Therefore, in the first instance all those must be annihilated who are especially harmful to the revolutionary organization, and whose sudden and violent deaths will also inspire the greatest fear in the government and, by depriving it of its cleverest and most energetic figures, will shatter its strength.

17. The second category must consist of those who are granted temporary respite to live, solely in order that their bestial behavior shall drive the people to inevitable revolt.

18. To the third category belong a multitude of high-ranking cattle, or personages distinguished neither for any particular intelligence nor for energy, but who, because of their position, enjoy wealth, connections, influence, and power. They must be exploited in every possible fashion and way; they must be enmeshed and confused, and, when we have found out as much as we can about their dirty secrets, we must make them our slaves. Their power, influence, connections, riches, and energy thus become an inexhaustible treasure house and an effective aid to our various enterprises.

19. The fourth category consists of politically ambitious persons and liberals of various hues. With them we can conspire according to their own programs, pretending that we are blindly following them, while in fact we are taking control of them, rooting out all their secrets and compromising them to the utmost, so that they are irreversibly implicated and can be employed to create disorder in the state.

20. The fifth category is composed of doctrinaires, conspirators, revolutionaries, all those who are given to idle peroration, whether before audiences or on paper. They must be continually incited and forced into making violent declarations of practical intent, as a result of which the majority of them will vanish without a trace and real revolutionary gain will accrue from a few.

21. The sixth, and an important category, is that of women. They should be divided into three main types: first, those frivolous, thoughtless, and vapid women who we may use as we use the third and fourth categories of men; second, women who are ardent, gifted, and devoted, but do not belong to us because they have not yet achieved a real, passionless, and practical revolutionary understanding: these must be used like the men of the fifth category;

and, finally there are the women who are with us completely, that is, who have been fully initiated and have accepted our program in its entirety. We should regard these women as the most valuable of our treasures, whose assistance we cannot do without.

---

The *Catechism* has been translated many times.
It is reprinted here from M. Confino, *Daughter of a Revolutionary* (Alcove Press, London, 1974), with the kind permission of author and publisher.

NIKOLAI MOROZOV

# THE TERRORIST STRUGGLE

W HAT IS THE LIKELY FATE of this new form of revolutionary struggle which could be called "terroristic revolution"?

In order to give a more or less positive answer to this question, it is important to review the meaning of the movement and its conditions.

Matters were as follows: at the head of the country was the all-powerful government with its spies, prisons, and guns, with its millions of soldiers and voluntary government servants who either knew or were ignorant of what they represented. It is the government against whom all the national uprisings and all the open revolutionary attempts of youth were helpless. It was a government that managed the country with an iron hand and was capable with one gesture of its leader to destroy tens of thousands of the obvious enemies. Against this large organization, the depressed, intelligent Russian youth brought forth a handful of people insignificant as to numbers but strong and terrible in their energy and elusiveness. The active, spontaneous revolutionary struggle was concentrated in this small group. To the pressure of the all-powerful enemy it opposed impenetrable secrecy.

This small group was not afraid of the enemy's numerous spies since it protected itself by the way it carried on the struggle. Revolutionaries did not need to get close to a lot of strange, little-known people and were able to choose only those men for comrades in their small group who were already tested and trustworthy. The Third Section [the secret police] knows how few members of this group fell into the hands of the government through the activity of the government's spies.

The revolutionary group is not afraid of bayonets and the government's army because it does not have to clash, in its struggle, with this blind and insensible force, which strikes down those whom it is ordered to strike. This force is only dreadful to the obvious enemy. Against the secret one it is completely useless.

The real danger lies in the carelessness among the revolutionaries since it may destroy individual members of the organization. But this destruction will be only temporary anyway. Elements from a better segment of society, which are hostile to government, will produce new members who will continue to work for the cause.

The revolutionary group is immortal because its way of struggle becomes a tradition and part of people's lives.

The secret assassination becomes a terrible weapon in the hands of such a group of people. "The 'malicious will' eternally bent to one viewpoint becomes extremely resourceful and there is no possibility of saving oneself from its assault." In such a way Russian newspapers described another attempt on the tsar's life. It is true that human resourcefulness is unlimited.

No one would have believed before November 19 that in spite of all the police measures it would be possible to mine the railroad during the tsar's return from Livadja. Before November 19 no one would have believed that the conspirators could penetrate to the tsar's castle. But terroristic struggle has exactly this advantage—that it can act unexpectedly and find means and ways which no one anticipates.

All that the terroristic struggle really needs is a small number of people and large material means.

This presents really a new form of struggle.

It replaces by a series of individual political assassinations, which always hit their target, the massive revolutionary movements, where people often rise against each other because of misunderstanding and where a nation kills off its own children, while the enemy of the people watches from a secure shelter and sees to it that the people of the organization are destroyed. The movement punishes only those who are really responsible for the evil deed. Because of this the terroristic revolution is the only just form of a revolution.

At the same time, it is also the most convenient form of a revolution.

Using insignificant forces it had an opportunity to restrain all the efforts of tyranny which seemed to be undefeated up to this time.

"Do not be afraid of the tsar, do not be afraid of despotic rulers because all of them are weak and helpless against secret, sudden assassinations," it says to mankind.

This is the meaning of the movement which is now developing in Russia. Never before in history have there been such convenient conditions for the existence of a revolutionary party and for such successful methods of struggle.

When a whole new row of independent terroristic societies arises in Russia together with the already existing terroristic groups and when these groups come to know each other during their struggle, they will all unite into one common organization. If this organization starts its activities against the government, and if the hard two-year struggles of Russian terrorists left any impressions on Russia's youth, then there can be no doubt that the last days of the monarchy and of brutal force will soon be over. A wide path will be open for socialist activities in Russia.

Terroristic movement in Russia has another distinctive feature, which we, its contemporaries, hardly notice, but which has an important meaning. This feature alone can bring about a turning point in the history of revolutionary struggle.

Hatred toward national oppressors was always powerful in mankind, and many times selfless people tried to destroy the life of the one who personified violence, at the price of their own lives. However, each time they tried, they perished. The act of human justice against tyranny had been accomplished but it was also followed by retribution.

In the deathly silence of depressed witnesses the bloody executioner's block arose, human sacrifice was offered to the idol of monarchy, and our national nemesis lowered again its slightly raised head. The momentary satisfaction of higher justice was now dimmed by the destruction of a generous and selfless man. The very thought of the tsar's assassination finally turned into something terrible and tragic. It soon evoked a notion of hopeless despair and magnanimous suicide rather than the idea of irreconcilable struggle with oppression. This thought told the people of terrible moral sufferings, of unbearable internal agony which the tsar's killer had to live through, before he finished his account with life and accomplished his feat, which appeared to be exceptional, unattainable, and not normal. The tsar knew that such magnanimous heroes were very few, and when he recovered from the first shock, he continued his reign of violence.

Contemporary terroristic struggle is not like this at all. Justice is done here, but those who carry it out remain alive. They disappear without a trace and thus they are able to fight again against the enemy, to live and to work for the cause. Sad feelings do not tarnish the realization of restored human dignity.

That was the struggle of despair and self-sacrifice; this is the struggle of force against force, of equal against equal; the struggle of heroism against oppression, of knowledge and education against bayonets and gallows.

Now the struggle does not speak to people of hopelessness and self-sacrifice. No, now it tells them about the powerful love of freedom which is capable of making a hero out of a man, which can give people gigantic strength to accomplish almost superhuman deeds.

The tsars and despots who oppress the nation cannot live peacefully any longer in their palaces. The unseen revenger will let them know by a deafening explosion that their time has come and the despots will feel that the earth is collapsing under their feet among the sounds of music, the frightened screams of innumerable crowds, during the dessert at a refined dinner.

Terroristic struggle is equally possible under the absolute force or under the constitutional brutal force, in Russia as well as in Germany. Brutal force and despotism are always concentrated either in a few or more often in one ruling person (Bismarck, Napoleon) and stop with his failure or death. Such people should be destroyed in the very beginning of their careers, be they chosen by an army or plebiscite. The wide and easy road opened in the country for ambitious people trying to strengthen their power on the remains of national freedom should be made hopeless and dangerous by anti-government terrorists. Thus, not too many volunteers will try to make use of it. In Russia, where rough force and despotism became traditional in the present dynasty, the course of terror became considerably complicated and perhaps a number of political assassinations and tsar killings are necessary. However, the contemporary terrorists who for two years fought the government, being supported only by the strength of their convictions, have shown that, even without clarifying the ideas of their struggle, it has many chances to succeed, even in this kingdom of despotism. Success of the terroristic movement will be inevitable if the future terroristic struggle becomes a deed of not only one separate group, but of an idea, which cannot be destroyed by people. Then in place of those fighters who will perish, new ones and new revolutionaries will appear until the goal of the movement is achieved.

The goal of the terroristic movement in our country should not become concentrated only on disarraying contemporary Russian despotism. The movement should make the struggle popular, historical, and grandiose. It should bring the way of struggle into the lives of people in such a manner that every new appearance of tyranny in the future will be met by new groups of people from the better elements of society, and these groups will destroy oppression by consecutive political assassinations. "Every man has a right to kill a tyrant and a nation cannot take away this right even from one of its citizens," said St. Just during the trial of Louis Capet. These words should become a slogan for the future struggle and violence.

There is no possibility to suppose that there won't be the necessary elements for this kind of struggle. Devotion to the idea, heroism and selflessness did not disappear from humanity during its darkest period of history, when it seems that oppression would crush the last gleam of life and consciousness of people. The gleam sparkled secretly in the heart of the country and broke free here and there as with a shot from Wilhelm Tell, or Babeuf's conspiracy, or the Decembrists' attempted struggle. The spontaneous, massive struggle against oppression throughout history was parallel to another struggle, which although unconscious and not systematic, nevertheless was continuous and irreconcilable. This other movement became evident because of a number of attempts at political assassinations. With every centennial this struggle became more energetic and active and never were the attempts on the tsar's life so numerous as in the last thirty years. There were the following facts concerning the struggle of underground fighters from 1848, without taking into account numerous assassinations and attempts at assassination of public statesmen of Russia and America: attempt on the life of the Count of Modena; attempt to assassinate a Prussian prince; attempt on the life of Queen Victoria; seriously wounding Emperor Francis Joseph on the bastions of Vienna; attempt on the life of Victor Emmanuel; assassination of Ferdinand III of Parma; attempt on the life of the Spanish queen; wounding of Ferdinand of Naples by bayonets; shooting of the queen of Greece; assassination of Prince Mikhail of Serbia; attempt on life of Humbert; two attempts on life of King Alfonso during his short reign; four attempts on life of Wilhelm, wounding him twice seriously; six attempts to assassinate Napoleon III in all possible ways; six attempts on life of Emperor Alexander II, of which only one was discovered while being carried out.

All these actions, which were carried out continuously and consequently at the time when the terroristic struggle had not yet been turned into a system, deprives of all foundation the assumption that these actions would cease in the future when terror acquires theoretical foundation.

But there is another reason which makes such assumption unlikely. We know that any historical struggle, any historical development, will move along the line of least resistance. All offsprings of movement turning to another direction bruise themselves against the obstacles they encounter on their way. Terroristic struggle which strikes at the weakest spot of the existing system will obviously be universally accepted in life. The time will come when the present, unsystematic attempts will merge into one wide stream and then no despotism or brutal force will be able to stand up against them. The task of the contemporary Russian terrorists is to summarize theoretically and to systematize practically this form of revolutionary struggle, which goes on for a long time. Political assassinations alone should become an expression of this rich, consistent system.

We know the importance of the influence of ideas on man. In distant antiquity these ideas brought about Christianity and from fires and crosses they foretold near freedom to the world. In the dark calm of the Middle Ages they were responsible for the crusades and for many years they attracted people to the dry and unfertile plains of Palestine. In the last one hundred years these ideas summoned revolutionary and socialist movements, and the fields of Europe and America were covered with the blood of new fighters for freedom and humanity.

When a small handful of people appears to represent the struggle of a whole nation and is triumphant over millions of enemies, then the idea of terroristic struggle will not die once it is clarified for the people and proven that it can be practical. Each act of violence and force will give birth to new revengers and each tyrant will create new Solovjevs and Nobilings. Thus, the very existence of despotism and monarchy will quickly become impossible.

Furthermore, it will not be difficult for the revolutionaries-terrorists, once they have succeeded, to direct their efforts to the preparation of social revolution of the whole nation. All the same, the ideas of the revolutionaries will live in the memories of the masses, and every manifestation of violence (on the part of government) will bring forth new terroristic groups. It will not be known where these groups will disappear to, or where they will come from.

Russian terrorists have two highly important tasks:

1. They should clarify theoretically the idea of terroristic struggle, which up to now is understood differently by different people. Along with the preaching of socialism, preaching on future struggle is essential among these classes of population where propaganda is still possible despite the unfavorable conditions. This can be accomplished because these classes, by their customs and traditions, are close to the revolutionary party. Only then will the struggle receive an influx of fresh forces from the population, and these forces are essential for a determined and long struggle.
2. The terroristic party should show in practice the usefulness of the means it employs. The party should bring about the final disorganization, demoralization, and weakening of government for its actions of violence against freedom. This should be achieved through a consistent, punishing system used by terrorists. This system should make the government weak and incapable of taking any measures for the oppression of freedom of thought and against actions carried out for the national welfare.

By accomplishing these two tasks the terroristic party will establish its way of struggle as a traditional one and will destroy the very possibility of despotism's recurrence in the future.

The future will show if the contemporary terrorists will live up to their standards. We are, however, deeply convinced that the terroristic movement will overcome all the obstacles in its way. The triumph of the cause will show all the antagonists that the terroristic movement fully satisfies the conditions of contemporary reality, which put this form of struggle in the forefront.

Nikolai Morozov, *Terroristicheskaya Borba* (Geneva, 1880). This translation is reprinted from Feliks Gross, *Violence in Politics* (Mouton & Co., the Hague, 1972) with the kind permission of author and publisher.

## G. TARNOVSKI

# TERRORISM AND ROUTINE

THE TERRORIST REVOLUTION is a pointed manifestation of the abnormalities of social relations in Russia. This is the "direct correlation"; in other words, these are the causes of terrorism.

As to its significance and consequence, even here our author [Dragomanov] does not betray himself; he does not acknowledge its social significance although he does not deny its political meaning.

Do you realize, Mr. Dragomanov, that in these matters it is now time to stop imparting a special importance to the titles of school textbooks and to stop looking at public life as if it was a set of categories with political types in one section and social life in quite a different one?

You ask, what significance can a few crowned heads have in the annihilation of social slavery? We do not know whether there can be any such question from the point of view of routine word games or appropriateness, but, as far as real progress is concerned, there can be no question at all. Where the full social liberation of mankind is concerned, political freedom, as we have defined it above, and the republic, are the first steps without which the rest is impossible. This is the real metaphysical point of view on this question; the existence of crowned vampires, kings, and czars is far from being a matter of indifference.

When you speak about self-defense and public defense (terrorism), you refer to the latter as "secret," wishing to imply something dirty by the use of this title. Kovalsky defended his fiat against evil-doers and robbers, gun in hand; as you so truly observe, amongst honorable people there can be no two opinions about this. But some people have made a generalization about this and have wished to strike one of the main perpetrators of death, not just Kovalsky. These people have decided to strike a blow at the very system of crime enmeshing Russia. In other words, they have moved from their own to a public point of view. "This," you say, "is dirty."

In your opinion the necessary defense of an isolated individual is praiseworthy. You say, however, that the public conscience denies the whole nation's right to necessary defense.

This is what we shall say to you this time, Mr. Dragomanov. Terrorists, the defenders of the people, have the right to ignore the public conscience which "always denies" the defense of the people. This is the conscience of the society whose representatives are the Alexander IIs, the Totlebens, the Tolstoys, persons with interests hostile to the people. If their "conscience" rises against terrorists, that is perfectly natural. And the fact that you were unable to renounce the views of this "society" and decided to look at terrorists through their moral glass is very, very sad.

With regard to the attacks on the moral aspect of terrorism, let us set down a few words. Let us suppose you, Mr. Dragomanov, to be "in the gray depths of eternity." Let us take any revolt aiming to save one's homeland—let us take the revolt led by Mucius Scaevola. Was that not a lofty, even heroic exploit, so morally beyond dispute that it is even glorified in children's school textbooks?

But we are now bounded by the prosaic present. Before us is a gang of worthless louts exploiting poor, hungry Russia, writhing in a wild frenzy on ground spattered with the blood of its finest people. At its head is the czar, without heart or reason, who has made it his aim to stifle all those who show signs of life. The defense of public life has passed into the hands of people who have decided to rid Russia of the tyrant, whatever the cost. What will you say to that? "Immoral," replies your article. One case is lofty and the other, exactly the same, is disgusting. It is only disgusting because it is "not accepted," it is only immoral because it is taking place in front of your very eyes in circumstances to which you are used to applying the narrow criterion of the status quo.

No, Mr. Dragomanov, if the main aim of your work is to preserve "innocence" of this kind, you should not allow yourself into the sphere of politics and national liberation. Here, there are other aims and another criterion. For the good of the homeland we have to sacrifice this foreign way of life and not stand too much in awe of our own way of life. Here, he who takes upon himself the courage to judge such historical facts as revolution, whether of the masses or of terrorists, must be able to renounce conventional morality and raise himself to the natural laws of justice and morality. And from this point of view of the highest justice, all revolution as a means of liberating the people is moral—already moral—because it gives the people the possibility of living a moral way of life.

Morals are inconceivable without freedom. Under the pressure of despotism there is subjection, hypocrisy, venality. There are not and cannot be morals because there is neither individual free choice nor self-determination. Thus are the development of society and the well-being of a nation the consequences of a successful revolution. And in the social sense only that is moral which furthers society's freedom, development, and material benefit. Everything hostile to this is immoral and is destined to destruction in the view of every thinking person. And that is not all.

Every member of society must, in the name of these same morals, be determined that the suffering borne by the people during the revolution should be reduced to the minimum and should not be in vain—that is to say, that the revolution should achieve its aim to the greatest extent possible. Furthermore, it should remove the very possibility of repeating in the future those actions which were the cause of the people's suffering. In this regard one must not forget that steps toward freedom were and are made in history only under the excesses of tyranny and in the face of historical movement. Consequently, it is only in such a movement that the people can find a safe measure against the encroachments of despotism. These are the bases on which to estimate the moral worth of revolution. And if we compare, for example, popular revolution (on which you comment further) as a means of attaining political freedom with terrorist revolution, with a system of political murders, then it is not hard to convince oneself which form to prefer.

During a popular revolution the greatest strength of the nation, its soldiers, perish, while those same perpetrators of evil calmly observe the conduct of the battle and at the critical moment bolt from the rear wing, as did Louis Philippe, or remain in their place, having temporarily put on sheep's clothing, but ready at the first opportunity to cast it off and take up their former trade again. Sometimes this is the essence of tragicomedy in reality: the blood of the innocent flows in rivers and the results are the more trivial as more blood is spilled and as the people grow more weary.

Terrorist revolution is not like this. Even when a few innocent people do suffer, as with the soldiers during the explosion at the Winter Palace, that is a straightforward *casus belli*. Terrorism directs its blows against the real perpetrators of evil. When the suffering of the people is ended, the meaning of the revolt will crystallize. It will become more intelligible to the public consciousness and will educate the people to despise despotism. The government itself helps in this; as is its usual custom, it intensifies its atrocities which are purposeless, even harmful to itself, but it relies on everything that is savage, uncontrollable, and mindless in such circumstances.

Like everything new and unprecedented, terrorist revolution at first brings a certain perturbation into society, but the greater part of society has understood what it stands for. This initial confusion changes to jeers and anger directed against the despot and it moves to sympathize with the revolution. Its outcome is practically assured; it now depends solely on the mind and energy of those who practice it.

Also, the position of the representatives of autocracy is completely changed by the presence of terrorism as a system.

From the point of view of a healthy social morality, the removal of those individuals who bring down a whole nation to the level of a herd in order to exploit and humiliate it is a duty prescribed by the laws of natural justice for everyone who still retains even a fraction of consciousness or humanity untainted by slavery.

The life of a tyrant changes from one of luxurious, sensuous ease to that of a tormented life full of tragedy of the kind paraded in front of our eyes by the czar, trembling every moment for his criminal existence. And nowhere will he find a word of compassion; everyone, gazing at these Macbeth-like agonies will say maliciously, "Thieves never prosper." The true value of the czar's position will become clear.

This is the wise way to national liberation. *"C'est une revolution vraiment scientifique,"* as a certain Frenchman said of Russian terrorism. Understand that well, gentlemen, and don't forget it! Remember that terrorist revolution is completely moral in its aims, more reasonable, humanitarian, and consequently more ethical in the methods which it uses than mass revolution.

Considering terrorism from the point of view of "purity of methods," we shall not bore ourselves and our readers by analyzing the models of deep thinking and consistency with which Mr. Dragomanov's essentially petty article is crammed. Let us move on directly to the finale and to Mr. Dragomanov's concluding suggestion.

Here is what the author of "Terrorism and Freedom" says on page eleven of his article: "We believe that political murders, even setting aside their moral inconvenience" (how he loves this word "convenience"), "have only a negative significance: they humiliate the government but do not subvert it." (But surely subversion is not a negative manifestation.) "In our view only an open attack on the political structure can lead Russia into a new path." (Here the same attack already appears to be positive; there is even a guide on the "new path.") "This attack by word and deed on the part of properly organized political societies is composed of citizens and soldiers in all Russia's territories and among all her peoples."

Mr. Dragomanov does not agree with the "authors of the Petersburg Proclamations"; he believes that terror cannot achieve freedom. Why? Because the results will only be negative. What a truly pedestrian argument!

At the beginning of this century, when railways were being constructed in France, the "eminent" Thiers disputed their value, arguing that such an undertaking was impracticable because "the wheels would not turn 'round." This advocate of conservatism was, of course, completely ignorant about engineering but had to think up some "sufficient basis" for argument against this innovation which no well-run state had ever tried before. That is why he stated that "the wheels will not turn 'round." Our author, too, in trying to find similar "bases" for his argument, has come up with the phrase "negative results." How could you lose sight of the fact that the difference between negative and positive results is relative and has no objective meaning? We can express one and the same idea both positively and negatively. We can say that a man is full or not hungry, stupid or not clever. If you like, one can express the term "progress" negatively as the destruction of arbitrary rule and exploitation in all its forms. If you do not find these examples of plain common sense quite clear or sufficiently convincing, remember Hegel's famous abstract, and yet entertaining, words "Life and non-life are identical," and hold on to his meaning.

And now tell me, is it possible to construct a negation of terrorism on such a negative basis? What will happen is that you will not deny its results but will only obscure them with a kind of mist with which you will adorn your final proposal "to lead Russia into a new path." What do you mean by this "open attack"? If you see here mass revolution, do you consider it possible and reasonable to arouse the Russian common man to fight for political freedom, bearing in mind his historical separation from the intelligentsia, his life of want, and his hard struggle for a piece of bread? He will have to be truly imbued with the need for political freedom.

Is it so hard to understand that all your "citizens and soldiers," all your "peoples" belong essentially to the intelligentsia? This intelligentsia is thus obliged, yes obliged, to bear political freedom in Russia upon its shoulders, using terror as its means.

You, however, deny terrorism because of its "moral inconvenience." What will remain of your "program of action" after such denial and self-denial? "Pure means," "absolutely pure methods," "moral comfort," in other words, "Misery have a heart."

We draw this conclusion: it is unsuitable to launch out onto the open sea of national liberation with a moral compass and ill-assorted luggage fit only for home life. You will not heed this until you find yourselves on a tow-boat with the czar's henchmen.

---

G. Tarnovski (G. Romanenko), *Terrorizm i Rutina*
(Geneva, 1880)

# UNDERGROUND RUSSIA

T HE GOVERNMENT SEEMED BENT on exasperating not only the liberals but also the revolutionists. With a vile desire for vengeance, it re-doubled its cruelty against the socialists, whom it had in its power. The Emperor Alexander II even went so far as to annul the sentence of his own senate, which, under the form of a petition for pardon, acquitted most of the accused in the trial of the 193.

What government, therefore, was this which acted so insolently against all the laws of the country, which was not supported, and did not wish to be supported, by the nation or by any class or by the laws which it had made itself? What did it represent except brute force?

Against such a government everything is permitted. It is no longer a guardian of the will of the people or of the majority of the people. It is organized injustice. A citizen is no more bound to respect it than to respect a band of highwaymen who employ the force at their command in rifling travelers.

But how shake off this camarilla entrenched behind a forest of bayonets? How free the country from it?

It being absolutely impossible to overcome this obstacle by force, as in other countries more fortunate than ours, a flank movement was necessary so as to fall upon this camarilla before it could avail itself of its forces, thus rendered useless in their impregnable positions.

Thus arose the terrorism.

Conceived in hatred, nurtured by patriotism and by hope, it grew up in an electrical atmosphere, impregnated with the enthusiasm awakened by an act of heroism.

On August 16, 1878—that is, five months after the acquittal of Zassu-lic—the terrorism, by putting to death General Mesentzeff, the head of the police and of the entire camarilla, boldly threw down its glove in the face of autocracy. From that day forth it advanced with giant strides, acquiring strength and position, and culminating in the tremendous duel with the man who was the personification of despotism.

I will not relate its achievements, for they are written in letters of fire upon the records of history.

Three times the adversaries met face to face. Three times the terrorist by the will of fate was overthrown, but after each defeat he arose more threatening and powerful than before. To the attempt of Solovieff succeeded that of Hartman, which was followed by the frightful explosion at the Winter Palace, the infernal character of which seemed to surpass everything the imagination could conceive. But it was surpassed on March 13. Once more the adversaries grappled with each other, and this time the omnipotent emperor fell half dead to the ground.

The terrorist had won the victory in his tremendous duel, which had cost so many sacrifices. With a whole nation prostrate he alone held high his head, which throughout so many tempests he had never bent.

He is noble, terrible, irresistibly fascinating, for he combines in himself the two sublimities of human grandeur: the martyr and the hero.

He is a martyr. From the day when he swears in the depths of his heart to free the people and the country, he knows he is consecrated to death. He faces it at every step of his stormy life. He goes forth to meet it fearlessly, when necessary, and can die without flinching, not like a Christian of old, but like a warrior accustomed to looking death in the face.

He has no longer any religious feeling in his disposition. He is a wrestler, all bone and muscle, and has nothing in common with the dreamy idealist of the previous luster. He is a mature man, and the unreal dreams of his youth have disappeared with years. He is a socialist fatally convinced, but he understands that a social revolution requires long preparatory labor, which cannot be given until political liberty is acquired. Modest and resolute, therefore, he clings to the resolution to limit for the present his plans that he may extend them afterward. He has no other object than to overthrow this abhorred despotism, and to give to his country what all civilized nations possess—political liberty—to enable it to advance with a firm step toward its own redemption. The force of mind, the indomitable energy, and the spirit of sacrifice which his predecessor attained in the beauty of his dreams, he attains in the grandeur of his mission, in the strong passions which this marvelous, intoxicating, vertiginous struggle arouses in his heart.

What a spectacle! When had such a spectacle been seen before? Alone, obscure, poor, he undertook to be the defender of outraged humanity, of right trampled underfoot, and he challenged to the death the most powerful empire in the world, and for years and years confronted all its immense forces.

Proud as Satan rebelling against God, he opposed his own will to that of the man who alone, amid a nation of slaves, claimed the right of having a will. But how different is this terrestrial god from the old Jehovah of Moses! How he hides his trembling head under the daring blows of the terrorist! True, he still stands erect, and the thunderbolts launched by his trembling hand often fail; but when they strike, they kill. But the terrorist is immortal. His limbs may fail him, but, as if by magic, they regain their vigor, and he stands erect, ready for battle after battle until he has laid low his enemy and liberated the country. And already he sees that enemy falter, become confused, cling desperately to the wildest means, which can only hasten his end.

It is this absorbing struggle, it is this imposing mission, it is this certainty of approaching victory, which gives him that cool and calculating enthusiasm, that almost superhuman energy, which astounds the world. If he is by nature a man capable of generous impulses, he will become a hero; if he is of stronger fiber, it will harden into iron; if of iron, it will become adamant.

He has a powerful and distinctive individuality. He is no longer, like his predecessor, all abnegation. He no longer possesses, he no longer strives after, that abstract moral beauty which made the propagandist resemble a being of another world. For his look is no longer directed inwardly but is fixed upon the hated enemy. He is the type of individual force, intolerant of every yoke, who fights not only for the people, to render them the arbiters of their own destinies, not only for the whole nation stifling in this pestiferous atmosphere, but also for himself; for the dear ones whom he loves, whom he adores with all the enthusiasm which animates his soul; for his friends, who languish in the horrid cells of the central prisons, and who stretch forth to him their skinny hands imploring aid. He fights for himself. He has sworn to be free and he will be free, in defiance of everything. He bends his haughty head before no idol. He has devoted his sturdy arms to the cause of the people. But he no longer deifies them. And if the people, ill-counseled, say to him "Be a slave," he will exclaim "No!" And he will march onward, defying their imprecations and their fury, certain that justice will be rendered to him in his tomb.

Such is the terrorist. . . .

The isolation of the Russian government can only be compared with that of a hated foreigner in a conquered country. The best proof of this is, as I have already said, its inability to overcome the terrorists. To illustrate this, however, I will relate a few little incidents of revolutionary life.

It must be admitted to begin with that as conspirators the Russian revolutionists, with few exceptions, are not worth much. The Russian disposition, generous, listless, undisciplined; the love of openness; the habit of doing everything "in common," render it little adapted to conform to the vital principle of conspiracy: to tell what is to be told only to those to whom it is essential to tell it, and not to those to whom it may merely be told without danger. Examples such as Perovskaia or Stefanovic are very rare among the Russians. Thus, the revolutionary secrets are usually very badly kept, and no sooner have they passed out of the organization than they spread abroad with incredible rapidity throughout the nihilist world, and not unfrequently pass from city to city. Notwithstanding this, the government never knows anything.

Thus, before the publication of the newspaper *Zemlia i Volia,* conducted by "illegal" men, a secret revolutionary and socialist journal was issued in St. Petersburg—*Nacialo,* which was not the organ of the organization, but of an isolated "circle," and its conductors were four or five "legal" men. All St. Petersburg knew them, and could name them. But the police, although they were run off their legs in search of traces of this newspaper, knew nothing, and never learnt anything about it; so that some of the conductors of the paper, who have not been compromised in other matters, remain safe and sound to this day.

The sale of the most terrible of the terrorist papers, the *Narodnaia Volia,* is carried on in St. Petersburg in the most simple manner imaginable. In every higher school, in every class of society, and in all the principal provincial towns, there are men, known to everybody, who undertake this commission; and receiving a certain number of copies of the paper, sell it to everybody who wants it, at twenty-five kopecks in St. Petersburg and thirty-five in the provinces.

Here is another fact, which will seem much more strange, but which, notwithstanding, is perfectly true.

The immense dynamite conspiracy, organized by the executive committee in 1879, for the emperor's journey to and from St. Petersburg and the Crimea, was perhaps the greatest undertaking ever organized by a secret society. This conspiracy was on too grand a scale to be carried out by the forces of the organization alone, so outsiders had to be taken from that vast world around it which is always ready to render it any kind of service. It is not to be wondered at that, with so many people, the secret of the attempts in preparation should leak out and quickly spread throughout all Russia. The precise places were not known, certainly, but every student, every barrister, every writer not in the pay of the police, knew that "the imperial train would be blown up during the journey from the Crimea to

St. Petersburg." It was talked about "everywhere," as the phrase runs. In one city a subscription was even got up, almost publicly, for this purpose, and about fifteen roubles were collected, all of which were paid into the coffers of the committee.

Yet the police knew nothing. Of the six attempts belonging to that period, one alone was discovered—that of Logovenco—by mere chance. The arrest of Goldenberg with a supply of dynamite, which also occurred by mere chance, at the Elisabetgrad station, was the circumstance which aroused suspicion that something was in preparation, and caused precautions to be taken in the arrangements of the trains.

These facts, and others of the same kind which I could multiply indefinitely, give an idea, it appears to me, of the respective positions of the government and the revolutionists.

The terrorists have before them a government not in the European sense of the word—for then, owing to the disproportion of strength, the struggle would be impossible—but a camarilla, a small and isolated faction, which represents only its own interests and is not supported by any class of society.

Thus the struggle, although extremely difficult, becomes possible, and may last for years and years.

What will be the end?

That depends upon the line of conduct adopted by the government.

One thing is evident: it will never succeed in putting down the terrorism by retaliation. Precisely because they are few, the terrorists will remain invincible. A victory obtained over a revolution like that of Paris gives to the conqueror at least ten or fifteen years of peace, for with a hundred thousand victims, all that is noblest, most generous, and boldest in a nation is exterminated, and it languishes until a fresh generation arises to avenge its slaughtered fathers. But what avails in a country like Russia, the loss of a handful of men, which from time to time the government succeeds in snatching from the ranks of the organization?

The survivors will continue the struggle with an ardor increased by the desire of vengeance. The universal discontent will provide them with pecuniary means. The young men, animated as they are by the example of so many heroes, are near to supply an immense and inexhaustible source of new recruits; and the struggle will continue still more fiercely.

But if the terrorists cannot be overcome, how are they to overcome the government?

A victory, immediate, splendid, and decisive, such as that obtained by an insurrection, is utterly impossible by means of terrorism. But another victory is more probable, that of the weak against the strong, that of the "beggars" of Holland against the Spaniards. In a struggle against an invisible, impalpable, omnipresent enemy, the strong is vanquished, not by the arms of his adversary, but by the continuous tension of his own strength, which exhausts him, at last, more than he would be exhausted by defeats.

Such is precisely the position of the belligerent parties in Russia.

The terrorists cannot overthrow the government, cannot drive it from St. Petersburg and Russia. But having compelled it, for so many years running, to neglect everything and do nothing but struggle with them, by forcing it to do so still for years and years, they will render its position untenable. Already the prestige of the imperial government has received a wound which it will be very difficult to heal. An emperor who shuts himself up in a prison from fear of the terrorists is certainly not a figure to inspire admiration.

On this point I could already cite many things which circulate in the army, and among the people. What will be said if he remains shut up another year or two? And how can he do otherwise than remain shut up if he continues his policy?

But it is not on the moral side alone that the government is the worse off.

In this struggle between liberty and despotism, the revolutionists, it must be confessed, have on their side an immense advantage, that of time. Every month, every week, of this hesitation, of this irresolution, of this enervating tension, renders the position of their adversary worse, and consequently strengthens their own.

---

Serge Stepniak-Kravchinski,
*Underground Russia* (London, 1883).

PYOTR KROPOTKIN

# THE SPIRIT OF REVOLT

T HERE ARE PERIODS IN THE LIFE of human society when revolution becomes an imperative necessity, when it proclaims itself as inevitable. New ideas germinate everywhere, seeking to force their way into the light, to find an application in life. These ideas are opposed by the inertia of those whose interest it is to maintain the old order; they suffocate in the stifling atmosphere of prejudice and traditions. The accepted ideas of the constitution of the state, of the laws of social equilibrium, of the political and economic interrelations of citizens, can hold out no longer against the implacable criticism which is daily undermining them whenever occasion arises—in drawing room as in cabaret, in the writings of philosophers as in daily conversation. Political, economic and social institutions are crumbling. The social structure, having become uninhabitable, is hindering, even preventing, the development of the seeds which are being propagated within its damaged walls and being brought forth around them.

The need for a new life becomes apparent. The code of established morality, that which governs the greater number of people in their daily life, no longer seems sufficient. What formerly seems just is now felt to be a crying injustice. The morality of yesterday is today recognized as revolting immorality. The conflict between new ideas and old traditions flames up in every class of society, in every possible environment, in the very bosom of the family. The son struggles against his father, he finds revolting what his father has all his life found natural. The daughter rebels against the principles which her mother has handed down to her as the result of long experience. Daily, the popular conscience rises up against the scandals which breed amidst the privileged and the leisured, against the crimes committed in the name of "the law of the stronger," or in order to maintain these privileges. Those who long for the triumph of justice, those who would put new ideas into practice, are soon forced to recognize that the realization of their generous, humanitarian and regenerating ideas cannot take place in a society thus constituted. They perceive the necessity of a revolutionary whirlwind which will sweep away all this rottenness, revive sluggish hearts with its breath, and bring to mankind that spirit of devotion, self-denial, and heroism, without which society sinks through degradation and vileness into complete disintegration.

In periods of frenzied haste toward wealth, of feverish speculation and of crisis, of the sudden downfall of great industries and the ephemeral expansion of other branches of production, of scandalous fortunes amassed in a few years and dissipated as quickly, it becomes evident that the economic institutions which control production and exchange are far from giving to society the prosperity which they are supposed to guarantee. They produce precisely the opposite result. Instead of order they bring forth chaos; instead of prosperity, poverty and insecurity; instead of reconciled interests, war—a perpetual war of the exploiter against the worker, of exploiters and of workers among themselves. Human society is seen to be splitting more and more into two hostile camps, and at the same time to be subdividing into thousands of small groups waging merciless war against each other. Weary of these wars, weary of the miseries which they cause, society rushes to seek a new organization. It clamors loudly for a complete remodeling of the system of property ownership, of production, of exchange and all economic relations which spring from it.

The machinery of government, entrusted with the maintenance of the existing order, continues to function, but at every turn of its deteriorated gears, it slips and stops. Its working becomes more and more difficult, and the dissatisfaction caused by its defects grows continuously. Every day gives rise to a new demand. "Reform this," "Reform that," is heard from all sides. "War, finance, taxes, courts, police, everything must be remodeled, reorganized, established on a new basis," say the reformers. And yet all know that it is impossible to make things over, to remodel anything at all because everything is interrelated; everything would have to be remade at once. And how can society be remodeled when it is divided into two openly hostile camps? To satisfy the discontented would be only to create new malcontents.

Incapable of undertaking reforms, since this would mean paving the way for revolution, and at the same time too impotent to be frankly reactionary, the governing bodies apply themselves to half-measures which can satisfy nobody, and only cause new dissatisfaction. The mediocrities who, in such transition periods, undertake to steer the ship of state, think of but one thing: to enrich themselves against the coming debacle. Attacked from all sides they defend themselves awkwardly, they evade, they commit blunder upon blunder and they soon succeed in cutting the last rope of salvation. They drown the prestige of the government in ridicule, caused by their own incapacity.

Such periods demand revolution. It becomes a social necessity; the situation itself is revolutionary.

When we study in the works of our greatest historians the genesis and development of vast revolutionary convulsions, we generally find under the heading "The Cause of the Revolution" a gripping picture of the situation on the eve of events. The misery of the people, the general insecurity, the vexatious measures of the government, the odious scandals laying bare the immense vices of society, the new ideas struggling to come to the surface and repulsed by the incapacity of the supporters of the former regime—nothing is omitted. Examining this picture, one arrives at the conviction that the revolution was indeed inevitable, and that there was no other way out than by the road of insurrection.

Take, for example, the situation before 1789 as the historians picture it. You can almost hear the peasant complaining of the salt tax, of the tithe, of the feudal payments, and vowing in his heart an implacable hatred toward the feudal baron, the monk, the monopolist, the bailiff. You can almost see the citizen bewailing the loss of his municipal liberties, and showering maledictions upon the king. The people censure the queen; they are revolted by the reports of ministerial action, and they cry out continually that the taxes are intolerable and revenue payments exorbitant, that crops are bad and winters hard, that provisions are too dear and the monopolists too grasping, that the village lawyer devours the peasant's crops and the village constable tries to play the role of a petty king, that even the mail service is badly organized and the employees too lazy. In short, nothing works well, everybody complains. "It can last no longer, it will come to a bad end," they cry everywhere.

But, between this pacific arguing and insurrection or revolt, there is a wide abyss—that abyss which, for the greatest part of humanity, lies between reasoning and action, thought and will the urge to act. How has this abyss been bridged? How is it that men who only yesterday were complaining quietly of their lot as they smoked their pipes, and the next moment were humbly saluting the local guard and gendarme whom they had just been abusing—how is it that these same men a few days later were capable of seizing their scythes and their iron-shod pikes and attacking in his castle the lord who only yesterday was so formidable? By what miracle were these men, whose wives justly called them cowards, transformed in a day into heroes, marching through bullets and cannon balls to the conquest of their rights?

How was it that *words,* so often spoken and lost in the air like the empty chiming of bells, were changed into *actions?*

The answer is easy. Action. The continuous action, ceaselessly renewed, of minorities brings about this transformation. Courage, devotion, the spirit of sacrifice, are as contagious as cowardice, submission, and panic.

What forms will this action take? All forms—indeed, the most varied forms, dictated by circumstances, temperament and the means at disposal. Sometimes tragic, sometimes humorous, but always daring; sometimes collective, sometimes purely individual, this policy of action will neglect none of the means at hand, no event of public life, in order to keep the spirit alive, to propagate and find expression for dissatisfaction, to excite hatred against exploiters, to ridicule the government and expose its weakness, and above all and always, by actual example, to awaken courage and fan the spirit of revolt.

When a revolutionary situation arises in a country, before the spirit of revolt is sufficiently awakened in the masses to express itself in violent demonstrations in the streets or by rebellions and uprisings, it is through *action* that minorities succeed in awakening that feeling of independence and that spirit of audacity without which no revolution can come to a head.

Men of courage, not satisfied with words, but ever searching for the means to transform them into action—men of integrity for whom the act is one with the idea, for whom prison, exile, and death are preferable to a life contrary to their principles, intrepid souls who know that it is necessary to *dare* in order to succeed—these are the lonely sentinels who enter the battle long before the masses are sufficiently roused to raise openly the banner of insurrection and to march, arms in hand, to the conquest of their rights.

In the midst of discontent, talk and theoretical discussions, an individual or collective act of revolt supervenes, symbolizing the dominant aspirations. It is possible that at the beginning the masses will remain indifferent. It is possible that while admiring the courage of the individual or the group which takes the initiative, the masses will at first follow those who are prudent and cautious, who will immediately describe this act as "insanity" and say, that "those madmen, those fanatics will endanger everything."

They have calculated so well, those prudent and cautious men, that their party, slowly pursuing its work would, in a hundred years, two hundred years, three hundred years perhaps, succeed in conquering the whole world. And now the unexpected intrudes! The unexpected, of course, is whatever has not been expected by them—those prudent and cautious ones! Whoever has a slight knowledge of history and a fairly clear head knows perfectly well from the beginning that theoretical propaganda for revolution will necessarily express itself in action long before the theoreticians have decided that the moment to act has come.

Nevertheless the cautious theoreticians are angry at these madmen, they excommunicate them, they anathematize them. But the madmen win sympathy, the mass of the people secretly applaud their courage, and they find imitators. In proportion as the pioneers go to fill the jails and the penal colonies, others continue their work. Acts of illegal protest, of revolt, of vengeance, multiply.

Indifference from this point on is impossible. Those who at the beginning never so much as asked what the "madmen" wanted are compelled to think about them, to discuss their ideas, to take sides for or against. By actions which compel general attention, the new idea seeps into people's minds and wins converts. One such act may, in a few days, make more propaganda than thousands of pamphlets.

Above all, it awakens the spirit of revolt: it breeds daring. The old order, supported by the police, the magistrates, the gendarmes, and the soldiers, appeared unshakable, like the old fortress of the Bastille, which also appeared impregnable to the eyes of the unarmed people gathered beneath its high walls equipped with loaded cannon. But soon it became apparent that the established order has not the force one had supposed. One courageous act has sufficed to upset in a few days the entire governmental machine, to make the colossus tremble. Another revolt has stirred a whole province into turmoil, and the army, till now always so imposing, has retreated before a handful of peasants armed with sticks and stones. The people observe that the monster is not so terrible as they thought; they begin dimly to perceive that a few energetic efforts will be sufficient to throw it down. Hope is born in their hearts, and let us remember that if exasperation often drives men to revolt, it is always hope—the hope of victory—which makes revolutions.

The government resists; it is savage in its repressions. But, though formerly persecution killed the energy of the oppressed, now, in periods of excitement, it produces the opposite result. It provokes new acts of revolt, individual and collective. It drives the rebels to heroism, and in rapid succession these acts spread, become general, develop. The revolutionary party is strengthened by elements which up to this time were hostile or indifferent to it. The general disintegration penetrates into the government, the ruling classes, the privileged. Some of them advocate resistance to the limit; others are in favor of concessions; others, again, go so far as to declare themselves ready to renounce their privileges for the moment, in order to appease the spirit of revolt, hoping to dominate again later on. The unity of the government and the privileged class is broken.

The ruling classes may also try to find safety in savage reaction. But it is now too late; the battle only becomes more bitter, more terrible, and the revolution which is looming will only be more bloody. On the other hand, the smallest concession of the governing classes, since it comes too late, since it has been snatched in struggle, only awakes the revolutionary spirit still more. The common people, who formerly would have been satisfied with the smallest concession, observe now that the enemy is wavering. They foresee victory, they feel their courage growing, and the same men who were formerly crushed by misery and were content to sigh in secret, now lift their heads and march proudly to the conquest of a better future.

Finally, the revolution breaks out, the more terrible as the preceding struggles were bitter.

First published in *Le Revolte* (Geneva, 1880),
translated by Arnold Roller (aka Siegfried Nacht)

JEAN MAITRON

# THE ERA OF THE ATTENTATS

W HAT GAVE RISE to these notorious attacks, for three years a constant theme of press reports, and why did they diminish after the Trial of the Thirty and eventually disappear altogether at the end of 1894? This is a question of historical philosophy rather than of history, variously answered according to individual judgment.

On the theoretical level, we have seen that "propaganda by deed," primarily conceived as a lesson in matters of socialism, came to be considered exclusively to be an act of terrorism and was propagated in that form from 1880 to 1888 by the French anarchist groups. Disregarding the events at Montceau les Mines, which had some characteristics of a collective revolt, and the bomb in the Bellecour Theater in Lyons, responsibility for which was never claimed, it cannot be said that, at that time, this terrorist propaganda led to effective action. It is not difficult to understand the reasons for this. In essence, they are to be found in two facts: on the one hand, the workers, the object of this propaganda, were too wise in revolutionary experience to indulge themselves in acts only too clearly fruitless; on the other hand, with all the possibilities of legal action available under the state, they must first be used, perhaps combined with some unlawful activity, but without lapsing into a nihilism whose violence barely hid its impotence.

It is nevertheless the case that, although displaced in time by some ten years, a terrorist era did begin in 1892. The essentially individual acts involved certainly reflected the traditional kind of anarchist activity. Yet why did they come to the fore in 1892 rather than at the time when every single issue of the anarchist press counseled them?

The reason is simple and it was indicated by the accused themselves. It was to avenge Decamps, Dardare and Leveille, the victims of police brutality on May 1, 1891, that Ravachol planted his bombs. Once raised to the status of a martyr for anarchy's sake, Ravachol inspired avengers who, martyrs in their turn, engendered new terrorists. Such was the chance cause which lay at the root of the attacks and outrages....

Certain other factors helped to spread the epidemic rather than check it. In this connection, the attitude of socialist groups, particularly the Guesdist party, may be considered. Their hostility could scarcely be distinguished from that of the bourgeois parties and may, by reaction, have reinforced the comrades' solidarity with the propagandists by deed.

Terrorist action also fed upon the corruption among the nation's elected representatives, one third of whom were implicated in the Panama scandal. Well might Drumont write ... From the mud of Panama are born men of blood—grotesque, misshapen beings like the monsters which emerged from the silt of the Flood—men prey to a dreadful neurosis, who have killed for killing's sake, destroyed for the sake of destruction."

It should also be noted how far the press contributed to a collective psychosis about the attacks. Throughout those troubled years the newspapers maintained a daily dynamite column. They piled on interviews and reports on the subject which to some extent could only encourage the trend.

The reasons for the ending of the outbreak after the murder by Caserio have still to be discussed.

It has been stated that the judicious verdict given at the Trial of the Thirty helped to calm tempers down: this appears incontrovertible. It has also been said that the defensive measures taken against anarchists discouraged the comrades. It is quite true that certain procedures inaugurated at that time had some effect. For example, a report dated April 23, 1894, observes that in Paris and the suburbs "each morning and sometimes even two or three times a day, a policeman goes to these peoples' dwellings" (i.e., those of the anarchists under surveillance) and "takes every care to let it be understood by these people, and even openly shows them, that the police have an eye on them and will not let them out of sight for a single day." However, it was under this system of close watch that two of the most spectacular attacks took place—those carried out by Emile Henry and Caserio. It is therefore clear enough that these preventive measures would have been inadequate in the absence of some weightier reason tending toward the cessation of the attacks. This determinant cause, in my opinion, was essentially inherent in the form taken by the class war at that time. The relationship between the bourgeois-proletariat forces had undergone, within the space of two years, far-reaching changes. A new feeling of collective force which might prove capable of leading to workers' emancipation was gradually redirecting the energies of libertarian propaganda. The new force involved was trade unionism and its panacea—the general strike identified with the revolution. In 1892 the Guesdist syndical federation existed only in a somewhat skeletal form and as a federation was wholly oriented toward reformism and the subjugation of public authority. From 1892 to 1894, there developed a federation of labor resources and in 1895 the anarchist Pelloutier became its general secretary. In 1894, this federation of labor resources held a unique congress, the Congress of Nantes, with the Guesdist syndicates. This represented a first blazing of the trail toward a general labor confederation, which was to be brought into being as an accomplished fact—at least in theory—at the Congress of Limoges in the following year.

It is impossible not to feel some skepticism toward opinions like those of Louzon, who saw the bomb attacks of 1892–94 as acts of decisive importance in the history of the labor movement "since their operation is like the striking of a gong which roused the French proletariat from the state of prostration and despair into which it had been plunged by the massacres of the Commune. In this way the attacks became the prelude to the establishment of the CGT and the mass trade union movement of 1900–1910. ..." The trade union movement, largely stimulated and inspired by the anarchists, was nothing else but a reaction against the childhood disease of anarchism—terrorism.

On this point, it is worthwhile to trace as closely as possible the slow process of this significant evolution in anarchist thinking. Its basic characteristics are disparagement of propaganda by deed as a factor in social emancipation, exaltation of collective action linked with individual action and calling the comrades to active militancy within the trade unions.

In the course of 1888, sustained pro-terrorist propaganda in the anarchist press ceased. The first clearly stated counter to a particularly one-sided view of the term "propaganda by deed" is to be found in 1886. An article in *La Revolte* (September 4–10, 1886) is quite precise: "By this expression 'propaganda by deed' three-quarters of the comrades mean nothing more than armed demonstrations, executing of exploiters, setting fire to sweatshops, etc. Having developed at the time when the Russian terrorists were unleashing their wonderful war of reprisals against their autocrats, the anarchist movement is more or less permeated by this way of doing things ... True, if the movement could establish itself and achieve continual action, that would be wonderful ... But, in our view, it would be losing ourselves in illusion and Utopia to believe that such acts could become the aim of a rational, active, sustained propaganda. ..." The article goes on to point out "how many opportunities for *action* occur every day, perhaps not quite so brilliantly as in our dreams, but just as effectively."

Five years later, in 1891, Kropotkin, no longer content to indicate that other kinds of action existed besides bombs, denounced propaganda by deed, when conceived solely as terrorism, as a mistake. His actual words are: "...While the development of the revolutionary spirit gains immensely from individual acts of heroism, it is nonetheless true...that revolutions are not made by heroic acts....Revolution is above all a popular movement...That was...the mistake of the anarchists in 1881. When the Russian revolutionaries had killed the Czar... the European anarchists imagined that, from then on, a handful of fervent revolutionaries, armed with a few bombs, would be enough to bring about the social revolution..A structure founded on centuries of history is not going to be destroyed by a few kilos of explosive...."

After remarking that the mistake was not without its uses, since, in his view, it meant that the anarchists could maintain their ideal in all its purity, Kropotkin nevertheless concluded that the time for it had passed and that it was now necessary "for the anarchist and communist idea to pervade the masses." (*La Revoke,* March 18–24, 1891.)

There ought, therefore, to be no cause for surprise that the earliest bombs, far from inspiring enthusiasm, created among the militants some tendency to hold back. Without going so far as to condemn those who plant bombs at the risk of their own lives, *La Revolte* (April 16–22, 1892) admits that "they do more harm than good to the evolution of anarchy." From that time on, during the whole tragic period, *never once* does an anarchist journal unreservedly seek to vindicate terrorism; reading between the lines, judgment has been passed upon it.

The year 1894, therefore, is a notable date in the history of the anarchist movement. Thereafter, without renouncing their principles, the comrades endeavored to assert themselves by other means. The era of individual attacks had ended and that of minorities operating at the heart of the masses was about to begin....

Jean Maitron, *Histoire du Mouvement Anarchiste en France, 1880–1914* (Paris, 1955).

# ADVICE FOR TERRORISTS

## I. ATTACK IS THE BEST FORM OF DEFENSE

*From Freiheit, September 13, 1884*

Since we believe that the propaganda of action is of use, we must be prepared to accept whatever attendant circumstances it involves.

Everyone now knows, from experience, that the more highly placed the one shot or blown up, and the more perfectly executed the attempt, the greater the propagandistic effect.

The basic preconditions of success are methodical preparation, deception of the enemy in question and the overcoming of any obstacles that stand between the one who is to carry out the deed, and the enemy.

The expense incurred by such undertakings is, as a rule, quite considerable. Indeed, one could go so far as to say that the possibility of such an action succeeding usually depends on whether the financial means are available to overcome the difficulties. Nowadays, money opens a number of doors one could not break open with an iron bar.

The persuasive clinking of coins turns men blind and dumb. The power of the bank account overrules any ukase.

A man who has no money cannot so much as set foot in "high society" without making himself "suspicious," without being put under surveillance and either summarily arrested or at the least prevented in some other way from carrying out his revolutionary intent. By contrast, by making himself appear elegant and "distinguished," the same man may circulate freely and inconspicuously in those circles where he needs to do some reconnoitering and will even possibly deal the decisive blow, or set in motion some engine of hell concealed beforehand in some good hiding place.

If, then, some comrades are inspired by ideas such as these, if they come to a decision to risk their lives to perform a revolutionary action, and if—realizing that the workers' contributions are but a drop in the ocean—they confiscate the means wherewith to carry out the deed, in our opinion their actions are entirely correct and in no way abnormal.

We are, in fact, firmly convinced that there is no possibility of any noteworthy operations being carried out at all unless the necessary funds have been confiscated in advance from the enemy camp.

Hence, anyone who, while approving an operation against some representative of the modern "order of thieves," at the same time turns up his nose at the manner in which the funds for it are acquired, is guilty of the grossest inconsistency. No one who considers the deed itself to be right can take offense at the manner in which the funds for it are acquired, for he would be like a man rejoicing in his existence who curses his birth. So let us hear no more of this idiotic talk of "moral indignation" at "robbery" and "theft"; from the mouths of socialists, this sort of blathering is really the most stupid nonsense imaginable. Since year in and year out the working people are robbed of everything bar the absolute bare necessities of life, he who wishes to undertake some action in the interests of the proletariat against its enemies is obliged to mix with the privileged robbers and thieves in order to confiscate at least as much as he is able of what has been created by workers, and use it for the correct purposes. In such cases, it is not theft and robbery we are dealing with, but precisely the opposite.

Those, therefore, who condemn financing operations of the kind we have been discussing, are also against individual revolutionary acts. Those who abhor such acts are totally unserious, are deceiving themselves when they call themselves revolutionaries, are unnerving the most active and dedicated pioneers of the proletariat, are playing the whore with the workers' movement, and are, when seen in a clear light, nothing better than treacherous blackguards.

Furthermore, any "illegal" action—whether it is only an action preparatory to some directly revolutionary action or not—may easily precipitate unforeseen circumstances which of their nature only ever present themselves in the middle of a critical situation.

It follows from our argument so far that these secondary circumstances (chance occurrences) cannot be separated off from the action itself and judged according to special criteria.

For example, if a revolutionary, in the process of carrying out an act of vengeance or similar, or of confiscating the means for such an act (money, weapons, poison, explosives, etc.), suddenly finds someone obstructing him, and if this puts the revolutionary in the gravest danger, then he not only has the right, from the usual standpoint of self-defense and self-preservation, to destroy whoever it is has betrayed him by his intervention—for this person's arrival may send him to prison or the gallows—but he even has a duty, for the sake of the cause for which he is fighting, to brush the unexpected obstacle out of his path.

## II. WHEN ARE THE PEOPLE "READY" FOR FREEDOM?

*From Freiheit, November 15, 1884*

"Not yet, by a long chalk!" is what the world's blackguards have been answering since time immemorial. Today, things are not so much better as worse in this regard, since we have people agreeing with this sentiment who otherwise behave as if they were working for the highest possible human happiness.

It is easy to understand some crown prince or other declaring that the people are not "ready" for freedom; after all, if he were to say the opposite, he would be showing just how superfluous he is and signing his own death warrant.

In the same way, unless he is going to deny his own right to exist, no aristocrat, bureaucrat, lawyer or other mandarin of the government or the "law" can concede that the people might be "ready." True, we know from the proverb that the world is ruled with unbelievably little wisdom; but however stupid these state layabouts may be, they still have enough gumption to realize that a people fit for freedom will soon cease to put up with their slavery.

All the clerical and literary preachers whose existence, indeed, entirely depends on being the guardians of the people, and who therefore exert themselves to the utmost to try and befuddle the human brain with their twaddle about the Bible and the Talmud, their newspaper humbug and theatrical garbage, their sophistry and trashy novels, their falsifications of history and their philosophical rubbish—in short, with hundreds of different sorts of hogwash—will always be trotting out something about the "immaturity" of the people.

The swells and other fat-faced philistines who, though one can read their stupidity on their faces, feel, in their positions as exploiting parasites and state-protected robbers, as happy in this stage of unfreedom as pigs in muck, naturally rub their hands in glee and nod well-contented approval when their mouthpieces, declaiming from their pulpits, lecterns, desks, and podiums, seek to prove to the people that they are not ready for freedom and that therefore they must be plundered, pillaged, and fleeced.

The average man in the street has something of the ape or parrot about him. This explains why it is that hundreds of thousands go round cutting their own throats by squawking to others what those cunning mind-warpers have proclaimed. We are too stupid for freedom—alas, how stupid, stupid, stupid we are!

This is all perfectly comprehensible. What, however, is not comprehensible is that people who make themselves out to be advocates of the proletariat likewise hawk round this hoary old legend about the people's "unreadiness" and the resulting temporary impossibility of allowing them to take possession of their freedom.

Is this just ignorance or a deliberate crime?

Let these people speak for themselves: they show clearly and distinctly enough in both their speeches and writings that:

1. the consequences of modern society will in themselves bring about its destruction;
2. one of the most terrible consequences of the system we have today is the gradually increasing deterioration of large sectors of the population, their physical enervation and spiritual demoralization; and,
3. today's state of enslavement must be succeeded by a state of freedom.

In other words, what they are saying is this: in the first case, the society we have now is heading for inevitable collapse; in the second case, the people grow steadily more and more wretched (i.e., less and less "ready" for freedom) the longer the present setup persists.

Hence, when such philosophers, despite such statements, exclaim in moving tones that the people are not yet "ripe" for freedom, they cannot do other than concede, in conformity with their own doctrine, that this "readiness" will be even more lacking later on.

Is it, then, that these people are incapable of following the train of their own thought from established fact to resulting conclusion? If this were the case, they would indeed be dunderheads and, at the very least, not sufficiently "mature" to set themselves up as educators of the people. Or is their crippled logic perfectly clear to them, and are they—in order to play the whore with the people—making them dance around on crutches on purpose? If this were the case, they would be criminal blackguards.

"Wait!," someone cries in defense of these people, "we have found a way of counteracting the degenerating effects of capitalism and making the people ready for freedom despite everything. We *enlighten*."

All well and good! But who has told you that the speed at which things are evolving will leave you enough time to carry out your so-called enlightenment in a systematic way? You yourselves do not believe in that kind of magic.

But what do *you* want?

We provoke, we stoke the fire of revolution and incite people to revolt in any way we can. The people have always been "ready" for freedom; they have simply lacked the courage to claim it for themselves.

We are convinced that necessity is, and will remain, the overriding factor in the struggle for freedom and that therefore hundreds of thousands of men and women will in time appear on the scene as fighters for freedom without ever having heard our call to arms. And we are content, as it were, to construct—by training those who we are able to reach now—sluices which may well prove apt to direct the natural lava-flow of social revolution into practical channels.

As in every previous great social cataclysm, the "readiness" of the people will reveal itself in all its majesty at the moment of conflict—not before, nor after. And then, too, as always, it will become apparent that it is not the theorists and "enlightened" pussy-footers who will provide the reeling society with a new solid foundation, but those miraculous forces which rise up as if raked up out of the earth at the great moment when they are needed. Practical children of nature who, until that point, have lived quiet and modest existences, reach out suddenly to take steps of which no philosopher in the whole wide world could ever have dreamed in a hundred years. The readiness for freedom is then customarily documented in the most astonishing fashion.

It is, therefore, a piece of monstrous idiocy on the part of any socialist to maintain that the people are not "ready" for freedom.

Everyone who does not number among the exploiters complains that others are more privileged than he. Far and wide, it is clear that the people are dissatisfied with their lot. And if they do not know yet what to replace the present setup with, they will discover it at the moment when something practical can be done in this regard, which is—*immediately*.

## III. ACTION AS PROPAGANDA

*From Freiheit, July 25, 1885*

We have said a hundred times or more that when modern revolutionaries carry out actions, what is important is not solely these actions themselves but also the propagandistic effect they are able to achieve.

Hence, we preach not only action in and for itself, but also action as propaganda.

It is a phenomenally simple matter, yet over and over again we meet people, even people close to the center of our party, who either do not or do not wish to understand. We have recently had a clear enough illustration of this over the Lieske affair. ...

So our question is this: what is the purpose of the anarchists' threats—an eye for an eye, a tooth for a tooth—if they are not followed up by action?

Or are perhaps the "law and order" rabble, all of them blackguards extraordinary a la Rumpff, to be done away in a dark corner so that no one knows the why and the wherefore of what happened?

It would be a form of action, certainly, but not action as propaganda.

The great thing about anarchist vengeance is that it proclaims loud and clear for everyone to hear that this man or that man must die for this and this reason; and that at the first opportunity which presents itself for the realization of such a threat, the rascal in question is really and truly dispatched to the other world.

And this is indeed what happened with Alexander Romanov, with Messenzoff, with Sudeikin, with Bloch and Hlubeck, with Rumpff and others. Once such an action has been carried out, the important thing is that the world learns of it *from the revolutionaries*, so that everyone knows what the position is.

The overwhelming impression this makes is shown by how the reactionaries have repeatedly tried to hush up revolutionary actions that have taken place, or to present them in a different light. This has often been possible in Russia, especially, because of the conditions governing the press there.

In order to achieve the desired success in the fullest measure, immediately after the action has been carried out, especially in the town where it took place, posters should be put up setting out the reasons for the action in such a way as to draw from them the best possible benefit.

And in those cases where this was not done, the reason was simply that it proved inadvisable to involve the number of participants that would have been required; or that there was a lack of money. It was all the more natural in these cases for the anarchist press to glorify and explicate the deeds at every opportunity. For it to have adopted an attitude of indifference toward such actions, or even to have denied them, would have been perfectly idiotic treachery.

*Freiheit* has always pursued this policy. It is nothing more than insipid, sallow envy which makes those demagogues who are continually mocking us with cries of "Carry on, then, carry on" condemn this aspect of our behavior, among others, whenever they can, as a crime.

This miserable tribe is well aware that no action carried out by anarchists can have its proper propagandist effect if those organs whose responsibility it is neither give suitable prominence to such actions, nor make it palatable to the people.

It is this, above all, which puts the reactionaries in a rage.

## IV. THE ARMAMENT QUESTION

### From Freiheit, March 27, 1886

If one suggests the acquisition of rifles, one can be sure to be labeled an "old fogey" by the ultra-radicals, because revolvers are "more handy." If one had suggested the latter oneself, the other side would no doubt have sung a hymn of praise to ordinary rifles.

If one is inclined to concede the merits of both types of weapon and to give each its due, it is a hundred to one odds that someone will come along claiming that all firearms are old hat and recommending dynamite.

This explosive, too, is then willingly accepted and emphatically recommended from every quarter, with the single observation that rifles, revolvers, *and* dynamite are better than dynamite alone. What an outcry this causes! Dynamite is now obsolete as well, the mysterious rumor runs; there are other things. And these new miraculous inventions tumble out one after another until finally we are even hearing about bombs that can fly around corners.

We consider that they should go and tell this sort of twaddle to the Marines, and we could perhaps afford to smile at infantility of this ilk, were it not that unfortunately it attracts too much attention to be passed over so lightly.

The immediate and first consequence of these bickerings and arguments is that some who would otherwise do so do not arm themselves at all. The second consequence is that they kill all faith in a certain type of weapon and thus frustrate the energy of many armed comrades. In particular however, they lead to the most disastrous confusion.

All of the blithering nonsense that is spoken in this regard should be forcefully combatted as soon as and wherever it is heard. What one should be doing, instead of indulging in debates idiotic enough to make the enemies of the proletariat split their sides laughing, is making propaganda on behalf of any sort of arms. Let us for goodness sake allow room for individual preference and talent in this domain as well!

Instead of conceitedly proclaiming that anyone who does not get himself this or that special weapon is a numbskull, we should be glad that members of the proletariat are arming themselves at all.

It also sounds extremely arrogant when people turn up their noses at the workers supposedly "playing at being proper soldiers and sharpshooters," since apart from the fact that nothing of the kind even goes on, so that all of this kind of talk is shown to be the web of trumped-up lies it is, we must not be lured into thinking that drill, and the cultivation of a feeling of "belonging" among those bearing arms, is ludicrous or trivial....

One often hears the view expressed that when the moment for battle comes, the people will take the arms it needs. To be sure, or rather, perhaps! Perhaps, on the other hand, the confiscation of arms will not go quite so smoothly. In any case, this much is certain, that fifty or a hundred well-armed and well-trained people are going to find it easier to clear out an arsenal and ensure that the pickings find their way into the right hands than a crowd of people—no matter how big—who have assembled by pure chance and have only their bare hands to fight with.

Moreover, the actual possession of arms is only half the story; one must also know how to use them. It is easy to shoot, but appreciably more difficult to hit anything.

Far too little credit has hitherto been given to the importance of this fact and not a few revolutionaries have already paid with their lives for having suddenly taken a shot at some representative of "law and order" without first having made himself into a marksman.

For it does take some while, with either a revolver or a rifle, to get the feel of a weapon. Each weapon has, as it were, its own particular characteristics, which need to be studied and respected. Using the first weapon that comes to hand, even the most expert marksman will not be able to score the successes he can achieve with his own gun, which he knows backwards.

The same applies to modern explosives, dynamite, etc.

Numerous incidents—notably in England—have shown just what a fool one can make of oneself if one does not know how to handle these substances properly. Practice, again, must come only after study.

It may be that, at the moment, active revolutionaries comprise only a small minority when compared to the population as a whole, yet this is no reason for telling oneself that there is for the time being little or no point in providing them with proper arms and training, on the grounds that at present they cannot even entertain the idea of declaring war on a hostile world.

111

On the contrary, their firm resolve must be to make up in quality for what they lack in quantity.

The firing line of the proletariat must consist of marksmen, i.e., each man must be sufficiently expert to be able, ultimately, to pick off his man with certainty over the varying distances the weapon covers, and to make every shot a bull's-eye.

While the main bulk of the people will charge against the general hangers-on of the bourgeoisie, the revolutionary marksman must lie in wait in order to be able to pick off an enemy officer or other weighty opponent with every single shot he fires.

HENRY DAVID

# PRELUDE TO HAYMARKET

ALTHOUGH IT WAS SOMETIMES PROPOSED that the private-property "beast" might be destroyed by passive measures, the real meaning of the term "all and every means" is best taken as "any and every type of force." For a short while, some of the leaders insisted that if everybody refused to receive and give pay for goods and services, the capitalist system would collapse, and they seriously advocated such action. At the Thanksgiving Day demonstration in 1884, a resolution was adopted to the effect that no man shall either pay or receive pay for anything, and that no man should deprive himself of what he desires if the object of his desire is useful and not being utilized. At the same time, however, a resolution was adopted which recommended the use of force and all types of arms and explosives to wipe out the existing system. Evidently little faith was placed in the first method, for it was quickly abandoned.

"Down with pay," exclaimed the *Alarm*, "and dynamite the man who claims it; and hang him who will not let his energies produce something. This," concluded the writer, "is socialism." "Workingmen of America, learn the manufacture and use of dynamite," advised the *Alarm*. "It will be your most powerful weapon; a weapon of the weak against the strong.... Then use it unstintingly, unsparingly. The battle for bread is the battle for life.... Death and destruction to the system and its upholders, which plunders and enslaves the men, women and children of toil."

One I.W.P.A. group, in the course of discussing the question "How can the idle obtain employment?," proposed that the "unemployed should attack the life and property of those who have robbed them of their labor products and so turn them adrift to starve." Again and again it was asserted that only when the workers "arm themselves and by force acquire the right to life, liberty and happiness" will they secure their "stolen birthright." "Each workingman ought to have been armed long ago," declared the *Arbeiter-Zeitung*. "Daggers and revolvers are easily to be gotten. Hand grenades are cheaply ... produced; explosives, too, can be obtained...." "A number of strikers in Quincy ... ," observed the same paper, "fired upon their bosses, and not upon the scabs. This is recommended most emphatically for imitation." It was suggested at mass meetings that "If we would achieve our liberation from economic bondage and acquire our natural right to life and liberty, every man must lay by a part of his wages, buy a Colt's navy revolver ... a Winchester rifle ... and learn how to make and use dynamite. ... Then raise the flag of rebellion. ... "

The conviction that force was the sole infallible means to destroy the existing order and inaugurate the glorious new society, together with the consequent constant appeal to and encouragement of its use, was marked by four very general characteristics. No real appreciation of the difference between individual deeds and expressions of mass violence was evident, and both were advised. The use of force was encouraged both for defensive—in resistance to the police, militia, Pinkertons and the like—and aggressive purposes. While every type of violence and every method of destruction was accepted, the use of dynamite and similar explosives was especially encouraged. Finally, unusual stress was placed upon the purely practical aspects of the employment of force.

Thus, the *Alarm* and the *Arbeiter-Zeitung*, frequently following the lead of and reproducing items from the *Freiheit*, published articles on the manufacture of dynamite, gun-cotton, nitroglycerine, mercury and silver fulminates, and bombs. They also offered instruction in the use of dangerous explosives. One article in the *Alarm* bore the heading "A Practical Lesson in Popular Chemistry—The Manufacture of Dynamite Made Easy." Another on the manufacture of bombs was subtitled "The Weapon of the Social Revolutionist Placed Within the Reach of All." The files of both papers are liberally studded with such items. The *Arbeiter-Zeitung* ran a notice through December, 1885 and the first three months of 1886 which offered free instruction in the handling of arms to workers "at No. 58 Clybourn Avenue. ... " And the *Alarm* urged its readers who desired additional information on the manufacture and use of bombs to communicate with it. Sometimes the mad "Revolutionary Catechism" of Nechaev was quoted. Lengthy discussions were frequently published on plans and methods of street fighting, means of combating the militia, the preparation necessary for revolutionary action, the perpetration of the individual deed, the danger of discovery, and the like.

Upon explosives, and upon dynamite in particular, the greatest emphasis was placed. Dynamite was the great social solvent—it was the "emancipator." The "right of property" could be destroyed, asserted the *Alarm,* and a glorious "free" society inaugurated "simply by making ourselves masters of the use of dynamite, then declaring we will make no further claims to ownership in anything, and deny every…person's right to be owner of anything, and administer instant death, by any and all means, to any and every person who attempts to claim personal ownership of anything. This method, and this alone, can relieve the world of this infernal monster called the 'right of property.'"

No article lauding the admirable qualities of dynamite or editorial hymn praising its revolutionary virtues compares with the fantastic and unbelievable contribution of one T. Lizius which was published in the *Alarm* as a letter to the editor:

"Dynamite! Of all the good stuff, this is the stuff. Stuff several pounds of this sublime stuff into an inch pipe (gas or water pipe), plug up both ends, insert a cap with a fuse attached, place this in the immediate neighborhood of a lot of rich loafers who live by the sweat of other people's brows, and light the fuse. A most cheerful and gratifying result will follow. In giving dynamite to the downtrodden millions of the globe, science has done its best work. The dear stuff can be carried around in the pocket without danger, while it is a formidable weapon against any force of militia, police or detectives that may want to stifle the cry for justice that goes forth from the plundered slaves. It is something not very ornamental but exceedingly useful. It can be used against persons and things, it is better to use it against the former than against bricks and masonry. It is a genuine boon for the disinherited, while it brings terror and fear to the robbers. It brings terror only to the guilty, and consequently the Senator who introduced a bill in Congress to stop its manufacture and use, must be guilty of something. He tears the wrath of an outraged people that has been duped and swindled by him and his like. The same must be the case with the 'servant' of the people who introduced a like measure in the Senate of the Indiana legislature. All the good this will do! Like everything else, the more you prohibit it, the more it will be done. Dynamite is like Banquo's ghost, it keeps on fooling around somewhere or other in spite of his satanic majesty. A pound of this good stuff beats a bushel of ballots all hollow, and don't you forget it. Our lawmakers might as well try to get down on a crater of a volcano or a bayonet as to endeavor to stop the manufacture or use of dynamite. It takes more justice and right than is contained in laws to quiet the spirit of unrest. If workingmen would be truly free, they must learn to know why they are slaves. They must rise above petty prejudice and learn to think. From thought to action is not far, and when the worker has seen the chains, he need but look a little closer to find near at hand the sledge with which to shatter every link. The sledge is dynamite."

The campaign of violence included items which ranged from Mrs. Parsons' pointed advice to tramps to learn to use explosives so that they could annoy the rich during hard times, to C. S. Griffin's article on assassination. In the latter, which patently reflects the influence of Nechaev and Russian terrorism, Mr. Griffin declared that:

"The moment the abolition of a government is suggested, the mind pictures the uprising of a hundred little despotic governments on every hand, quarreling among themselves and domineering over the unorganized people. This fact suggests the idea that the present governments must be destroyed, only in a manner that will prevent the organization or rise of any and all other governments, whether it be a government of three men or three hundred million. No government can exist without a head, and by assassinating the head just as fast as a government head appears, the government can be destroyed, and by the same process all other governments can be kept out of existence. ... Those governments least offensive to the people should be destroyed last. ... He alone is free who submits to no government. All governments are domineering powers and any domineering power is a natural enemy to all mankind, and ought to be treated as such. Assassination will remove the evil from the face of the earth.

The author himself observed that this was the policy of the Nihilists, and in closing said that "Assassination properly applied is wise, just, humane, and brave. For freedom, all things are just."

---

Henry David, *The History of the Haymarket Affair*
(New York, 1936)

# O'DONOVAN ROSSA'S DYNAMITERS

### From *Irish World*, August 28, 1880

FIVE YEARS AGO O'Donovan Rossa, through the columns of this paper, made known to the Irish people the idea of skirmishing. ...

He did not himself write the address that was published. Rossa called for $5,000. The first notion seemed to rise no higher than the rescue of a few Fenian prisoners then held in English jails. He wanted badly to knock a feather out of England's cap. That sort of theatrical work did not satisfy us.

Nor did it commend itself to some others either. Rossa then said he was willing to burn down some shipping in Liverpool. "Why not burn down London and the principal cities of England?" asked one of the two whom Rossa, in the beginning, associated with him in the movement. Rossa said that he was in favor of anything. The question of loss of life was raised. "Yes," said he, who had put forward the idea. "Yes, it is war," said Rossa and in all wars life must be lost; but in my opinion the loss of life under such circumstances would not be one tenth that recorded in the least of the smallest battles between the South and the North." Someone suggested that plenty of thieves and burglars in London could be got to do this job. Here we interposed. "Why should you ask others to do what you yourself deem wrong? After all, would it not be yourself that would be committing the sin? Gentlemen, if you cannot go into this thing with a good conscience you ought not to entertain the notion at all."

Here now, two questions presented themselves: (1) Was the thing feasible? (2) If feasible, what would be the probable result?

That the idea could be carried into execution, that London could be laid in ashes in twenty-four hours was to us self-evident. England could be invaded by a small and resolute band of men, say ten or a dozen, when a force of a thousand times this number, coming with ships and artillery, and banners flying, could not effect a landing. Spaniards in the days of the Invincible Armada, and Zulus today, could not do what English-speaking Irishmen can accomplish. Language, skin color, dress, general manners, are all in favor of the Irish. Then, tens of thousands of Irishmen, from long residence in the enemy's country, know England's cities well. Our Irish skirmishers would be well-disguised. They would enter London unknown and unnoticed. When the night for action came the night that the wind was blowing strong—this little band would deploy, each man setting about his own allotted task, and no man, save the captain of the band alone, knowing what any other man was to do, and at the same instant strike with lightning the enemy of their land and race ... In two hours from the word of command London would be in flames, shooting up to the heavens in fifty different places. Whilst this would be going on, the men could be still at work. The blazing spectacle would attract all eyes, and leave the skirmishers to operate with impunity in the darkness.

*simultaneous attack*

# LOMASNEY

WILLIAM MACKEY LOMASNEY was one of the most remarkable men of the Fenian movement. A small man of slender build, who spoke with a lisp, modest and retiring in manner, one who did not know him well would never take him for a desperate man, but no man in the Fenian movement ever did more desperate things. He was better known in Cork for his raids for arms in Allport's gunshop and other places after the Rising, than for the part he played at Ballyknockane. They were done in broad daylight and he showed great coolness and daring. When he was arrested he shot the Peeler who had seized him. The Peeler, although severely wounded, did not die and Lomasney was tried for attempted murder. Judge O'Hagan, who had been a Young Irelander and later became Lord Chancellor of Ireland, was the trial judge and undertook to lecture him on the enormity of his crime, but Lomasney turned the tables on him by reminding him that he was himself once a rebel and that he (Lomasney) was only following the example O'Hagan had set in 1848.

The Peeler, a big, powerful man, had knocked Lomasney down and had him under him while they were struggling for possession of Lomasney's revolver. It went off in the struggle and Lomasney had no intention of killing him. O'Hagan was stung by Lomasney's sharp rebuke and imposed a sentence of fifteen years' penal servitude, for which he was severely censured by even the English and the Tory Irish papers. Lomasney took the sentence calmly, although he had only recently been married. It was in Millbank Prison that I first met him, and we became fast friends.

In America, years later, when the dynamite warfare was on foot, he was warned by the "Triangle" that I was a "traitor" and he must not have anything to do with me, but he told Aleck Sullivan that I was an honest man with a right to my opinions and that he would not obey any order to treat me as a man disloyal to Ireland. Sullivan needed Lomasney to hold his grip on the executive of the organization, which he controlled, so he let the matter drop.

Lomasney then explained his policy and methods to me, and they were entirely different from those of the "Triangle." He wanted simply to strike terror into the government and the governing class and "would not hurt the hair of an Englishman's head" except in fair fight. We then discussed the policy fully and I told him the most he could expect through terrorism was to wring some small concessions from the English which could be taken back at any time when the government's counter-policy of terrorism achieved some success. Lomasney admitted this, but contended that the counter-terrorism would not succeed; that the Irish were a fighting race who had through the long centuries never submitted to coercion; that their fighting spirit would be aroused by the struggle; that the sympathy of the world would eventually be won for Ireland, and that England could not afford to take back the concessions, which could be used to wring others, and that in the end Ireland would win her full freedom.

I freely admitted that if honestly carried out on his lines the policy of terrorism might succeed, but that I utterly disbelieved in the sincerity of those men who were directing it; that they were only carrying on a game of American politics, using the bitter feeling of Irishmen here to obtain control of the organization and turn it into an American political machine to achieve personal purposes. I pleaded for a broader policy that would win the intellect of the Irish at home and abroad and make the race a formidable factor in the counsels of the world, and an ally worth dealing with in England's next big war. I further pointed out to him that the temper of the race would upset all his ideas about "not hurting the hair of an Englishman's head"; that once their blood was up, the honest fighting men who would have to carry on the work would kill all the Englishmen they could and that England, having the ear of the world and control of all the agencies of news supply, would see to it that the world was duly shocked.

I wasted my time and made no impression whatever upon him. He was as cool and calm during the argument as if we were discussing the most ordinary subject and, while his manner was animated, there was not the slightest trace of heat or passion in it. He even denied the right of the Home Organization to decide the policy for the whole race when I told him the Supreme Council was as firm as the Rock of Cashel against anything being done within its jurisdiction of which it did not fully approve. He was a fanatic of the deepest dye, and all the harder to argue with because he never got heated or lost his temper.

Such was the man who was blown to atoms under London Bridge with his brother, his brother-in-law, and a splendid man named Fleming, a short time after my talk with him. The explosion only slightly damaged one of the arches, and I have always believed that this was all he intended to do. He was, in my opinion, carrying out his policy of frightening the English government and England's ruling class. And that it did frighten them, as all the other dynamite operations did, there can be no reason to doubt.

---

J. Devoy, *Recollections of an Irish Rebel*
(New York, 1929).

# Terrorism in the Twentieth Century

# INTRODUCTORY NOTE

F ROM THE TURN OF THE CENTURY to the 1960s, terrorism was mainly the work of nationalist-separatist movements and extreme right-wing groups. There were a few major exceptions such as the second wave of left-wing terrorism in Russia (1904–1907) and the industrial and political terrorism indigenous to Spain. But the centers of action were Ireland, Macedonia, Palestine (before and after World War II) and, to a lesser degree, after Asian and African countries such as India and Egypt. Terrorist tactics were used by some fascist parties in Central Europe and the Balkans and, after the Second World War, in the struggle which accompanied decolonization, for instance, in Cyprus, Aden, and Algeria. In preparation for their military offensives, North Vietnamese communists used individual terrorism to eliminate their Trotskyite political opponents in the cities and the headmen loyal to the government in the villages. The recrudescence of left-wing terrorism in the 1960s was limited, on the whole, to small sectarian groups; the publicity accorded to their actions was in inverse ratio to their real importance. This is particularly true of groups and individuals in the United States, West Germany, and Japan, which, acting separately or in unison ("Carlos Marighella's multinational terrorism"), frequently had the support of sympathetic governments other than their own.

The use of terrorism as surrogate political warfare is by no means a new phenomenon; a famous precedent was the support Italian fascism lent to the Croatian Ustasha who killed King Alexander in Marseilles in 1934. During the 1960s and 1970s, state-supported terrorism became an established practice, especially in the Middle East and North Africa, with Libya, Algeria, Iraq, South Yemen, and Somalia as the main sponsors, and it was also in evidence on occasion in Latin America (Cuba). There are certain links between multinational terrorism and the Soviet bloc. Some of the terrorist groups of the 1960s tended to the left, others to the right; some defied definition in clear-cut ideological terms and combined concepts and practices of the extreme left and right. Extreme left-wing terrorism was of political significance in Latin America (the Tupamaros in Uruguay, the Argentinian ELP, and the Montoneros), but their activities inevitably resulted in a violent backlash on the part of the extreme right. Historical experience has shown that terrorism has lasted only when it functioned within the framework of a wider political movement (almost always of a nationalist-separatist character) or when it was supported by powerful outside forces (as evidenced in Ulster and by the Basques, Croats, Palestinian Arabs, and other such groups). Furthermore, experience has taught us that while the terrorism of the 1960s and 1970s has professed to fight tyranny, it has hardly ever appeared and has never succeeded where repression is at its greatest. Terrorism is a weapon that can only be used effectually against democratic and ineffective authoritarian regimes.

The Inner Macedonian Revolutionary Organization (IMRO), established in the 1890s to fight the Turks and achieve independence for Macedonia, continued its struggle for four decades but, after World War I, it became the tool of successive Bulgarian governments for use against internal and external enemies and was itself liquidated when it was no longer needed by its paymasters.

Political terrorism was widely used in the early 1920s in Germany by the precursors of the Nazis; the assassination of Walther Rathenau, foreign minister of the Republic, was the most famous of many terrorist incidents. Other fascist movements such as the Rumanian Iron Guard applied individual terrorism on a wider scale than the Italian fascists and the Nazi party, which preferred, on the whole, an open struggle for power. *Vier Jahre politischer Mord* (Berlin, 1922), a documentary record denouncing the activities of right-wing "patriots," was prepared by a young Heidelberg professor, Emil Julius Gumbel (1891–1966), much to the disgust of the academic authorities who were opposed to such extracurricular activities. After his emigration from Germany, Gumbel taught statistics at Columbia University.

The "Philosophy of the Bomb," a manifesto by a small left-wing Indian group, the Hindustan Socialist Revolutionary Army, was published in January, 1930. It was written by Bhagwat Charan and took issue with Gandhi's policy of nonviolence which guided the Indian Congress party at the time. As it turned out, terrorism was equally advocated (and more frequently practiced) by extreme right-wing Hindu fundamentalist circles, from among which Gandhi's murderer emerged.

The history of the IRA has been related in considerable detail, yet novels and movies (such as, for instance, *The Informer* and *Odd Man Out)* are probably of greater benefit than the official ideological pronouncements in yielding an understanding of the motivation of Irish (and Ulster Protestant) terrorists. Furthermore, any similarity between the theory of ideological pronouncement and practice in the street is usually quite accidental. According to recent doctrinal statements made by the IRA, the British army is the sole enemy of the IRA provisionals, and they have nothing in principle against Protestant Irishmen. In actual fact not a single British soldier lost his life in Belfast between September, 1974, and October, 1976, whereas hundreds of Catholic and Protestant civilians were killed in the same period in what is essentially a civil war split along sectarian lines. The anonymous Easter Week ballad of 1916 and the equally anonymous open letter by an extremist Protestant organization published in a Belfast newspaper in 1972 convey a more accurate impression of the mood prevailing among the warring factions than any lengthy manifestos. In a similar way, the publications of the various Palestinian Arab organizations are no reliable guide to their actions: they dwell on the strategy of popular resistance and mass action, whereas the real manifestations of their terrorist tactics, such as the hijacking of planes, are all but never discussed. The publications of Iranian terrorists are, in this respect, far more outspoken; the excerpts published here are from Bizham Jazani's (1937–1975) *Armed Struggle in Iran*. According to the official Teheran version the author was shot "while trying to escape from prison." He belonged to the Marxist-Leninist *Siahkal,* a group named after the small town near the Caspian Sea where one of its first armed actions took place in 1971.

Menahem Begin (1913–1992) was the leader of the IZL *(Irgun Zvai Leumi)* from 1943 to its dissolution in 1948; he was head of the Likud party in Israel and prime minister of Israel. In the 1930s, IZL split away from the Hagana, the irregular Palestinian Jewish defense forces. Earlier than other Zionist parties it advocated the establishment of a Jewish state on both banks of the Jordan. The IZL was outflanked by the smaller, more radical, more militant, and, in certain respects, more "left-wing" Stern Gang (Fighters for the Freedom of Israel).

Latin America was the predominant scene of terrorist activities during the 1960s and 1970s. The Venezuelan communists had been pioneers in this respect, but it was only after the failure of the various rural guerrilla groups, in particular, Che Guevara's small band in 1967, that the terrorist wave reached its highest point. The chief political advocate of "urban guerrilla" was Abraham Guillen; excerpts from his writings can be found in my *Guerrilla Reader*. More influential, albeit mainly restricted to a discussion of military strategy, was Carlos Marighella's famous *Minimanual*. A long-time Brazilian communist, Marighella, left the party in 1967 because it was not sufficiently militant and he was killed in a shoot-out with the police in Sao Paulo in 1969. "Urbano" was a leader of the Uruguayan Tupamaros, which, prior to their defeat in 1971, was the most successful terrorist group in Latin America. In an interview with Urbano that appeared in a Cuban publication some aspects of the political and tactical approach of the Tupamaros are discussed.

Finally, there are the small terrorist factions that developed out of the remnants of the New Left in the United States, western Europe, and Japan. Their publications, of which *Prairie Fire,* published by the SDS in 1974, and *Das Konzept Stadtguerilla,* published by Baader-Meinhof group in April, 1971, are quite representative, are mainly devoted to statements of general political principles and expectations. No survey of recent terrorist literature would be complete without them, but they do not offer much that is novel in comparison with terrorist groups of previous ages, except for the fact that their activities, like those of the fascist groups of the inter-war period, were directed against democratically elected governments. This might account for the sense of isolation that is distinctly evident beneath the veneer of ultra-radical phraseology.

ST. CHRISTOWE

# TWILIGHT OF THE IMRO

OR FIFTY YEARS THE MACEDONIANS have been spilling blood profusely, their own and that of their enemies. I do not believe that the words autonomy, liberty and independence hold such magic for any other people as they do for the Macedonians. To free peoples the word liberty has lost some of its real significance. They accept it as one of the appurtenances of life, or as one of the necessities, like air, like water. But to the Macedonians liberty has become the highest goal for which man can strive. The *comitadjis*, with all their faults, are not *comitadjis* for the sport of it: Theirs is not a profession. It is true some have become *comitadjis* for sheer adventure, others because it offered them a livelihood, and still others have been forced into the movement; but most of them have been conscientious lovers of liberty, men that were ashamed to remain a subjugated people in an age of freedom and independence.

And yet at times the *comitadjis have* behaved like gangsters. The last decade of *comitadji* history deals more with internal warfare and self-annihilation than with a consistent and determined pursuit of the goal itself. Since Michailoff's ascent to power the IMRO has seen a series of sanguinary spectacles among the *comitadjis* themselves, with an occasional revolutionary act in the enemy camp performed by some terrorist at the cost of his or her life. There is little that is virtuous and humane to distinguish or redeem Michailoff's epoch. The pistol and the dagger have been the solution of all internal conflicts and schisms. Michailoff's reign in IMRO history will go down as one of bloodletting and mutual extermination.

Michailoff is a persuasive talker. He is endowed with a brilliant mind and is patient and kind and modest. He is not an impulsive person and does not jump into fights as does a man of impetuous temperament and belligerent character. On the contrary, he is noted for his cold, rigid logic and his blueprint thinking. He tries every conceivable way of conciliation, but he remains as firm and unyielding as a rock. And when he has talked himself out and has exhausted all other ways of effecting peace and harmony, he invariably seeks recourse in bloodshed. A less rigid, less adamant attitude, a certain elasticity, and even an occasional compromise would at least have moderated, if not entirely prevented, the fierce internal clashes and saved the movement from the discredit, the blemishes, and the final wreck....

Following the wars nearly one-half of the Macedonian Bulgars escaped into Bulgaria. Naturally this half was the more virile, the more buoyant ethnically, and from it the movement derived its principal strength. From this same more vigorous national element the movement drew its strength afterward also, but where before it was on its own soil, now it was on foreign soil, which makes a great difference. This gave IMRO the features of a foraying, sniping, outlaw society, its bands emerging sporadically in Yugoslav and Greek Macedonia and quickly retreating to their base in Bulgaria for recuperation and rearming.

When the Serbs and the Greeks took even more drastic measures against these bands, and crossing into either part of Macedonia meant certain death, IMRO transformed itself into a sheerly terroristic society in order to maintain a semblance of revolutionary life in Greek and Yugoslav Macedonia. Thus, in its history of forty years the organization went through three distinct stages of development. First, it was a society of secret civilian committees. From these it evolved into a mass organization with a permanent semimilitary armed force—the *comitadjis.* It was as such that Alexandroff attempted to reestablish it and partly succeeded. But as time went on, the Greeks and Serbs destroyed practically every band that crossed over into their jurisdictions, besides putting the local population where such bands were sighted through the most brutal tortures. Under Michailoff, IMRO went through still another development, becoming a dreaded band of plotting terrorists and depending for its effects almost entirely upon individual heroics.

But in Bulgarian Macedonia and in Bulgaria proper, IMRO was something quite different. Here it was a mass revolutionary organization. But here there was no need whatever for any rebel activity. The *comitadjis* committed no outrages in Bulgaria except against themselves. They made of the Petrich district a kind of *comitadji* Hollywood, with no grinding cameras but with plenty of actors and directors. The old form of *comitadjism*—romantic, picturesque, with its breathless secrecy, its spectral nocturnality, its eerie omnipresence, but with none of the old-time danger that breathed living reality into it—was here recreated. To it were added such modern innovations as whizzing automobiles, telephonic communication, and typewriters.

Michailoff proved himself an able administrator and tax collector as well. He put IMRO on a business basis. The organization took on the character of a holding corporation, with its finger in all economic enterprises in the district, as well as in most national Macedonian cooperative and commercial ventures in old Bulgaria. Nothing could be done in the Petrich district without permission from IMRO. One could not even build a fence around a field unless one had first consulted with the local IMRO agent. Michailoff appointed schoolteachers, municipal clerks, tax collectors (for the Sofia government) and mayors of towns and villages. No one could hold a position with the official government in this territory unless he was persona grata to IMRO.

There were no popular elections here; the eleven deputies in the Sofia parliament representing the district were IMRO appointees. The political party machines did not extend into this newly acquired Bulgarian land. Michailoff wanted unity in his "little kingdom" and would not permit the Bulgarian politicians to spread partisan issues and animosities among his people. Partisanship is a serious business in the Balkans. Two Bulgarians belonging to two different parties are like two men of different nationalities. There was one party in Bulgarian Macedonia, and that was IMRO; one political objective, and that was the union of the three parts of Macedonia into a single independent state. Once the Macedonians had attained that objective, they could form as many political parties as they desired and could air their political convictions as much as they wished. Until then, all Macedonians were needed for the struggle, and any one that tried to sow dissension among them or to wean any away from their national duty was an enemy of the cause and would be fought by IMRO.

---

St. Christowe, *Heroes and Assassins*, New York, (Holt, 1935). Reprinted with the permission of the publishers.

EMIL JULIUS GUMBEL

# ORGANIZED MURDER

T HE MOST SHOCKING MURDERS are those which have been committed during periods of complete calm, when there was neither a real nor a fictitious left-wing revolt. Here the excuses and extenuations we have encountered hitherto will not do. We are left with just two methods. The first method is to say that it is not worth making such a commotion about. The man was mad anyway, he suffered from persecution mania. He was convinced he was going to be killed one day. Is that not proof enough that he knew what his fate was going to be? We can see what sort of people the Left is composed of. By robbing the dead man of his one possession, his good name, they exonerate themselves by such desecration of the dead, from any responsibility. Nevertheless, the government pledges to hold a thorough inquiry. The periodical reports of how things are proceeding in an orderly fashion grow shorter and shorter. New political problems fill the newspapers and after a while the flood of leaflets abates. Only a few papers continue to cry and yelp. Soon the dead man is forgotten.

Or the murder is made acceptable to the people in advance. The victim must be so inculpated that his assassination is regarded as an act of liberation, an heroic deed. "Germany has finally been freed of a man who brought so much misery to his fatherland." A great deal of detailed work, high culture, masterful preparation and methodical cooperation are involved in bringing about the victim's downfall. "This man is a wrecker. He must be removed. The National United Front alone can help." Thus snarls the press, and goes on snarling until even the last inhabitant of much-binding-in-the-marsh knows it.

## ARE THERE ASSASSINATION ORGANIZATIONS?

Assassination organizations in the proper sense of the term (i.e., organizations whose sole purpose is political assassination) probably do not exist in present-day Germany. However, there are certainly organizations which condone political assassination either as a secondary aim or as a means to an end. Their true goals, comprising three essentially distinct aims, are nationalist in character. The first is monarchist. This is the first reason why these organizations attack the Republic and, first and foremost, its representatives. At the same time, however, the various organizations that exist disagree both over the form of the future monarchy (whether it should be absolute or constitutional), its scope (Unified German State or return of former rulers), and the person of the monarch himself (whether he should be a Wittelsbach or a Hohenzollern). There is, above all, no sufficiently popular candidate for the throne. This piece of good fortune may perhaps save the Republic, as a similar one saved France in 1870.

The second tendency is the imperialist. The Versailles Peace Treaty dismembered Germany and took away from it territories with German populations. In view of this, efforts to regain those areas cut off from Germany against their wills and to improve Germany's economic situation are entirely justified. Furthermore, these associations advocate an explicitly imperialist policy, in particular a war of revenge.

The third current within these movements is anti-Semitism, which derives from highly exaggerated ideas of the importance and influence of the Jews.

To a considerable extent, these three aims of policy are not officially acknowledged. In public, they appear more in the guise of professional, scientific, and cultural demands or other political objectives. Some organizations still even insist on maintaining the fiction of political neutrality. In all of them, one finds the most active members are almost always members of the old army.

The three movements are customarily fused. The majority of *Geheimbündler* are simultaneously monarchists, imperialists, and anti-Semites. The organizations' extremist attitudes lead them to believe that by killing one's political opponent one can thereby do away with the ideas he stands for. A second, and essentially different, root-cause of political assassination is an occasional necessity, as it seems, to remove uncomfortable accomplices who, it is feared, may betray the organization.

## SECRET COMMUNIST ORGANIZATIONS

It is beyond question that there have also been secret Communist organizations. This party's mentality, as exemplified in their responsibility for the March, 1921 uprising, makes it barely possible to doubt their existence. But the reports about them have in every single case proved to be grossly exaggerated. In those cases where such organizations have actually existed, a major role has been played by stool pigeons and provocateurs from right-wing organizations, the reason being that the party as a whole has been heavily infiltrated by stool pigeons. In Munich, informers have even been uncovered holding positions as district leaders, i.e., officials of the party.

## THE SOCIAL STRUCTURE OF THE GEHEIMBÜNDE

A number of these organizations live only for a short while and then disappear. A series of new ones are then founded. The process appears entirely haphazard and chaotic, yet is in fact very simple. The way in which these organizations fragment into hiking clubs, study groups, sports organizations, regimental associations, rifle clubs, veterans' organizations, officers' federations and organizations of *volkisch,* nationalist and monarchist revival, with some of these groups continually disappearing and new ones emerging, is only intended as a camouflage. It allows the organizations to be continued in the event of a ban, makes it possible for any links to be denied, any identity to be challenged and, furthermore, for any informers who may have crept in to be rendered harmless by a rapid change in the character of the organization. The lines of communication between the leaders and the movement's errand boys are sometimes very loose. The top leadership must always be in a position to be able to disavow any such connection.

How loose these lines of communication can be kept, without impairing the strong mutual trust that exists, is illustrated by the attack on Harden, when those involved communicated with each other exclusively by post and the instigator of the attack did not even know the name of the superior who was providing him with money. Communications work so well that the authorities have still not succeeded in pinpointing the men who commissioned and funded Rathenau's murder. The maître chefs have been arrested, but not the cooks who actually brewed the whole business up.

A large proportion of the membership is made up of young people. It is students and secondary school children who comprise the main force of these organizations. Seventeen-year-old students played a decisive role in Rathenau's murder. As, despite all the social democratic ministers of education we have had, the children of today still study the old textbooks, which are tailored to the emperor and imperial rule, they can hardly escape being convinced that empire is the only true form of government and that the Republic is a regrettable aberration to be corrected as soon as possible. The younger terrorists are therefore acting in absolute good faith and believe themselves to be the true successors of Harmodios, Aristogeiton and Brutus if they kill the few Republicans that Germany possesses.

One must not allow the large number of these organizations to mislead one into thinking that they are all independent of each other. Their membership is to a large extent drawn from the same people. One and the same person is often affiliated to ten such organizations under ten different names. The total figure of those belonging to illegal or semi-legal German nationalist organizations would very probably not exceed one quarter of a million. As for arms, the highest estimate would be in the region of one hundred and fifty thousand rifles with ten rounds of ammunition per rifle, and two thousand light and five hundred heavy automatic weapons. It is unlikely that these organizations possess any heavy artillery worth mentioning.

## PUBLIC OPINION AND THE MURDERERS

Even before the victim has stopped twitching, the press begins to make the appropriate noises. "Frightful, frightful," scream the *Local News*, the *Times*, the *Daily Clarion*, the *German Daily News*, etc.: "We condemn political assassination from any quarter." But one can already discern a subdued undertone, which soon becomes increasingly loud: "Is it in fact certain that it was the German nationalists who were responsible?" The crocodile tears fall in torrents. For a few minutes, the government shakes off its lethargy; there will be tough legislation to protect the Republic. The Left levels loud accusations against the murderers. Then the undertone grows even more distinct: "We are against such excesses" (i.e., we disapprove of people being sincerely and honestly against assassination, we dislike a spade being called a spade and the German nationalist *Geheimbund-ler* being called murderers.)

The murderers escape. The bold headlines in the papers fade away. Committed anti-Republicans easily bend the "Laws for the Protection of the Republic" to suit their own purposes. The newspapers speak of paid assassins sent by a foreign "Communist state": "A German could never do such a thing."

The most interesting aspect is the reaction immediately after the murder. There is great perturbation throughout the country, especially among the workers, and in a few cases among the bourgeoisie, too. Depending on their various attitudes, the workers' parties call for mass action, protest strikes or marches. It is common knowledge that, as a result of the high level of discipline that is generally to be found in the organized socialist parties, a demonstration of this kind can pass off quite peacefully if the police behave sensibly and more especially if they are taken off the streets altogether. Hundreds of marches have shown this to be the case. But for such marches to pass off without event is decidedly not in the interests of those on the Right. Paid agents, provocateurs who deliberately stir up unrest, and the provocative behavior of the police ensure that there is disruption. At some point there is a clash between marchers and police. From some direction, the notorious first shot is fired. (Later it proves impossible to discover from which side it came.) Ruthlessly, the well-organized police begin to club, shoot at, beat and trample on the unarmed mass of demonstrators. Dozens of dead marchers—but no dead policemen—are littered over the field of battle. This the press takes as sufficient reason to condemn in the strongest terms the continuing terror from the Left and the excesses not, as one might have thought, of the police, but of the demonstrators, and to conclude that democracy, freedom, and the constitution are under threat—not, one must understand, from the assassins, no, but from the "masses of the workers spurred on by troublemakers." This line of argument is especially effective if, in the course of a demonstration, the workers have destroyed a few symbols of empire.

---

Emil Julius Gumbel, *Vier Jahre politischer Mord*
(Berlin, 1922)

# A DUBLIN BALLAD

Who fears to speak of Easter Week
That week of famed renown,
When the boys in green went out to fight
 The forces of the Crown.

With Mausers bold and hearts of gold
And the Countess dressed in green
And high above the G.P.O.
The rebel flag was seen.

Then came ten thousand khaki coats
Our rebel boys to kill
Before they reached O'Connell Street
Of fight they got their fill.

They'd Maxim guns and cavalry
And cannon in galore
But it's not our fault that ne'er a one
Got back to England's shore.

They shot our leaders in a gaol
Without a trial, they say.
They murdered women and children, too
Who in their cellars lay.

They dug their grave with gun and spade
To hide them from our view

Because they could neither kill nor catch
The Rebels so bold and true.

May the Lord have mercy on three men
Who faced the murderous foe;
There was Dixon, Sheehy-Skeffington
And McIntyre also.

T'was in a dismal barracks cell
They met their fate so cruel
Yes, they were shot with no clergy got
To prepare them for their doom.

For six long days we held them off
With odds at ten to one.
And through our lines they could not pass
For all their heavy guns.

And deadly poison gas they used
To try and crush Sinn Fein
And burn our Irish capital
As the Germans did Louvain.

But we shall love old Ireland
And shall while life remains,
And we shall say, God speed the day
The Rebels shall rise again.

Though Irish slaves and English knaves
Will try us to deceive
Remember those who died for you
And likewise James Connolly's grave.

—ORIGIN UNKNOWN

# FREEDOM STRUGGLE
# BY THE PROVISIONAL IRA

Q UITE FRANKLY IT SUITED IRA STRATEGY to carry out selective bombings in Belfast, Derry and other towns in occupied Ulster. They
see these actions as a legitimate part of war, the targets chosen
being military and police barracks, outposts, customs offices, administrative and government buildings, electricity transformers and pylons, certain
cinemas, hotels, clubs, dance halls, pubs, all of which provide relaxation
and personal comforts for the British forces, also business targets (e.g.,
factories, firms, stores—sometimes under the guise of CO-OPs) owned in
whole or part by British financiers or companies, or who in any way are a
contributory factor to the well-being of Her Majesty's invading forces, and
in certain instances residences of people known to harbor or be in league
with espionage personnel or *agents provocateurs*, namely the S.A.S., MRF,
and S.I.B. In many ways this campaign is reminiscent of that carried out by
the underground resistance in France during World War II.

In all cases IRA bomb squads give adequate warning though these
warnings are sometimes withheld or delayed deliberately by the British
army as a counter-tactic, with view to making optimum publicity out of
the injured and the dead in their propaganda war on the IRA. In
no instance has the "warning rule" been violated by the guerrilla forces
in sharp contrast with the "no warning" methods used by the unionist
gangs and British army *agents provocateurs*.

The Abercorn Restaurant, McGurk's Bar, Benny's Bar, and more recently McGlades' Bar are frightening examples of the latter type of instant
bombing. Naturally it presents less risk to the bombers in terms of
personal safety and lessens the chances of being apprehended. As
well as giving warnings, the IRA always claims full responsibility for
all military action taken even should this redound unfavorably on the
Republican Movement's popularity; E.B.N.I., and Donegall Street are clas-

138

sic examples of this. Over the years the press has learned to accept the veracity of Irish Republican Publicity Bureau statements, whereas, with the British army's constant propaganda handouts, various versions of incidents and blatant covering up of tracks, have created for them a gross credibility gap.

The effect of the IRA bombing campaign can be gauged in many different ways. Firstly, they have struck at the very root of enemy morale, confining and tying down large numbers of troops and armored vehicles in center city areas, thus relieving much of the pressure on the much-oppressed nationalist areas. In terms of direct financial loss (structural damage, goods, machinery), also in the crippling of industrial output and perhaps worst of all in the scaring off of foreign capital investments, IRA bombs have hit Britain where she feels it most—in her pocket.

England always found unfortunate soldiers quite dispensable and to a certain extent replaceable, but she always counted in terms of cost to the Treasury. Any peace through the granting of freedom emanating to rebellious colonies from London came by means of calculation—the cost of occupation. Since 1969 a bill of warfare running to at least a conservative £500,000,000 has not gone unnoticed back home in Britain where recent opinion polls showed that over 54 percent of the ordinary people wanted the troops withdrawn forthwith.

Already some fifteen hundred troops have left Northern Ireland never to return. In many cases death certificates have been issued as for fatal road accident victims to the unsuspecting next-of-kin of soldiers killed in action in a heartless attempt at cooking records and hiding telling manpower losses. Suddenly Northern Ireland has become England's Vietnam. In the knowledge that the will to overcome of a risen people can never be defeated by brute force or even overwhelming odds, more enlightened British politicians have seen the light and are themselves thinking along Tone's famous dictum: "Break the connection!"

Great Britain too, of course, has suffered losses other than bomb damage and loss of personnel. Her prestige and credibility in terms of world opinion and world finance have been severely shaken; her duplicity and selective sense of justice have been seriously exposed; her puerile hankering after "holding the last vestige of the Empire" has marked her as a recidivist nation, psychologically vulnerable, unstable, and mentally immature. These considerations have not been lost on the European Common Market countries, especially France and Monsieur Pompidou. Britain's dilemma in Ireland is of her own making and is now seen as a black mark against her in the new capital—Brussels. Time is running out along the Thames.

BHAGWAT CHARAN

# THE PHILOSOPHY
# OF THE BOMB

Recent events, particularly the congress resolution on the attempt to blow up the viceregal special on December 23, 1929, and Gandhi's subsequent writings in *Young India*, clearly show that the Indian National Congress in conjunction with Gandhi has launched a crusade against the revolutionaries. A great amount of public criticism both from the press and platform has been made against them. It is a pity that they have all along been, either deliberately or due to sheer ignorance, misrepresented and misunderstood. The revolutionaries do not shun criticism and public scrutiny of their ideals or actions. They rather welcome these as a chance of making those understand, who have a genuine desire to do so, the basic principles of the revolutionary movement and the high and noble ideals that are a perennial source of inspiration and strength to it. It is hoped that this article will help the general public to know the revolutionaries as they are and will prevent it from taking them for what interested and ignorant persons would have the public believe them to be.

Let us first take the question of violence and nonviolence. We think that the use of these terms in itself is a grave injustice to either party, for they express the ideals of neither of them correctly. Violence is a physical force applied for committing injustice, and that is certainly not what the revolutionaries stand for. On the other hand, what generally goes by the name of nonviolence is in reality the theory of soul force—the attainment of personal and national rights through courting suffering and hoping to finally convert your opponent to your viewpoint. When a revolutionary believes certain things to be his right, he asks for them, pleads for them, argues for them, wills to attain them with all soul force at his command, stands the greatest amount of suffering for them, is always prepared to make the highest sacrifice for their attainment, and also backs his efforts with all the physical force he is capable of. You may coin what other word you like to describe the revolutionary methods, but you cannot call it violence because that would constitute an outrage on the dictionary meaning of that word. Gandhi's satyagraha is insistence upon truth. Why press for the acceptance of truth by soul force alone? Why not add physical force to it? While the revolutionaries stand for winning independence by all the forces, physical as well as moral, at their command, the advocate of soul force would like to ban the use of physical force. The question is therefore not whether you will have violence or nonviolence but whether you will have soul force plus physical force or soul force alone.

The revolutionaries believe that the deliverance of their country will come through revolution. The revolution they are constantly working and hoping for will not only express itself in the form of an armed conflict between the foreign government and its supporters and the people, but it will also usher in the new social order. The revolution will bring the death knell of capitalism and class distinction and privileges. It will bring the nation into its own. It will give birth to a new state, a new society. Above all, it will establish the dictatorship of the proletariat and will forever banish social parasites from the seat of political power.

The revolutionaries already see the advent of the revolution in the restlessness of youth, in its desire to get free from the mental bondage and religious superstitions that hold them. As the youth will get more and more saturated with the psychology of revolution, it will come to have a clearer realization of the national bondage and a growing, intense, unquenchable thirst for freedom till, in their righteous anguish, infuriated youth will begin to kill the oppressors. Thus has terrorism been born in the country. It is a phase, a necessary and inevitable phase of the revolution. Terrorism is not complete revolution and the revolution is not complete without terrorism. This thesis can be supported by an analysis of any and every revolution in history. Terrorism instills fear in the hearts of the oppressors, it brings hopes of revenge and redemption to the oppressed masses. It gives courage and self-confidence to the wavering and it shatters the spell of the subject race in the eyes of the world, because it is the most convincing proof of a nation's hunger for freedom. Here in India, as in other countries in the past, terrorism will develop into the revolution and the revolution into independence, social, political and economic....

Gandhi has called upon all those who are nearest to reason to withdraw their support from the revolutionaries and condemn their actions so that our deluded patriots may, for want of nourishment to their violent spirit, realize the futility of violence and the great harm that violent activities have every time done. How easy and convenient it is to call people deluded, to declare them to be past reason, to call upon the people to withdraw its support and condemn them so that they may get isolated and be forced to suspend their activities, specially when a man holds the confidence of an influential section of the public. It is a pity that Gandhi does not understand and will not understand revolutionary psychology in spite of his lifelong experience of public life. It is a precious thing. It is dear to everyone. If a man becomes a revolutionary, if he goes about with his life in the hollow of his hand ready to sacrifice it at any moment, he does not do so merely for the fun of it. He does not risk his life because sometimes when the crowd is in a sympathetic mood it cries bravo in appreciation. He does it because his reason forces him to that course, because his conscience dictates it. A revolutionary believes in reason more than anything else. It is to reason and reason alone that he bows. No amount of abuse and condemnation, even [if] it emanates from the highest of the high, can turn him from his set purpose. To think a revolutionary will give up his ideals if public support and appreciation are withdrawn from him is the highest folly. Many a revolutionary has ere now stepped on the scaffold and laid his life for the cause, regardless of the curses that the constitutional agitators rained plentifully upon him. If you will have the revolutionaries suspend their activities, reason with them squarely. This is one way and the only way. For the rest, let there be no doubt in anybody's mind. A revolutionary is the last person on the earth to submit to bullying.

We take this opportunity to appeal to our countrymen, to the youth, to the workers and peasants, to the revolutionary intelligentsia to come forward and to join us in carrying aloft the banner of freedom. Let us establish a new order of society in which political and economic exploitation will be an impossibility. In the name of those gallant men and women who willingly accepted death so that we their descendants may lead a happier life, who toiled ceaselessly and perished for the poor, defamished [sic] and exploited millions of India.

We call upon every patriot to take up the fight in all seriousness. Let nobody toy with the nation's freedom, which is her very life, by making psychological experiments with nonviolence and such other novelties. Our slavery is our shame. When shall we have courage and wisdom enough to be able to shake ourselves free of it? What is our great heritage or our civilization and culture worth if we have not enough self-respect left in us to prevent us from bowing survilance [sic] to the commands of foreigners and paying homage to their king and flag.

There is no crime that Britain has not committed in India. Deliberate misrule has reduced us to paupers, has bled us white. As a race and as a people we stand dishonored and outraged. Do people still expect us to forget and forgive. We shall have our revenge, a people's righteous revenge on the tyrant. Let cowards fall back and cling for compromise and peace. We ask not for mercy and we give no quarter. Ours is a war to the end—to victory or death. Long live revolution.

---

Manifesto of HSRA illegally distributed in various parts
of India in January, 1930

MENAHEM BEGIN

# THE REVOLT

A T THE LAUNCHING OF THE REVOLT we divided the Irgun into a number of sections—in addition to the natural administrative and geographical divisions. We called these sections:

1. A.R.—Army of the Revolution
2. S.U.—Shock Units
3. A.F.—Assault Force
4. R.P.F.—Revolutionary Propaganda Force

We intended, therefore, to have four sections. But reality is stronger
than any decisions of a fighting command. The A.R. existed only in theory. It was supposed to serve as a reserve, embracing all the soldiers who
were in none of the three remaining sections. But this arrangement never
worked. Newcomers passed through it, and after their basic training were
transferred to one of the other sections. It had neither officers nor men
of its own. It had its day only when we emerged from the underground
into the battle with the Arab invaders—when every man in the Irgun was
drafted to a regular army unit: section, platoon, company, battalion.

The Shock Units were never actually set up. This was merely a new
name given to a unit that had existed before the revolt. It was known—to
those that knew of its existence—as the "Red Section" or the "Black
Squad." The idea behind this unit was very interesting. It was Yaacov
Meridor's idea. He assumed that the struggle for liberation would require
men especially trained to operate in the Arab areas, both in Eretz Israel
and in the Arab countries. The men chosen were, therefore, brave and
dark-skinned. They were given military training and lessons in Arabic.
The composition of the "Red Section" was to be kept absolutely secret

even from other members of the Irgun. This was the "underground within the underground" idea—which did not succeed. It was daring, but its execution caused a mixture of difficulties, some of them not unamusing. Suddenly the best men, and even officers, began leaving the Irgun. Loyal members who had gone with the Irgun through thick and thin wondered and could not understand. *He*—a deserter? And the deserter would add insult to injury. Not content with loud declarations that he had nothing more to do with the Irgun, he would curse and swear at it. This strange behavior of formerly devoted men and important officers was bound to lower morale in the ranks. It was impossible to explain, or even hint at, the truth. Despite this, however, the deserters were not followed by real ones. Our boys were fortified by the principle we had succeeded in embedding in their hearts: that the ideal is the important thing and not the man. So-and-so had left, such-and-such a one had deserted? What matter? You, the soldier, had taken a historic mission upon yourself out of inner conviction. You had to fulfill it without regard to what anybody might say or do in negation of that mission, whether it were your antagonists or your friends of the day before, or your comrades or your officers. As a soldier of freedom, your supreme commander was the cause itself.

The affair of the "Red Section," though it opened in sorrow, ended in joy and gladness. When the revolt began, all the deserters reappeared in their regular units. There was renewed surprise, but this time it was accompanied by happy relief. Only yesterday that so-and-so had been cursing the Irgun up hill and down dale, and now he was an officer in the front line? They rubbed their eyes. Friendships were reformed. Much-lowered morale rose up once more.

In the "Red Section" there were many excellent fighters and all, or almost all, looked like Arabs. But it is not only people from the Arab countries who are dark-skinned. There are many Ashkenazi Jews from Europe who are no less dark—and are sometimes darker—than the purest Sephardi. The only two members of the unit I knew personally came from Lodz, in Poland. It is true that many of the fighters in the Shock Units sprang from the eastern communities. Hence the story, disseminated particularly by the British press correspondents, of the "Black Squad" of the Irgun, allegedly composed only of Yemenites. This legend was helped along to no small extent by certain Jewish politicians. Wishing to belittle us, these gentlemen whispered, or said aloud, that the *whole* of the Irgun consisted only of Yemenites. Our enemies, who disseminated tales about "black Yemenites" on the one hand and "the scum of Eastern Europe" on the other, were trying to besmirch us. It is a pity that our Jewish political opponents stooped to this nasty "racial" invective so beloved of anti-

Semitic propagandists between the wars. The Nazis used to say: "Maybe not all Jews are Communists, but all the Communists are Jews." Similarly, some Zionists said of us: "Not all Yemenites are Irgunists, but all the Irgun people are Yemenites."

Nothing of the sort. In the Shock Units and in all the divisions of the Irgun we had members who came from all Jewish communities and of all classes. We had people from Tunis and Harbin, Poland and Persia, France and Yemen, Belgium and Iraq, Czechoslovakia and Syria; we had natives of the United States and Bokhara, of England, Scotland, Argentina and South Africa, and most of all, of Eretz Israel itself. We were the melting pot of the Jewish nation in miniature. We never asked about origins; we demanded only loyalty and ability. Our comrades from the eastern communities felt happy and at home in the Irgun. Nobody ever displayed any stupid airs of superiority toward them; and they were thus helped to free themselves of any unjustified sense of inferiority they may have harbored. They were fighting comrades and that was enough. They could, and did, attain the highest positions of responsibility. Shlomo Levi, the first chief of staff in the revolt, is a Sephardi. His brother, "Uzi," on his return from the Eritrea prison camp, became regional commander at Tel Aviv and commanded thousands of men until he fell, fighting heroically, in the decisive battle for Jaffa. Shimshon, regional commander at Haifa until he was betrayed to the British military authorities, came from Persia. We had a Gideon in Jerusalem, who led the historic operation against the G.H.Q. of the occupation army and led it with consummate bravery and coolness. He was a Sephardi, too. Two of the men who went to the gallows, Alkoshi and Kashani, were Sephardim. The "smear" with which our enemies and opponents tried to belittle us was to us a source of pride. People who had been humiliated and degraded became proud fighters in our ranks, free and equal men and women, bearers of liberty and honor. Statistics? We never counted along these lines. But I believe I shall be very near the truth if I say that in the various sections of the Irgun there were no less than 25 percent and no more than 35 percent Sephardim and members of the eastern communities. In the Shock Units, in view of the special emphasis on dark skins the proportion was probably greater, possibly between 40 and 50 percent.

The members of the Shock Units carried out the early operations of the revolt, but their separate existence was not justified in practical tests. In the course of time and with the deepening of the struggle, the Shock Units were united with the Assault Units and became the famous Assault Force of the Irgun, which delivered the heaviest blows against the oppressor and was directly responsible for the disintegration of the mandatory rule in the Eretz Israel. Of the four sections we had planned there remained in practice only two: the Assault Force and the Revolutionary Propaganda Force. And between them there was permanent conflict: every R.P.F. man wanted a transfer to the A.F., and no A.F. man ever agreed to go over to the R.P.F.

This was not the only conflict inside the underground. A fighting underground is a veritable state in miniature—a state at war. It has its army, its police, its own courts. It has at its disposal all the executive arms of a state. Above all, it bore the responsibility for life and death not only for individuals, but also for whole generations. Nor is it only in this sense that an underground resembles a state. Just as in the ministries and departments of government, so too in the underground and its divisions and sections there is cooperation and there are quarrels, arising from human nature itself. The regional commanders did not like the "autonomy" granted to the Shock Units and later to the Assault Force. "We," said the regional commanders, "handle all the work in the area under our command. We know what arms we have (or have not). We know our people. Why should we not be in charge of the preparations for battle operations and of the operations themselves?" This argument was quite logical. But the retort of the Assault Force commanders was no less so. "Battle operations," they said, "have often to be prepared very speedily. The regional commander is like a father of many children. He is preoccupied with scores of organizational problems. We can only be sure of maximum efficiency if we have direct contact with the local operational officers."

It was not easy to judge between the two sides, particularly as both were seeking only the best means of carrying on the struggle. At times I felt like the judge who had decreed both parties in a dispute to be right and who, when asked by his wife how this could possibly be, replied gently, "You are right too, my love!"

This dispute over autonomy that had been granted in the case of the Assault Force went on at the same time as another discussion over autonomy which was not granted. Our Intelligence Service never ceased asking for a certain measure of autonomy. This section did great work during the struggle. While the Assault Force belabored the enemy with iron and lead, the Intelligence fought him with brains. Indeed, the victory over the government forces depended largely on our Intelligence, its revelations, its information and the security belt it built, laboriously and with unerring common sense, round the fighting underground. Its members, headed by Yoel's deputy and successor, Michael, were anxious for even greater achievements and believed they could attain them if they were given a measure of freedom of action. Characteristically, they quoted in support of their argument the custom in many countries in which the intelligence and counter espionage services are under the direct control of the central government.

Thanks to the understanding and tolerance which all our comrades displayed, we succeeded in overcoming these internecine difficulties, which flowed from the necessary division of labor among many people and their eager desire to succeed in their tasks. It is no exaggeration to say that in the underground we all gained some experience of the machinery of state, with its light and shadow, its virtues and its defects. Generally we overcame the "interdepartmental" problems, but we never succeeded in putting an end to the sacred dispute between the Assault Force and the Revolutionary Propaganda Force.

---

Menahem Begin, *The Revolt* (London, n.d.) Reprinted
with the permission of the publisher, W.H. Allen.

# PLATFORM OF THE POPULAR FRONT FOR THE LIBERATION OF PALESTINE

1. Conventional War Is the War of the Bourgeoisie. Revolutionary War Is the People's War.

The Arab bourgeoisie has developed armies which are not prepared to sacrifice their own interests or to risk their privileges. Arab militarism has become an apparatus for oppressing revolutionary socialist movements within the Arab states, while at the same time claiming to be staunchly anti-imperialist. Under the guise of the national question, the bourgeoisie has used its armies to strengthen its bureaucratic power over the masses and to prevent the workers and peasants from acquiring political power. So far it has demanded the help of the workers and peasants without organizing them or without developing a proletarian ideology. The national bourgeoisie usually comes to power through military coups and without any activity on the part of the masses; as soon as it has captured power it reinforces its bureaucratic position. Through widespread application of terror it is able to talk about revolution while at the same time it suppresses all the revolutionary movements and arrests everyone who tries to advocate revolutionary action.

The Arab bourgeoisie has used the question of Palestine to divert the Arab masses from realizing their own interests and their own domestic problems. The bourgeoisie always concentrated hopes on a victory outside the state's boundaries in Palestine and in this way they were able to preserve their class interests and their bureaucratic positions.

The war of June, 1967 disproved the bourgeois theory of conventional war. The best strategy for Israel is to strike rapidly. The enemy is not able to mobilize its armies for a long period of time because this would intensify its economic crisis. The enemy gets complete support from U.S. imperialism and for these reasons it needs quick wars. Therefore, for our poor people the best strategy in the long run is a people's war. Our people must overcome their weaknesses and exploit the weaknesses of the enemy by mobilizing the Palestinian and Arab peoples. The weakening of imperialism and Zionism in the Arab world demands revolutionary war as the means to confront them.

2. Guerrilla Struggle Can Be a Form of Pressure for the "Peaceful Solution."

The Palestinian struggle is a part of the whole Arab liberation movement and of the world liberation movement. The Arab bourgeoisie and world imperialism are trying to impose a peaceful solution on this Palestinian problem, but this suggestion merely promotes the interests of imperialism and of Zionism, doubt in the efficacy of people's war as a means of liberation and the preservation of the relations of the Arab bourgeoisie with the imperialist world market.

The Arab bourgeoisie is afraid of being isolated from this market and of losing its role as a mediator of world capitalism. That is why the Arab oil-producing countries broke off the boycott against the West (instituted during the June war), and for this reason [the U.S.'s Robert] McNamara, as head of the World Bank, was ready to offer credits to them.

When the Arab bourgeoisie strive for a peaceful solution, they are in fact striving for the profit which they can get from their role as mediator between the imperialist market and the internal market. The Arab bourgeoisie are not yet opposed to the activity of the guerrillas and sometimes they even help them, but this is because the presence of the guerrillas is a means of pressure for a peaceful solution. As long as the guerrillas don't have a clear class affiliation and a clear political stand they are unable to resist the implication of such a peaceful solution, but the conflict between the guerrillas and those who strive for a peaceful solution is unavoidable. Therefore, the guerrillas must take steps to transform their actions into a people's war with clear goals.

3. There Can Be No Revolutionary War Without a Revolutionary Theory.

The basic weakness of the guerrilla movement is the absence of a revolutionary ideology, which could illuminate the horizons of the Palestinian fighters and would incarnate the stages of a militant political program. Without a revolutionary ideology the national struggle will remain imprisoned within its immediate practical and material needs. The Arab bourgeoisie is quite prepared for a limited satisfaction of the needs of the national struggle, as long as it respects the limits that the bourgeoisie sets. A clear illustration of this is the material help that Saudi Arabia offers Al Fatah while Al Fatah declares that it will not interfere in the internal affairs of any Arab countries.

Since most of the guerrilla movements have no ideological weapons, the Arab bourgeoisie can decide their fate. Therefore, the struggle of the Palestinian people must be supported by the workers and peasants, who will fight against any form of domination by imperialism, Zionism, or the Arab bourgeoisie.

4. The War of Liberation Is a Class War Guided by a Revolutionary Ideology.

We must not be satisfied with ignoring the problems of our struggle, saying that our struggle is a national one and not a class struggle. The national struggle reflects the class struggle. The national struggle is a struggle for land and those who struggle for it are the peasants who were driven away from their land. The bourgeoisie is always ready to lead such a movement, hoping to gain control of the internal market. If the bourgeoisie succeeds in bringing the national movement under its control, which strengthens its position, it can lead the movement under the guise of a peaceful solution into compromises with imperialism and Zionism.

Therefore, the fact that the liberation struggle is mainly a class struggle emphasizes the necessity for the workers and peasants to play a leading role in the national liberation movement. If the small bourgeoisie take the leading role, the national revolution will fall victim to the class interests of this leadership. It is a great mistake to start by saying that the Zionist challenge demands national unity, for this shows that one does not understand the real class structure of Zionism.

The struggle against Israel is first of all a class struggle. Therefore, the oppressed class is the only class which is able to face a confrontation with Zionism.

5. The Main Field of Our Revolutionary Struggle Is Palestine.

The decisive battle must be in Palestine. The armed people's struggle in Palestine can help itself with the simplest weapons in order to ruin the economies and the war machinery of their Zionist enemy. The moving of the people's struggle into Palestine depends upon agitating and organizing the masses more than depending upon border actions in the Jordan valley, although these actions are of importance for the struggle in Palestine.

When guerrilla organizations began their actions in the occupied areas, they were faced with a brutal military repression by the armed forces of Zionism. Because these organizations had no revolutionary ideology and so no program, they gave in to demands of self-preservation and retreated into eastern Jordan. All their activity turned into border actions. This presence of the guerrilla organizations in Jordan enables the Jordanian bourgeoisie and their secret agents to crush these organizations when they are no longer useful as pressure for a peaceful solution.

6. Revolution in Both Regions of Jordan.

We must not neglect the struggle in east Jordan, for this land is connected with Palestine more than with the other Arab countries. The problem of the revolution in Palestine is dialectically connected with the problem of the revolution in Jordan. A chain of plots between the Jordanian monarchy, imperialism and Zionism have proved this connection.

The struggle in east Jordan must take the correct path—that of class struggle. The Palestinian struggle must not be used as a means of propping up the Jordanian monarchy under the mask of national unity, and the main problem in Jordan is the creation of a Marxist-Leninist party with a clear action program according to which it can organize the masses and enable them to carry out the national and class struggle. The harmony of the struggle in the two regions must be realized through coordinating organs whose tasks will be to guarantee reserves inside Palestine and to mobilize the peasants and soldiers in the border territories.

This is the only way in which Amman can become an Arab Hanoi—a base for the revolutionaries fighting inside Palestine.

YEHOSHAFAT HARKABI

# AL FATAH'S DOCTRINE

IT IS NOT BY SHEER ACCIDENT that the third Fatah pamphlet entitled "The Revolution and Violence, the Road to Victory" is a selective precis of Frantz Fanon's book *The Wretched of the Earth*. Fanon's influence is manifested in other Fatah writings, especially on the psychological impact of Israel on the Arabs and on the transformations that their armed struggle will produce in the Palestinians. "Violence," "violent struggle," and "vengeance" are expressions of great frequency in Fatah literature. The reader of these texts is introduced to a world of simmering frustrated hatred and a drive for unquenchable vengeance.

Violence is described as imperative in wiping out colonialism, for between the colonialist and the colonized there is such a contradiction that no coexistence is possible. One of the two has to be liquidated. (Descriptions of the Arab-Israel conflict as both a zero-sum game and a deadly quarrel are frequent in Arab publications.) Such a conflict is "a war of annihilation of one of the rivals, either wiping out the national entity, or wiping out colonialism. ... The colonized will be liberated from violence by violence." The "Palestinian revolution" is such a cataclysmic event that it can only be achieved by violence.

Violence liberates people from their shortcomings and anxieties. It inculcates in them both courage and fearlessness concerning death.

Violence has a therapeutic effect, purifying society of its diseases. "Violence will purify the individuals from venom, it will redeem the colonized from inferiority complex, it will return courage to the countryman." In a memorandum to Arab journalists, Fatah stated: "Blazing our armed revolution inside the occupied territory [i.e., Israel—it was written before the Six-Day War] is a healing medicine for all our people's diseases."

The praising of violence as purgative may imply also an element of self-indictment for flaws which will now be rectified, and a desire to exorcize the record of failings. The praising of violence may have as well the function of giving cathartic satisfaction as a substitute for operational action.

Violence, Fatah asserts, will have a unifying influence on people, forging one nation from them. It will draw the individuals from the pettiness of their ego and imbue them with the effusiveness of collective endeavor, as bloodshed will produce a common experience binding them together. Thus, "the territoriality (i.e., the fragmentation into different Arab states), which was imposed by imperialism and Arab leaderships and which was sustained by traditional circumstances in the societies, will end."

The struggle, besides its political goals, will have as a by-product an important impact on those who participate in it. It is "a creative struggling" (*nidalia khallaqa*). Violence, revolutionarism, activism, "the battle of vengeance," "armed struggle," all coalesce in an apocalyptic vision of heroic and just aggression, meting out revenge on Israel....

The parts of Fatah's writings which deal with the phases of war make uneasy reading. Fatah's terminology and formulation may seem both esoteric and highfalutin. However, what may be more wearisome for the reader who is not versed in such parlance is the generality and abstraction of the discussion. It contains a mixture of a terminology influenced by Marxist literature, attempting to interpret developments in a rational way, with mythical overtones expressed in figures of speech like the "ignition" or "detonation" of a revolution, and leaves the reader wondering how it is to be done.

The organizational stages symbolize the expansion of the circles of those involved in the revolution or war. The first stage is the Formation of the Revolutionary Vanguard. This is achieved by "the movement of revolutionary gathering of the revengeful conscious wills." "The individual of the Revolutionary Vanguard is distinguished by his revolutionary intuition." His task is "to discover the vital tide in his society, for its own sake and for its usefulness for action and movement and then to realize what obstacles hamper his movement in accordance with history's logic." Thus, "the Revolutionary Vanguard signifies the type of human who interacts positively with the reality [of his predicament] and so elevates himself by his consciousness until he releases himself from reality's grip in order to pursue the superseding of this reality by another, which differs basically in its values and traits. To take a concrete example, the reality of Arab Palestinian people is fragmented, disfigured and corrupted, and shows signs of stagnation. However, despite this stagnation and immobility, the historical direction imposes the existence of a current of vitality among the Palestinian people, so long as the Palestinian man treasures vengeance on this reality. As this wish for vengeance grows, the current of vitality congeals in the form of a Revolutionary Vanguard."

The second stage is the formation of the Revolutionary Organization. In it the Revolutionary Vanguard achieves a psychological mobilization of the Palestinian masses by stimulating their urge for revenge, until "the constructive revolutionary anxiety embraces all the Palestinian Arabs." It is thus called the stage of Revolutionary Embracing (*Al Shumul al-Thauri*). Indoctrination of the masses will not precede the staging of the armed struggle but will be achieved by it. "Mistaken are those who advocate the need for rousing a national consciousness before the armed struggle assumes a concrete form.... Ineluctably the armed struggle and mass consciousness will go side by side, because the armed struggle will make the masses feel their active personality and restore their self-confidence." The Vanguard will galvanize the masses by means of its example and sacrifice in guerrilla activities.

Fatah's publications state that irresistible might is stored in the Arab masses. They are "latent volcanoes," they are the main "instrument" of the struggle. This explosive capacity has to be activated and this task is allotted to the Vanguard.

The revolution's success is dependent on cooperation between the Vanguard and the masses. "The revolution in its composition has a leadership and a basis, necessitates the accomplishment of a conscious interaction between the basis, which is the masses, and the leadership, in order to ensure the revolution's success and continuation."

The third stage is the formation of the Supporting Arab Front. Popular support for the "Palestinian revolution" is to be secured in all Arab countries in order to safeguard rear bases in Arab countries for the war, and as a means of putting pressure on the Arab governments not to slacken or deviate from aiding the Palestinian revolution by pursuit of their local interests. The Supporting Arab Front is thus expressed on two levels, the popular and the governmental. The popular support is used as an instrument of pressure against the Arab governments.

In the same publications the overall development of the revolution is divided into two major stages: one, Organization and Mobilization, called elsewhere the Phases of Revolutionary Maturing, comprises the organizational stages already enumerated. The second stage is called that of the Revolutionary Explosion (*Marhal atal-Tafjir al-Thauri*). The stage of the Revolutionary Explosion is described in colorful language: "The hating revengeful masses plunge into the road of revolution in a pressing and vehement fashion as pouring forces that burn everything that stands in their way." In this stage "tempests of revenge" will be let loose. However, the

Vanguard should ensure mass discipline to prevent violence going berserk. "The revolution's will should obey its regulating brain."

While the first stage is preparatory, the second is the main, interesting stage. Unfortunately, Fatah's description of it is rather rudimentary. Even the question of the timing of its beginning is not clear. Fatah specified, "Our operations in the occupied territory can never reach the stage of the aspired revolution unless all Palestinian groups are polarized around the revolution." Fatah does have an ambition to become the central leader of all the Palestinians, proving that the other movements, which have not matured round what has been described as a Revolutionary Vanguard like itself, are artificial and "counterfeited." Thus, the stage of revolution will arrive only when Fatah has mobilized *all* Palestinians.

---

Reprinted by special permission from *Adelphi Papers*,
No. 53 (December 1968).
Institute of Strategic Studies, London.

BIZHAM JAZANI

# ARMED STRUGGLE IN IRAN

## THE MAIN FORM OF ADVENTURISM IN THE ARMED MOVEMENT

1. To ignore the objective conditions which are relevant to the growth of the revolutionary movement; to consider the role of the vanguard out of its context; and to peddle the notion that the sensational sacrifice of some elements of the vanguard will immediately (or in a short time) attract the support of the masses, or even encourage their active participation in the struggle, is adventuristic. Such conceptions about armed struggle should be replaced by a Marxist understanding of the dynamics of society and of the revolutionary movement in general. Today, we live in conditions where all factors are combined against the evolution. To believe that all these factors are amenable to change by one single factor, namely, the role of the vanguard—a vanguard in its most elementary form, for that matter—is an unscientific approach to society and to the movement. To persist in such a theory is to deny the role of the masses in the movement. *To deny the masses their role in the movement—although those guilty might vehemently deny this—is the main form of adventurism.*

2. Paying scant attention to revolutionary theory, concentrating only on "practical" and delimited actions and attention to tactical matters while ignoring strategic questions are all forms of adventurism.

   When we fail to recognize that a guerrilla is an informed individual who performs a military assignment armed primarily with revolutionary theory; when we pay little or no attention to political studies and hurriedly try to exploit the excitement caused by a revolutionary action and wish immediately to transform whosoever may join the movement into an exemplary practitioner; and when we imagine that revolutionary theory is merely about tactical questions and sensational literature, then we are only revealing our adventuristic tendencies, and this can be reflected in the revolutionary movement as a whole.

3. An absolute insistence on armed tactics of a particular nature in urban guerrilla struggle, making dogmas out of these tactics and underestimating the value of other tactics besides armed tactics, is only a form of adventurism. To put too much value on sensational tactics, and to pay no attention to tactics that can excite the physical support of the masses for the movement, can alienate the former from the latter and ultimately defeat the movement.

   Too much emphasis on the role of the "Fedaee," resorting to constant invocations of "Martyrdom" to offset the absence of a mass movement, and the belief that the sacrifice of blood is sufficient for the start of the revolution are aspects of adventurism.

4. An incorrect knowledge of the potential forces, seeing the struggle merely within the limits of available forces, employing tactics that can only satisfy the latter, disregarding genuine revolutionary forces merely because these will turn to struggle at a later date are deviationary phenomena. Marxist-Leninist organizations are liable to succumb to the temptation of putting aside the special features of their ideology in order to get hold of the available forces offered by certain sections of the petit bourgeoisie. Such acts can effectively cut off the organizations from the proletariat. This, in effect, means that they will have to make do with a limited force and ignore the potential force in whose hands the revolution will triumph. This is another form of adventurism.

5. Expressions of weariness about the struggle, demonstrations of impatience when the struggle drags on, and complaints about the masses which can turn into pessimism about them is an aspect of adventurism. To employ vengeful tactics in order to offset the absence of a mass movement and to make continuous demands on the members for more and more sacrifices to fill such a vacuum is a natural consequence of the same thing. To merely examine small tactical matters in an attempt to find the causes of defeat, to explain away the fundamental shortcomings of the movement by looking only at one part of the whole picture, and to blame oneself for the movement's inadequacies is also adventurism.

**6.** Underestimating the enemy, indulging in self-satisfied expressions because of some victories, exaggerating one's power and ignoring the power of other forces who face the ruling cliques and imperialism is a further form of adventuristic tendency which will prevent us from making a continuous effort in looking for new tactics, correcting the old ones, and recognizing our shortcomings.

7. Adventurist tendencies can also appear in various other aspects of our work, e.g., in understanding and evaluating the real potentials of different individuals and their political as well as ideological training, in our moral discipline, and in our personal and collective conduct.

The petit bourgeois deviationary tendency, which manifests itself in the form of leftist and pseudorevolutionary attitudes, is liable to keep us apart from those more straightforward individuals who come to the movement. It can also drive us toward hypocrisy and false humility and prevent us from carrying out fundamental ideological training.

These are the main forms of adventuristic tendencies in groups and organizations, attached to the armed movement. The less experienced an organization the more exposed it is to the dangers of these tendencies. Some forms of leftism have a great attraction for inexperienced Marxist individuals, and it is quite true that "leftism" is "an infantile disorder" within the revolutionary working-class movement. Left to itself the disease can spread throughout the whole movement. Those comrades who prescribe the fatal medicine of leftism in order to cure an allegedly "rightist attitude," those comrades who in any way "criticize" a "leftist stand," which in practice is nothing short of an encouragement of this disease, are in effect the most dangerous protagonists of adventurism.

A determined fight against opportunism, in whatever position, the recognition of what are deviationary tendencies and a timely war against them, and a sober defense of revolutionary policy and ideology constitute the central task facing all elements and groups who are attached to the working classes. Failure to do this is tantamount to leaving the fate of the movement to unforeseen future events....

Armed struggle is bound to grow, despite the inevitable ups and downs which are natural in the development of any movement. Urban guerrilla organizations will expand and armed struggle will assume bigger dimensions and more effective forms. Nevertheless, the following impediments prevent this form of struggle from becoming a mass movement:

a. Urban guerilla tactics are complicated. Urban guerrilla tactics are, from a technical point of view, extraordinarily complicated. In such a struggle every guerrilla will have to be a highly experienced commando. A complete command of the technicalities of struggle against the police—technicalities that continually become more and more complicated—and an extraordinary mobility is an absolute must for every guerrilla. The workers and urban proletariat who have not had sufficient training are unable to use these tactics. The use of these tactics will also be fraught with danger for an ordinary intellectual.

In an urban guerrilla war it is not possible to accept volunteers from among the workers and hope that a few experienced comrades will be able to command them. A commander in such a situation has limited possibilities to guide his men who require leadership at all hours of the day in their various assignments. In such a struggle, every man plays a decisive role in protecting himself and his comrades-in-arms. The great mass of people turn to a struggle in large numbers and suddenly. Hence, the above-mentioned features effectively rule out their participation in an urban guerrilla war.

b. Our towns have limited capacity to accommodate guerillas. Even the largest towns in our country have a limited capacity to accommodate guerrillas. A guerrilla force in Teheran, which is an exceptionally large town, cannot exceed an estimated number of a few hundred—between one to two thousand, if we include the auxiliary units. If we look at the way in which an urban guerrilla unit operates, we will realize that this figure represents an extraordinary force, and is the optimum capacity for military assignments in a town. If the capacity of a town for military actions and concealment is such that the actions of two or more groups overlap each other or cause problems for other groups, thus depriving them of important room for maneuver in the face of possible enemy search-and-destroy operations, then the continuation of a guerrilla existence in that town will become precarious. In such a case the expansion of a guerrilla force is a detrimental factor for us. Those who believe that townspeople will eventually join urban guerrilla organizations in their thousands or tens of thousands have, unfortunately, no clear picture of the masses. Nor do they have a clear understanding of the characteristics of our struggles. These are the people who occasionally start to murmur about a liberated zone in urban areas.

Urban guerrilla groups and their reserve units (i.e., sympathizers) are formed from conscious and progressive elements. The masses, despite their tremendous size and quality, are unable to participate in urban armed struggle.

c. The intellectuals are better prepared. The intellectuals are better prepared than workers and other proletarians to take part in this struggle. That is why the main force of the urban guerrilla struggle is composed of revolutionary intellectuals.

This composition, with some increase in favor of the workers, will on the whole be maintained through the next stages of the struggle.

In contrast to these limitations and shortcomings, the armed struggle has the following possibilities in the mountains and rural areas:

• In the countryside ordinary rural elements can turn to struggle and, after an initial training by experienced cadres, take part in direct actions. There is no impediment to accepting the rural masses into armed combat units, and the reason for dispatching urban guerrilla units to the rural areas is because of the military unpreparedness of the rural population. Not only farmers but also workers and other urban elements can engage in rural armed struggle and develop their potentialities in such a struggle.

• The limitations of armed struggle in the towns and its expansion outside does not contradict the primary role of the urban areas in the first stage. In this stage, towns have various advantages over rural areas. These advantages were noted and emphasized by the movement with considerable results. These limitations of urban guerrilla struggle and the possibility of better opportunities in the rural areas, are being analyzed in relation to the armed struggle becoming a mass movement. Armed struggle outside the towns is vital to the future of the movement and it is very important in the total mobilization of the masses in an armed movement.

• Thus, the present realities of the situation manifest themselves in two essential ways.

The first is that, parallel to the growth of armed struggle, the urban masses will become active through participation in economic and political movements, the continuation of which will depend on the growth of armed struggle.

• The second is that armed struggle will become a mass movement in the rural areas. With the expansion and development of armed struggle in the rural areas, the urban and rural masses will join the struggle. Therefore, we shall in the future—i.e., at the end of the first and throughout the second stages—witness the increase of political and economic protests by the urban population. The expansion of these protests is a result of the growth in social contradictions, and the effect that armed struggle will have on these contradictions in order to reactivate them. . . .

## THE EFFECT OF ARMED STRUGGLE ON THE PEOPLE

From the start the people showed an interest in the guerrillas. Although they had no clear understanding of what a "guerrilla" was, they were thoroughly familiar with the regime. This was the result of a long process of struggle over some generations. The nature of the regime and especially its head, the shah, was perfectly clear to the masses, not in the form of a political awareness but instinctively. The regime and the shah's determination to remain in power for such a long time helped this understanding. Therefore, the people's initial reaction to the movement was based on the simple mechanism of "the enemy of the regime is a friend of the people." This mechanism does not always hold good, as it can and has been used by demagogues and the pawns of imperialism to deceive the masses.

Thus, even before the nature and characteristics of the "guerrillas" were clear, people displayed favorable sentiments toward them. These were expressed in the form of the various rumors in favor of the guerrillas, although the rumors tended to create a larger-than-life impression about their qualities and numbers. After Siahkal, it was rumored that the northern woods were bristling with guerrillas and the regime's expeditionary force to the north was therefore thought to be on a massive scale. There was, consequently, an exaggerated idea of the enemy's casualties and about the guerrillas' bravery. The news of the guerrillas' defeat was received with incredulity.

It might be said that "rumors" are on a par with lies and fabrication. However, a scientific analysis of "rumors" yields a different picture. In order for a rumor to spread quickly and to grow, it needs a suitable social background. The area in which a rumor tends to spread has to have political, economic and cultural affinity with it. Otherwise, not only rumor but even straightforward facts will fail to penetrate the people of that area. Within two days of General Farsio's execution, it was rumored all over the country that he had died immediately (this was in fact the case), whereas the regime was desperately trying to show that he was alive. After this incident, if any of the regime's military political personalities failed to appear in public for a few days, rumor would have it that they had been executed by the guerrillas. . . .

PRAIRIE FIRE

# POLITICAL STATEMENT
# OF THE WEATHER
# UNDERGROUND, 1974

A RMED STRUGGLE HAS COME INTO BEING in the United States. It is an indication of growth that our movement has developed clandestine organizations and that we are learning how to fight.

The development of guerrilla organization and armed activity against the state is most advanced in the black community, where the tradition and necessity for resistance is highest. The crises of the society provide the training grounds; for third world people the conditions of prison, the army, the streets and most oppressive jobs produce warriors, political theorists, and active strategists.

The Black Liberation Army (fighting for three years under ruthless attack by the state), the fighters in prisons, and recently the Symbionese Liberation Army are leading forces in the development of the armed struggle and political consciousness, respected by ourselves and other revolutionaries.

At this early stage in the armed and clandestine struggle, our forms of combat and confrontation are few and precise. Our organized forces are small, the enemy's forces are huge. We live inside the oppressor nation, particularly suited to urban guerrilla warfare. We are strategically situated in the nerve centers of the international empire, where the institutions and symbols of imperial power are concentrated. The cities will be a major battleground, for the overwhelming majority of people live in the cities; the cities are our terrain.

We believe that carrying out armed struggle will affect the people's consciousness of the nature of the struggle against the state. By beginning the armed struggle, the awareness of its necessity will be furthered. This is no less true in the U.S. than in other countries throughout the world. Revolutionary action generates revolutionary consciousness; growing consciousness develops revolutionary action. Action teaches the lessons of fighting and demonstrates that armed struggle is possible.

We are building a foundation. In four years of armed work, we have come to appreciate the complexity of doing it right and the difficulty of sustaining it. These are contradictions we are working with:

☐ We live in a whirlwind; nonetheless, time is on the side of the guerrillas. Fighting the enemy is urgent, and we have a duty to do all we can. Yet it takes time to win the people's trust; it takes time to build an organization capable of surviving the hunt; it takes time to recover and learn from mistakes, to prepare, train, study, and investigate. This is an observation. It is not offered as an argument for delay.

☐ There is constant resolution between carrying forward the struggle and the necessity of preserving valuable cadre and supporters. Sometimes this is not a matter of choice–the guerrillas are forced, because of the torture and murder committed by the repressive apparatus, to escalate and move beyond what can be immediately sustained.

☐ Armed struggle brings the resistance to a sharper and deeper level of development. The greater the resistance, the greater will be the force and scope of the state repression brought to bear upon the people. When resistance is at a high level, the enemy takes measures against the people. But treading lightly will not assuage the rulers. Violent repression is built into the status quo. Guerrilla strategy has to resolve the contradiction between the necessary progress of the struggle and what the people can sustain at any given time.

☐ Armed actions push forward people's consciousness and commitment; they are a great teacher and example. Yet they must be clearly understandable to the people, identify our enemy precisely, and overcome his massive lies and propaganda.

Attacks by the Weather Underground have been focused and specific. These actions were a catalyst for thousands of politically directed armed actions between 1970 and 1972, almost all of which complemented mass struggles.

These bombings were carried out by the Weather Underground to retaliate for the most savage criminal attacks against black and Third World people, especially by the police apparatus:

• Haymarket police statue, Chicago, October 1969 and October 1970

- Chicago police cars, following the murder of Fred Hampton and Mark Clark, December 1969
- New York City Police Headquarters, June 1970
- Guard Headquarters, Washington, D.C., after the murders at Jackson State and Kent State, May 1970
- Presidio Army Base and MP Station, San Francisco, July 26, 1970
- Federal Offices of HEW (Health, Education and Welfare), (women's brigade), San Francisco, March 1974
- Liberation of Timothy Leary from California Men's Colony, San Luis Obispo, September 1970

Mass struggle and movements are not mere spectators in revolutionary war; armed struggle cannot become a spectacle. It is the responsibility of mass leaders and organizations to encourage and support revolutionary armed struggle in open as well as quiet ways. Actions are more powerful when they are explained and defended. The political thrust of each armed intervention can be publicly championed and built on. Parallel mass support will further both the mass and military struggle.

There are many faces to militant resistance and fighting, a continuum between guerrilla and mass work. An examination of recent history points to: *acts of resistance* ... draft card burnings, sabotage in the military, on the job, in government, and attacks on the police; *mass demonstrations* ... Marches on the Pentagon, Stop the Draft Week, African Liberation Day rallies, International Women's Day marches, Chicano Moratorium marches; *demands for control and power through seizures of institutions* ... community control of hospitals and schools, occupations of land such as Wounded Knee, or symbols such as the Statue of Liberty, People's Park, prison rebellions and takeovers; *clandestine propaganda* ... spray painting, pouring blood on draft files, the Media, Pa., FBI ripoff; *popular rebellion* ... Watts, Detroit, Chicago, Cleveland, Newark; *outrage expressed violently and collectively* ... Jackson/Kent/Cambodia, bank burning at Isla Vista, TDAs, Days of Rage.

There are connecting lines between these different forms of fighting. All are forms of resistance by the people and forms of attack against the state. Militancy and armed struggle are consistent threads in revolutionary movements—they cannot be wished or forced away. They will continue to be practiced as long as imperialism exists. Together they constitute the fullness of revolutionary war.

The greater part of the revolution remains before us. We need to evaluate our strengths and weaknesses to go on from here. Our present strategy is rooted in our interpretation of the struggles of the last fourteen years.

# THE CONCEPT OF THE URBAN GUERRILLA

I F WE ARE CORRECT IN SAYING that American imperialism is a paper tiger, i.e., that it can ultimately be defeated, and if the Chinese Communists are correct in their thesis that victory over American imperialism has become possible because the struggle against it is now being waged in all four corners of the earth, with the result that the forces of imperialism are fragmented, a fragmentation which makes them possible to defeat—if this is correct, then there is no reason to exclude or disqualify any particular country or any particular region from taking part in the anti-imperialist struggle because the forces of revolution are especially weak there and the forces of reaction especially strong.

As it is wrong to discourage the forces of revolution by underestimating their power, so it is wrong to suggest they should seek confrontations in which these forces cannot but be squandered or annihilated. The contradiction between the sincere comrades in the organizations—let's forget about the prattlers—and the Red Army Fraction, is that we charge them with discouraging the forces of revolution and they suspect us of squandering the forces of revolution. Certainly, this analysis does indicate the directions in which the fraction of those comrades working in the factories and at local level and the Red Army Fraction are overdoing things, if they are overdoing things. Dogmatism and adventurism have since time immemorial been characteristic deviations in periods of revolutionary weakness in all countries. Anarchists having since time immemorial been the sharpest critics of opportunism, anyone criticizing the opportunists exposes himself to the charge of anarchism. This is something of an old chestnut.

The concept of the urban guerrilla originated in Latin America. Here, the urban guerrilla can only be what he is there: the only revolutionary method of intervention available to what are on the whole weak revolutionary forces.

The urban guerrilla starts by recognizing that there will be no Prussian order of march of the kind in which so many so-called revolutionaries would like to lead the people into battle. He starts by recognizing that by the time the moment for armed struggle arrives, it will already be too late to start preparing for it; that in a country whose potential for violence is as great and whose revolutionary traditions are as broken and feeble as the Federal Republic's, there will not—without revolutionary initiative—even be a revolutionary orientation when conditions for revolutionary struggle are better than they are at present, which will happen as an inevitable consequence of the development of late capitalism itself.

To this extent, the urban guerrilla is the logical consequence of the negation of parliamentary democracy long since perpetrated by its very own representatives; the only and inevitable response to emergency laws and the rule of the hand grenade; the readiness to fight with those same means the system has chosen to use in trying to eliminate its opponents. The urban guerrilla is based on a recognition of the facts instead of an apologia of the facts.

The student movement, for one, realized something of what the urban guerrilla can do. He can make concrete the agitation and propaganda which remain the sum total of left-wing activity. One can imagine the concept being applied to the Springer Campaign at that time or to the Heidelberg students' Cabora Bassa Campaign, to the squads in Frankfurt, or in relation to the Federal Republic's military aid to the *comprador* regimes in Africa, in relation to criticism of prison sentences and class justice, of safety legislation at work and injustice there.

The urban guerrilla can concretize verbal internationalism as the requisition of guns and money. He can blunt the state's weapon of a ban on communists by organizing an underground beyond the reach of the police. The urban guerrilla is a weapon in the class war.

The urban guerrilla signifies armed struggle, necessary to the extent that it is the police that make indiscriminate use of firearms, exonerating class justice from guilt and burying our comrades alive unless we prevent them. To be an "urban guerrilla" means to not let oneself be demoralized by the violence of the system.

The urban guerrilla's aim is to attack the state's apparatus of control at certain points and put them out of action, to destroy the myth of the system's omnipresence and invulnerability.

The urban guerrilla presupposes the organization of an illegal apparatus, in other words apartments, weapons, ammunition, cars, and papers. A detailed description of what is involved is to be found in Marighella's *Mini-manual for the Urban Guerrilla*. As for what else is involved, we are ready at any time to inform anyone who needs to know because he intends to do it. We do not know a great deal yet, but we do know something.

What is important is that one should have had some political experience in legality before deciding to take up armed struggle. Those who have joined the revolutionary left just to be trendy had better be careful not to involve themselves in something from which there is no going back.

The Red Army Fraction and the urban guerrilla are that fraction and praxis which, because they draw a clear dividing line between themselves and the enemy, are combatted most intensively. This presupposes a political identity, presupposes that one or two lessons have already been learned.

In our original concept, we planned to combine urban guerrilla activity with grass-roots work. What we wanted was for each of us to work simultaneously within existing socialist groups at the work place and in local districts, helping to influence the discussion process, learning, gaining experience. It has become clear that this cannot be done. These groups are under such close surveillance by the political police, their meetings, timetables, and the content of their discussions so well monitored, that it is impossible to attend without being put under surveillance oneself. We have learned that individuals cannot combine legal and illegal activity.

Becoming an urban guerrilla presupposes that one is clear about one's own motivation, that one is sure of being immune to *Bild-Zeitung* methods, sure that the whole anti-Semite-criminal-subhuman-murderer-arsonist syndrome they use against revolutionaries—all that shit that they alone are able to abstract and articulate and that still influences some comrades' attitude to us, that none of this has any effect on us.

---

Rote Armee Fraktion (RAF), *Das Konzept Stadtguerilla*
April, 1971.

# Interpretations of Terrorism

# INTRODUCTORY NOTE

THE STUDY OF TERRORISM has given rise to a great many theories and interpretations because terrorism itself has varied so much in character, origins, and causes. Some of these interpretations are discussed in my *Terrorism* (Boston: Little, Brown; and London: Weidenfeld, 1977). The excerpts presented in this section are fairly typical of their kind.

Lucien de la Hodde, a member of many French secret societies of the 1830s and 1840s, was the chief police spy of the period; his life reads like that of a character in a Balzac novel. In a book published in 1850, after his role as informer had been revealed, he listed the reasons people join a revolutionary movement. Sometimes this sounds like a caricature, at other times its resemblance to the true revolutionaries is uncomfortably close. A more detached view is offered by Cesare Lombroso (1835–1909), the most respected criminologist of the second half of the nineteenth century, who devoted several books to political crimes and their putative causes. Emma Goldman (1869–1940), one of the patron saints of anarchism, argued, not without reason, that it was quite wrong to assume that all terrorists were anarchists; most of them were not. As for those anarchists who had opted for violence, Emma Goldman claimed that intolerable pressure had driven them to commit acts of despair. Regarding terrorism the views of Marx and Engels, Lenin, and Trotsky are documented in some detail. With them we reach the contemporary period.

No one should be deterred by the fact that there is no "general scientific theory" of terrorism, let alone universal agreement about its character. A general theory is *a priori* impossible because the phenomenon has so many different roots and manifestations. But this is not to say that all the theories are equally true and deserve the same measure of respect. On the whole, terrorism is not a complicated issue, and its basic patterns are not shrouded in secrecy.

Chalmers Johnson was Professor of Political Science at the University of California, Los Angeles; Paul Wilkinson taught at University College, Cardiff; Feliks Gross was Professor of Politics at Brooklyn College; Dr. Hans Josef Horchem was head of the *Bundesamt fuer Verfassungsschutz* in Hamburg.

170

LUCIEN DE LA HODDE

# THE DISAFFECTED

Whatever may be done to the contrary, it is very certain that no form of government among us will ever escape the pest of conspiracies; for there is always a large class of men who think that the government under which they live is the worst one that they could have. And as these men also think that all our insurrections have been the work of secret societies, these societies are hence held by them in very particular esteem.

But in fact not one of our revolutions during the last sixty years has been the work of conspirators. However blasphemous this assertion may appear to the grumblers of the mob, we hold it to be true.

There is but one maker of revolutions in France, and that is Paris—idle, sophistical, disappointed, restless, evil-minded Paris. We all know her … But this Paris does not overthrow the government on a fixed day, and according to a settled plan; for every time she takes the initiative she is crushed at once. Witness the affair of June, 1832, of May, 1839, and several other similar affrays. To meet with success, it is necessary that the bourgeoisie, either in a fit of passion, as in 1830, or from a misdirection of ideas, as in 1848, should set the insurrection in motion. And above all, Providence itself must permit one of those incomprehensible contingencies—such, for instance, as that of sovereign power giving way to a revolt without the test of a combat.

This Paris, which is always lying in wait to seize power by the throat and strangle it, is composed of the following elements, viz:

1. *The Youth of the Schools* (as they are called). It is the nature of these gentlemen to be opposed to the government. The most of them would consider it ridiculous to have the same ideas as their neighbor, the bourgeois, who defends the existing order of things, because they give him and his family the means of an honest livelihood. And

then schoolboys, we know, are fond of noise, fracas, and sudden events; indeed, they expect to be recognized by such traits. Everyone has heard of their traditions of the *Pre aux Clercs*; they are a species of puerility which would be amusing if these young men, as well by their real courage as from the prestige which is accorded them, and from the facility with which they become instruments in the hands of the factious, did not, in fact, possess a considerable weight in our revolutions. The majority of students, it is well known, are occupied in the study of law, of medicine, or some other science, and not in reforming the government at the point of the bayonet. Hence, in speaking of the youth of the schools, we mean only those of whom the anarchical journals take it upon themselves to be the interested flatterers—those who parade at the clubs, political meetings, and other rude places. The students who are occupied with their studies have never had the honor of attracting the attention of our patriot editors.

The youth of the schools have their chiefs, some of whom have never taken the papers, and others have ceased to take them for the last ten years, for they go directly to the *pure* fountainhead, to the offices of the papers themselves, and there receive their instructions. When an order of the day is given, they hasten to all the estaminets in the Latin quarter of the town, where they are sure to meet with their fellows—some of the youths of the schools frequent such places, too. The leaders resort thither also and then are distributed those documents which, at one and the same time, enlighten the faithful and invite the curious.

Rumors have spread that the schools are to be removed beyond the limits of Paris, and it is certain that the government might thus cut off *one* of the arms of the insurrectional Briareus. The English, who have a genius for order and public tranquility, have long since excluded from their capital this interesting but rather dangerous portion of the community. Besides the political question involved, it is a sufficient reason for the government that those students who now spend their time at billiards, or in revolutionary maneuvers, would be much better off in the provinces under the eyes of their parents than at Paris, and that those who really wish to devote themselves to study have no need of the too numerous distractions of the capital.

2. *The Imbeciles.* In this class are included lawyers without clients, doctors without patients, writers without readers, merchants without customers, and all that troupe of hopeful men who, having studied their parts in the politics of the newspapers, aspire to enact them as men of the state. Some few of them are indeed capable of the

posts to which they aspire, but they find it intolerable to arrive at them like the rest of the crowd, by diligence and perseverance. Others of their number are not capable, and these are by far the most ardent and ambitious. They are all imbecile, for they fail in the first evidence of strength, which is patience. The organizers of secret societies and schemers of insurrection come from this class.

3. *The Gypsies.* These exist everywhere, and especially among us—a class of imaginative persons who have an utter horror of ordinary life. The generality of mortals usually understand that pleasure and repose are the rewards only of labor and privation, but the gypsies expect never to work and always to enjoy. As this kind of life, however, in order to be conveniently practiced, requires some fat rents, which they have not, they are obliged to have recourse to the expedient of establishing a sort of vagrancy, of which the obscurest estaminets become the courts of miracles. The provinces count but a few of these individuals, for they generally alight upon the capital, the only place where idleness flourishes and where certain wickednesses thrive at their ease. To determine from what quarter this variety of the social world comes is not easy; it comes from no matter where, from the highest as well as the lowest. Some few of them remain very nearly honest men, especially if they are not of too excitable a temperament or are wanting in the courage of crime; but the greater part of them have the instincts of debauchees, which they gratify at all hazards.

It is in this class that are found the chiefs of sections, the commandants of barricades, etc.

4. *The Sovereign People* (that is to say, the workmen of Paris, either native or those who have become acclimated in the suburbs). Brave by nature, and a fighter by habit, the workman expects to make a fortune out of every political tumult. A lofty sentiment of independence, acquired by the reading of revolutionary rhapsodies, renders him impatient of the restraints of authority. He never likes the master by whom he is employed, generally detests all others, and the rich and the dignitaries of the government he considers himself bound to execrate. This is not a mere portrait of our own inventing, for M. Louis Blanc, who will recognize some of his own workmanship in it, declares that the people are gross and brutal. Now there is but one people for M. Louis Blanc and men of his like, and those people are the people of Paris. This organizer of labor adds, it is true, that it is not the fault of the people that

they are so. Agreed. But it is something very astonishing that with two such important qualities, courage and intelligence, the people of Paris should remain so deplorably deficient in polish. Those socialists who are candid frankly confess the fact, and if they would open their eyes and confess the whole truth, they would acknowledge that they themselves are the cause of it.

It is useless to deny that this workman—gross, brutal, quarrelsome, ignorant of his duty, in opposition always to the law—is not in the majority in Paris. We mean, of course, those who are wheedled by the patriots—those who are told, and really believe it themselves, that they alone are the masters of the destinies of the country.

5. *The Fly Catchers.* This is a class of persons who are rather to be pitied than condemned. They are good men at bottom, but they listen to M. Bareste, maker of almanacs, who tells them that the country is horribly governed; to M. Proudhon, that detestable mystifier, who tells them that property is theft; to M. Ledru-Rollin, a millionaire overwhelmed with debts, who tells them that the patriots are dying from hunger. Through foolish or shameless newspapers, they are made to see every day that black is white, and white black. The same falsehood presented in a hundred different ways, the same deception practiced in a hundred different forms, is offered to them every morning, in the most natural manner in the world—with the most perfect air of assurance. The friends are near to support the cause; the papers of the opposite opinion are never read, because *they* are *sold.* If good advice happens to be given, *that* comes from a renegade or a spy; and thus a large mass of honest men give themselves up to foolish schemes, harassing miserably their own lives, and those of others. From the National Guard which introduces the Republic with the shout of "Hurrah for reform!" down to the innocent citizen who swallows everything that is told him, they are fly catchers, political and socialist, from every class of society, and of every shade and variety of color and complexion.

These honest souls serve as the lever, as the plastron, or as the make-weights of the revolutions.

6. *The Disaffected.* This class, also, is composed of an infinitude of elements; but we design especially to speak of those persons who, by the fall of former governments, have been injured either in their fortunes or affections. They never take a part in the insurrection as mere common soldiers; some are led into it for the sake of excitement, and others for a consideration. The latter, men practiced in the routine of political life, are too skillful to leave any traces of their

maneuvers. Instructions, advice, material aid, everything of this kind, reaches its destination among them only from the third or fourth person. The police alone has been able to follow this train of bribes and intrigues into its obscure shades; but thus far it has seldom been able to detect the plotters in the fact.

These men, who are the very leprosy of the body politic, are incontestably the most dangerous of all others to every government.

7. *Political Refugees.* This class of men is a virus with which France has become inoculated, and which adds to her revolutionary maladies. The abettors of revolt from all countries, drawn among us by an imprudent generosity on our part, are constantly busied in fomenting insurrections, knowing well that a disturbance in France is a signal to other countries.

8. *The Bandits.* The social condition of a country is always very much disturbed during revolutionary times; it is then, in particular, that malefactors have rare picking. A few good men, it is true, during the disturbances of February, posted notices of "Death to Robbers!"; but this did not prevent the Duchess of Orleans' shawls from being stolen, nor the wine casks of M. Duchatel from being emptied, nor the jewels of the family of Orleans from being sold throughout Europe. That some few of the mob endeavored to preserve the police cannot be denied; we render justice to whom it is due. But what a fine pretension is here set up! Ah! we must know these fellows who live upon the wealth of others. No sooner does the disturbance break forth, than, seized with patriotic zeal, they rush with a lantern in one hand and a musket in the other, demanding only to be posted at the best places, reserving the time and mode of action to themselves.

But robbers are not the only ones who profit by an insurrection. There are a few well-meaning men, it is true, who, after having shouted, "Hurrah for the charter! Hurrah for reform!" and having borne the brunt of the fight, then withdraw, in all the pride of integrity, to die in their garrets. But there are some very accomplished rascals, on the other hand, who, when the revolution is over, are found living in comfortable ease on their suddenly acquired rents. Indeed, it is beyond a doubt that the thieves, robbers, and assassins of Paris never fail to furnish some of the *heroes* of our revolutions.

Such, then, are the eight divisions of the forces which are usually employed in an insurrection. Sometimes they may be seen all assembled together; but this depends upon circumstances; for, if the affair appears to be badly managed, some of the forces draw off, but when things take a favorable turn, and success seems probable, then the whole army may be found drawn up in line.

---

Lucien de la Hodde, *History of Secret Societies*
(New York, 1864)

CESARE LOMBROSO

# THE MILITANTS

We suffer above all from our defective economic order—not that it is really worse than that of our fathers. Indeed, famine, which formerly carried off millions of victims, today accounts for only a few hundred, and our working women have more linen to wear than the proudest of *chatelaines* in former times. But the needs of the people have increased to an extent disproportionate with their incomes, together with a repugnance for the means of satisfying them. Charity, as dispensed by the convents and monasteries, is still the most widespread remedy for acute poverty, though it does not so much relieve the need for basic necessities as cause irritation to the natural pride of modern man. As for cooperatives, their field of action is too limited; indeed, in our country districts, they are almost altogether lacking.

Even if both sources of assistance were fruitful and efficient, they would not suffice to calm our people, because social and economic fanaticism, blind and violent like all fanatical movements, is rising...This is because the ideals of religion, of family life and of patriotism, together with those of local loyalties, inherited rank, caste, and esprit de corps, have disappeared before our eyes.

And since men have always need of some ideals, they now cling to economic betterment, as positive and relevant to the necessities of life, and not subject, like the others now discredited, to the ruthless logic of modern analysis. Here they concentrate all the energies formerly disseminated among the others so that if we no longer feel the advantages of those ideals overthrown (such as generosity, tolerance, and the spirit of self-sacrifice), sufficient relics of the old order remain to make us realize the injuries and constraints we suffered from it. Thus, if history has duly punished the two higher social strata, history has not wiped out all the evils they engendered.

We still have to endure them and those that have succeeded them. Feudal arrogance and overbearing behavior, for instance, religious hypocrisy and intolerance, etc., continue in many places together with, and in addition to, the arrogance of the third estate.

Theocratic dominance faded from our customs long ago, at least to all appearance. But try to bring into the open some question into which, even remotely, that of religion enters (such as, for instance, that of divorce, or anti-Semitism, or the suppression of the clerical schools), and you will see the opposition that is aroused—of course disguised in the most diverse forms, even the most liberal—bringing into play individual freedom, respect for womanhood, the protection of children, and so on. The domination of the military class, too, has not been with us for many centuries. Nevertheless, try to sound this note, if not to members of the general public, at any rate, in official or semi-official circles, and you will inevitably create hostility toward yourself. The state finances show millions spent on the maintenance of hundreds of gold-braided, useless generals, while meager salaries are meted out to impoverished teachers who merely receive unprofitable praise, and promises that are never carried out. Meanwhile, approaching bankruptcy is blatantly disregarded, as is, worse still, the starvation of the exhausted peasantry.

The same can be said of patriotic and aesthetic ideals; they are undermined, it is true, but go and tell the French common people to have done with its hatred for the Italians, the English, and half the rest of the world. Tell the Italian middle classes how ridiculous they are with their false adoration of the classics (which, in fact, they neither appreciate nor understand), while on their altar they waste the best hours of their sons' lives, and they will pretend not to understand you, or will be scandalized.

Against the greed for gain of the industrialists, the fourth estate, which protests about everything, is already raising its voice. They are maintaining that there is no kind of proportion between the profits and the amount of labor expended by the three upper levels of society, and the scanty gains and hard work which are their own lot.

This is all the more felt and vigorously proclaimed now where poverty is least in evidence, because it is easiest there to create a reaction. The poor Indians, dying by millions of hunger, have no strength to react, nor can the Lombards who are dying of pellagra. On the other hand, the peasants of Germany and the Romagna, who are relatively better off than the rest, like the workers of Australia, have more strength of initiative and are able to protest on behalf of those poorer than themselves. And in fact the anarchists are not among the poorest of the workers, indeed many of them are comparatively well off.*

(And then it is undeniable that whether under the form of a republic or a monarchy, at least for the Latin races, all our social and governmental institutions are a great conventional sham, as we all admit in our hearts but deny with our lips.)

Faith in parliamentary government, which every day lays bare its dismal impotence, is a falsehood. Also false is our faith in the infallibility of the heads of state, who are often inferior to the least of us; and false our faith in a form of justice which, weighing heavily on the shoulders of honest men, strikes at scarcely 20 percent of the true culprits, the majority of whom are of low intelligence and leaves the rest free, obeyed and admired, amid the weak and innocent destined to be their victims.

We no longer possess even a hands-breadth of dominion over the sea that surrounds us. We have not cleansed our uncultivated lands, and we are playing the fool like children in an area no better than a desert which may cost us much blood, without bringing us the slightest gain.

Against the deep-seated evils that are gnawing at our vitals—against pellagra, alcoholism, and superstition, against legal injustice and ignorance in our educational system—we react with theatrical demonstrations, rhetorical phrases, and bureaucratic formulas, winning time if possible, if not to make matters worse, at least to give an impression of dealing with them.

The society of the capital, headed like that of Japan by a Mikado and a Shogun, is ravaged by a crowd of wretched rhetoricians, who on a small scale sum up all the ills of Italy.

We have a clergy, powerless in theory but in fact still influential over the two extremes of the social structure—the common people and the aristocracy—a caste that officially has inherited the power but not the prestige of both, and which is scarcely superior to them in abilities or in energy. So that mediocrity dominates everywhere and, unconscious of its own ineptitude, strives to achieve some effect, without forseeing or caring about the outcome.

(This is why, for want of any solid basis from his education, the young man seizes upon any new idea, however erroneous and ill-adapted to the times, if it reminds him of a remotely glimpsed antiquity.) Whoever doubts this should remember the classicism of the revolutionaries of '89 and read Valles' book, *Le bachelier et l'insurge*. He will see there how greatly this education, so out of key with modern times, contributes to the formation of unsettled and rebellious youth.

This abuse of classical education prompts our ready agreement to set up a monument or celebrate a centenary rather than to inaugurate a school or an industry, or to drain a swamp. And from this education is derived that adoration of violence which has been the point of departure of all our

179

revolutionaries, from Cola da Rienzi to Robespierre.

("...All our classical education," writes Guglielmo Ferrero *(Riforma sociale,* 1894), "what is it if not a continual glorification of violence, in all its forms? Beginning with the apotheosis of the assassinations committed by Codrus or by Aristogeiton and leading up to the regicides headed by Brutus. And all the history of the Middle Ages and all modern history, and the history of our Risorgimento itself, as it is taught today almost everywhere, what is it if not the glorification, from a particular point of view, of brutal and violent acts? Has not a poet, regarded by everyone as the moral representative of the new Italy, felt able to write, amid general applause:

'Steel and wine I must have... steel to strike down the tyrants, wine to celebrate their obsequies...'.

"Here the evil is so deep-seated that all parties are in agreement: the clericals give cheers for Ravaillac's stabbing of Henry IV; the conservatives for the mass shooting of the *communards* of 1871; and the republicans at Orsini's bombs. All are of one mind in celebrating the sanctity of violence when it turns out useful to themselves. The new hero of the last years of this century is neither a man famed for great learning nor a great artist, but Napoleon I."

---

Cesare Lombroso, *Gli Anarchisti*, Chap. 1 (Turin, 1895).

---

*According to statistics, certainly neither exact nor impartial, from the Paris prefecture, there are 500 anarchists in Paris (they themselves claim that there are 7,500 in Paris and 4,000 in France. Of the 500 there are two classes, the propagandists and the real initiates: among the propagandists there are 10 journalists, 25 printers, and 2 proofreaders; among the skilled workers 17 tailors, 16 shoemakers, 20 workers in the food industries, 15 cabinetmakers, 12 barbers, 15 mechanics, 10 bricklayers, and 250 belonging to various professions, viz: 1 architect, 1 ex-doorkeeper, 1 singer, 1 bank messenger, 1 insurance agent, etc. These figures are doubtless incomplete. In any case, they cannot represent excessive poverty, nor do they in the case of H. Dupont, one of the leaders and a rich man, nor in that of Prince Kropotkin, nor Gori and Molinari, professional men and landowners, nor in the Bohemian bomber Drexken, a member of a very rich family.

*Dubois, in Le peril anarchiste (1893), calculates the anarchists in France as numbering 20,000 to 30,000, the majority of them sedentary workers; shoemakers, carpenters, weavers and mineworkers, followed by dyers and upholsterers; therefore, not by any means indigent.*

EMMA GOLDMAN

# THE PSYCHOLOGY OF
# POLITICAL VIOLENCE

T O ANALYZE THE PSYCHOLOGY of political violence is not only extremely difficult but also very dangerous. [If such acts are treated with
understanding, one is immediately accused of eulogizing them.] If,
on the other hand, human sympathy is expressed with the *Attentäter,* one
risks being considered a possible accomplice. Yet it is only intelligence and
sympathy that can bring us closer to the source of human suffering and
teach us the ultimate way out of it.

The primitive man, ignorant of natural forces, dreaded their approach,
hiding from the perils they threatened. As man learned to understand nature's phenomena, he realized that though these may destroy life and cause
great loss, they also bring relief. To the earnest student it must be apparent
that the accumulated forces in our social and economic life, culminating
in a political act of violence, are similar to the terrors of the atmosphere,
manifested in storm and lightning.

To thoroughly appreciate the truth of this view one must feel intensely
the indignity of our social wrongs. One's very being must throb with the
pain, the sorrow, the despair millions of people are daily made to endure.
Indeed, unless we have become a part of humanity, we cannot even faintly
understand the just indignation that accumulates in a human soul—the
burning, surging passion that makes the storm inevitable.

The ignorant mass looks upon the man who makes a violent protest
against our social and economic iniquities as upon a wild beast, a cruel,
heartless monster, whose joy it is to destroy life and bathe in blood; or at
best, as upon an irresponsible lunatic. Yet nothing is further from the truth.
As a matter of fact, those who have studied the character and personality
of these men, or who have come in close contact with them, are agreed that

it is their super sensitiveness to the wrong and injustice surrounding them that compels them to pay the toll of our social crimes. The most noted writers and poets, discussing the psychology of political offenders, have paid them the highest tribute. Could anyone assume that these men had advised violence, or even approved of the acts? Certainly not. Theirs was the attitude of the social student, of the man who knows that beyond every violent act there is a vital cause.

Bjornstjerne Bjornson, in the second part of *Beyond Human Power,* emphasizes the fact that it is among the anarchists that we must look for the modern martyrs who pay for their faith with their blood, and who welcome death with a smile, because they believe, as truly as Christ did, that their martyrdom will redeem humanity.

Francois Coppee, the French novelist, thus expresses himself regarding the psychology of the *Attentater*:

> The reading of the details of Vaillant's execution left me in a thoughtful mood. I imagined him expanding his chest under the ropes, marching with firm step, stiffening his will, concentrating all his energy, and, with eyes fixed upon the knife, hurling finally at society his cry of malediction. And, in spite of me, another spectacle rose suddenly before my mind. I saw a group of men and women pressing against each other in the middle of the oblong arena of the circus, under the gaze of thousands of eyes, while from all the steps of the immense amphitheater went up the terrible cry, *Ad leones!* and, below, the opening cages of the wild beasts.
>
> I did not believe the execution would take place. In the first place, no victim had been struck with death, and it had long been the custom not to punish an abortive crime with the last degree of severity. Then, this crime, however terrible in intention, was disinterested, born of an abstract idea. The man's past, his abandoned childhood, his life of hardship, pleaded also in his favor. In the independent press generous voices were raised in his behalf, very loud and eloquent. "A purely literary current of opinion," some have said, with no little scorn. *It is, on the contrary, an honor to the men of art and thought to have expressed once more their disgust at the scaffold....*

That every act of political violence should nowadays be attributed to anarchists is not at all surprising. Yet it is a fact known to almost everyone familiar with the anarchist movement that a great number of acts, for which anarchists had to suffer, either originated with the capitalist press or were instigated, if not directly perpetrated, by the police.

For a number of years acts of violence had been committed in Spain, for which the anarchists were held responsible, hounded like wild beasts, and thrown into prison. Later it was disclosed that the perpetrators of these acts were not anarchists, but members of the police department. The scandal became so widespread that the conservative Spanish papers demanded the apprehension and punishment of the gang leader, Juan Rull, who was subsequently condemned to death and executed. The sensational evidence, brought to light during the trial, forced Police Inspector Momento to exonerate completely the anarchists from any connection with the acts committed during a long period. This resulted in the dismissal of a number of police officials, among them Inspector Tressols, who, in revenge, disclosed the fact that behind the gang of police bomb throwers were others of far higher position, who provided them with funds and protected them.

(This is one of the many striking examples of how anarchist conspiracies are manufactured.) Counter terrorism → terroristic

That the American police can perjure themselves with the same ease, that they are just as merciless, just as brutal and cunning as their European colleagues, has been proven on more than one occasion. We need only recall the tragedy of November 11, 1887, known as the Haymarket Riot.

No one who is at all familiar with the case can possibly doubt that the anarchists, judicially murdered in Chicago, died as victims of a lying, bloodthirsty press and of a cruel police conspiracy. Has not Judge Gary himself said, "Not because you have caused the Haymarket bomb, but because you are anarchists, you are on trial"?

The impartial and thorough analysis by Governor Altgeld of that blotch on the American escutcheon verified the brutal frankness of Judge Gary. It was this that induced Altgeld to pardon the three anarchists, thereby earning the lasting esteem of every liberty-loving man and woman in the world....

But, it is often asked, have not acknowledged anarchists committed acts of violence? Certainly they have, always however ready to shoulder the responsibility. My contention is that they were impelled, not by the teachings of anarchism, but by the tremendous pressure of conditions, making life unbearable to their sensitive natures. Obviously, anarchism, or any other social theory, making man a conscious social unit, will act as a lesson for rebellion. This is not a mere assertion, but a fact verified by all experience. A close examination of the circumstances bearing upon this question will further clarify my position.

Let us consider some of the most important anarchist acts within the last two decades. Strange as it may seem, one of the most significant deeds of political violence occurred here in America, in connection with the Homestead strike of 1892.

During that memorable time the Carnegie Steel Company organized a conspiracy to crush the Amalgamated Association of Iron and Steel Workers. Henry Clay Frick, then chairman of the company, was entrusted with that democratic task. He lost no time in carrying out the policy of breaking the union, the policy which he had so successfully practiced during his reign of terror in the coke regions. Secretly, and while peace negotiations were being purposely prolonged, Frick supervised the military preparations, the fortification of the Homestead Steel Works, the erection of a high board fence, capped with barbed wire and provided with loopholes for sharpshooters. And then, in the dead of night, he attempted to smuggle his army of hired Pinkerton thugs into Homestead, which act precipitated the terrible carnage of the steel workers. Not content with the death of eleven victims, killed in the Pinkerton skirmish, Henry Clay Frick, good Christian and free American, straightway began the hounding down of the helpless wives and orphans, by ordering them out of the wretched company houses....

If such a phenomenon can occur in a country [India] socially and individually permeated for centuries with the spirit of passivity, can one question the tremendous, revolutionizing effect on human character exerted by great social iniquities? Can one doubt the logic, the justice of these words:

"Repression, tyranny, and indiscriminate punishment of innocent men have been the watchwords of the government of the alien domination in India ever since we began the commercial boycott of English goods. The tiger qualities of the British are much in evidence now in India. They think that by the strength of the sword they will keep down India! It is this arrogance that has brought about the bomb, and the more they tyrannize over a helpless and unarmed people, the more terrorism will grow. We may deprecate terrorism as outlandish and foreign to our culture, but it is inevitable as long as this tyranny continues, for it is not the terrorists that are to be blamed, but the tyrants who are responsible for it. It is the only resource for a helpless and unarmed people when brought to the verge of despair. It is never criminal on their part. The crime lies with the tyrant."*

Even conservative scientists are beginning to realize that heredity is not the sole factor molding human character. Climate, food, occupation, nay, color, light, and sound must be considered in the study of human psychology.

If that be true, how much more correct is the contention that great

---

* *The Free Hindustan.*

social abuses will and must influence different minds and temperaments in a different way. And how utterly fallacious the stereotyped notion that the teachings of anarchism, or certain exponents of these teachings, are responsible for the acts of political violence.

Anarchism, more than any other social theory, values human life above things. All anarchists agree with Tolstoy in this fundamental truth: if the production of any commodity necessitates the sacrifice of human life, society should do without that commodity, but it cannot do without that life. That, however, nowise indicates that anarchism teaches submission. How can it, when it knows that all suffering, all misery, all ills, result from the evil of submission?

Has not some American ancestor said, many years ago, that resistance to tyranny is obedience to God? And he was not an anarchist even. I would say that resistance to tyranny is man's highest ideal. So long as tyranny exists, in whatever form, man's deepest aspiration must resist it as inevitably as man must breathe.

Compared with the wholesale violence of capital and government, political acts of violence are but a drop in the ocean. That so few resist is the strongest proof how terrible must be the conflict between their souls and unbearable social iniquities.

High-strung, like a violin string, they weep and moan for life, so relentless, so cruel, so terribly inhuman. In a desperate moment the string breaks. Untuned ears hear nothing but discord. But those who feel the agonized cry understand its harmony; they hear in it the fulfillment of the most compelling moment of human nature. Such is the psychology of political violence.

---

Emma Goldman, *Anarchism and Other Essays*
(London, 1910)

KARL MARX AND FRIEDRICH ENGELS

# COMMENTS ON TERRORISM

## INTRODUCTORY NOTE

**M**ARX AND ENGELS BELIEVED in revolution and the collective struggle, not in individual terror. They ridiculed Heinzen, regarded Most as a semi-educated charlatan, and bitterly attacked Bakunin. They were pro-Irish but emphatically condemned the terrorist activities of the Fenians (such as the Clerkenwell prison explosion in 1867) and of the "Invincibles" (including the Phoenix Park murder in 1882). Engels thought that the bombing campaigns of the Irish dynamiters and the French anarchists were counterproductive. Their attitude was more positive toward the Russian revolutionary terrorists of the 1870s and 1880s. When Plekhanov published "Our Differences" in 1884, Engels dryly noted that the *Narodniki* were "the only people in Russia who were doing something." Earlier, in 1879, he had anticipated a "decisive movement" in Russia. The agents of the government had committed incredible atrocities. "Against such wild beasts one ought to defend oneself to the best of one's ability with powder and lead. Political murder is the only way open to intelligent and decent people of strong character to defend themselves against the agents of unheard-of despotism" (*La Plebe,* March 30, 1879.) Marx's comment about the assassins of Alexander II in 1881 is worth recalling: "They were sterling people through and through." They had been simple, businesslike, and heroic, and had endeavored to show Europe that their chosen modus operandum was specifically Russian and historically inevitable. One could no more argue for or against an assassination than one could take a moral stance regarding an earthquake. "Russia is the France of this century," Engels told Lopatin, the Russian emigre.

And, in a letter to Vera Zasulich, he wrote that the revolution might break out any day in Russia, only the slightest push was needed. Perhaps Blanqui and his fantasies had been right after all—with regard to Russia, of course. Perhaps a small conspiracy could overthrow an entire society. Perhaps this was one of the few cases in which a handful of people could "make" a revolution. Engels later admitted that he and Marx had exaggerated the prospects for terrorism in Russia: It had no future, after all.

The Bolsheviks and their allies did not oppose terrorism in principle. Total rejection of terrorism was philistine, Lenin wrote. But terrorism was advisable only at the right time and place and then only if executed "together with the people." There were endless polemics between Lenin and the Social Revolutionaries (who believed in terrorism) about what "together with the people" really meant. Both Lenin and Leon Trotsky had strong misgivings about the indiscriminate use of terror by the Social Revolutionaries. Lenin believed terrorism was a specific kind of struggle practiced by the intelligentsia. Trotsky would say, in an ironic vein, that it was "our national Russian achievement." Terrorism made organizational and political work among the people more difficult. "Easy tactics" were never of great value. Patient organization and propaganda were far more effective. Terrorism was only likely to spread harmful illusions that the Tsarist autocracy could easily be defeated. In a revolutionary situation, on the other hand, the bomb could be used as well as other weapons of guerrilla warfare and terrorism. Interestingly, Trotsky noted after the failure of the first Russian revolution of 1905 that, though terrorism was dead in Russia, it might have a future in what would be called in later years the "Third World"; it was "part of the political awakening" in these countries.

The attitudes of communist parties toward individual terrorism have been somewhat ambiguous ever since. On the doctrinal level, they have always considered terrorism fundamentally opposed to the teachings of Marxism-Leninism. But in practice, individual communist parties have occasionally engaged in terrorist tactics in the struggle for power. This is true with regard to Spain after the First World War, Bulgaria and Germany in the 1920s, and, of course, Vietnam and some Latin American countries. But it is equally true that terrorism was never regarded by the communists as their main and most telling weapon. In this respect they differed from some other radical groups which genuinely believed that terrorism was a cure for all society's ills.

## MARX TO ENGELS

*December 14, 1867*

Dear Fred,

The last exploit of the Fenians in Clerkenwell was a very stupid thing. The London masses, who have shown great sympathy for Ireland, will be made wild by it and driven into the arms of the government party. One cannot expect the London proletarians to allow themselves to be blown up in honor of the Fenian emissaries. There is always a kind of fatality about such a secret, melodramatic sort of conspiracy.

## ENGELS TO MARX

*December 19, 1867*

The stupid affair in Clerkenwell was obviously the work of a few specialized fanatics; it is the misfortune of all conspiracies that they lead to such stupidities, because "after all something must happen, after all something must be done." In particular, there has been a lot of bluster in America about this blowing up and arson business, and then a few asses come and instigate such nonsense. Moreover, these cannibals are generally the greatest cowards, like this Allen, who seems to have already turned Queen's evidence, and then the idea of liberating Ireland by setting a London tailor's shop on fire!

## ENGELS TO MARX

*December 29, 1867*

As regards the Fenians you are quite right. The beastliness of the English must not make us forget that the leaders of this sect are mostly asses and partly exploiters and we cannot in any way make ourselves responsible for the stupidities which occur in every conspiracy. And they are certain to happen....

## MARX TO PAUL AND LAURA LAFARGUE

*March 5, 1870*

Here, at home, as you are fully aware, the Fenians' sway is paramount. Tussy is one of their head centers. Jenny writes on their behalf in the *Mar-*

*seillaise* under the pseudonym of J. Williams. I have not only treated the same theme in the Brussels "*Internationale*," and caused resolutions of the Central Council to be passed against their jailers. In a circular, addressed by the Council to our corresponding committees, I have explained the merits of the Irish Question.

You understand at once that I am not only acted upon by feelings of humanity. There is something besides. To accelerate the social development in Europe, you must push on the catastrophe of official England. To do so, you must attack her in Ireland. That's her weakest point. Ireland lost, the British "Empire" is gone, and the class war in England, till now somnolent and chronic, will assume acute forms. But England is the metropolis of landlordism and capitalism all over the world.

## ENGELS TO KARL KAUTSKY

### February, 1882

...I therefore hold the view that *two* nations in Europe have not only the right but even the duty to be nationalistic before they become internationalistic: the Irish and the Poles. They are most internationalistic when they are genuinely nationalistic. The Poles understood this during all crises and have proved it on all the battlefields of the revolution. Deprive them of the prospect of restoring Poland or convince them that the new Poland will soon drop into their lap by herself, and it is all over with their interest in the European revolution.

## ENGELS TO EDUARD BERNSTEIN

### June 26, 1882

...Therefore, all that is left to Ireland is the constitutional way of gradually conquering one position after the other; and here the mysterious background of a Fenian armed conspiracy can remain a very effective element. But these Fenians are themselves increasingly being pushed into a sort of Bakuninism .... Thus the "heroic deed" in Phoenix Park appears if not as pure stupidity, then at least as pure Bakuninist, bragging, purposeless *propagande par le fait*. If it has not had the same consequences as the similar silly actions of Hodel and Nobiling, it is only because Ireland lies not quite in Prussia. It should therefore be left to the Bakuninists and Mostians to attach equal importance to this childishness and to the assassination of Alexander II, and to threaten with an "Irish revolution" which never comes.

One more thing should be thoroughly noted about Ireland: never praise a single Irishman—a politician—unreservedly, and never identify yourself with him before he is dead. Celtic blood and the customary exploitation of the peasant (all the "educated" social layers in Ireland, especially the lawyers, live by this alone) make Irish politicians very responsive to corruption. O'Connell let the peasants pay him as much as £30,000 a year for his agitation. In connection with the Union, for which England paid out £1,000,000 in bribes, one of those bribed was reproached: "You have sold your motherland." Reply: "Yes, and I was damned glad to have a motherland to sell."

## ENGELS TO J. BECKER IN GENEVA

### December 16, 1882

...The anarchists commit suicide every year and arise anew from the ashes every year; this will continue until anarchism is persecuted in earnest. It is the only socialist sect which can really be destroyed by persecution. For its perpetual resurrection is due to the fact that there are always would-be great men who would like on the cheap to play an important role. It seems as if anarchism were specially made for this purpose. But to run a risk—that is no go! The present persecutions of anarchists in France, therefore, will harm these people only if they are not just pretense and police humbug. Those who are bound to suffer are those poor fellows—the miners of Montceau. Incidentally, I have got so used to these anarchist buffoons that it seems quite natural to me to see alongside the real movement this clownish caricature. The anarchists are dangerous only in countries like Austria and Spain, and even there only temporarily. The Jura, too, with its watchmaking, which is always carried on in scattered cottages, seems to have been destined to become a focus of this nonsense, and your blows will probably do them good.

## ENGELS TO P. IGLESIAS IN MADRID (DRAFT)

### March 26, 1894

As for the anarchists, they are perhaps on the point of committing suicide. This violent fever, this salvo of insane outrages, ultimately paid for and provoked by the police, cannot fail to open the eyes even of the bourgeoisie to the nature of this propaganda by madmen and provocateurs. Even the bourgeoisie will realize in the long run that it is absurd to pay the police and, through the police, the anarchists, to blow up the very bourgeois who pay them. And even if we ourselves are now liable to suffer from the bourgeois reaction against the anarchists, we shall gain in the long run because this time we shall succeed in establishing in the eyes of the world that there is a great gulf between us and the anarchists.

## MARX AND ENGELS: REPORT OF THE HAGUE CONGRESS OF THE INTERNATIONAL, JULY, 1873

In the student unrest Bakunin discovers "an all-destroying spirit opposed to the state...which has emerged from the very depths of the people's life." He congratulates "our young brothers on their revolutionary tendencies....This means that the end is in sight of this infamous Empire of all the Russias!..."

> The Russian people, Bakunin continues, are at present living in conditions similar to those that forced them to rise under Czar Alexei, father of Peter the Great. Then it was Stenka Razin, the Cossack brigand chief, who placed himself at their head and showed them "the road" to "freedom." In order to rise today the people are waiting only for a new Stenka Razin; but this time he "will be replaced by the legion of declassed youth who are already living the life of the people... Stenka Razin, no longer an individual hero but a collective one" [!] and "consequently they have an invincible hero behind them. Such a hero are all the magnificent young people over whom his spirit already soars."

To perform this role of a collective Stenka Razin, the young people must prepare themselves through ignorance:

> "Therefore abandon with all speed this world doomed to destruction. Leave its universities, its academies, its schools and go among the people," to become "the midwife of the people's self-emancipation, the uniter and organizer of their forces and efforts. Do not bother at this moment with learning, in the name of which they would blind you, castrate you.... Such is the belief of the finest people in the West....The workers' world of Europe and America calls you to join them in a fraternal alliance...."

Citizen B acclaims here for the first time the Russian brigand as the type of true revolutionary and preaches the cult of ignorance to young Russians under the pretext that modern science is merely official science (can one imagine an official mathematics, physics, or chemistry?), and that this is the opinion of the finest people in the West. Finally, he ends his leaflet by letting it be understood that through his mediation the International is proposing an alliance to these young people, whom he forbids even the *learning* of the Ignorantines....

By the law of anarchist assimilation Bakunin assimilates student youth:

"The government itself shows us the road *we* must follow to attain *our* goal, that is to say, the goal of the people. It drives *us* out of the universities, the academies, the schools. We are grateful to it for having thus put us on such glorious, such strong ground. Now we stand on firm ground, now we can do things. And what are we going to do? Teach the people? That would be stupid. The people know themselves, and better than we do, what they need" (compare the secret statutes which endow the masses with "popular instincts," and the initiates with "the revolutionary idea"). "Our task is not to teach the people but to rouse them." Up to now "they have always rebelled in vain because they have rebelled separately...we can render them invaluable assistance, we can give them what they have always lacked, what has been the principal cause of all their defeats. We can give them the unity of a universal movement by rallying their own forces."

This is where the doctrine of the Alliance, anarchy at the bottom and discipline at the top, emerges in all its purity. First by rioting comes the "unleashing of what are today called the evil passions" but "in the midst of the popular anarchy, which will constitute the very life and energy of the revolution, there must be an organ expressing unity of revolutionary idea and action." That organ will be the universal "Alliance," Russian section, the *Society of the People's Judgment.*

But Bakunin is not to be satisfied merely with youth. He calls all brigands to the banner of his Alliance, Russian section....

In the second leaflet, "The Principles of Revolution," we find a development of the order given in the secret statutes for "not leaving a stone standing." Everything must be destroyed in order to produce "complete amorphism," for if even "one of the old forms" be preserved, it will become the "embryo" from which all the other old social forms will be regenerated. The leaflet accuses the political revolutionaries who do not take this amorphism seriously of deceiving the people....

Here, then, the existence of the *international brothers,* so carefully concealed in the West, is exposed before the Russian public and the Russian police. Further, the leaflet goes on to preach systematic assassination and declares that for people engaged in practical revolutionary work all argument about the future is "criminal because *it* hinders *pure destruction* and delays the march of revolution. We believe only in those who show their devotion to the cause of revolution by deeds, without fear of torture or imprisonment, because we renounce all words that are not immediately followed by deeds. We have no further use for aimless propaganda that does not set itself a definite time and place for realization of the aims of revolution. What is more, it stands in our way and we shall make every effort to combat it....We shall silence by force the chatterers who refuse to understand this."

These threats were addressed to the Russian emigres who had not bowed to Bakunin's papal authority and whom he called doctrinaires.

"We break all ties with political emigres who refuse to return to their country to join our ranks; and, until these ranks become evident, with all those who refuse to work for their public emergence on the scene of Russian life. *We make exception for the emigres who have already declared themselves workers of the European revolution.* From now on we shall make no further repetitions or appeals.... He who has ears and eyes will hear and see the men of action, and if he does not join them his destruction will be no fault of ours, just as it will be no fault of ours if all who hide behind the scenes are cold-bloodedly and pitilessly destroyed, along with the scenery that hides them."

At this point we can see right through Bakunin. While enjoining the émigrés on pain of death to return to Russia as agents of his secret society—like the Russian police spies who would offer them passports and money to go there and join in conspiracies—he grants himself a papal dispensation to remain peacefully in Switzerland as "a worker of the European revolution," and to occupy himself composing manifestos that compromise the unfortunate students whom the police hold in their prisons.

"While not recognizing any other activity but that of destruction, we acknowledge that the forms in which it manifests itself may be extremely varied: poison, dagger, noose, etc. The revolution sanctifies all without distinction. The field lies open!...Let all heads that are young and healthy undertake at once the sacred work of killing out evil, purging and enlightening the Russian land by fire and sword, joining fraternally with those who will do the same thing throughout Europe."

Let us add that in this lofty proclamation the inevitable brigand figures in the melodramatic person of Karl Moor (from Schiller's *Robbers),* and that No. 2 of *The People's Judgment,* quoting a passage from this leaflet, calls it straight out *"a proclamation of Bakunin's"* ...

## ENGELS: ENEMIES OF THE RUSSIAN REVOLUTION

There were three major explosions within fifteen minutes in London on January 24, [1885] around two in the afternoon which caused more damage than all previous ones together and which killed at least seven people and perhaps as many as fifteen, according to other estimates. ...

Who profits from these explosions? Who has the most interest in these otherwise purposeless false alarms, the victims of which were not just simple policemen and bourgeois but also workers, their wives and children? Who indeed? The few Irishmen driven to despair in prison partly through government brutality who, according to conjecture, did plant the dynamite? Or the Russian government which cannot achieve its aim [an extradition treaty] without exerting extraordinary pressure on the British government and people, fanning public opinion to blind and mad rage against the dynamiters?

This way of struggle has been dictated to the Russian revolutionaries by dire necessity, by the action of their enemies. They are responsible to their people and to history for the means they apply. But the gentlemen in western Europe who needlessly parody this struggle like schoolchildren, who reduce the revolution to actions á la Schinderhannes* and who direct their arms not against their real enemies but against the public in general, these gentlemen are not the heirs and successors of the Russian revolutionaries but their worst enemies.

---

"Kaiserlich Russische Wirkliche Geheime Dynamitraete,"
published in *Der Sozialdemokrat*, January 29, 1885

## ENGELS TO V. I. ZASULICH IN GENEVA
*April 23, 1885*

What I know, or think I know, about the situation in Russia leads me to believe that the Russians are approaching their 1789. Revolution must break out within a certain time, but it may break out any day. Under these conditions the country is like an unexploded mine which only needs the fuse to be lit. This is especially so since March 13.** It is one of those exceptional circumstances when a handful of people can succeed in making a revolution. With one small push they can topple a whole system which is in a precarious state of balance (to use Plekhanov's metaphor) and can liberate with one action, insignificant in itself, explosive forces which will subsequently be impossible to contain. And if ever the Blanquist vision of using a small explosion to shock a whole society had any foundation, then it is in Petersburg. Once the powder is set alight, once the forces are unleashed and potential national energy is transformed into action (also one of Plekhanov's favorite and most successful images), the people who light the fuse will be caught in the explosion which will seem a thousand times stronger than they. The explosion will occur where it may, subject to economic forces and economic resistance.

Let us suppose that these people imagine that they can seize power. What of it? Let them only make the breach which will destroy the dike, then the flood will swiftly put an end to their illusions. But if these illusions were to give them greater strength of will, would it be worth complaining about? People boasting that they have made a revolution are always convinced next day that they did not know what they were doing and that the revolution they have made is not at all the one they wanted to make. This is what Hegel called the irony of history, the irony which very few historical figures have escaped. Look at Bismarck, an unwilling revolutionary, and at Gladstone, who in the end became caught up in his beloved monarch's ideas.

It is important for Russia to be given a push so that revolution may break out. Whether the signal is given by this faction or that, whether it will take place under this flag or that, is of little importance. Be it even a palace conspiracy, it will be swept away the very next day. Where the situation is so tense, where revolutionary elements have gathered to such a degree, where day by day the economic situation of the vast mass of the people is becoming less bearable, where every stage of social development from the primitive commune to modern heavy industrialization and powerful financiers is represented, and where all these contradictions are held together by the force of despotism which has no equal, despotism that the young, the embodiment of the reason and worth of the nation, are finding harder and harder to bear—there, in such a country, it is well worth initiating a 1789, for a 1793 will not be long in following.

---

*Schinderhannes was the head of a famous gang of robbers in eighteenth-century Germany.

** Engels has in mind the murder of Alexander II on March 13, 1881 [Ed.]

# REVOLUTIONARY
# ADVENTURISM

## ISKRA, AUGUST–SEPTEMBER, 1902

In their defense of terrorism, which the experience of the Russian revolutionary movement has so clearly proved to be ineffective, the Socialist Revolutionaries are talking themselves blue in the face in asseverating that they recognize terrorism only in conjunction with work among the masses, and that therefore the arguments used by the Russian Social Democrats to refute the efficacy of this method of struggle (and which have indeed been refuted for a long time to come) do not apply to them. Here something very similar to their attitude toward "criticism" is repeating itself. "We are not opportunists," cry the Socialist Revolutionaries, and at the same time they are shelving the dogma of proletarian socialism, for reason of sheer opportunist criticism and no other. We are not repeating the terrorists' mistakes and are not diverting attention from work among the masses, the Socialist Revolutionaries assure us, and at the same time enthusiastically recommend to the party acts such as Balmashov's assassination of Sipyagin, although everyone knows and sees perfectly well that this act was in no way connected with the masses; and, moreover, could not have been by reason of the very way in which it was carried out—that the persons who committed this terrorist act neither counted on nor hoped for any definite action or support on the part of the masses. In their naïveté, the Socialist Revolutionaries do not realize that their predilection for terrorism is causally most intimately linked with the fact that, from the very outset, they have always kept, and still keep, aloof from the working class movement, without even attempting to become a party of the revolutionary class which is waging its class struggle. Over-ardent protestations very often lead one to doubt and suspect the worth of whatever it is that requires such strong seasoning. Do not these protestations weary them? I often think of these words, when I read assurances by the Socialist Revolutionaries: "by terrorism we are *not* relegating work among the masses into the background." After all, these assurances come from the very people who have already drifted away from the Social Democratic labor movement, which really rouses the masses. They come from people who are continuing to drift away from this movement, clutching at fragments of any kind of theory.

The leaflet issued by the "Party of the Socialist Revolutionaries" on April 3, 1902, may serve as a splendid illustration of what has been stated above. It is a most realistic source, one that is very close to the immediate leaders, a most authentic source. The "presentation of the question of terrorist struggle" in this leaflet "coincides in full" also "with the party views," according to the valuable testimony of *Revolutsionnaya Rossiya.*

The April 3 leaflet follows the pattern of the terrorists' "latest" arguments with remarkable accuracy. The first thing that strikes the eye is the words, "we advocate terrorism, not in place of work among the masses, but precisely for and simultaneously with that work." They strike the eye particularly because these words are printed in letters three times as large as the rest of the text (a device that is of course repeated by *Revolutsionnaya Rossiya).* It is all really so simple! One has only to set "not in place of, but together with" in bold type, and all the arguments of the Social Democrats, all that history has taught, will fall to the ground. But just read the whole leaflet and you will see that the protestation in bold type takes the name of the masses in vain. The day "when the working people will emerge from the shadows" and "the mighty popular wave will shatter the iron gates to smithereens,"alas! "is still a long way off, and it is frightful to think of the future toll of victims!" Do not these words "alas, still a long way off" reflect an utter failure to understand the mass movement and a lack of faith in it? Is not this argument meant as a deliberate sneer at the fact that the working people are already beginning to rise? And, finally, even if this trite argument were just as well founded as it is actually stuff and nonsense, what would emerge from it in particularly bold relief would be the inefficacy of terrorism, for *without* the working people all bombs are powerless, patently powerless.

Just listen to what follows: "Every terrorist blow, as it were, takes away part of the strength of the autocracy and transfers [!] all this strength [!] to the side of the fighters for freedom.... And if terrorism is practiced systematically [!], it is obvious that the scales of the balance will finally weigh down on our side." Yes, indeed, it is obvious to all that we have here in its grossest form one of the greatest prejudices of the terrorists: political assassination of itself "transfers strength"! Thus, on the one hand you have the theory of the transference of strength, and on the other—"not in place of, but together with".... Do not these protestations weary them?

But this is just the beginning. The real thing is yet to come. "Whom are we to strike down?" asks the party of the Socialist Revolutionaries, and replies: the ministers, and not the czar, for "the czar will not allow matters to go to extremes" (How did they find that out?), and besides "it is also easier" (This is literally what they say!): "No minister can ensconce himself in a palace as in a fortress." And this argument concludes with the following piece of reasoning, which deserves to be immortalized as a model of the "theory" of the Socialist Revolutionaries. "Against the crowd the autocracy has its soldiers; against the revolutionary organizations its secret and uniformed police; but what will save it ... " (What kind of "it" is this? The autocracy? The author has unwittingly identified the autocracy with a target in the person of a minister whom it is easier to strike down!) " ... from individuals or small groups that are ceaselessly, and even in ignorance of one another [!!], preparing for attack, and are attacking? No force will be of avail against elusiveness. Hence, our task is clear: to remove every one of the autocracy's brutal oppressors by the only means that has been left [!] us by the autocracy—death." No matter how many reams of paper the Socialist Revolutionaries may fill with assurances that they are not relegating work among the masses into the background or disorganizing it by their advocacy of terrorism—their spate of words cannot disprove the fact that the actual psychology of the modern terrorist is faithfully conveyed in the leaflet we have quoted. The theory of the transference of strength finds its natural complement in the theory of elusiveness, a theory which turns upside down, not only all past experience, but all common sense as well.

Nor does the leaflet eschew the theory of excitative terrorism. "Each time a hero engages in single combat, this arouses in us all a spirit of struggle and courage," we are told. But we know from the past and see in the present that *only* new forms of the mass movement or the awakening of new sections of the masses to independent struggle really rouses a spirit of struggle and courage *in all*. Single combat, however, inasmuch as it remains *single combat* waged by the Balmashovs, has the immediate effect of simply creating a short-lived sensation, while indirectly it even leads to apathy and passive waiting for the next *bout*. We are further assured that "every flash of terrorism lights up the mind," which, unfortunately, we have not noticed to be the case with the terrorism-preaching party of the Socialist Revolutionaries.

We are presented with the theory of big work and petty work. "Let not those who have greater strength, greater opportunities and resolution rest content with petty [!] work; let them find and devote themselves to a big cause—the propaganda of terrorism among the masses [!], the preparation of the intricate [the theory of elusiveness is already forgotten!] ... terrorist ventures." How amazingly clever this is in all truth: to sacrifice the life of a revolutionary for the sake of wreaking vengeance on the scoundrel Sipya-gin, who is then replaced by the scoundrel Plehve—that is big work. But to prepare, *for instance,* the masses for an armed demonstration—that is petty work. ...

## A TACTICAL PLATFORM FOR THE UNITY CONGRESS

### *March 1906*

We are of the opinion, and propose that the Congress should agree that:

1. the party must regard the fighting guerrilla operations of the squads affiliated to or associated with it as being, in principle, permissible and advisable in the present period;
2. the character of these fighting guerrilla operations must be adjusted to the task of training leaders of the masses of workers at a time of insurrection, and of acquiring experience in conducting offensive and surprise military operations;
3. the paramount immediate object of these operations is to destroy the government, police and military machinery, and to wage a relentless struggle against the active Black Hundred organizations which are using violence against the population and intimidating it;
4. fighting operations are also permissible for the purpose of seizing funds belonging to the enemy (i.e., the autocratic government) to meet the needs of insurrection, particular care being taken that the interests of the people are infringed as little as possible; and,
5. fighting guerrilla operations must be conducted under the control of the party in such a way as to prevent the forces of the proletariat from being frittered away, and to ensure that the state of the working class movement and the mood of the broad masses of the given locality are taken into account.

LEON TROTSKY

# THE COLLAPSE
# OF TERRORISM (I)

INDIVIDUAL TERRORISM AS A METHOD of political revolution is a specifically Russian feature. Of course, the murder of "tyrants" is almost as
old as the institution of "tyrants," and poets in almost every age have
composed many odes in honor of those who liberate by means of the
knife. But systematic terror that sets itself the task of removing satrap after
satrap, minister after minister, monarch after monarch, "Ivan after Ivan,"
as was formulated by a certain member of the "People's Freedom Movement" of the '80s as a program of terror—this terror, which adapts itself to
the bureaucratic hierarchy of absolutism and founds its own revolutionary
bureaucracy—is an original product of the Russian intelligentsia. Naturally
there must be profound reasons for this, and one must seek them firstly in
the nature of Russian autocracy and secondly in the nature of the Russian
intelligentsia.

So that the idea of mechanically annihilating absolutism may gain popularity, the state apparatus must present itself as being completely set apart
from the organization of force, as not having any roots in the organization
of society. But Russian autocracy appeared to the revolutionary intelligentsia as precisely this. Its historical foundation was based on this very illusion. Czarism was founded under pressure from more cultured western
states. To survive competition it had to fleece the masses without mercy
and, by so doing, tear up the economic ground from under the feet of even
the privileged classes. They were not even successful in raising themselves
to the political level of their counterparts in the West. And in the nineteenth century the powerful pressure of the European currency exchange
was added to this. As the sums it lent czarism increased, so did Czarism's
direct relation to the economic conditions of its own country decrease. It

200

armed itself with European military technology at Europe's expense and thus grew into a (relatively speaking) self-sufficient organization raising itself above all other classes of society. From this grew the idea of using dynamite to blow this superstructure of foreign origin sky-high.

It was the intelligentsia which felt the call to undertake this task. Like the state it had developed under the direct influence of the West (as had its enemy), it too had outrun the economic development of the country. The state had done so technologically, the intelligentsia ideologically. At the time when revolutionary ideas were developing more or less parallel with broad revolutionary forces in older European societies, in Russia the intelligentsia, accustomed to the West's ready-made cultural and political ideas, was spiritually revolutionized before the economic development of the country could give birth to revolutionary classes on which it could have counted for support. Under such conditions nothing remained for it but to increase its revolutionary enthusiasm by using the explosive strength of nitroglycerine. It was thus that the terrorism of the classic "People's Freedom Movement" arose. In two or three years it reached its zenith, then rapidly fizzled out to nothing, having burnt in its own fire the supply of military force which the intelligentsia, so weak in numbers, could have mustered.

The Socialist Revolutionaries' terror is due both in general and particular to the same historical causes: on the one hand, the "self-contained" despotism of the Russian state and, on the other, the "self-contained" revolutionary character of the Russian intelligentsia. But twenty years have not passed in vain and the second wave of terrorists are already emerging as imitators noted by the press as historically behind their time. The capitalist period of *Sturm und Drang* of the '80s and '90s created and nurtured a numerous industrial proletariat, penetrated the strong defenses of the village, and closely linked it to the factory and the town. There was no revolutionary class behind the "People's Freedom Movement"; the Socialist Revolutionaries just did not want to see the revolutionary proletariat, or at least they did not know how to value its historic significance.

Of course one can easily select from the Socialist Revolutionaries' literature several dozen quotations to the effect that they would create terror, not instead of the struggle of the masses but together with the struggle of the masses. But these quotations bear witness only to the struggle which came to be fought between the ideologists of terror and the Marxists, the theoreticians of the mass struggle. This does not alter the facts, however. By its very nature terrorist work demands the kind of concentration of energy on "the great moment," the evaluation of the significance of personal heroism, and finally the "hermetic" secrecy of conspiracy which, if not logically, then psychologically, absolutely excluding agitation and organization among the masses. For the terrorist only two fruitful points exist in each political field—the government and the fighting organization. "The government is ready to make temporary peace with the existence of all other movements," wrote Gershuni to his friends who were awaiting the death sentence, "but it has decided to concentrate all its strength on crushing the Socialist Revolutionary party." "I fervently hope," wrote Kalyaev at the very same time, "that our generation, with the fighting organization at its head, will make an end to autocracy."

Everything that is not understood by terrorism is only a condition of war and, even at best, a subsidiary means. In the blinding flames of exploding bombs, distinctions between political parties and boundaries of class struggle disappear without trace. And we hear the greatest romantic and finest exponent of the new terrorism, Gershuni, demanding of his friends "not to split up either the revolutionary ranks or those of the opposition."

"Not instead of the masses, but together with the masses." Terrorism is, however, too "absolute" a form of struggle to be content with playing a relative and subordinate role in any party. Conceived in the absence of a revolutionary class, born as a consequence of lack of faith in the revolutionary masses, terrorism can best support its own existence only by exploiting the weakness and disorganized state of the masses by belittling their achievements and magnifying their defeats. During Kalyaev's trial, the lawyer Zhdanov said of terrorists, "They have seen how impossible it is against modern weapons for the masses, armed with pitchforks and boathooks, those hallowed weapons in the people's armory, to destroy present-day Bastilles. After the Ninth of January [1905] they now know to what this leads; against machine guns and rapid-fire arms they set revolvers and bombs; these are the barricades of the twentieth century." The revolvers of solitary heroes replace the people's boathooks and pitchforks; bombs replace barricades. Such is the true formula of terrorism. And whatever subordinate place "artificial" party theoreticians may give it, terrorism will always hold the advantage; in fact, the fighting organization which the official party hierarchy puts beneath the Central Committee appears unavoidably to be above it, above the party and all its work until a cruel fate places it below the police department. It is just because of this that the downfall of the police conspirators' fighting organization will be the unavoidable signal for the political downfall of the party.

---

*Przeglad Socyal—demokratyczny,* May, 1909

# THE COLLAPSE OF TERRORISM (II)

T ERRORISM IN RUSSIA IS DEAD, thanks to Bakai, that counterrevolutionary double agent, a terrorist Anabaptist who helped to transform terrorists into corpses in Warsaw and who now with his godfather, Burtsev, is trying to provoke a spark of life from the corpse of terrorism. If, however, he can succeed in creating the conditions needed for a second double agent organization in the style of Azev, it will be (at best) less than a tenth as successful as the first.

Revolutionary terrorism has removed itself far to the east—to the regions of the Punjab and Bengal. There, the slow political awakening of a 300 million-strong nation provides a sympathetic atmosphere in which it can flourish. The ruling class there appears to be even more absolute in its despotism over society, even more foreign and a matter of "chance," for the politico-military apparatus of the East Indies was exported from England together with calico and business ledgers. That is why the Indian intelligentsia, accustomed from its school days to communicate with the ideas of Locke, Bentham, and Mill, and in its ideological evolution having left behind the political development of its country, is naturally predisposed to seek the strength it lacks in the bottom of an alchemist's retort. Perhaps other Eastern countries, too, may be fated to live through a period of flourishing terrorism. But in Russia it is already considered to be the property of history....

Our class enemies are in the habit of complaining against our terrorism. What they mean by terrorism is not always clear. They would particularly like to brand with the name of terrorism all those acts of the proletariat directed against their interests. In their view, strikes are the chief method of terrorism. The threat of a strike, the economic boycott of a blood-sucking

boss, the organization of a strike picket, and the moral boycott of a traitor
in their own ranks they call by the name of terrorism. If one understands
as terrorism every act that brings fear to the enemy or causes him to suffer
damage, then of course the class war is none other than terrorism. One
may only question whether bourgeois politicians have the right to pour
onto proletarian terrorism the floods of their moral indignation when their
whole state apparatus, with its laws, police, and army, is none other than
the apparatus of capitalist terror.

One must say, though, that when they reproach us with terrorism, they
are trying, however bad the reasoning, to give this word a more narrow
and direct meaning. The merciless beating-up of an employer, the threat of
setting fire to a factory or killing its owner, an armed attempt on the life of
a minister are all terrorist acts in the true meaning of the word. However,
anyone who knows anything about the true nature of international social
democracy must be aware that it has always fought implacably against this
type of terrorism....

Only a thinking and well-organized working class is capable of sending strong representatives who will be vigilant on behalf of proletarian
interests to parliament. However, it is not necessary to have the organized
masses behind one simply to kill an important official. Recipes for making
explosives are available to all and a Browning can be obtained anywhere.

Firstly, there is the social struggle, the ways and means of which forc-
ibly flow from the very nature of the ruling social order. Secondly, there is
purely mechanical coercion, the same everywhere, obvious in its external
form (murder, explosion, etc.) but which is quite harmless to the social
structure.

Even the most minor strike brings social consequences in its wake; it
strengthens the confidence of the workers, helps the trade unions to grow,
and often even succeeds in taking over the machinery of production. The
murder of a factory owner only results in police action and makes no
change in the social significance of the owners.

Whether or not a terrorist attempt, even a "successful" one, throws ruling circles into confusion will depend on concrete political circumstances.
In any case this confusion must only be of short duration; the existence
of the capitalist state does not depend on its ministers and cannot be destroyed with them. The classes which it serves can always find new people;
the mechanism will remain whole and will continue to function.

But a far worse confusion can be caused by attempting to carry a terrorist action into ranks of the working masses themselves. If one can achieve
one's aims armed only with a pistol, what is the point of the efforts of class
struggle? If a thimbleful of gunpowder and a tiny piece of lead are enough

to shoot the enemy through the neck, what need is there for class organization? If the thunder of an explosion can intimidate high personages, what is the need for a party? What is the point of meetings, mass agitation, and elections when it is so easy to aim at the minister's bench from the parliamentary gallery?

The reason why individual terrorism is, in our view, not permissible is precisely because it lowers the political consciousness of the masses, causes them to acquiesce in their own lack of strength, and directs their gaze and hopes to a great avenger and liberator who may come one day to do their work for them.

Anarchist prophets of "propaganda by deed" may discuss to their hearts' content the elevating and stimulating influence of terrorist attempts on the masses. Theoretical considerations and political experience prove the exact opposite. The more "effective" terrorist acts are, the greater the impression they make, the more the attention of the masses is concentrated upon them, the more will the masses' interest in self-education decline.

But the smoke of the explosion is drifting away, panic is subsiding, the murdered minister's successor is here; once again life settles into its old rut. The wheels of capitalist exploitation turn round as before. Only police repression becomes more brutal and shameless and, as a result, in place of burnt-out hopes and artificially aroused awareness, we have disillusionment and apathy. Reactionary attempts to stop strikes and the mass movement generally have always and everywhere ended in failure. Capitalist society needs an active, mobile, and intelligent proletariat; it cannot, therefore, keep it bound hand and foot for long. On the other hand, the anarchist program of action has always shown that the state is more strengthened by the use of physical destruction and the mechanics of repression than are terrorist groups....

Before it is raised to the level of being a method of political struggle, terrorism appears in the form of isolated acts of revenge. So it was in Russia, the classical country of terrorism. The flogging of political prisoners roused Vera Zasulich into giving vent to the general feeling of indignation by her attempt on the life of General Trepov. This example was imitated in the circles of the revolutionary intelligentsia, which did not have the support of the masses behind it. What started as an instinctive feeling of revenge developed from 1879 to 1881 into an entire system. Anarchist attempts in western Europe and America always flare up after government atrocities—for instance, after the shooting of strikers or after executions. The search to find expression for the feeling of revenge is always an important psychological source of terrorism.

It is not necessary to expand the fact that the Social Democrat has nothing in common with those moralists who, on the occasion of every terrorist attempt, pontificate triumphantly about the "absolute value" of human life. They are the same people who in other circumstances, in the name of other absolute values, for example, the honor of the nation or the prestige of the monarchy, are ready to push millions of people into the hell of war. Today their hero is the minister who gives orders to shoot unarmed workers in the name of the most sacred right of property. Tomorrow, when the hand of the desperate unemployed clenches into a fist or takes up a weapon, they will mouth empty words about the inadmissibility of violence.

Whatever moral eunuchs and pharisees may say, the feeling of revenge has its right. The working class has greater moral probity because it does not look with dull indifference at what is happening in this, the best of all worlds. The proletariat's unsatisfied feeling of revenge should not be extinguished; on the contrary, it should be aroused again and again; it should be deepened and directed against genuine examples of every kind of wrong and human baseness. This is the task of the Social Democrat.

If we rise against terrorist acts, it is only because individual revenge does not satisfy us. The account that we must settle with the capitalist status quo is too great to present to an official calling himself a minister. We must learn to see the monstrous evidence of the class structure in all crimes against the individual, in every attempt to maim or stifle a human being, body and soul, so that we may direct all our strength toward a collective struggle against this class structure. This, then, is the method by which the burning desire for revenge can achieve its greatest moral satisfaction.

---

*Der Kampf,* November 1911.
Translated here from the Russian.

# PART TWO
# THE GUERRILLA READER

# The Age
# of Small War

# INTRODUCTORY NOTE

G UERRILLA AND PARTISAN WARS have been fought throughout history, but a systematic doctrine of the small war first appeared only in the eighteenth century. The French had some free corps even before 1740, and more were established in subsequent years. The Austrians freely used semi-regular Hungarian and Croatian units during and after the Spanish War of Succession. Under daring commanders such as Franz von der Trenck these highly mobile units effectively disrupted enemy lines of supply and communication. The discipline of these groups was low, however; they robbed and burned without discrimination, and there were complaints that they did as much harm to their own side as to the enemy.

The leading military thinkers of the period differed sharply in their appraisals of these units. Guibert claimed that they were useless; neither Gustavus Adolphus nor Turenne had believed in them. But with the (harmful) expansion of armies a function had to be found for the many new cavalry units. As a result, contemporary observers came to attribute to the small war a role out of all proportion to its real importance. Frederick II of Prussia thought that the small war would never be decisive and, though he had suffered some unpleasant setbacks as the result of surprise attacks by Austrian irregulars, he preferred to ignore them rather than to be deflected from his course of action. Napoleon also took a dim view of irregulars, whether they appeared as partisans (in Spain, Russia, or Tyrol) or militias; they would never decide the fate of a campaign, let alone a war. Other lesser writers of the period attributed more significance to the small war: because armies had grown quickly, their losses had increased, and they had become more dependent on supplies. Was it not true that, as a result, the cost effectiveness (as one would now say) of small, semi-independent units had become much greater? They would not be able to force a decision, but, by gathering intelligence, cutting off the enemy's supply lines, and harassing and misleading him, they could make a major contribution to victory. Only later on, in the Napoleonic Wars, did the idea of national resistance appear—or to be precise, reappear. Even if the regular army was defeated and the capital of the country occupied, the war against the invader could and would be continued.

Maurice, Count de Saxe (1696-1750), Marshal of France, was an early convert to the importance of the small war. The excerpt reprinted here is part of a letter to Augustus II, King of Saxony, dated 1732 and first published in his *Mes reveries* (Reveries or Memoirs Upon the Art of War [London, 1757]).

Little is known about de Grandmaison and De Jeney. The former was a lieutenant-colonel of cavalry in the Corps des Volontaires de Flandre; de Jeney served with the French army of the Rhine.[1] De Jeney's work, which was translated into German and English, was the first systematic treatise on partisan warfare; it included maps, sketches, and even advice on first aid.

Andreas Emmerich (1737–1809) and his contemporary and compatriot, Johann von Ewald (1744–1813), the American War of Independence. Von Ewald became a lieutenant-general in the Danish army. Emmerich, called whom von Ewald "the first partisan of our age," was executed by the French following the Marburg insurrection in 1809.[2] Georg Wilhelm Freiherr von Valentini (1775–1834), subsequently a Prussian lieutenant-general, participated as a young officer in the war against the French Republic (1792–94). On the basis of his experience, he wrote a treatise on the small war which was at the time of its appearance the most comprehensive work on the subject.[3]

The authors mentioned so far were almost exclusively preoccupied with the technique of the small war within the wider framework of a large war. Carl von Clausewitz's (1780–1831) writings after the Napoleonic Wars shift the discussion to the strategic, and political, function of the people's war. The excerpts published here are from Chapter 26 of *On War* and from a lecture course on small wars (1810–11). Major von Clausewitz was addressing the Prussian War Academy. His copious notes, covering almost four hundred printed pages, were first published in 1966. [4]

---

1 De Grandmaison, *De la petite guerre* . . . (Paris, 1756); De Jeney, Le partisan, ou *l'art de faire la petite guerre avec succes, selon le genie de nos jours* (La Haye, 1759).

2 Von Ewald, *Abhandlung über den kleinen Krieg* (Kassel, 1790); A. Emmerich, *The Partisan in War or the Use of a Corps of Light Troops to an Army* (London, 1789); the English original could not be located and it has been translated here from the German translation of Der Parteigdnger im Krieg (Dresden, 1791).

3 Von Valentini, *Abhandlung uber den kleinen Krieg und über den Gebrauch der leichten Truppen* (Berlin, 1799).

4 Von Clausewitz, *Schriften-Aufsätze-Studien-Briefe*, ed. W. Hahlweg, Vol. I (Göttingen, 1966).

# HERCULES AGAINST SCHOOLBOYS

Sir,

I was honored with your Majesty's letter bearing date the 20th of last month. My silence in the conversation which passed upon the subject of light horse proceeded from my ideas concerning the importance of the object. But, in compliance with your Majesty's commands, I shall now speak my sentiments with that martial freedom which you are so good as to require of those whom you condescend to admit to your friendship.

An army unprovided with light horse, or not having a sufficient number to oppose against those of the enemy, may be compared to a man armed *cap-a-pie,* who is to encounter a troop of schoolboys without any other offensive weapons than clods of earth. This Hercules will presently be obliged to retire, struggling for want of breath and confounded with shame.

In 1713, your Majesty had twelve troops of Walachians, which performed great things because the Swedes had no light horse, which was what gave us the superiority over them in the field. For the Walachians were perpetually insulting, even their grand guards: our forages, and pastures were never exposed to the least interruption or danger, whilst theirs were frequently attacked. Neither could they make any detachments of which we had not immediate intelligence, and were in a capacity to defeat...

But a superior number of light horse is, notwithstanding, far from being the most eligible remedy to obviate all these inconveniences, because they are attended with a great expense, and, as you are not to lay any stress or dependance upon them for solidity, do not add to your strength in cavalry on the day of action. Large bodies of them upon the flanks of your army are even dangerous, which we have but too often experienced in the war with the Swedes in Poland, and that even at the battle of Kalish,* which your Majesty is very sensible of. It is necessary, therefore, to have recourse to other measures. The French have established certain bodies of light horse, under the name of free companies, to remedy these evils, which are posted in houses in the environs of their camps from whence they make some excursions. But, being no better mounted than dragoons, they are incapable of moving much from their quarters. And although they may contribute a little toward the ease and relief of the army, yet they are far from answering the purpose effectually.

There is not a sovereign in Europe who has it so much in his power to establish an excellent body of light horse, as your Majesty. Your troops have been accustomed for these twenty-six years past, in different wars, to fight against light horse and to contend with superior numbers. The grand point is to keep steady and maintain their ground, which method of behavior they have naturally learnt from a consciousness of the impossibility of flying upon horses so large and heavy as theirs. If they were mounted upon light horses and lightly accoutred, I am persuaded they would presently put a stop to the insults of the enemy's irregulars, which proceed from nothing but the impunity that attends them, and the facility of their flight ...

If then your Majesty approves of my reflections upon this subject, a thousand of the shortest-sized men must be chosen out of all your army, and such officers appointed to command them as are noted for courage, skill, and understanding. They must be formed into twelve troops, according to which division a troop will consist of about eighty; so that if, by any means, there should happen to be a future deficiency of even thirty, there will still remain fifty, which is the usual number of a troop of cavalry in time of war in all regular services.

I have already observed that the smallest-sized men are the best, because it has frequently been proved that a horse which will carry a man thirty leagues in a day whose weight does not exceed eight or nine stones, which is usually about that of a man of five feet two inches high, will hardly be able to carry one of from ten to twelve stone half that same distance; and, in swiftness, will lose from a hundred to a hundred and fifty paces in a thousand.

All their arms, as well as accoutrements, are to be extremely light. With regard to horses, your Majesty may furnish yourself with very good ones out of the strings brought by the Walachian dealers to Otakir, from Rou-

---

* The King of Poland was present at this battle.

giac, from lower Arabia, and from Romelic, which are infinitely better, swifter, larger, and higher mettled than the Hungarian ones. Neither will they cost more than those from Holstein, which are made use of in the Saxon cavalry...

Maurice, Count de Saxe, *Reveries or Memoirs Upon the Art of War* (London, 1757).

# THE USES OF SMALL WAR

W HILE THE USEFULNESS OF TROOPS engaged in small war and that of partisan leaders has been generally recognized throughout all ages and all nations, the necessity for them is even more strongly proved in our present century by the torrent of the Queen of Hungary's light irregular troops which has overwhelmed Bohemia, Bavaria, and Alsace in a situation where France finds herself entirely lacking in such troops.

Without harking back to when the Numidian cavalry rendered immense service to Hannibal, above all in the famous Battle of Cannae, and when the Parthians preserved their liberty against the whole might of Rome by their swiftness and agility in combat, we may note that the French at various times and under different names have formed advance troops to fight in campaigns, obtain intelligence about the enemy, intercept his convoys, storm his outposts, and fall upon his equipment during an action. The Stradiots [light Albanian cavalry: scout (estrader)] did so at the Battle of Fornoue. By means of an unexpected charge upon the supply convoy of the army of King Charles VIII of France, they swung the balance of victory between him and the federated Princes of Italy, to whom the raid proved disastrous rather than advantageous because of this light cavalry's obstinate seizure of booty throughout the action.

In the following century, Captains Montluc and Bayard and their adventurers carried out some remarkable feats. Henri IV himself found it necessary to engage in partisan exploits on many occasions.

Under Louis the Great, the famous leaders Jacob-Pasteur, Lacroix, Dumoulin, Kleinholds, and others gave signal service to the state by their bold enterprises and lucky achievements. Lastly, France is not unaware of the harm which it suffered in the last war because of the abundance of nations subject to the Queen of Hungary whose troops were lightly equipped and nimbly mounted. They harried us incessantly, stormed our convoys, our sick quarters, our baggage, our foragers, our detachments, and great numbers of our raiders; and this destroyed the finest armies ever to cross the Rhine, who neither saw nor fought any troops other than Hungarians, Slavonians, Waradins, Lincanians, Croats, Rascians, Banalists, and Pandours, against whom we could oppose only a few French companies and two regiments of Hussars devastated by desertion and by the great superiority of their adversaries.

De Grandmaison, *La petite guerre ou traité du service des troupes legères en campagne* (Paris, 1756).

DE JENEY

# SOME QUALITIES REQUIRED OF A PARTISAN

A MONG ALL THE BRANCHES of military service, there is none which in essence demands so many uncommon qualities as those of a partisan. Without entering into too great detail, I shall cite only the most indispensable: on the one hand, the natural advantages; on the other, the habits acquired by his own efforts, all of which he should have.

A good partisan should possess:

1. an imagination fertile in schemes, ruses, and resource;
2. a shrewd intelligence, to orchestrate every incident in an action;
3. a fearless heart in the face of all apparent danger;
4. a steady countenance, always confident and unmoved by any token of anxiety;
5. an apt memory, to speak to all by name;
6. an alert, sturdy, and tireless constitution, to endure all and inspire all;
7. a rapid and accurate glance, to grasp immediately the defects and advantages, obstacles, and risks presented by a terrain, or by anything it scans; and,
8. sentiments that will engage the respect, confidence, and affection of the whole corps.

Lacking such aptitudes, success in this art is impossible. It is useless for anyone to presume on some other talent or to flatter himself that, by taking pains or by good fortune, he may expect to win renown; experience, reason, and duty deny such a presumption. Notwithstanding the value and excellence of his other virtues, his honor fails of its object. Besides this, the partisan must know Latin, German, and French so as to make his meaning clear when he may meet men of all nations. He should also have a perfect knowledge of military practice, chiefly that of light troops, and not forget that of the enemy. He should possess the most exact map of the theater of war, examine it well, and master it thoroughly. It will be highly advantageous to him to keep some able geographers under his orders who can draw up correct plans of the armies' routes, their camps, and all places to be reconnoitered.

Nor should he be at all parsimonious, if he can thereby obtain from able spies sure information of the enemy's line of march, his forces, his intentions, and his position. All such disclosures will enable him to serve his general to great advantage; they will be of incalculable benefit to the army's security and to his own corps' standing, good fortune, and glory.

His own interest and his honor also require that he should retain a secretary to draw up the diary of his campaign. In it, he will cause to be set down all orders received and given, as in general all his troop's actions and marches, so that he may always be in a position to account for his conduct and justify himself when attacked by criticism, which never spares partisans.

As a leader, he owes to his troop the example of blameless conduct, entirely commensurate with the care and affection of a father for his children. He will thereby inspire them all with respect, love, zeal, and vigilance, and will win all hearts to his service.

Such an officer would run great risk should he entertain the least attachment to women, wine, or wealth. The first is conducive to neglect of duty and is often the cause of ruinous treachery. The second prompts dangerous indiscretions and always attracts contempt. The third leads to crime and extinguishes honor.

---

De Jeney, *Le partisan ou l'art de faire la petite guerre*
(La Haye, 1759).

JOHANN VON EWALD

# CUNNING, SKILL, SPEED, SECRECY

B Y RIGHTS, THE PHRASE "SURPRISE ATTACKS" should be unknown in wartime; and if all officers were to reflect upon the insulting implications of this term, there would be few, if any, cases of this kind. For
to be attacked means in reality to have forfeited through one's own negligence, ignorance, or willfulness one's honor, freedom, and possibly life, as
well as that of large numbers of others entrusted into one's care. Can, then,
an officer who has brought such a calamity upon himself through his own
fault suffer a worse insult than the comment, "He was taken by surprise!"
However much an officer who has been entrusted with a post in the field
may be on his guard, cases of this kind will always occur in wars; for he
who chances an attack will seldom fail, and it is those very attacks that the
common run of men considers impossible that customarily meet with the
greatest success.

The large measure of cunning, skill, speed, and secrecy that the launching of such "surprise attacks" requires is well rewarded when they are
successful, for these attacks are of great use in wartime, dealing a harsh
blow to the morale of those exposed to them. To be in a position to deal
the enemy such a blow, one must first make a particular effort to get to
know the terrain and region where the attack is to be staged. One must
have both good scouts and good guides. The former are needed to inform
us of the enemy's strength, how his outposts are manned and of what kind
they are; to tell us whether he is neglectful of his duties, where and how
far his patrols go, how strong they are, how often they are sent out, and
how far the nearest outpost is to the one we intend to attack; and further,
to discover what sort of man the commanding officer is, whether he is per-

haps easygoing or given to extravagant behavior. The latter, the guides, are necessary to lead us to the enemy by a roundabout route and to show us exactly where all the points of access are so that one can cut off the enemy completely. For if these lightning attacks are only half-successful, or fail, then one makes oneself look ridiculous in the eyes of the enemy and loses the respect of one's men. To take an example, on the occasion of the attack on Baumbruck in the spring of 1777, the English cavalry should have advanced a quarter of an hour earlier from the point where they crossed the Raritan River if they were to succeed in cutting the Americans off from the pass leading to Morristown. It was because they failed to do so that General Lincoln and all but two hundred of eight hundred men escaped. The same mistake was made on the occasion of the attack on the Marquis de Lafayette's corps near Germantown in the spring of 1778.

One must also know of more than one way back so that after a successful, or unsuccessful, raid, one can find the shortest route home. The night is the most favorable time for such attacks, since at night panic rapidly spreads among the enemy. When he sees he is being attacked from all sides, he cannot make out our movements; he cannot distinguish between a real attack and false one; in his fright he sees two of everything and even mistakes trees and bushes for human beings. I myself have experienced a false alarm at first hand only once. It is difficult to imagine just how great an effect fear has on men who are groggy with sleep. The incident I refer to happened during the Pennsylvanian campaign, when General Howe was making to cross the Chalkill after the Battle of Brandywine River. The Hesse and Anspach rifle corps were encamped in a wood not far from French Creek. They had been told to act as rear guard and were resting, weapons in hand, ready to move at a moment's notice. A few shots were heard from the direction of one of the pickets. These sparked off shouting and screaming among the inhabitants of nearby plantations. All at once someone yelled, "Run for your lives; we're being attacked!" At this, the whole corps started to run amok. It took about an hour to calm down the men, and it was well nigh impossible to convince them that the "attack" was only a false alarm. Fog, mist, strong winds with driving snow or rain contribute to the success of an attack, for in bad weather there are seldom any patrols on the roads because the enemy thinks the weather will prevent an attack. Fog enables one to creep up on the enemy unnoticed.

When strong wind and driving rain are blowing into the faces of the sentries, they often drop their heads and forget themselves, turning their backs to the wind and rain and making it easy to creep up and kill them. I myself have succeeded in approaching very close to sentries who, because they were guarding the most dangerous outposts, were constantly aware that the slightest negligence on their part could bring death or disaster, and have remained for some time standing right in front of them without being discovered. At such times, therefore, one cannot be too assiduous about visiting outposts.

---

Johann von Ewald, *Abhandlung über den kleinen Krieg*
(Kassel, 1790).

ANDREAS EMMERICH

# THE PARTISAN IN WAR

No ARMY CAN DO WITHOUT light troops in time of war because it depends upon them not only for what it can or cannot undertake but also for its sustenance.

The detachments of light troops should be made up of fusiliers with drawn muskets, light infantry with bayonets, and light dragoons or hussars, though occasionally, as the English have done, they may consist of battalions drawn from the light infantry of various regiments supported by grenadiers.

A corps made up of these three kinds of light troops should never number below a thousand men or above seventeen hundred. Moreover, the troops recruited should be volunteers, as it would be dangerous to force people into this kind of service...

It is important that the person commanding a corps of light troops be an officer of proven good conduct and great experience and a man in whom one can place great trust without risk. This is vital because from time to time the commanding general may need to divulge to him—epending on the nature of the mission—both the password and the war-cry, the discovery of which by the enemy could be of dire consequence for the whole army. It is of no less importance that he should be strong of body, lively of mind, and capable of enduring great hardships.

The other officers of a large partisan corps must be chosen with similar care, for without exception they must be men of proven moderation, energy, loyalty, and physical resilience. Their duties are more unsettled and exacting than those of any other kind of troops, as they are never encumbered with tents and as the security of the army largely depends upon their vigilance.

Conversely, if the partisan ever allows himself to be taken by surprise,

222

he has no excuse. He may of course be attacked, even cut to pieces, but he must never, either in the field or in his quarters, let himself be taken by surprise....

Earlier, I mentioned the qualities required of a partisan. Here I feel I must add that the skill necessary for this extremely important branch of military science is rarely acquired in the course of normal service....

If a partisan discovers an enemy spy in his own camp, by judicious treatment he will be able to use him for the furtherance of his own interests; it is only good sense to defer all punishment until one has tried every means of bringing him over to one's side. One must have the spy's every movement carefully watched in order to discover whether he has an associate in the corps itself or in the vicinity of the post. The partisan should look for a favorable moment to approach the spy because, with his knowledge of this type of person, he will probably be able to elicit some useful information, if not indeed to persuade the spy to act on his behalf. If the partisan is successful in this latter attempt, the spy will have an important part to play in the execution of the partisan's plans since he has free passage into the ranks of the opposing army. The information he provides should, however, never be believed entirely until other information has substantiated it and removed all grounds for doubting the spy's loyalty and reliability....

Of the duties of an officer, none requires more wisdom or adroitness than the management of spies. These people are as a rule motivated solely by greed, yet no commanding general can afford to do without them, much less a partisan who is continually in an advanced position and from whom his general thus expects the most precise information. It would be quite superfluous for me to describe the great variety of ways in which spies can be used. I shall limit myself to a few words on the subject as a whole.

Spies are to be found among all classes of society and even among both sexes. Should circumstances require their services, they must be paid well and punctually and never be made to wait even a second for their remuneration, so that their identity does not become known to anyone–be he officer or soldier—but the commander who gives him his instructions.

---

Andreas Emmerich, *Der Parteigänger im Krieg*
(Dresden, 1791).

GEORG WILHELM FREIHERR VON VALENTINI

# WHAT KIND OF TRAINING?

WHAT I UNDERSTAND BY THE PHRASE "SMALL WAR" are all those actions undertaken in time of war which further an army's or corps' operations without themselves being directly connected with the conquest or retention of territory. In other words the "small war" entails the protection, even the concealment, of the main army besides those operations intended to inflict minor injury on the enemy.

Although at first it might appear that the results of the small war have no significant bearing on the outcome of the war as a whole, they are nevertheless of importance: they contain the means whereby that higher goal of warfare may be attained. Moreover, a successfully conducted small war weakens the enemy by reducing his capacity to hold out in the field. Such was the case in the French Revolutionary War (1791–92). The French, being untrained civilian soldiers and in no position to engage their properly trained enemy in open combat, fell back on a more natural form of fighting—that of marksmen.

Their *tirailleurs,* harrying and tormenting the enemy from every side like a pack of dogs, gave the armies of the Allies, which were accustomed to fighting only in serried ranks, not a moment's peace. When numbers, the lay of the land, and the time of year favored them, they gained the upper hand. Thus, in the winter campaign of 1793, the Austrian army in Alsace, unable to hold out any longer, was forced to retreat from the Hagenau and Weissenburg lines, this momentous withdrawal occurring without any decisive battle.

Later, in the Netherlands, the French emerged the victors from much larger encounters and battles. Nevertheless, it was the systematic harrying of the defeated armies and the practice of continuously pestering and plaguing them with sharpshooters that proved the overriding reason why periods of respite in traditional winter quarters vanished from war and why the allied armies found no rest until they were back on the other side of the Rhine....

Napoleon's furious campaigns, however, all but put an end to small war as we have defined it. "In recent times," Bevenhorst wrote in 1809, "large-scale warfare has almost entirely swallowed up the small war, for in the campaigns of 1805, 1806, and 1809 no real small war was fought. Perhaps fighting on a small scale will return in the future. But for the present, when Napoleon, in glorious isolation, is riding the crest of war like Neptune on the waves of the ocean, coursing ahead of all the unleashed sons of Aeolus, for the present, when overthrow and enslavement are the order of the day for kings and the peoples, there will be little thought of that other trifling pastime of the goddess of war so long as this hero lives, breathes, and wages war."

Clearly, what the witty commentator whose words I have so gladly reproduced here was referring to were those small-scale, separate actions against the enemy for which Napoleon left us no time. Yet this prophecy that "fighting on a small scale" would perhaps return in the future was very soon fulfilled in Spain, where it was crowned with success surpassing even the boldest expectations. That the enemy was driven from the peninsula, and even put under pressure in his own country, was of course primarily due to the victories of the Duke of Wellington. But anyone who has merely glanced at the history of this war knows how the peasants' war—as it is called—contributed to those victories and how it prevented the enemy from enjoying in tranquillity the fruits of its initial successes.

ANY DEFENSIVE WAR in which the people play a purposeful role through supporting the operations of the allied forces by waging a small war at the enemy's rear will meet with the same grand success. Even after he has won a battle, the enemy will never be able to gain a firm foothold in the country, except in fortified places he has either overpowered or laid out himself. Every detachment he sends out and every fresh supply of reinforcements, armaments, or food are exposed to attacks by waiting partisans. Fought in this manner on a large scale, small wars become wars of extermination for the enemy armies.

The war in the Vendee, however, cannot be described as a small war. The peasants who fought there so bravely for king and country were intent upon *completely* destroying the opposing forces. Versed in the skills of hunting, they exploited to the full the hedges, bushes, and concealed meandering paths that ran among them to creep up on the blue hordes, surrounded them on every side, and shoot them down with well-directed musket volleys. Then, when this musket fire had caused the enemy to falter, they would charge upon him at exactly the right moment and finish him off in the shortest possible time in hand-to-hand fighting. Artillery fire, the efficacy of which was considerably impaired by the restricted range possible in that wooded country, was rendered harmless by the peasants' practice of hurling themselves to the ground when the cannons were fired. Then they would overpower the artillery in the final assault.

When the war began, no more than a minority of the peasants were armed with muskets, and even some of these were ordinary hunting guns. The remainder of the peasants were used for close-quarter combat. Until the moment for the charge had arrived, the few muskets available were given to the best marksmen, while others reloaded them. Whenever they seemed to be getting the worst of a skirmish, the nimble peasants would jump over the hedges and vanish down winding lanes. There appears to have been no more than a minimum of leadership and organization among them. The volunteers were informed only of the purpose of a raid and the place where it was to take place; as the men involved were completely at home in the terrain, this was sufficient.

The war in the Tyrol affords a similar picture. It is striking how in mountainous areas and generally in regions where men must wrestle with nature to survive and make a living, the inhabitants receive a training of mind and body that well fits them for war. This training instills in them a natural tactical sense suited to the terrain which is almost impossible to inculcate by artificial methods. Teaching those who live on the plains and pursue their trades in cities or in leisurely fashion plowing the open fields how to wage war after the manner of those pugnacious highland people will be no easy matter....

I now come to the question of what kind of training the commanding officer of light troops, or a commanding officer in wartime in general, should receive. It has long been a matter of dispute whether war is to be considered a mathematical science or a game of chance. I do not wish to enter into the argument here, but in my opinion the partisan is of all leaders in war the most justified in tempting fate and, by trusting to his own eye and talent for making snap decisions, in thumbing his nose at the sacred rules constructed on mathematical principles. In order that he may not be lacking in these qualities, let him develop his military gifts to the highest degree and, above all, let him acquire that *attentiveness* which allows us to exploit the present moment to the full and enables us to learn more from practical life than from books. Let him spend more time in the fields and woods than in his study or in company indoors so that he may know his way around in the terrain that is to be the setting for his actions. A speculative disposition and pettymindedness are two dangerous liabilities for any commanding officer in time of war. The first estranges him from nature and people, preventing him from being able to coolly reflect upon what is in front of his eyes; the second causes him to miss the essential for the inessential. Most necessary of all, however, to the man who would be a leader, is that moral courage which lifts us above events and carries others along with us at the crucial moment.

Here we find the explanation of the successes of men who have had no great preparation or long practice in peacetime and of half-trained men who, placed at the head of armies or regiments by virtue of their blood or turbulent times, nonetheless have led their troops to glory and triumph in the field. They possessed this practical gift of which I have been speaking; they did not allow their minds to be ruled by a fixed idea. Thanks to this openness of mind they rapidly acquired from experience the knowledge they needed to become great generals.

It is this experience, our own and that gleaned from military history, that should be our mentor. It is by gathering together the practical rules we have derived from experience and then applying them to the matter at hand that we form our theory of the small war. Examples illustrated in the actual terrain in which they took place will provide valuable practice both for eye and judgment, thereby giving the reader wide scope for the development of his own ideas.

---

Georg Wilhelm Freiherr von Valentini, *Abhandlung über den kleinen Krieg ünd liber den Gebrauch der leichten Truppen* (Berlin, 1799), and many later editions.

CARL VON CLAUSEWITZ

# A BATTALION IN BATTLE

IT IS A CHARACTERISTIC OF TROOPS fighting in small-scale wars that, side by side with great audacity and daring, they show a far greater aversion to actual danger than do those fighting in large-scale war. The enterprising spirit of the lone hussar or fusilier and his trust in himself and his luck can scarcely be imagined by a man who has never been outside the ranks. Accustomed by experience to undertaking a variety of difficult missions, the former remains calm and collected when the latter would be nervous and fearful. But, in contrast, the hussar and fusilier are much more mindful of danger in a normal battle than are troops of the line. Unless absolutely necessary, the former will never expose themselves to danger and will withdraw and seek cover whenever they can....

This characteristic of the light troops is a necessary one. If they did not possess this aversion, how could they ceaselessly place themselves right under the enemy's nose, how could they go on giving battle almost daily without being completely destroyed in one campaign? Therefore, I am by no means reproaching the light troops for their circumspection; it is a quality they must have. They must alternate between great daring and prudent caution according to different circumstances, and each man must be capable of both in equal measure. No man needs to be taught a fear of danger; nor do the light troops. Natural instinct teaches them to avoid it. The same would be true of the other troops if one did not do everything to suppress it. In large battles, one must brave danger, for here the individual's cleverness and cunning can achieve nothing. It is in the broad planning of the commands of the main parties that cleverness and coordination are needed. In a particular position, great energy and the most ferocious defiance of danger make the best sense.

A battalion in a battle or large engagement will rarely have an opportunity to distinguish itself by clever maneuvers; it distinguishes itself by its bravery, courageous charge, and steadfast, disciplined endurance of hours of bombardment. To say that a battalion has lost half or two-thirds of its men in a battle is to need to say no more. This is not true in the case of light troops. In a fixed battle, the masses of men are pressed up close to each other and small units have less opportunity for combinations. Provided that it had already been exchanging fire with the enemy, a battalion that recklessly threw itself against it without paying any attention to the battalions next to it might bring about its own destruction. Yet this danger does not compare with the advantage such an action might bring, for a charge at this spot might alter the course of the whole battle and perhaps lead to final victory. There is no telling how many victories such an action could lead to, and one wishes that many battalions would indulge in this kind of recklessness. In small-scale wars, a similar advance by an isolated troop may bring advantages, but they will rarely be large or decisive. Moreover, that the forces in small-scale wars are spread over large areas means there is much opportunity for combinations and that the advancing troop could easily be destroyed without creating any prospect of a great victory. It is the inventiveness and improvisation that small-scale wars permit and the skillful combination of boldness and caution (in other words, the happy composition of daring and fear) which make them so superlatively interesting.

---

Carl von Clausewitz, *On War* (J. J. Graham, trans.)
(London, 1873).

CARL VON CLAUSEWITZ

# PEOPLE'S WAR

A PEOPLE'S WAR IN CIVILIZED EUROPE is a phenomenon of the nineteenth century. It has its advocates and its opponents. The latter either considering it in a political sense as a revolutionary means, a state of anarchy declared lawful, which is as dangerous as a foreign enemy to social order at home; or on military grounds, conceiving that the result is not commensurate with the expenditure of the nation's strength. The first point does not concern us here, for we look upon a people's war merely as a means of fighting, therefore, in its connection with the enemy. But with regard to the latter point, we must observe that a people's war in general is to be regarded as a consequence of the outburst which the military element in our day has made through its old formal limits, as an expansion and strengthening of the whole fermentation process which we call war. The requisition system, the immense increase in the size of armies by means of that system, and the general liability to military service, the utilizing militia, are all things which lie in the same direction, if we make the limited military system of former days our starting point; and the *levee en masse,* or arming of the people, now lies also in the same direction. If the first-named of these new aids to war are the natural and necessary consequences of barriers thrown down, and if they have so enormously increased the power of those who first used them that the enemy has been carried along in the current and obliged to adopt them likewise, this will be the case also with people's wars. In the generality of cases, the people who make judicious use of this means will gain a proportionate superiority over those who despise its use. If this be so, then the only question is whether this modern intensification of the military element is, upon the whole, salutary for the interests of humanity or otherwise—a question which it would be about as easy to answer as the question of war itself. We leave both to philosophers. But the opinion may be advanced that the resources swallowed up in people's wars might be more profitably employed if used in providing other military means. No very deep investigation, however, is necessary to be convinced that these resources are for the most part not disposable and cannot be utilized in an arbitrary manner at pleasure. One essential part that is the moral element is not called into existence until this kind of employment for it arises.

We therefore do not ask again, "How much does the resistance which the whole nation in arms is capable of making, cost that nation?" But we ask, "What is the effect which such a resistance can produce? What are its conditions, and how is it to be used?"

It follows from the very nature of the thing that defensive means thus widely dispersed are not suited to great blows requiring concentrated action in time and space. Its operation, like the process of evaporation in physical nature, is according to the surface. The greater that surface and the greater the contact with the enemy's army, consequently the more that army spreads itself out, so much the greater will be the effects of arming the nation. Like a slow, gradual heat, it destroys the foundations of the enemy's army. It requires time to produce its effects, so whilst the hostile elements are working on each other, there is a state of tension which either gradually wears out if the people's war is extinguished at some points and burns slowly away at others, or leads to a crisis if the flames of this general conflagration envelop the enemy's army and compel it to evacuate the country to save itself from utter destruction.

In order that this result should be produced by a national war alone, we must suppose either a surface extent of the dominions invaded, exceeding that of any country in Europe, except Russia, or suppose a disproportion between the strength of the invading army and the extent of the country, such as never occurs in reality. Therefore, to avoid following a phantom, we must imagine a people's war always in combination with a war carried on by a regular army, and both carried on according to a plan embracing the operations of the whole. The conditions under which alone the people's war can become effective are that:

1. the war is carried on in the heart of the country;
2. it cannot be decided by a single catastrophe;
3. the theater of war embraces a considerable extent of country;
4. the national character is favorable to the measure; and,
5. the country is of a broken and difficult nature, either from being mountainous, or by reason of woods and marshes, or from the

peculiar mode of cultivation in use. Whether the population is dense or otherwise is of little consequence, as there is less likelihood of a want of men than of anything else. Whether the inhabitants are rich or poor is also a point by no means decisive, at least it should not be; but it must be admitted that a poor population accustomed to hard work and privations usually shows itself more vigorous and better suited for war. One peculiarity of country, which greatly favors the action of war carried on by the people, is the scattered sites of the dwellings of the country people, such as is to be found in many parts of Germany. The country is thus more intersected and covered; the roads are worse, although more numerous. The lodgement of troops is attended with endless difficulties, but especially that peculiarity repeats itself on a small scale which a people's war possesses on a great scale—namely, that the principle of resistance exists everywhere but is nowhere tangible. If the inhabitants are collected in villages, the most troublesome have troops quartered on them, or they are plundered as a punishment, and their houses burnt, etc., a system which could not be very easily carried out with a peasant community of Westphalia.

National levies and armed peasantry cannot and should not be employed against the main body of the enemy's army, or even against any considerable corps of the same. They must not attempt to crack the nut, they must only gnaw on the surface and the borders. They should rise in the provinces situated at one of the sides of the theater of war, and in which the assailant does not appear in force, in order to withdraw these provinces entirely from his influence. Where no enemy is to be found, there is no want of courage to oppose him, and at the example thus given, the mass of the neighboring population gradually takes fire. Thus, the fire spreads as it does in heather, and reaching at last that part of the surface of the soil on which the aggressor is based, it seizes his lines of communication and preys upon the vital thread by which his existence is supported. For although we entertain no exaggerated ideas of the omnipotence of a people's war, such as that it is an inexhaustible, unconquerable element o'er which the mere force of an army has as little control as the human will has over the wind or the rain—in short, although our opinion is not founded on flowery ephemeral literature, still we must admit that armed peasants are not to be driven before us in the same way as a body of soldiers who keep together like a herd of cattle and usually follow their noses. Armed peasants, on the contrary, when broken, disperse in all directions, for which no formal plan is required. Through this circumstance, the march of every small body of troops in a mountainous, thickly wooded, or even broken country becomes a service of a very dangerous character, for at any moment a combat may arise on the march. If in point of fact no armed bodies have even been seen for some time, yet the same peasants already driven off by the head of a column may at any hour make their appearance at its rear. If it is an object to destroy roads or to block up a defile, the means which outposts or detachments from an army can apply to that purpose bear about the same relation to those furnished by a body of insurgent peasants as the action of an automaton does to that of a human being. The enemy has no other means to oppose to the action of national levies except that of detaching numerous parties to furnish escorts for convoys to occupy military stations, defiles, bridges, etc. In proportion as the first efforts of the national levies are small, so the detachments sent out will be weak in numbers, from the repugnance to a great dispersion of forces. It is on these weak bodies that the fire of the national war usually first properly kindles itself. They are overpowered by numbers at some points, courage rises, the love of fighting gains strength, and the intensity of this struggle increases until the crisis approaches which is to decide the issue. According to our idea of a people's war, it should, like a kind of nebulous, vapory essence, never condense into a solid body; otherwise the enemy sends an adequate force against this core, crushes it, and takes a great many prisoners; their courage sinks; everyone thinks the main question is decided, any further effort useless, and the arms fall from the hands of the people. Still, however, on the other hand, it is necessary that this mist should collect at some points into denser masses and form threatening clouds from which now and again a formidable flash of lightning may burst forth. These points are chiefly on the flanks of the enemy's theater of war, as already observed. There the armament of the people should be organized into greater and more systematic bodies, supported by a small force of regular troops, so as to give it the appearance of a regular force and fit it to venture upon enterprises on a larger scale. From these points, the irregular character in the organization of these bodies should diminish in proportion as they are to be employed more in the direction of the rear of the enemy, where he is exposed to their hardest blows. These better organized masses are for the purpose of falling upon the larger garrisons which the enemy leaves behind him. Besides, they serve to create a feeling of uneasiness and dread and increase the moral impression of the whole. Without them the total action would be wanting in force, and the situation of the enemy upon the whole would not be made sufficiently uncomfortable.... After these reflections, which are more of the nature of subjective impressions than an objective analysis, because the subject is one as yet of rare occurrence generally, and has been but imperfectly treated of by those who have had actual experience for any length of time, we have only to add that the strategic plan of defense can include in itself the cooperation of a general arming of the people in two different ways—that is, either as a last resource after a lost battle or as a natural assistance before a decisive battle has been fought.... No state should believe its fate, that is, its entire existence, to be dependent upon one battle, let it be even the most decisive. If it is beaten, the calling forth fresh power and the natural weakening which every offensive undergoes with time may bring about a turn of fortune, or assistance may come from abroad. No such urgent haste to die is needed yet; and as by instinct the drowning man catches at a straw, so in the natural course of the moral world a people should try the last means of deliverance when it sees itself hurried along to the brink of an abyss. However small and weak a state may be in comparison to its enemy, if it foregoes a last supreme effort, we must say there is no longer any soul left in it. This does not exclude the possibility of saving itself from complete destruction by the purchase of peace at a sacrifice. But neither does such an aim on its part do away with the utility of fresh measures for defense; they will neither make peace more difficult nor more onerous, but easier and better. They are still more necessary if there is an expectation of assistance from those who are interested in maintaining our political existence. Any government, therefore, which, after the loss of a great battle, only thinks how it may speedily place the nation in the lap of peace and, unmanned by the feelings of great hopes disappointed, no longer feels in itself the courage or the desire to stimulate to the utmost every element of force, completely stultifies itself in such case through weakness, and shows itself unworthy of victory, and perhaps just on that account, was incapable of gaining one. However decisive, therefore, the overthrow may be that is experienced by a state, still, by a retreat of the army into the interior, the efficacy of its fortresses and an arming of the people may be brought into use. In connection with this it is advantageous if the flank of the principal theater of war is fenced in by mountains, or otherwise very difficult tracts of country, which stand forth as bastions, the strategic enfilade of which is to check the enemy's progress.

---

Carl von Clausewitz, *Schriften-Aufsätze-Studien-Briefe,* ed. W. Hahlweg, Vol. I, (Gottingen, 1966).

# Napoleon and After

# INTRODUCTORY NOTE

F OLLOWING THE NAPOLEONIC WARS, greater attention was paid to the political aspects of partisan warfare. This section opens with the chapter on national war from *Precis de l'art de guerre* published by Antoine Henri de Jomini in Paris in 1838. Swiss by origin, General de Jomini (1779–1869) had served in Napoleon's army.

Francisco Espoz y Mina (1781–1836) was the best-known Spanish guerrilla leader of his time; he fought with less success in the first Carlist War. His *Memorias* were published posthumously. The excerpt presented here is from *A Short Extract from the Life of General Mina Published by Himself* (London, 1825).

Denis Vasilevich Davydov (1784–1839), Russian poet and cavalry officer, was the outstanding partisan commander among those fighting the French army near Moscow in 1812. He is the author of a fascinating diary about partisan operations, from which the present excerpts are taken,[1] and of a theoretical essay on partisan warfare (1821).

Jean Frédéric-Auguste Lemière de Corvey (1770–1832) and Carl von Decker (1784–1844) are the authors of the two definative classic nineteenth-century books on partisan warfare. For many decades these works provided inspiration to authors all over Europe.[2] Lemiere de Corvey, also known as a composer, had fought as an officer in the Napoleonic army in the Vendée and Spain. He emphasized that partisan war, far from being primitive, was essentially novel. He argued that it was pointless to treat partisans as mere brigands, and that the application of traditional military doctrine was of little use in combatting them. General Carl von Decker also stressed that partisan warfare was more difficult than conventional war—even a mediocre talent could make a useful contribution in regular warfare. Partisan warfare however, called for very special qualities.

In this political context the Italian and Polish guerrilla literature of the

---

[1] *Voennie Zapiski* (Moscow, 1940).

[2] Lemière de Corvey, *Des partisans et des corps irreguliers* (Paris, 1823). Carl von Decker, Der Kleine Krieg im Geiste der neueren Kriegsführung (Berlin, 1822).

nineteenth century is by far the most important, for it provides the link between radical politics and partisan warfare tactics. The ideas of "bases," political indoctrination, the use of terrorism, and the gradual transformation of guerrilla war into regular war is to be found in the writings of the contemporary authors. The Polish and Italian writers represented in this section knew each other and collaborated on various occasions. Karol Bogumir Stolzman and Carlo Bianco helped to prepare Mazzini's ill-fated invasion of Savoy. Chrzanowski was chief of staff of the Piedmontese army at one time. Giuseppe Mazzini (1805–72), the hero of the Risorgimento, was not a military leader, but among his writings were *Istruzione per le bandi nazionali* (1853), from which the excerpts below have been taken. More important as a military theorist was Carlo Bianco, Conte di St. Jorioz (1795–1843). The son of an ennobled Turin lawyer, he served in the army in Spain and later became a member of the radical-democratic wing of the Italian nationalist underground. His two-volume magnum opus was written and published in Malta.[3] His last years were spent in impoverished exile in France, Switzerland, and Belgium. Wojciech Chrzanowski (1793–1861) participated in Napoleon's invasion of Russia as a young lieutenant and was subsequently an officer in the Russian army. He was chief of staff of the rebel Polish units in 1831. Later he became a military and political adviser to the British government and a general in the Italian army. Karol Bogumir Stolzman (1793-1854) also participated in the last phase of the Napoleonic Wars and later served in the Russian army. He took part in the Polish insurrection of 1830 and, as an émigré, represented his native country on Mazzini's Young Europe committee. After 1835, England became his permanent home.[4]

Gingins-La Sarraz (1790–1863), author of *Les partisans et la defense de la Suisse* (Lausanne, 1861), was an amateur botanist and historian of some standing with a particular interest in medieval and regional history.

Antoine-Fortune de Brack (1789–1850) began his military career during the Napoleonic Wars and later became known as a successful regimental commander, *beau sabreur,* and important military writer. The excerpts on partisan units are taken from the English translation of *Avant-postes de cavalerie legere—Advanced Posts of Light Cavalry* (London, 1850).

---

[3] *Della guerra nazionale d'insurrezione per bande applicata all'ltalia. Trattato dedicato ai buoni Italiani da un amico del paese,* 2 vols. (Italia, 1830). Soon after, an abridged and slightly modified version appeared from which these excerpts were taken, *Manuale pratico del rivoluzionario italiano . . .* (Italy, 1833).

[4] Chrzanowski's *O wojnie partyzanckiej* (Paris, 1835) was not accessible and the present translation is from *Über den Parteigdnger-Krieg* (Berlin, 1846). Stolzman's main work is *Partyzanka czyli wojna dla ludow powstajacych najwlasciwsza* (Paris, 1844).

ANTOINE HENRI DE JOMINI

# NATIONAL WARS

N ATIONAL WARS, TO WHICH WE HAVE REFERRED in speaking of those of invasion, are the most formidable of all. This name can only be applied to such as are waged against a united people, or a great majority of them, filled with a noble ardor and determined to sustain their independence. Then every step is disputed, the army holds only its camp ground, its supplies can only be obtained at the point of the sword, and its convoys are everywhere threatened or captured.

The spectacle of a spontaneous uprising of a nation is rarely seen; and, though there be in it something grand and noble which commands our admiration, the consequences are so terrible that, for the sake of humanity, we ought to hope never to see it. This uprising must not be confounded with a national defense in accordance with the institutions of the state and directed by the government.

This uprising may be produced by the most opposite causes. The serfs may rise in a body at the call of the government, and their masters, affected by a noble love of their sovereign and country, may set them the example and take the command of them. Similarly, a fanatical people may arm under the appeal of their priests; or a people enthusiastic in their political opinions, or animated by a sacred love of their institutions, may rush to meet the enemy in defense of all they hold most dear.

The control of the sea is of much importance in the results of a national invasion. If the people possess a long stretch of coast, and are masters of the sea or in alliance with a power which controls it, their power of resistance is quintupled, not only on account of the facility of feeding the insurrection and of alarming the enemy on all the points he may occupy, but still more by the difficulties which will be thrown in the way of his procuring supplies by the sea.

The nature of the country may be such as to contribute to the facility of a national defense. In mountainous countries the people are always most formidable; next to these are countries covered with extensive forests.

The resistance of the Swiss to Austria and to the Duke of Burgundy, that of the Catalans in 1712 and in 1809, the difficulties encountered by the Russians in the subjugation of the tribes of the Caucasus, and, finally, the reiterated efforts of the Tyrolese, clearly demonstrate that the inhabitants of mountainous regions have always resisted for a longer time than those of the plains—which is due as much to the difference in character and customs as to the difference in the natural features of the countries. Defiles and large forests, as well as rocky regions, favor this kind of defense; and the Bocage of La Vendée, so justly celebrated, proves that any country, even if it be only traversed by large hedges and ditches or canals, admits of a formidable defense.

The difficulties in the path of an army in wars of opinions, as well as in national wars, are very great, and render the mission of the general conducting them very difficult. The events just mentioned, the contest of the Netherlands with Philip II, and that of the Americans with the English, furnish evident proofs of this. But the much more extraordinary struggle of La Vendee with the victorious Republic, those of Spain, Portugal, and the Tyrol against Napoleon—and, finally, those of the Morea against the Turks, and of Navarre against the armies of Queen Christina—are still more striking illustrations.

The difficulties are particularly great when the people are supported by a considerable nucleus of disciplined troops. The invader has only an army: his adversaries have an army, and a people wholly or almost wholly in arms, and making means of resistance out of everything, each individual of whom conspires against the common enemy; even the noncombatants have an interest in his ruin and accelerate it by every means in their power. He holds scarcely any ground but that upon which he encamps. Outside the limits of his camp everything is hostile and multiplies a thousandfold the difficulties he meets at every step.

These obstacles become almost insurmountable when the country is difficult. Each armed inhabitant knows the smallest paths and their connections. He finds everywhere a relative or friend who aids him. The commanders also know the country and learning immediately the slightest movement on the part of the invader, can adopt the best measures to defeat his projects; while the latter, without information of their movements, and not in a condition to send out detachments to gain it, having no resource but in his bayonets, and certain safety only in the concentration of his columns, is like a blind man. His combinations are failures, and when, after the most carefully concerted movements and the most rapid and fatiguing marches, he thinks he is about to accomplish his aim and deal a terrible blow, he finds no signs of the enemy but his camp fires. While, like Don Quixote, he is attacking windmills, his adversary is on his line of communications, destroys the detachments left to guard it, surprises his convoys and his depots, and carries on a war so disastrous for the invader that he must inevitably yield after a time.

In Spain I was a witness of two terrible examples of this kind. When Ney's corps replaced Soult's at Corunna, I had camped the companies of the artillery train between Betanzos and Corunna, in the midst of four brigades distant from the camp from two to three leagues, and no Spanish forces had been seen within fifty miles. Soult still occupied Santiago de Compostela, the division Maurice-Mathieu was at Ferrol and Lugo and Marchand's at Corunna and Betanzos. Nevertheless, one fine night the companies of the train—men and horses— disappeared, and we were never able to discover what became of them. A solitary wounded corporal escaped to report that the peasants, led by their monks and priests, had thus made away with them. Four months afterward, Ney with a single division marched to conquer the Asturias, descending the valley of the Navia, while Kellermann debouched from Leon by the Oviedo road. A part of the corps of La Romana which was guarding the Asturias marched behind the very heights which enclose the valley of the Navia, at most but a league from our columns, without the marshal knowing a word of it. When he was entering Gijon, the army of La Romana attacked the center of the regiments of the division Marchand, which, being scattered to guard Galicia, barely escaped, and that only by the prompt return of the marshal to Lugo. This war presented a thousand incidents as striking as this. All the gold of Mexico could not have procured reliable information for the French; what was given was but a lure to make them fall more readily into snares.

No army, however disciplined, can contend successfully against such a system applied to a great nation, unless it be strong enough to hold all the essential points of the country, cover its communications, and at the same time furnish an active force sufficient to beat the enemy wherever he may present himself. If this enemy has a regular army of respectable size to be a nucleus around which to rally the people, what force will be sufficient to be superior everywhere, and to assure the safety of the long lines of communication against numerous bodies?

The Peninsular War should be carefully studied, to learn all the obstacles which a general and his brave troops may encounter in the occupation or conquest of a country whose people are all in arms. What efforts of patience, courage, and resignation did it not cost the troops of Napoleon,

Massena, Soult, Ney, and Suchet to sustain themselves for six years against three or four hundred thousand armed Spaniards and Portuguese supported by the regular armies of Wellington, Beresford, Blake, La Romana, Cuesta, Castanos, Reding, and Ballasteros! If success be possible in such a war, the following general course will be most likely to insure it—namely to make a display of a mass of troops proportioned to the obstacles and resistance likely to be encountered, calm the popular passions in every possible way; exhaust them by time and patience; display courtesy, gentleness, and severity united; and, particularly, deal justly. The examples of Henry IV in the wars of the League, of Marshal Berwick in Catalonia, of Suchet in Aragon and Valencia, of Hoche in La Vendee are models of their kind, which may be employed according to circumstances with equal success. The admirable order and discipline of the armies of Diebitsch and Paskevitch in the late war were also models, and were not a little conducive to the success of their enterprises.

The immense obstacles encountered by an invading force in these wars have led some speculative persons to hope that there should never be any other kind, since then wars would become more rare, and conquest, being also more difficult, would be less a temptation to ambitious leaders. This reasoning is rather plausible than solid; for, to admit all its consequences, it would be necessary always to be able to induce the people to take up arms, and it would also be necessary for us to be convinced that there would be in the future no wars but those of conquest, and that all legitimate though secondary wars, which are only to maintain the political equilibrium or defend the public interests, should never occur again. Otherwise, how could it be known when and how to excite the people to a national war?

For example, if one hundred thousand Germans crossed the Rhine and entered France, originally with the intention of preventing the conquest of Belgium by France, and without any other ambitious project, would it be a case where the whole population—men, women, and children—of Alsace, Lorraine, Champagne, and Burgundy should rush to arms to make a Saragossa of every walled town, to bring about, by way of reprisals, murder, pillage, and incendiarism throughout the country? If all this be not done, and the Germans, in consequence of some success, should occupy these provinces, who can say that they might not afterward seek to appropriate a part of them, even though at first they had never contemplated it? The difficulty of answering these two questions would seem to argue in favor of national wars.

But is there no means of repelling such an invasion without bringing about an uprising of the whole population and a war of extermination? Is there no mean between these contests, between the people and the old regular method of war between permanent armies? Will it not be sufficient, for the efficient defense of the country, to organize a militia, or *Landwehr*, which, uniformed and called by their governments into service, would regulate the part the people should take in the war, and place just limits to its barbarities?

I answer in the affirmative; and, applying this mixed system to the cases stated above, I will guarantee that fifty thousand regular French troops, supported by the National Guards of the East, would get the better of this German army which had crossed the Vosges. For, reduced to fifty thousand men by many detachments, upon nearing the Meuse or arriving in Argonne it would have one hundred thousand men on its hands. To attain this mean, we have laid it down as a necessity that good national reserves be prepared for the army, which will be less expensive in peace and will insure the defense of the country in war. This system was used by France in 1792, imitated by Austria in 1809, and by the whole of Germany in 1813.

I sum up this discussion by asserting that, without being a Utopian philanthropist, or a condottiere, a person may desire that wars of extermination may be banished from the code of nations, and that the defenses of nations by disciplined militia, with the aid of good political alliances, may be sufficient to insure their independence. As a soldier, preferring loyal and chivalrous warfare to organized assassination, if it be necessary to make a choice, I acknowledge that my prejudices are in favor of the good old times when the French and English guards courteously invited each other to fire first—as at Fontenoy—preferring them to the frightful epoch when priests, women, and children throughout Spain plotted the murder of isolated soldiers.

---

Antoine Henri de Jomini, *Precis de l'art de la guerre*
(Paris, 1838) [in English: Philadelphia, 1862].

FRANCISCO ESPOZ Y MINA

# FIGHTING IN SPAIN

I KEPT IN CHECK IN NAVARRE twenty-six men for the space of 53 days, who otherwise would have assisted at the battle of Salamanca, as they were on their march to join Marmonft's army; and by cutting down the bridges, and breaking up the roads, I prevented the advance of eighty pieces of artillery, which would otherwise have been employed in that battle.

I contributed to the happy result of the decisive battle of Vittoria; for if, by the maneuvers I executed, I had not prevented the junction of the French divisions Claussel and Foi, which consisted of from twenty-seven to twenty-eight thousand men and intercepted their correspondence, the issue would have been very doubtful...

The French, rendered furious by the disasters they experienced in Navarre, and by their fruitless attempts to exterminate my troops, began a horrible mode of warfare upon me in 1811, hanging and shooting every soldier and officer of mine who fell into their hands. They also killed the friends of the volunteers who served with me, and carried off to France a great number of families. On December 14th of the same year, I published a solemn Declaration, composed of twenty-three articles, the first of which ran thus: "In Navarre, a war of extermination, without quarter, is declared against the French army, without distinction of soldiers or chiefs, not excepting the Emperor of the French." And this sort of warfare I carried on for some time, keeping always in the valley of Roncal a great depot of prisoners, so that if the enemy hung or shot one of my officers, I did the same with four of his; if one of my soldiers, I did the same with twenty of his. In this manner I succeeded in terrifying him...

I never suffered a surprise. Once, on April 23, 1812, at break of day, having been sold by the Partisan Malcarado, who had previously made his arrangements with General Panetier, and had withdrawn the advanced guard from before Robres, I saw myself surrounded in the town by one thousand infantry and two hundred cavalry, and was attacked by five hussars at the very door of the house where I lodged. I defended myself from these latter with the bar of the door, the only weapon I had at hand, while my attendant, Louis Gaston, was saddling my horse; and mounting immediately, with his assistance, I sallied forth, charged them, followed them up the street, cut off an arm of one of them at one blow, immediately collected some of my men, charged the enemy several times, rescued many of my soldiers and officers who had been made prisoners, and continued the contest for more than three-quarters of an hour, in order that the remainder might escape. This Louis Gaston I always retain about my person as a friend. The next day I caused Malcarado and his attendant to be shot, while three alcaldes and a parish priest, likewise concerned in the plot, were hanging.

Amidst the numberless toils and anxieties by which I was continually surrounded, and which scarcely allowed me a moment's repose, *never having counted upon any assistance from the government, either pecuniary or otherwise* (these very words are in the government's statement of my services), I found means to raise, organize, discipline, and maintain a division of infantry and cavalry, composed of nine regiments of the first and two of the latter class, whose total amount at the end of the campaign was thirteen thousand five hundred men.

My division took from the enemy, at different periods, thirteen strong places and fortresses, and more than fourteen thousand prisoners (not including those made during the time that no quarter was given), with an immense number of pieces of artillery, quantities of arms, clothing, stores, provisions, etc. The delivery of this number of prisoners at Valencia, Alicante, Lerida, the Cantabrian coast, and at other points to which I ordered them to be taken, I have officially authenticated.

From an examination of the returns of killed, wounded, and prisoners, the result is a loss on my side of five thosuand men, while that of the enemy, including their prisoners, does not fall far short of forty thousand.

The Spanish prisoners whom I rescued amount to above four thousand among them some generals, many chiefs and officers, and not a few partisan leaders.

I was several times wounded by musket balls, sabers, or lances. I have still a ball in my thigh, which the surgeons have never been able to extract.

I had four horses killed under me, and several wounded in action.

A price was set upon my head by the enemy from the end of 1811 till the conclusion of the war.

---

Francisco Espoz y Mina, *A Short Extract from the Life of General Mina,* (Published by himself, London, 1825).

DENIS DAVYDOV

# ON GUERRILLA WARFARE

T HE CONCEPT OF GUERRILLA WARFARE which still predominates is the result of a one-sided attitude or an apparently cautious view of the subject. Seizing prisoners and making them talk, committing to flames one or two enemy storehouses located near the army, suddenly smashing the advance guard, or viewing the multiplication of small detachments as the systematic and pernicious fragmentation of the army's effectiveness—these are usually the essential definitions of this type of warfare. All are erroneous! Guerrilla warfare consists neither of quite minor enterprises nor of those of the first order of magnitude, for it is not concerned with the burning of one or two granaries, nor with smashing pickets, nor with striking direct blows at the main forces of the enemy. Rather, it embraces and traverses the whole length of the enemy lines, from the opposing army's rear to the area of territory assigned for the stationing of troops, provisions, and weapons. Thus, guerrilla warfare stops up the source of the army's strength and continuing existence and puts it at the mercy of the guerrillas' own army while the enemy army is weakened, hungry, disarmed, and deprived of the saving bonds of authority. This is guerrilla warfare in the fullest sense of the word!

There is no doubt that this kind of warfare would be less effective were it waged only between low-powered armies that did not require large quantities of food and supplies and that fought only with cold steel. However, the invention of gunpowder and firearms, the great increase in the size of military forces, and the preference for the concentration rather than fragmentation of forces posed impossible obstacles to the procurement of food supplies from the occupied territory. Also immense difficulties were encountered in the manufacture of charges in laboratories, the training of recruits, and the mustering of reserves amidst the alarms, engagements, and general accidents of war.

Under these circumstances, it became necessary to provide troops with all the necessities of war in a way that would not entail their procurement from the occupied area, something which would be impossible because of the disproportion between the number of consumers and the amount producible. The solution was to obtain the necessities from areas beyond the range of military operations. Hence there came about the division of the ter of war into two fields, the battlefield and the reserves field, the former being supplied by the produce of the latter. This produce would come not all at once or in bulk but as the army used up the provisions and military equipment it carried with it. Thus troops would not be burdened with excessive loads that would hamper their movement. Naturally, however, this invention led to a counter-invention with which the enemy could obstruct the delivery of supplies of the produce so vital to the efficiency of the opposing side. Two ways of achieving this aim were immediately obvious: action on the battlefield by detachments against the rear of the army where newly supplied ammunition and provisions are distributed and newly arrived reserve troops deployed, or action by these same detachments on the reserves field itself.

But then it was discovered that the first of these, the battlefield, was difficult to access owing to the close proximity of the enemy to the place appointed for the attack; and that the second, the reserves field, was usually protected by fortifications enclosing the stores of provision, the ammunition factory, and the reserve formations. There remained the ground over which these three items were transported to the army. This is the field of guerrilla operations. It presents none of those obstacles that abound on both the battlefield and the reserves field because the enemy's main forces and fortifications, being located at its extremities, are in no position to defend it—the former because all their efforts are directed at fighting the main army of their adversary, the latter by reason of their natural immobility.

Hence it follows that guerrilla warfare cannot exist when the opposing army is situated on the reserves field itself. But the greater the distance separating the battlefield and the reserves field becomes, the more effective and decisive guerrilla warfare can be. Prudent commanders do not fail to provide the entire length of the main supply route across the aforesaid territory with fortified stages or shelters to protect transports during halts or night stops and to supply troop detachments to cover these transports while they are on the march between stages. These sensible measures are nonetheless vastly inadequate in the face of attacks by numerous active brigades, as indeed any defensive operation is inferior to an offensive one. Another consideration is that the fortified stages, however spacious they may be, cannot accommodate the number of carts that go to make up even the smallest transport required by the armies of our times. The cover, however numerous it may be, can never operate as a single body for the reason that, in order to protect the entire length of the transport, it is obliged to spread out along its whole length during marches and therefore must always be weaker at any pressure point than a detachment operating as a whole. In addition to these inconveniences, much military strength is required to provide the army with fortified halts, the number of which increases as the army advances, its successes luring it farther away from its reserves field.

As a definitive illustration of the great importance of guerrilla warfare in modern operations involving huge armies and concentrations of supplies, let us ask some questions and give the answers.

First: by whom is war waged? By people, joined together in an army.

Second: can people do battle empty-handed? No. War is not like fist-fighting. These people need weapons. But now that gunpowder has been invented, even weapons alone are insufficient. Soldiers need cartridges and charges for their weapons. As these charges and cartridges are almost completely discharged during the course of each battle and since their manufacture is difficult during troop movements and operations, new supplies must be sent directly from the place where they are prepared. This is a clear demonstration that an army with weapons but without cartridges and charges is no better than an organized crowd of people with bear spears, a crowd which will scatter at the first shot from the enemy or, if it accepts battle, which will perish in so doing. In short, there is no strength in an army, for since the invention of gunpowder, an army without charges and cartridges is no army at all.

Third: does an army require reinforcement during the course of a war? Yes, it does. Men and horses are lost in battles, skirmishes, and exchange of fire; they become casualties to wounds received in battle or to diseases which run increasingly rampant because of the intense pressure of campaigns, inclement weather, and strains and shortages of all kinds. An army unable to refurbish itself will inevitably dwindle and disappear.

Fourth (although it seems superfluous): does the soldier need food? A man without food cannot exist, let alone fight. Because of its large size, the army of modern times cannot make do with the produce of the area it occupies. It therefore needs regular food supplies. Without these it will either die of hunger or scatter beyond the radius of military operations in search of sustenance, thereby degenerating into a corrupt horde of robbers and vagrants that will perish without protection or glory.

So, what method should be selected to deprive the enemy of these three fundamental elements of the vital strength and military might of his army? There is no other method than to destroy them by guerrilla warfare while they are being transported from the reserves field to the battlefield. What venture will an enemy embark upon without food, ammunition, or replacement troops? He will be compelled to cease his operations either by making peace, surrendering into captivity, or scattering with no hope of being reunited—three dismal consequences totally opposed to those an army seeks when it opens hostilities. Besides the mortal threat that guerrilla warfare represents to these three fundamental elements of the strength and existence of an army, it poses danger to the secondary needs of an army that are so closely bound up with its welfare and no less exposed to danger than food, or ammunition, or transports of reserves. These secondary elements are clothing, footwear, and arms to replace those worn by excessive use or mislaid in the chaos of battle; surgical and hospital equipment; and messengers and aides-de-camp sometimes carrying vitally important orders to and from enemy headquarters and remote areas in the rear, command posts, and particular corps and detachments. The combined action of these units is disrupted and destroyed by guerrilla operations. Other targets may be transports of sick and wounded men on their way from the army to hospitals, teams of invalids who have recovered and are returning from hospital to the army, high-ranking officials traveling from one place to another to inspect particular units or take up a particular command, and so forth.

But this is not all. Guerrilla warfare can also have an effect upon the main operations of the opposing army. The army's strategic movements during the course of a campaign must inevitably encounter enormous difficulties when they can immediately be reported to the commander on the opposite side by guerrilla units or when they can be delayed by these same units building abatis or destroying fording places. Also an army can be attacked by all the opposing forces when it has left one strategic point but not reached the next—a situation reminiscent of Seslavin at Maloyaroslavets. Similar obstacles are also a threat to the enemy during his retreat. Erected and defended by guerrilla detachments, these barriers allow the pursuing army to constrict the retreating one and exploit the advantages of the locality to bring about its final destruction—a spectacle we witnessed in 1812 during the retreat of the Napoleonic hordes from Moscow to the Nieman.

Still this is not all. Scarcely less important than the material aspect of this kind of operation is the moral one. Raising the lowered spirits of the inhabitants of areas at the enemy rear; distracting mercenary-minded troublemakers from giving assistance to the enemy by seizing all kinds of spoils from the enemy army and dividing them among the inhabitants; boosting the morale of one's own army by frequent deliveries and parades of captured soldiers and officials, transports and provisions, stock, and even guns; and, besides all this, stunning and disheartening the men in the opposing armies—such are the fruits of skillfully directed guerrilla warfare. What consequences will we not see when the success of guerrilla detachments leads to their winning over the entire population of regions in the enemy rear and when news of the horror sown along the enemy's lines of communication is broadcast among the ranks of its army? When the realization that there is no escape from the guerrilla bands robs each soldier of his reliance on the reserves field, the effect will be to cause timidity and circumspection and then looting, which is one of the chief reasons for a fall in discipline, and with it, the total destruction of an army.

C A R L   V O N   D E C K E R

# ON PARTISAN WAR

INSUFFICIENT IMPORTANCE IS ATTACHED to partisan warfare; it is thought easier than it really is. Hence so many men reckon themselves, far from truly, as good partisans.

Partisan war can be more difficult than large-scale war since the partisan rarely possesses adequate resources. Such warfare requires special talents in the commander and unusual qualities in the men. By contrast, large-scale war provides a suitable place even for the most ordinary talents, and all rankers, if only they are brave, find their proper function....

Insufficient importance is attached to partisan warfare; it is thought easier than it really is. Hence so many men reckon themselves, far from truly, as good partisans.

In all cases, the selection of new men should be guided by the utmost discretion. Even more is this so in creating a band of partisans; success depends upon making a good choice.

Partisan leaders should never forget that a handful of brave soldiers can do wonders, whereas with a host of cowards not even an expedition of the smallest value can be mounted against the enemy. Above all, they will beware of cashiered officers or those who have been obliged to leave their regiments under a cloud. They will not accept the view that in wartime a man's past is of no moment. True courage in an officer is founded on blameless morality; blind and unthinking boldness is no more than a fleeting excess of intoxication. In general, partisan actions are carried out with small numbers; hence, an officer must choose his men well because their usefulness lies not in number but in intrinsic merit. If the ranks possess this value as individuals, some whims may be overlooked—for example, theatrical uniforms or some eccentricities in their dress. However, where there are no real and material qualities to excuse such childishness, the free corps will rather resemble the well-known "travestied Aeneas" (Enee Tombo-lino) and his operatic heroes.

A partisan will endeavor in every possible way to win over the local inhabitants. If he does not succeed in this or if the nature of things is unfavorable, he will never be of great use: this was clearly proven by the best-known partisans of the allied armies during the French campaign of 1814. However, even when a partisan has the people on his side, he ought never to stay long in one place but be nowhere and everywhere.

A partisan, furthermore, must be able at all costs to win over spies and secret agents of all classes. Therefore, he should possess a knowledge of the world, an elegant manner, and authoritative, persuasive, and ingratiating ways. If he can invest himself with a certain brilliance, so much the better. If he knows how to achieve influence over women, he will take care not to neglect this approach; he will owe his surest information to them. A secret which neither women nor clergy can divulge will probably never be revealed.

The partisan must be welcome everywhere; to this end, he will maintain strict discipline in his band and will know how to present himself in a disinterested guise. He should be able to have the elements to fulfill his needs brought to him without having to take them; but when he must requisition them, he will ensure that everything is paid for in ready money so that he is not classed with freebooters. The country should consider him its liberator, shielding it from enemy vexation, and gratefully offer him its best.

For this reason, partisans often achieve their greatest success at the very moment when the large-scale army is in a disadvantageous position and when, in one sense, Schiller's words given to Wallenstein are applicable: "It must be night, that Friedland's star may shine in all its splendor."

It is not easy to impart the waging of partisan warfare in all its fine points and variations. How can one prescribe to a genius what to invent in a given case or what resources to employ? How can one foresee and foreordain the means he should use to attain his purpose? It would be simpler to teach the way in which partisan war should not be fought.

Examples alone can serve as lessons here: not fictitious examples such as certain writers have attempted to invent but real ones drawn from the great book of experience. Therefore, we refer our readers to the history of war. Of the books written on partisan warfare, those of Ewald and Emmerich have interested us above all others. In truth, they do not possess the flowery, brilliant style brought from the universities by our modern writers; but they contain sound practical rules and unvarnished truths, and their simple language, speaking to the imagination as well as to good sense, owes its pleasing effect to this circumstance....

In the case of a special mission, it is the mission itself which should be paramount to the partisan above all other considerations. He ought never to deviate from his purpose, never, above all, at the expense of his mission, whatever inviting opportunities may tempt him. In short, the partisan should be a man of absolute reliability.

When he has no special mission, the partisan should take as his sole aim the infliction of appreciable losses on the enemy. Today, the taking of hundreds of prisoners counts for little; that would be but a trifle and, if information is to be obtained, there must not be too many.

The foremost enterprises that a partisan should carry out are:

1. to carry off or destroy munitions, weapons, and clothing;
2. to seize horse yards or supply columns;
3. to carry off or destroy vehicles of war, supply depots, and baggage trains (above all in sieges);
4. to seize provisions which the enemy must bring up from far at his rear and which he cannot find in the area of conflict;
5. to carry off military and other public coffers;
6. to destroy arms manufactories, powder factories, and other military establishments or to hinder the destruction of our own;
7. to carry off material for military construction, such as wood for bridges, tools to construct entrenchments, etc.;
8. to free prisoners;
9. to carry off enemy generals, high civil authorities, and hostages, and to levy ransoms;
10. to intercept enemy dispatches; and
11. to pass on or seek out important information about an enemy corps, a fortress, etc. ...

A partisan will avoid contact with the enemy insofar as the object of his expedition can be achieved without fighting if for no other reason than that he is not always his own master in providing for the needs of the wounded, nor can he count on anyone to replace his losses. However, if a free corps cannot avoid an engagement, each man must be inspired by the greatest bravery. No partisan should ever dream of laying down his arms, if only because he must consider himself and his men as outlaws. If a partisan band is scattered, each man must know the general meeting place and do his utmost to reach it.

On the failure of an undertaking, the locality must be left at once. This, however, holds good after a successful stroke too, for the enemy will certainly take steps to recoup his setback. Consequently, whether his operations fall out well or badly, the leader of a partisan band cannot stay long in the same spot or area. Nothing is more wretched for a partisan than to remain penned up in one district, to be fettered to the army, to commandeer its best provisions, and yet to be unable to furnish any scrap of information that could not be obtained much more cheaply and simply from the army's outposts. We recall one partisan (or so he called himself) who was obliged to retire at speed from a village because the army headquarters was due to arrive there that same day. This could hardly be called glorious.

To detail the conduct to be maintained in the eleven cases we have enumerated would scarcely be possible or useful. In such warfare, the permutations are infinite and each has its variants. Ruse, surprise, force, boldness, chance, and, above all, *luck*—these are the means that every intelligent partisan must know how to turn to advantage. Sometimes one, sometimes another will lead to his object. His salvation of today may destroy him tomorrow. Here all rules fall short and theory is of no avail.

Almost always, the partisan is weaker than the enemy he confronts; method, therefore, no longer applies, for all method is based on some equality of forces.

---

Carl von Decker, *Der Kleine Krieg im Geiste der neueren Kriegsführung* (Berlin, 1822).

J. F. A. LEMIÈRE DE CORVEY

# UN PEU DU FANATISME

D URING THE THREE YEARS I SPENT IN SPAIN, I admired the courage of
Ration. It was able to defend its independence against a formidable invasion with no other resources than ill-armed, ill-disciplined
bands of partisans inspired by love of their country who were known under
the name of guerrillas. I was astonished at the way they waged war; their
devotion to the national cause, their courage, and their patience foiled the
tactics of the French soldiers. These guerrillas worked on the principle of
avoiding any engagement in line with our armies, and perseverance in this
plan thwarted all our schemes. By attacking small detachments, under-
strength escorts, or any isolated men they met, they beat us point by point,
undermined us, and imperceptibly destroyed so many men that the Spanish War cost France more than five hundred thousand men throughout the
seven years it lasted.

At the beginning of the revolution, I observed how the Vendeans organized their armies. I was struck by their new tactics and by their division
of their territory into bishoprics, cantons, and parishes. But, in my opinion, they failed in their object for, although they had a central point for
this or that general commanding the district of a bishopric, they had no
such center for the whole countryside they occupied. Every general commanded over his district at his own pleasure, and although they did sometimes join forces, this was by arrangement among the generals. There was
no one among them who was empowered to order an overall movement;
they recognized no leader but the king or the French princes. I have since
compared their tactics with those of the Spaniards and have found many
points of resemblance between the partisan warfare of these two peoples.
I shall only observe that the Vendeans, having several *departements* wholly
enlisted in their cause, could have assembled together a larger body of

men than could the Spaniards and could have fought battles. But if the Spaniards, whose principal towns we occupied, had been able to muster a national army headed by staunch leaders, then it is more likely that such an army, together with the corps of guerrillas, would have driven the enemy invaders from their territory than that Spain would have been subjected to the conqueror's yoke. In undertaking a national war to preserve independence and make a stand against a foreign invasion, a war of extermination must be waged and the enemy must perforce be driven away, otherwise the defending nation will be overrun, giving the victor the right to treat it as a conquered country. This has happened more than once. However, if the conquest is to be sustained, the vanquished must be treated gently; that is the way to win them over. Unfortunately, every war in which a mass rising occurs is nourished by some fanaticism, be it the spirit of faction, religion, etc.; otherwise, such wars of extermination with their fearful results would not exist.

The manner in which these two peoples marshaled their plan of defense has given rise to some interesting observations upon their organization and tactics. I have seen the advantage which bold and able leaders were able to make of irregular bands. I have thought therefore that if this manner of fighting could be brought under fixed rules, a great service would be rendered to all countries which, following an unsuccessful war, have found themselves exposed to invasion and subjection. No one has yet treated this subject thoroughly; writers on the art of war have mentioned partisans only very superficially. They have no doubt regarded these volunteer bands as unimportant auxiliaries. I myself, having a different viewpoint, have undertaken this work, believing it useful for all civilized nations, since, by providing rules for this means of defense on home ground, I prove to conquering peoples the folly of wishing to overrun a country when the nation threatened is disposed to make an impressive stand.

Energy is needed to repel an invasion and similarly to rise spontaneously in a body. It is necessary therefore that the motivating power should have so forceful an energy as to be able to communicate it to the entire nation. Otherwise, a general council must be appointed. Provided this general council enjoys widespread confidence, it will have that energy and will perform miracles...

When earlier I discussed the manner of protecting an unfortified city against a surprise attack, I mentioned Berlin and Paris and based my example on the latter, since it is known to all. But neither Paris nor any great city will successfully defend itself against an army unless it is galvanized by some fanaticism. The reason is simple: in all great cities the property owners, merchants, or other established persons are not, or are no longer, military men. The cares of their business preoccupy them and, as to defending themselves, they say: "What need have I to match myself against professional soldiers? Who will back me up? Men who will perhaps abandon me at the first musket shot? I ought to stay at home to defend my family and property." If the enemy deals gently with these men, they will not stir. But if a bomb burns down the house of one of them or if a shell-burst or a charge of grapeshot kills or dangerously wounds his wife or child, then he will take up arms and seek an opportunity to avenge himself. Almost all men allow themselves to be guided by private considerations. How many mediocre persons pass for great men because the motives behind their actions are unknown! ...

This is the system Spain used against us. One hundred and fifty to two hundred guerrilla bodies throughout Spain each took a vow to kill thirty or forty Frenchmen a month, making six to eight thousand men a month for all the guerrilla bands. Unless possessing superior forces, they never attacked soldiers traveling in bodies. Instead they fired on all isolated men, attacked small escorts, and endeavored to make away with enemy resources, dispatch riders, and, above all, supply trains. Since all the inhabitants served as spies to their fellow citizens, the date of departure and the strength of escorts were known. Thus the bands could join together to be at least twice the enemy number. They knew the country well and attacked violently in the most favorable spot; success often crowned their undertaking, and, as many men were always killed, their object was fulfilled. As there are twelve months in a year, we lost at least seventy-two thousand men a year without any pitched battles. The Spanish War lasted seven years, so there were over five hundred thousand French soldiers killed, as I postulated in the preface. But I only speak of those killed by the guerrillas. If we add to the battles of Salamanca, Tallaveyra, Vittoria, and several others lost by our soldiers the sieges laid by Marshal Suchet, the defense of Saragossa, the fruitless attack on Cadiz, and then subjoin the invasion and evacuation of Portugal and the fevers and various sicknesses inflicted by the climate upon our soldiers, you will see that three hundred thousand men over those seven years can assuredly be added to that number.

And who were these guerrilla leaders who defeated our worthy captains? No doubt they were distinguished retired officers, skilled in military tactics? Not at all; the principal leaders of those bands so audaciously resisting the French armies were a miller, doctor, shepherd, curate, some monks, a few deserters, but not a single man of mark before that time. ...

Their boldness in attack and perseverance often gave them the advantage in the war against our armies. They relied on local terrain and on their way of fighting; there was a touch of fanaticism, too. To make a good

defense of one's country in an invasion, one must decide on a war of extermination. Here a touch of fanaticism is essential, for enemy armies practice
reprisals and are all the more severe in their judgment because they see no
regular army confronting them. They deal with those who cannot otherwise be overcome as rebels and brigands, although if these were making
regular war, they would be treated as soldiers. This is why wars of opinion,
inspired by religious differences or for some cause which each party believes itself obliged to defend, are terrible wars. Each faction, regarding its
own side as a private cause to be avenged, often becomes cruel in victory.
Even the leaders sometimes make use of this factional spirit to inspire their
soldiers. In the Vendee, ill-armed peasants, quite undisciplined, were seen
to rush at pieces of ordnance and carry them away. Afterward they turned
them against the republican armies. Since artillery is useless to irregulars,
they would dismount and spike them if the affair ended in their favor or,
in the contrary case, they would cut the traces and take the horses with
them.

This kind of warfare breeds terror. Regular soldiers think twice before
pursuing an enemy in unfamiliar circumstances, for they do not know his
strength and always fear an ambush.

---

J. F. A. Lemière de Corvey, from *Des partisans et des corps
irreguliers* (Paris, 1823).

CARLO BIANCO

# A HANDBOOK FOR
# REVOLUTIONARY BANDS

## GENERAL RULES FOR INSURRECTIONARY WARFARE

The rules of military tactics are designed to prevent any breakup of an army's forces and to provide against all occurrences that might lay the troops open to such a danger. Regular troops are trained to take up positions in line, column, and close formation, and to change front. This is done always with the aim of not losing contact with their military base such as a fortified town, an entrenched camp, or a locality protected by the nature of the ground itself where artillery, arms and ammunition, baggage, provisions, money, and stores of every kind necessary for the maintenance of an army obliged to stay in a compact body can be kept. War today no longer aims at driving the enemy from a given area but rather at occupying those places which contain the material elements of his power. Thus, an advance is made only to a predetermined point: the enemy is expelled from a position and pursued to where it is judged advisable to stop. Such a judgment is always made with the view of not running out of the army's means of supply, since in regular warfare these are held almost of more account than men. A general, therefore, has to limit his operations to his available material resources. This is the system we have to fight.

All individual effort, all the energies of the nation must come into play when a desperate war is undertaken against a tenacious and implacable enemy. All the rules of war cease to apply the moment that insurrection breaks out. All means are sacrosanct when their sole aim is the annihilation of the country's enemies. *To obtain the liberation of Italy* is the only law.

Actions regarded as barbarous in regular warfare must be resorted to in order to terrorize, unnerve, and destroy the enemy. In this way Spain buried eight hundred thousand Frenchmen in the war against Napoleon Bonaparte.

Ardent patriotism, perspicacity, vigor, and stubborn determination are essential qualities for this war; also needed is energetic action combined with an understanding of the proper use of prudence.

The chief care of insurgent bands must be to thwart and render ineffectual the principles and rules of military tactics. Consequently, patriots will for the most part take up positions around the area where the enemy is stationed so that they can harass him with feints and forays and thus draw his forces away from their base. Such detachments, radiating out from their strategic center, their lines of communication weakening as they advance, will be exposed to attacks from the sides and rear by other bands who will cut them off from their base and overcome them.

The whole space between the enemy army and the periphery where the patriots are operating should be rendered of no possible use to the enemy.

The activities of the Italian combatants will thus be aimed at separating themselves from the enemy's base with land that they have laid waste by burning and flooding, so causing him serious shortages of fodder and provisions, indeed of everything needed by a regular army. In consequence, he will be obliged to send out frequent detachments of troops across this smoldering swamp to fight the bands beyond it and to obtain the necessities of life. Such units, cut off from contact with their base, will then easily be surrounded, attacked, and destroyed.

The flocks and herds together with stocks of grain and fruit having been withdrawn to the hills, the insurgents will leave the land around the enemy barren and devastated and will break up the roads by cutting deep ditches across them. They will lay mines in mountain passes and other narrow places through which the enemy has to go, timing the fuses to set off explosions when the troops are likely to be close to the spot; but even if one should go off before or after their passage, it will still do damage and have a useful effect in alarming the men and producing panic among them. Careful connections made between the dikes in the plain will cause the rivers and canals to overflow so that water near the part occupied by the army can be diverted to spread over the whole area. If the enemy persists in staying where he is, the army will suffer serious harm from the noxious air rising from this marshland which can result in pernicious fevers and consequent death. The north Italian plain, everywhere crossed by rivers and waterways, is well suited for such an operation. Bridges must be blown up, mills and bakeries destroyed, and wells and fountains poisoned; all crops not suitable to be taken away, trees, bushes, scattered houses in the plain, and finally the villages themselves, if within reach of the enemy, must be set on fire. In this way, deprived of everything around him, he will have to send for convoys of supplies from his headquarters; and because of his urgent need of food and stores, his lines of communication will be greatly extended, and his units, out of touch with their base and drawn farther and farther from it, will be open to attack from the flank and rear while the convoys will be endangered.

This is not a war between kings but a people's war, of insurgent masses formed into regular bodies of combatants against one or more professional armies. At such a time every Italian who loves his country and is brave of heart will pursue the barbarian oppressors with ardor, holding it a satisfying and indeed glorious occupation to bring about the death of the enemy.

## THE VOLUNTEER

Very different from the unhappy young man torn by force from the bosom of his family to serve under the flag of the tyrant or from the contemptible wretch who, to gain his bread, blindly sells himself for a pittance and for a term of years for employment in shameful and brutal acts against his suffering compatriots—very different from these is the Italian citizen who, animated by a sacred enthusiasm, freely dedicates his life and possessions to his country and joins the patriot bands as a volunteer and takes up arms to serve Italy and play his part with all his strength in the sublime purpose of her regeneration.

The youth torn from the arms of his father, mother, and sisters and from a pleasant, quiet life among his dear ones will be morose, aloof, and unwilling when he suddenly finds himself, against his natural inclinations, among coarse and licentious companions and expected to obey harsh, stupid, and arrogant superiors who fill him with bitter hatred for his condition. His temper becomes violent and, carrying out his duty badly, he has no heart to learn how to do it better. If, however, he is by nature dissolute, evil-minded, or a bully, he will inevitably become a hired cutthroat forced to abandon himself to depravity and vice of every sort and to offenses against his companions, friends, relatives, and compatriots. It is the attribute of the patriotic volunteer to be imbued with the pure joy that gladdens the life of one devoted to a good cause; with the ardent and clear-sighted valor of a man who feels a love for humanity and for what is just and true; and with the disinterestedness by which virtuous souls hold it a duty to sacrifice everything to the realization of a sublime idea for the good of mankind.

Patience that is proof against all trials, unshakable constancy, decision and unlimited resolution, strength of body, the eyes of a lynx, and firmness of hand and agile limbs must necessarily be the distinctive qualities inherent in the volunteer fighter.

His life is all poetic ardor, continual emotions and transports of joy, fearful dangers, physical privations, and moral satisfaction. He moves from place to place in a group of loyal brothers; he finds that he belongs to an affectionate family, a gathering of fine and honorable young men all conspiring for the liberation of their country and the good of humanity. Strong as lions, swift as the mountain deer, they enjoy almost complete independence when charged with performing special operations. Always in movement, sometimes on mountain heights, at other times in the forests of the plain, they do not wait for sunrise in the place where they were at sunset, but turning this way and that, they take the enemy by surprise and always defeat him, owing to their own resourcefulness and conviction that a free man is always a match for a dozen serfs or slaves. The volunteer moves about at night and sleeps by day in the woods; with no tent, no bed, and no roof for shelter, he lies wrapped in a blanket on the bare ground with a stone for a pillow. On rare occasions he lodges in a peasant's hut, a house abandoned by its rich owner, old ruins, underground quarries, aqueducts, or caves. He eats frugally, contenting himself with water and any crust that may come his way; hunger will make the coarsest food palatable to him and the fatigues of the day will render hard ground as comfortable as any bed. His time is spent happily in contributing toward the great intention: he aids the wretched, consoles the afflicted, and helps those who have been misled to find the right way. Thus are the powerful opposed and kings discomfited.

## PRELIMINARY OPERATIONS AND THE PROGRESSIVE GROWTH OF THE INSURGENT BANDS

In general, the smaller groups of insurgents are those first to be formed since it is easier for them to take the field before the government becomes aware of them.

These primary groups, and the flying columns that come already organized from beyond the frontiers or are set up as knowledge of their presence spreads, will not have to face such difficulties as the later ones. Those volunteers already expecting to take the field will either have or not have arms; in the latter case they must equip themselves by taking weapons from whomever has them. Supposing that twenty or thirty patriots have decided to start fighting, yet are not armed. It is unlikely that none possess pistols, fowling pieces, or other lethal weapons that they could use in raiding army stores for guns. Such volunteers will then decide individually but in agreement with their accepted leader on the safest and simplest way in which to arm themselves if, for instance, a detachment of troops, carabineers, or gendarmes is stationed in a volunteer's village or in one nearby and it would be possible to disarm them by a surprise attack. If this should appear too risky, each volunteer will lie in ambush not far from his own home (if possible) with a fowling piece or pistol and wait for the daily or periodic passing of the troops or others who have to make contact with or take over from the police. When he sees one who has fallen out from the main unit, he will fire at him and kill him, then strip him of weapons and equipment of use in the field and disappear into the country to join his band. If he misfires, he must flee and discard his weapons in the scrub. If caught, he must protest that he is unarmed and was running away out of fear, in which case the authorities will face the alternative of exonerating an enemy or executing a man found without arms and apparently inoffensive. Public opinion will be on the side of the volunteer, and if the government decides to condemn him, the citizens' indignation will increase hostility toward the regime and produce other volunteers to replace him. A number of such cases will cause the government to decide to send troops to reinforce the police guards; its opponents will grow in number and sufficient arms will be produced for one or more bands of insurgents. The troops will cause us casualties, but we shall kill many more of them in the way indicated above. Will they win the day? Since we are resolved to fight an unending war if necessary, reverses will only provoke us the more. If we are defeated, our daring will be redoubled.

In this way, and with the help of other groups and their established leaders, an insurrectionary force will begin by obtaining its equipment. But in this early phase the struggle must be purely defensive: the volunteer must not leave his home district. He must take advantage of his familiarity with the whole area and his personal relationship with his friends and family.

If the band, when formed, can already dispose of arms, it will not have to acquire them by the above methods. It will act in accordance with the situation obtaining in the town or village where it is located and will decide whether to continue with individual action or to move further off to a more promising area.

The band must be in constant, secret movement, above all in the early part of the war when it must hide by day and march at night and follow little-known and unfrequented mountain paths. It must take cover during the day in a wood, chapel, some unoccupied house, or a cavern. Sometimes it must stay for two or three days or more in barren regions almost impossible of access. Its movements must be swift, unaccountable, and unpredictable. Amid forests and mountain crags, in wooded valleys and plains, along rivers, on hidden, remote roads protected by thick hedges, and in isolated mountain ravines the group will find advantageous positions to occupy. To escape from enemy search parties it will break up the roads and make them unusable. It will avail itself of walls, buildings, farmyards, fields, or gardens to serve as defenses against the regular troops sent out to attack them. The leader of the band will post lookouts along the ways of approach to keep watch for the enemy. They will be posted in places from where a safe line of retreat can be kept open and through which by day or at night mail vans, stagecoaches, traveling carriages, and carriers have necessarily to pass. All these the patriots must stop if they are not escorted by guards in superior strength. Government mail must be seized and travelers strictly interrogated. If among the latter any are recognized as hostile to Italy, they must be kept back and dealt with, the others being allowed to proceed should it appear unlikely that their talk might endanger the existence or subsequent operations of the insurgent band.

The patriots must move with lightning speed from one position to another, keeping always in mind the fact that their safety and success depend entirely on such activity. Fighting in country well known to them, they alone will possess the secrets of the winding turns in the labyrinthine mountain tracks, of the abysses and ravines, inaccessible crags and precipices, the hollowed-out paths in the rocks covered with thorny scrub and the ill-defined ways through widespread intricate woodland where, amid dark bogs and quagmires, it would be easy to hold up or destroy an enemy who can never have a perfect knowledge of the area. If, despite such handicaps, enemy troops should persist in trying to attack the patriots, unwisely pressing on into the depths of the forest, they will find it impossible to advance in closed order and the men will have to break ranks. Moving forward individually, they will at any moment find themselves encircled by the patriots, who from high ground will roll down rocks upon them if they have the temerity to attempt escape by climbing up the mountainsides. If this form of defense turns out to be ineffectual and the enemy with great courage reaches a summit and threatens the safety of the band, the volunteers will scatter to reunite in some better position and will have the satisfaction of slipping away in sight of the enemy, who will be unable to stop them. The expedition will therefore have proved a failure, and the troops will return tired out and disgusted with such service.

On another occasion, a shrewd insurgent leader, profiting from his own knowledge of the practicable places for traversing the swamp, will lure the imprudent troops into the midst of it, where, having carried out a skillful countermarch, the patriot forces will fall on them from the flank and rear. Unable to withstand the onslaught in such conditions, the enemy troops will unfailingly be left submerged in the mire.

The Italian people, encouraged by the successes of the insurgents, will everywhere determine on action for supporting them. They will decide on immediate measures of attack and defense and will not lay down their arms until liberty, equality, unity, and independence for their country are assured. The enemy will be assailed on every side by all classes and with every kind of weapon and will find no protection or security in any part of the peninsula.

Young and old, women and children will share in some way in the liberation and salvation of their country. The whole Italian population will rise against its oppressors.

The spirit of the people, everywhere in sympathy with this sacred cause, will hasten the success of the struggle. Threats or promises will not avail to induce our peasants to betray those who are fighting for them. Nothing will please them more than to see the citizens, armed with guns, pikes, spears, or axes, seeking out the Austrians and their adherents. Indeed, they will feel it a duty to let the patriots know the whereabouts of the Austrians and their comrades, what road one or more Austrians may be expected to take, and where there is a safe hiding place from which to shoot them without risk. They will indicate the best way to escape pursuit by the enemy and the safest road or time for achieving their purpose. Sometimes, at the risk of their own lives, the peasants will save a few patriots by hiding them in their houses.

Those villages in no position to oppose the enemy, and whose inhabitants have not taken refuge in the hills or woods, will greet them in an amicable manner and let them pass. But as soon as the backs of the enemy troops are turned, the villagers will immediately block the roads, break up the bridges, cut off irrigation channels and ditches. Arming themselves with stones, fishing spears, and guns, the villagers will place themselves at doors, windows, and on roofs so that the troops on their return cannot pass through without serious damage to their artillery and baggage and injury to themselves. Finally, the villagers will succeed in instilling panic into the minds of the troops by random, unexpected assaults in places unfamiliar to them.

The whole nation will spontaneously take up arms with the one avowed intention of marching against the country's enemies. All fit men from the ages of sixteen to forty-five will join the insurgent bands or the Italian regular troops. The youngest and oldest, despite their disabilities or lack of strength, will still be able to kill an enemy from the cover of a parapet, rock, door, or window. They will be enrolled in the national guard. In every village, township, or city the national flag will be raised, and round it the people will gather to pledge their support. Their accepted leaders, with help from the mayor, will draw up a general register of all the inhabitants, which will be divided into groups and classified according to age and ability. All will be provided with such weapons as can be had in the circumstances. Each group, depending on its numerical strength and morale, will have an area assigned to it beforehand where it must assemble at the first stroke of the alarm bell, every man coming with victuals for several days. They will then divide into two groups. One will defend the houses, streets, and churches of the city or village, which they will be expected not to leave; the second group will issue forth into the countryside to collaborate with and support the insurgent bands and the patriotic troops operating in the area.

In the towns and fortified cities the inhabitants themselves will defend the ramparts, thus enabling the garrisons to be reduced and more fighting forces to be made available for the country districts. In the streets and town centers the patriot troops will be sustained and encouraged by the sight of the whole populace, well or badly armed and without distinction of class or sex, joining in manning the defenses, unsparing of themselves and performing prodigies of valor. Monks and priests will carry guns and cartridge belts over their cassocks as the volunteers and simple artisans carry them over their belted blouses.

None will be indifferent to the crisis facing the nation. All, young and old, will have their share in achieving success for the great purpose.

## WOMEN

This more delicate and attractive part of the nation will be called upon to assume important and interesting duties both in the early stages of this war and at the moment of mass rising at the height of the revolution. The women must set an example of more than manly strength of mind inspired by ardent love for their Italian fatherland. In those places where revolution has not yet broken out or which unfortunately are occupied by the enemy, they will not take it ill—indeed they will be proud—to be dubbed rebel women. Instead of attending social festivities they will gather at the prisons where their friends and relatives are confined. They will console them and encourage them not to yield to the fury of the tyrant but to remain firm, preferring imprisonment to infamy and death to servitude. They will per-

suade them that the evils they suffer will bear fruit in winning the inestimable blessing of liberty, which is man's birthright. Women will meet secretly
in some friendly house to lament the misfortunes of their country and to
discuss how best to deliver it from the anguish of foreign oppression. Also,
they will exhort and beseech their fathers, husbands, sons, and brothers to
be firm of purpose in not yielding to ill-fortune and in not letting their love
for their families be so strong that they forget what they owe to their country. The women will keep contact with the patriots in the field, letting them
know what happens in their hometown and what people are saying, hoping, or fearing. They will themselves prepare and coordinate the collection
of materials and the enlistment of helpers in disposing of stores. In short,
they will pave the way for a planned uprising and will find ways to entrap
the enemy. In towns where revolutionary warfare is active, great use will
be made of the powerful influence they can exert in rousing young men's
enthusiasm so that they will throw themselves on the enemy and overcome
him, even if he is superior in numbers, arms, and tactical training. They
will stir up the populace against the foreign troops and urge it to defend
itself by barricading or mining the streets and by incendiarism too, if the
moment is opportune. They will bring the wounded into their houses and
give them care and comfort. In fortified places they will help by going up
to the breaches and even to the advanced posts, in fact to wherever there is
need of support for the hard-pressed defenders. Some will tend the fallen;
others will do their utmost to bring them water, wine, and provisions of all
kinds. Altogether, they will share in all the operations of the patriot bands
and their allied forces in defending their homes.

## OLD MEN AND BOYS

At the glad moment when the Italian revolution breaks out, there will be
heard on every hand the noise of arms and the sound of trumpets and
drums. Everywhere men will be seen drilling and learning the use of weapons. Old and young, fathers and sons and women, too, will all be intent on
working for their country, some to learn and others to encourage and give
comfort to the rest.

The old and feeble and those not fit for any active form of service must
be aided by the young in collecting the ingredients necessary for making
gunpowder and the means for supplying it to the combatants. They must
melt lead and use some of it to make bullets and keep the rest to pour on
the enemy when, held up by the barricades in the streets, some may stop
beneath their windows. Other old people will sharpen daggers, clean and
repair guns, sabers, swords, and knives. Others will make spears, pikes,

hayforks, and iron-bound clubs. Old women, boys no more than twelve years old, and young girls can help by collecting victuals and taking them to the fighting men. They can prepare medicaments, dressings, and bandages for the wounded and watch beside them to relieve their needs. Finally, as their chief occupation by day and by night, they will make thousands of cartridges.

## GENERAL COOPERATION

When enthusiasm has become general, then every day and every moment will be marked by some great enterprise impossible in times of peace. Indispensable services of every sort will be rendered to the great advantage of the nation by general cooperation in the country districts. The inhabitants will join in procuring gunpowder and making all kinds of weapons and munitions. Working in isolated buildings, they will hide them skillfully to escape the enemy's vigilance. They will help to transport cannon and carry bullets and other instruments of war past enemy outposts in carts laden with dung and they will carry gunpowder in baskets of fruit, sacks of grain, or other farm produce. Those going to market will hide cartridges in packing cases of candles, and so on.

The peasant, plowing or hoeing his fields, will keep his loaded gun near at hand, covered with straw. When an army unit passes by, he will take no notice or else humbly salute the display of force. But once it is gone, if, owing to an accident or to fatigue or from a wish for diversion, one of the men falls out and stays behind, sure that he can make his way alone, as often happens in armies, the peasant-patriot will cautiously take out his gun and noiselessly move to a wall or hedge where he can lie in ambush until the straggler is within reach and then shoot him. Stripping the body of its equipment, he will hide his booty in one place and the corpse in another and then recharge his gun and calmly return to work.

Carlo Bianco, *Manuale pratico del rivoluzionario italiano* ... (Italy, 1833).

GIUSEPPE MAZZINI

# RULES FOR THE CONDUCT OF GUERRILLA BANDS

G UERRILLA WARFARE MAY BE CONSIDERED as the first stage of a national war. Guerrilla bands should therefore be so organized as to prepare the way for, and facilitate by their action, the formation of a national army.

The general method of organization, the authorization of leaders, the moral and political precepts regulating the conduct of the bands with regard to the country and to individuals should be under the superintendence of a Center of Action, whose duty it will be to ensure the greatest possible amount of uniformity even in their apparently most unconnected movements.

The political mission of the bands is to constitute the armed apostolate of the insurrection. Every band should be a living program of the morality of the party. The most rigorous discipline is at once a duty and a necessity among them. It is a sacred duty toward their country, and a necessity for the bands themselves, which could not long exist if their conduct were such as to deprive them of the sympathy of the people.

Respect for women, for property, for the rights of individuals, and for the crops, should be their motto.

Guerrilla bands are the precursors of the nation, and endeavor to rouse the nation to insurrection. They have no right to substitute themselves for the nation.

To the nation alone belongs the right of declaring its intentions and belief.

Toleration, a consequence of liberty of conscience, is among the first virtues of the republican. The bands are therefore bound to show respect for the churches and symbols of Catholicism, and to the priests, so long as they maintain their neutrality.

The right of compelling expiation, or executing justice upon those guilty in the past, belongs to the nation alone. The bands may not usurp this right. The vengeance of the country must not be entrusted to individuals, be they whom they may.

A commission, elected by the soldiers, and presided over by the captain, will be chosen to watch over and maintain the inviolability of these rules. The names of those soldiers who have either been punished or expelled for disobedience to any of these rules will be forwarded by the captain to the Center of Action for publication at the proper time.

The captain of each band is responsible to the Center of Action for the conduct of his men.

Any captain guilty of dishonorable conduct will be deprived of his commission by the Center of Action, and, if necessary, punished publicly.

When repeated complaints have been made of the collective misconduct of any band, proving it to be unworthy to represent the national cause, it will be immediately disbanded by the Center of Action. Should it disobey the command of the Center of Action, it will be regarded from that time forward as a mere horde of men without flag or mission.

Every band has the right to take measures for its own safety and preservation, and to promote the national insurrection. All acts of aggression or resistance, all information given to the enemy by the country people, and all acts of hostility shown to individual Italians will be speedily and severely punished by the bands.

The bands have a right to live, and it is their duty to increase the forces of the insurrection by adding to the means of the party.

The bands will subsist upon the booty taken from the enemy, treasure seized from the government, forced contributions imposed upon those of the wealthy notoriously adverse to the national cause, and supplies demanded from the provinces through which they pass.

All booty seized is the collective property of the band. It will be distributed either in value or substance, as equally as circumstances permit, among the officers and soldiers, according to the regulations voted by the bands themselves.

All governmental funds seized are the property of the national party. The captain will be responsible for them. He will leave a document with the official in custody of those funds, stating the amount. With regard to forced contributions, the captain will obey the orders of the Center of Action.

Demands and requisitions of victuals should be made as seldom as possible, and they are to be paid for whenever the band possesses the means of paying. When they have no such means, the captain or officer in command making such requisition will sign an acknowledgment of the amount of food received and leave it with the civil authorities of the place. By this means the nation will be enabled, when the war is ended, to note the contributions of each locality.

Whatever monies the captain can dispense with without injury to his band, he will forward to the Center of Action.

The captain will keep an exact account of all the pecuniary transactions of his band. A copy of this account will be audited by the civil commissioner to be employed in all possible cases by the Center of Action, whose duty it will be to watch over the observance of the rules above mentioned.

The bands will make it a general rule to seek to compromise all large cities and avert the vengeance of the enemy from all small localities.

In passing through small and unarmed localities, the captain will rather seek to repress than promote any revolutionary demonstration on the part of the inhabitants. Those patriots who are able to join the bands will enroll themselves as simple individuals and quit the locality.

It will be the aim of every band to increase its numbers, by admitting every possible element into its ranks. But so soon as the band shall have reached the maximum cipher indicated by the Center of Action as constituting a company in the future army, all fresh recruits will be regarded as forming the nucleus of a new band.

The captains of the first bands will naturally be either chosen or recognized by the Center of Action. The vacancies caused among the officers by war will be filled up upon the principle of universal suffrage, exercised progressively, from the ranks up to the captain. The captain of the new band, formed out of the superabundance of recruits joining the former band, will thus be chosen by the captain and officers next in rank belonging to the first band. The organization of each separate band, with a view to the formation of a company in the future army, will in no way interfere with the practical character of their operations as guerrilla bands.

In order to increase the facilities of obtaining subsistence without serious inconvenience to the country, and to enable them more rapidly to disband or conceal themselves, the bands will be divided into small bodies of from twenty-five to fifty men, acting as detachments under the orders of a single commander, and within the territory assigned to his operations.

The uniform of the bands will be a shirt or blouse. In the first period of the war it is perhaps better to avoid all uniform, and content themselves with the national cockade, which can be easily thrown away or hidden in cases where it is necessary abruptly to disband or disappear. A ribbon, or other distinctive mark, not visible at a distance, will be worn by the officers during action. If the blouse be adopted, the color should be the same both for the officers and the men.

The essential weapons are a musket or rifle with a bayonet and a dagger. Each soldier will carry his cartouche box, a case containing bread and spirits, a thin but strong cord, a few nails, and, if possible, a light axe. The clothes worn by the soldiers should be so made as to allow of rapidity of movement, and of a shape not calculated to betray them in case of dispersion.

The signals and commands will be sounded by a horn or trumpet. The following are the most important movements, and therefore those the bands must first be taught to distinguish: (1) assault in the front, (2) on the right, (3) on the left, (4) combined, (5) assault of riflemen, (6) reassembling, (7) retreat.

The noncommissioned officers will employ all leisure moments in drilling the men in the few movements most necessary in guerrilla warfare, teaching them to acquire rapidity in loading and firing, and in dispersing and reassembling.

The principal aim of the bands will be constantly to damage and molest the enemy with the least possible exposure or danger to themselves, to destroy their ammunition and supplies, shake their confidence and discipline, and reduce them to such a condition as will secure their defeat, so soon as the regular army or the united bands are able to give them battle.

The means by which to attain this aim are to attack the enemy as frequently as possible in the flank or rear; to surprise small detachments, escorts, vedettes, outposts, and stragglers; to seize upon their convoys of provisions, ammunition, or money; to interrupt their communications and correspondence by lying in wait for their couriers, destroying the roads, bridges, fords, etc.; to continually break in upon their hours of refreshment and sleep, and seize their generals and superior officers, and so on.

Guerrilla war is a war of judicious daring and audacity, active legs, and espionage.

The captain of a guerrilla band must be able to calculate and plan coolly, execute boldly, march unweariedly, retire rapidly, and keep himself thoroughly informed about the enemy's movements.

In this, as in regular warfare, the great secret is to preserve the means of communication. The possibility of contact and communication between the various detachments of each band, and between the different bands acting in the same province, must be jealously maintained, so as to insure simultaneous action at the decisive moment.

The greatest merit in the commander of regular troops is to know when to fight and conquer; the greatest merit of the guerrilla chief is to contrive constantly to attack, do mischief, and retire.

A band that is surrounded is lost. The retreat must always be left open.

The captain will never command an assault without first assigning a point of reunion for his men in case of dispersion.

The best time for attacking the enemy is at night, during refreshment, or after a long march.

Unless circumstances compel the adoption of a different method, the best mode of attack is for the bands to spread their forces like sharpshooters. The greater the extension of the ground they occupy, the less dangerous will be the enemy's fire.

Country abounding in hedges, forests, or broken ground, affords natural entrenchments for guerrilla bands. The mountains are their fortresses ...

*Life and Writings of Mazzini,* Vol. I (London, 1864).

WOJCIECH CHRZANOWSKI

# THE POLISH EXPERIENCE

HERE IS A BRIEF SUMMARY of the main principles of this type of warfare. A partisan war can of course be waged to great advantage
in hilly country, but it can be waged in flatter terrain too. It can
always be employed with profit in one's country, provided the inhabitants
possess at least sufficient courage to wish to defend themselves and resist
the insults, plundering, and, ultimately, the yoke of their enemy. In inaccessible, difficult terrain, where there are woods, marshes, dikes, gullies, and
ditches, the war can be fought by detachments on foot, just as in mountainous regions. In open, flat country, however, detachments of horse should
be used, the only difference being that entailed by the type of arms used
in each case.

Partisan warfare can succeed in destroying the enemy and forcing him
to quit the country he has invaded only when the size of his army is incom-
mensurate with the area of land he is occupying. Since this is rarely the
case, partisan warfare is most frequently waged in conjunction with the
regular army. Great benefit may be expected from partisan warfare when
it is waged against the enemy's flanks and rear. Any strongholds in the area
still in the hands of the national troops are of the greatest value for this
type of warfare because hard-pressed partisans can find refuge there to
rest after strenuous marches and replenish their supplies of ammunition.
Furthermore, should a corps of the national army be located in the vicinity of such a stronghold, then the detachments of partisans can undertake
bolder and more decisive actions from the very beginning. Finally, partisans are of two kinds: they consist of detachments selected from the main
army or of irregular, independent detachments formed for this one specific
purpose....

Each man in a company of partisans receives a number from a consecutive series and a special name (nom de guerre) under which he is entered in the log book and by which he is known thereafter. The partisan must be sober and cool-headed and no good-for-nothing. The man on foot must be a good marcher and a crack shot; the man on horseback must be a good rider and possess great stamina. The selection of partisans must be carried out as carefully and rigorously as possible. Quality, not quantity, is important; the flower of the nation should not be set alongside its dregs. The selection of officers naturally requires even greater care. They must enjoy a good reputation in the area in which the partisan detachment is being formed. Inquiries into their past conduct are not out of place in time of war. Above all one should guard against accepting officers who have been relieved of their duties at some earlier date because of poor leadership: true courage is grounded in morality. As a last point, it is by no means obligatory to select old soldiers to serve as officers. Among those who led the bands of guerrillas in Spain were doctors and provosts. They were brave, circumspect, and energetic people.

The dress of the local people is the best and simplest clothing for the partisans. Broad leggings and no more than a cockade worn in the hat should serve as an insignia. Officers ought to wear the same dress as their men, with woolen belts denoting their rank. Officers of lower rank can wear woolen braid to make themselves noticed. In a word, each man must be clothed in such a way that if he is forced to scatter, he can readily [hide his weapons and] dispose of his insignia....

Partisan war is of use only if it is of long duration. The two quailties needed for it more than any others are patience and stamina. The chances for the success of partisan war increase with time, for the longer a nation wages this kind of war, the better it grows at it. The longer an enemy army is involved in such a war, the weaker and more disorganized it becomes until it is eventually destroyed. The greatest evil, however, that can befall a nation is its enslavement.

The first exploits of an organized body of partisan troops are decisive for its later success. For this reason, partisans should initially avoid any direct engagement of the enemy and should restrict themselves to such smaller actions as disrupting postal communications at the enemy's rear, ambushing couriers, capturing generals and officials traveling without a proper guard, and picking off individual soldiers. Tactics of this sort force the enemy to protect his communications with numerous garrisons, place all his transports and couriers under escort, and constantly send out large numbers of moving columns (large patrols). This in turn offers the partisans a variety of opportunities for attacking the enemy and provides them with plenty of scope for action. Even if the detachments of partisans are not strong enough to launch direct attacks on enemy positions, they will nevertheless have sufficient men to give such positions a fight and to creep up on vedettes and sentries and kill them. Although seemingly insignificant, small losses of this nature will, if inflicted a hundred times a day, every day, finally be the ruin of any army, no matter how big it is....

Initially partisan groups should attack only isolated enemy soldiers. Success in their activities, however, will soon permit them to undertake actions against single enemy detachments. If later the number of companies in a particular province considerably increases and if both leaders and soldiers have grown accustomed to skirmishing and are sufficiently experienced, then they may even tackle enemy corps of a thousand men. They will still retain their idiosyncratic tactics, seeking as far as possible to destroy the enemy piecemeal. From this tactical principle it follows that partisans must never face an enemy corps en bloc, even when there is equality of numbers; they must spread themselves out in mile-long lines. If the enemy follows suit and divides into lines of similar length, then a few partisan detachments should gather on one flank in order to make an attack on one section of the line with superior forces....

---

Wojciech Chrzanowski: *Ueber den Parteigänger-Krieg*
(Berlin, 1846).

KAROL STOLZMAN

# TERRIFYING FOR THE STRONGEST ENEMY

T HE METHOD CONSIDERED HERE is guerrilla warfare. The Italians waged it in the Middle Ages. They did not appreciate either its power or its subtleties, as the national concept had not yet come into existence. Later the French became acquainted with guerrilla warfare in Calabria. Yet the Italians did not make immediate use of what they had acquired. Subsequent events were conditioned by the considerable cowardice displayed by their great revolutionary leaders, by obsolete prejudices, by the envy displayed by the military aristocracy, and by a naive trust in treaties.

Guerrilla war is truly a people's war; it uses means which are terrifying even for the strongest enemy. From time immemorial it was left exclusively to bandits, who used it for vile purposes. They taught, nevertheless, that it could be used against governments to good effect. The same Italians who took to shameful flight as a result of waging war by orthodox methods later gained renown in Spain as brave guerrilla fighters.

The efficacy of guerrilla warfare lies in the fact that it satisfies simultaneously both material and moral needs—two things which ought never be separated if good results are to be reaped from one's endeavor.

With regard to the material aspect, the people who rise in arms contribute maximum resources into the fight against the enemy. Thus, from their point of view this is the very best type of warfare because it makes the best use of these resources in a way most suited to their nature. The most advantageous war is the one which can be reinforced by the greatest amount of resources while forcing the enemy to use the maximum of his own forces. In such a war the result of a defeat is less decisive, but victories do not lose importance.

These are the conditions which are suited for guerrilla warfare. It is a war which points a way to activity and glory to anyone who feels he is strong enough, making him a creator and king in his realm. This kind of war gives rise to countless reasons for solidarity between one province and another, one district and another, and one man and another. It leaves room for personal talent, arouses the nation from its lethargy, and both cultivates and channels a feeling of independence so prejudicial to action in orthodox warfare. Yet such a war does not in the least hinder anyone who prefers the orthodox method and wants to join the national army. It helps, however, to bring out the most talented among the masses, those who desire to throw off as soon as possible their shameful shackles and who do not possess the knowledge of the art of war but are uneasy only because they want to move. Yet without steering, they will inevitably become a turbulent gang highly dangerous to the cause. Everyone will be glad to be of use whenever offered the chance if he is certain that his deeds, not mixed with the deeds of thousands, will bring him glory and profit. As far as the aim is concerned, the only choice that remains is the one between the banner of tyranny or a bandit's disgusting name and the national flag seized by brave men who gladly rally under the latter in order to satisfy their inborn' instinct of freedom. The people crave for action; let us provide them with a purpose. If we open a path toward it, the people will go on this path. In Spain, after the word was given, many people whose torpor infected the whole country and who were arms smugglers by trade became the terror of the French. Now they are included among the most ardent protagonists of the holy cause.

Our last uprising, designed to wage war the way it is being waged among great powers, has left inactive forces which have succumbed to lethargy, one from which a single word could wake them. They have renounced their intrinsic nature and have faded. Sentiments of hatred and vengeance were doomed to be eroded by the maledictions and inaction of the cold, diplomatic, and vague language of a government which only derisively could be called a revolutionary government. How advantageous could be the use of these sentiments so common in our country had they been used in the war? But this government did the the very opposite—it rejected those sentiments and gave orders to calm them down. How different would have been the results of the people's general enthusiasm which at that time was doomed to inaction because there was no room for it in the regular army. If only the then leaders had made the nation aware of its own power, acquainted it with war, which—instead of drill, study, military equipment, and slavish submissiveness—requires only enthusiasm, strong hands and feet, knowledge of localities, cunning, and sharpness of wit. Had they disseminated in all the appropriate places proclamations and general outlines of guerrilla warfare, had only a certain number of military veterans put themselves at the head of the youths who were ready to respond to any sign from them, had the banner of insurrection fluttered in the villages and been struck on the towers of the parish churches, matters would have been different.

Let us not seek examples from among other nations. Let us consider the Confederation of Bar.[1] It succeeded in maintaining its action for six years because it fought its battles according to the system of guerrilla warfare. But for the important fact that it was conducted solely by the gentry (*szlachta*), who did not call on the mass of population for support, it would have undoubtedly blocked, perhaps forever, the frontiers of Poland to the invader. The Russians used to compare this confederation to a hydra, that mythological, many-headed serpent whose heads, when cut off, were replaced by two others.

The Circassians, who to this very day fight successfully against the Muscovite army, are further proof that even the smallest nation can successfully resist the strongest enemy if guerrilla warfare is chosen as the basis of its resistance. The glorious deeds of Ziska, that great hero of the Czechs, and the fight of the Serbs for independence which was waged from 1804 until 1813 are the strongest arguments in favor of guerrilla warfare. They are proof that it is the only war for the people.

Indeed, guerrilla warfare, whose center is everywhere and whose range of activity is unlimited, is the most appropriate and effective war for a people rising in arms. It is for this reason that we can call it a popular war. There is no treason which could instantly extinguish it, as so often—almost always—happens in the case of orthodox warfare. The conquest of the capital by the enemy does not decide the fate of the uprising. No military action can thus ensure a decisive victory for the enemy. A regular army is rarely capable of resisting an enemy invasion—as our history teaches us. The converse is also true. What invasion would be powerful enough against a whole nation? There is no organization of the army of old which could prevent it dispersing its forces in order to lay siege to numerous guerrilla strong points. How can one reach an adversary and fight him when the adversary suddenly divides his forces into small mobile columns, scatters his forces in all directions (amidst natural obstacles, for instance) and slips away in small groups within the compass of the range of action taking place? More concretely, how can one reach a detachment operating within a mountain range or situated among the numerous rivers, lakes, and swamps in which Poland abounds,

---

1 "Confederation of Bar" was a patriotic Polish uprising against the Russians to prevent the partition of Poland.

or located in such extensive forests, like the forest of Biaowieza? How can one cut off their lines of communication when the number of points through which the rebel units could slip is countless?

What army would have to be used by the enemy to lie in wait for all of them? A regular army against which the rebels are waging war would have to advance on a two-pronged front and would either have to disperse its forces or concentrate them in order to occupy a certain area of the country. It is in this area, there and then, that the guerrillas would sting them by frontal attacks as well as by attacks from the rear and flanks. Or the enemy might have to disperse his forces so widely as to be incapable of manning every one of the thousands of positions suitable for offensive actions. It is there that the enemy might be attacked by forces stronger than his own. Thus, the regular forces would be forced into both defensive and offensive actions.

The impending revolution in Poland must be, in accordance with the spirit and strivings of this age, a people's revolution, not a revolution of privileged factions, military or civil. Therefore, the banner which has to lead the Polish insurrection ought to be dedicated to the people. Then the people will reveal themselves in their greatness.

But in order to achieve this, the people have to be emanicipated. They have to be enlisted. One has to entrust the fate of the homeland to their its hands. One also has to make the people aware of their own might and to convince it that no power in the world will be capable of crushing this might against its will.

This might has to be instructed in the methods of military activities. It has to become the embodiment of revolutionary thought. Thus, the people will be ordered to buy with their own blood both the right and independence of free men. This sacrifice will teach the people to live it and to keep it pure. This war will give birth to strength, trust, and free education for the people because struggle tempers nations and rebellion wipes out the stigma of bondage from the rebels' brows. Guerrilla warfare causes minds to adapt themselves to independence and to an active and heroic life. It makes nations great.

When every Pole has a heritage to defend and to pass on to his descendants when every inch of Polish soil becomes famed for heroic deeds and when our cornfields become consecrated with the bones of our brave men mingled with the bones of the invaders, who will dare to foul and violate this consecrated space? Which hated home or foreign power will venture to establish compounds of oppression or usurper camps on those fields on which the great deed of liberation has created a truly free nation which by means of an experience both sublime and triumphant has gained the knowledge of its own strength and of its right, not lost by prescription but given to it by the Creator? ...

We say once again to our fellow countrymen: do not look at the French because they have no need as urgent and as sacred as ours to rise in arms. It would, however, be a deadly sin to wait with folded arms for foreign help when our own strength is sufficient. To do so would mean that we were unable to appreciate our strength and that we sinned against the sacred mission Providence has imposed on every nation as part of mankind. Anyone who causes the sacred deed of liberation to depend on either chance or circumstance offends the sanctity of this deed and impresses the stigma of shame on his brow.

Let us not await events. Let the nobleman and the peasant join hands since all are Poles created by the same God and in His image. Above all, do not stand idly by and await with folded arms the fulfillment of the prophecy that the Turks will water their horses in the Vistula in order to achieve our redemption. Instead, make the greatest possible effort to ensure that our own cavalry horses should be able to taste the waters of our Polish rivers—the Niemen, the Dnieper, the Dniester, the estuary of the Warta, and the sources of the Vistula.

To arms, then, brothers. The future is ours.

---

Karol Stolzman, *Partyzanka czyli wojna dla ludow powstajacych najwlasciwsza* (Paris, 1844).

## ANTOINE-FORTUNE DE BRACK

# A HAZARDOUS PROFESSION

Q. What is the meaning of partisan?

A. A detachment is in partisan when it operates detached and isolated from the army, and under the genius of its leader, which is not controlled except by orders given in a general manner, and by the indications of the combined movements of the army.

A partisan is sent to raise a province; to harass the flanks and rear of the enemy's army; to carry off or destroy depots, convoys, etc.; to make prisoners; and sometimes to deceive the enemy as to the movements of our army.

Q. What is the first care of an officer directed to carry on partisan warfare?

A. It is to be scrupulously careful that the detachment which he commands is composed of bold and well-mounted troopers.

Q. And the second?

A. To receive from his general an accurate map of the country that is the locale of his operations as correct information as is procurable regarding the dispositions of the enemy, and the plans which he is supposed to have formed; and further to have an eye upon the present and future movements of our different *corps d' armee.*

Q. Why should he care about this last, when he is acting independently?

A. In order to know whither he should send his reports and to find a support to his retreat, should he find himself hard-pressed.

The profession of a partisan is a hazardous one. It can only be properly followed out by a skillful, rapid, and bold leader—and by a body of men resembling him. No more rest for the partisan; he ought always to have his eyes open, and if fatigue compels him to snatch a momentary slumber, it is necessary that an advanced line of spies should watch over and warn him.

The war, which he carries on, is piratical. The strength of his warfare lies in surprise. The kite unperceived, which makes a sudden swoop at its prey, bears it off, and vanishes, is the image of the partisan! Let him then inflict a decided, prompt, and, if necessary, even terrible, blow; and let no traces point out his retreat.

Every stratagem of war is at the disposal of the partisan. Let him combine his attack so judiciously, and fling his lasso so accurately around the enemy, whom he surprises, that not an individual can escape to give the alarm.

Such a one in an enemy's country maneuvers with the enemy, levies in his name contributions of clothing and horses, and fresh clothes, and re-mounts his detachment at the expense of the King of Prussia.

Such another strips his prisoners, clothes his men in their uniforms, and enters the unsuspecting bivouacs of the enemy, whom he surprises and cuts to pieces.

Another one, at twenty leagues in rear of the Russian army, recaptures our prisoners, whom he mounts upon the horses of their escort, and thus doubles his force.

Such another carries off a park of artillery. The enemy, informed of it, hastens up two hours afterward, and by the time that he reaches the smol-dering remains of his blown-up wagons, the partisan deals a blow equally severe three leagues to his rear.

The enemy, utterly ignorant of the numerical force of this daring band, halts, takes up a position, and forms those detachments in mass, which would have been a splendid reinforcement to his own army, and ours prof-its by the delay.

Such another, lastly, like the brave and illustrious Pole Uminski, at the head of a few squadrons, penetrates through the enemy's army, raises a province, makes a powerful diversion, and, after several victories, when compelled to retreat, rejoins the national army with his forces trebled.

The partisan, owing to the isolation in which he is placed and to his not being compelled to march immediately in such or such a direction—or to retire upon a certain point—is not trammeled or fettered in any way. He is master of the whole country which his eye takes in. Let him survey it with no ordinary intelligence, and let him conceive it in his imagination, not so much as viewed from the spot where he stands, as from the point of view of the enemy. Thus, let him calculate the hollows, the heights, the natural screens, in their connection with this point of view, and let him always post himself in such a manner as to intercept by these screens the visual ray which the enemy might direct toward him.

If he descend by this path, the rising ground on his right will conceal his movements. If he traverse the plain in that direction, the little wood, which is to be seen on his left, will mask his march for the next ten minutes, and these ten minutes will be sufficient to enable him to gain the ravine, in which he may conceal himself.

The partisan, acting only by surprise, takes up offensive positions which are invariably ambuscades. The closer they are to the point of attack, the better. But it is requisite that this proximity should always be calculated with reference to the greater or less confidence and vigilance of the enemy.

The partisan, after having boldly swept off a convoy, commences his retreat. It is necessary that this retreat should be prompt, for the enemy may receive intelligence and pursue with superior forces. He therefore compares the importance and the possibility of preserving the prize, which he has captured, with that of the attack which he may have to sustain, and of the rapidity with which he is obliged to make his retreat. This rapid comparison will cause him to destroy everything which would danger-ously retard him, and he retreats, not by the road, which he has followed in gaining the spot, but by that which contracts the distance that he will have to travel over in order to gain a place of safety. The undulations of the ground, the woods, the ravines, mask his retreat, and he does not halt until after he has been some hours on the road. He is aware that the pursuit of the enemy is never pushed beyond a certain distance, and that the further it is carried, the more languid and less dangerous it becomes, especially if the pursuers are led by the pursued over a difficult and intersected country, causing apprehensions of ambuscades.

If, however, the pursuing enemy appears at some distance and threatens to attack briskly and powerfully, the partisan does not hesitate to put him on a wrong scent. He makes the convoy file off under an officer, whom he enjoins to proceed rapidly, and, in the case of being attacked, to abandon everything which he deems it impossible to save. Then, with the bulk of his convoy, he proceeds either to the right or left, draws the misled enemy in that direction, whom he thus carries to a distance from his object.

A partisan, knocked out with long-continued duties, and who needs repose, ought either to gain one of our posts, situated at the rear of the enemy, and which is not invested by the enemy, or to throw himself sud-denly beyond the line of his operations. In general, this line, is confined to some roads, held by detachments on their way to rejoin, and patrolled to very short distances.

The partisan has, then, only a few leagues to traverse to place himself in safety. Nevertheless, in order to render this security more complete, he frequently changes his position.

If the partisan has some sick and wounded, he carries them along with him, and is lavish of his care of them. If the diseases or wounds are too severe to admit of the men laboring under them keeping up with him without retarding his rapid marches, he places them in the villages and entrusts them to men of mark upon their personal responsibility.

If the partisan has taken made prisoners, in order not to weaken his strength, he confides the care of them, in a friendly country, to the care of the national rural guards, who take them to our army by roundabout ways.

If the partisan has captured guns and cannot convey them in safety to our army, he buries them privately, and especially out of view of his prisoners, in a wood seldom frequented, and marks the spot where they are concealed. He then carries off the limbers* with him, which he destroys at some leagues farther off; thus the place of concealment is entirely unknown.

As a general rule, as the partisans ought to be in the highest state of mobility, they should retain nothing with them that can retard or encumber their march.

---

Antoine-Fortune de Brack, from *Advanced Posts of Light Cavalry* (London, 1850).

---

* A two-wheeled vehicle for which a gun or caisson may be attached.

# Partisan Warfare
# 1860–1938

# INTRODUCTORY NOTE

T HIS SECTION COVERS THE PERIOD between the American Civil War and
the outbreak of World War II. During that time the study of guerrilla war was not part of the curriculum of the military academies
despite the fact that European armies were engaged in many colonial wars
and partisans frequently played important roles in major wars. This certainly holds true with regard to the Civil War, the Franco-Prussian War,
the Boer War, and also, to a lesser degree, World War I. But it is also true
that victory in all these wars went to the stronger battalions, the overall outcomes being determined in massive battles between vast armies.
Military thinkers were almost exclusively concerned with issues such as
*Vernichtungsschlacht, Blitzkrieg,* and later with tank warfare and airpower.
The new weapons seemed to tip the balance even further against guerrilla
warfare. Political theory and military doctrine, "bourgeois" and Leninist
alike, accorded to guerrilla warfare only a limited role. Guerrilla warfare,
almost by definition, could succeed only if the internal or external enemy
was weak and if it was conducted within the framework of a prolonged
general war. The guerrillas could hope to challenge regular armies only
in certain exceptional conditions which rarely existed during the period
under review. Propitious conditions arose when the colonial powers collapsed during World War II. Neither was there pronounced interest in
guerrilla war among revolutionary leaders; indeed, guerrilla tactics were
used more frequently by the extreme right than the left during the Russian
civil war and elsewhere in Europe during the interwar period.

There were, nevertheless, some military experts who believed that it
was premature to write off guerrilla warfare altogether. Among these was
Friedrich Wilhelm Rüstow (1821–1878), one of the most original and
prolific (as well as controversial) German military writers of the period.
A radical democrat, he left Germany after the defeat of the revolution of
1848, served as Garibaldi's chief of staff, and settled in Switzerland where
he was the first professor of military science at the Zurich Polytechnic. His
*Die Lehre vom kleinen Krieg* was published in Zurich in 1864.

Francis Lieber (1800-1872) was another political émigré from Germany. Arrested as a liberal in his native country, he volunteered to fight in the Greek War of Independence and subsequently emigrated to the United States. He was editor of the *Encyclopaedia Americana* and in 1835 became professor of history and political economy at South Carolina College. In 1856 he accepted an appointment to the Columbia Law School. During the Civil War he was asked by the United States government to provide legal advice. One of his papers, "Guerrilla Parties, Considered with Reference to the Laws and Usages of War," is quoted in the present volume. Albrecht von Boguslawski (1834–1905) was a colonel (subsequently lieutenant-general) in the German army when his *Der kleine Krieg und seine Bedeutung für die Gegenwart* (Berlin, 1881) was published. He was also the author of a history of the war in the Vendee which is of considerable interest in the guerrilla context.

Karl Hron was an officer in the Austro-Hungarian army and later became a newspaper editor and writer on the topic of European and Oriental politics.

Charles Callwell (1859–1928) is the author of *Small Wars* (London, 1899). An artillery captain by training, he had been seconded to intelligence. He saw action in Afghanistan and South Africa but resigned from the army when he was passed over for promotion—apparently as the result of the publication of his indiscreet literary "Sketches from Military Life." Callwell was recalled to duty in 1914, became chief of operations in the War Office, and was promoted to major-general and then knighted. T. Miller Maguire (1849–1920) was a barrister and a successful army "coach" who lectured and wrote about strategy and great campaigns. Among his students were Allenby and Gough. He is the author of *Guerrilla or Partisan Warfare* (London, 1904).

Thomas Edward Lawrence (1888-1935) needs no introduction. The present excerpt is reprinted by permission of *Encyclopaedia Britannica,* 14th edition (1929).

Arthur Ehrhardt (1895-1971) was one of the very few German authors of the twentieth century to comment on guerrilla war. He was a lieutenant in the World War I and a captain with the *Abwehr* in World War II. A publisher in civilian life with apparently no pronounced political views before 1945, he became editor-in-chief of *Nation-Europa,* a monthly journal of the extreme right.

"Notes on Guerrilla Warfare" by Lieutenant T. H. C. Frankland of the Royal Dublin Fusiliers was published in the *United Service Magazine,* Vol. 33 (1912); Major Harold H. Utley's "An Introduction to the Tactics and Techniques of Small Wars" appeared in the *Marine Corps Gazette* of May

1931. They are reprinted here with the permission of the publishers. These articles are of interest because, early on, they drew attention to certain aspects of guerrilla warfare that became common knowledge only several decades later. Thus Frankland noted that the absence of civilization afforded great openings for to guerrilla warfare.

B. C. Dening stressed that modern guerrilla war would aim at draining the financial rather than the military resources of the Great Powers. Major Harold Utley, an American, emphasized the importance of Congress and domestic public opinion: "In small wars we are at peace no matter how thickly the bullets are flying..." In short, guerrilla warfare meant that the hands of the military would be tied.

FRANCIS LIEBER

# GUERRILLAS IN INTERNATIONAL LAW

T HE TERM "GUERRILLA" IS DIMINUTIVE of the Spanish word *guerra*, war, and means "petty war", that is, war carried on by detached parties generally in the mountains. Further, it means a party of men united under one chief engaged in petty war, which, in eastern Europe and the Levant is called a "captainry", a band under one *capitano*. The term guerrilla, however, is not applied in Spain to individual members of the party. Each is called a *guerrillero'* or, more frequently, a *partida,* which means partisan. Thus Nappier, in speaking of the guerrilla in his *History of the Peninsular War*, uses with rare exception the term *partidas* for the chiefs and men engaged in the petty war against the French. The dictionary of the Spanish academy gives as the first meaning of the word guerrilla, "a party of light troops for reconnaissance, and opening the first skirmishes." I translate from an edition of 1826, published long after the Peninsular War, since which the term guerrilla has passed into many other European languages. Self-constitution is not a necessary element of the meaning given by the Spaniards or by many writers of other nations to the word guerrilla, although it is true that the guerrilla parties in the Peninsular War were nearly all self-constituted, since the old government had been destroyed, and the forces which had been called into existence by the provisional government were no more acknowledged by the French as regular troops than were the self-constituted bands under leading priests, lawyers, smugglers, or peasants because the French did not acknowledge the provisional junta or *cortes.* Many of the *guerrilleros* were shot when made prisoners, and the guerrilla chiefs executed French prisoners in turn. It is the state of things, which the existence of these bands almost always leads to, due to their inherent character. Yet, when the *partidas* of Mina and Empecinado had swelled to the imposing number of twenty thousand and more, which fact of itself implies a degree of discipline, Mina made a regular treaty with the French for the passage of certain French goods through the lines. On these the partisan leader levied regular duties according to a tariff agreed upon by the belligerents.

What, then, do we in the present time understand by the word guerrilla? In order to ascertain the law or to settle it according to elements already existing, it will be necessary ultimately to give a distinct definition. Whatever may be our final definition, it is universally understood in this country that a guerrilla party means an irregular band of armed men carrying on an irregular war which is not able, according to its character as a guerrilla party, to carry on what the law terms a regular war. The irregularity of the guerrilla party consists in its origin, for it is either self-constituted or constituted by the call of a single individual, and not according to the general law of levy, conscription, or volunteering. It consists in its disconnection from the army as to its pay, provision, and movements. And it is irregular as to its permanency: it may be dismissed and called together again at any time. These are the constituent ideas of the term guerrilla as now used. Other ideas are associated with the term differently by different persons. Thus, many persons associate the idea of pillage with the guerrilla band because, not being connected with the regular army, the men cannot provide for themselves except by pillage, even in their own country. (Spanish *guerrilleros* sorely afflicted their own countrymen in the Peninsular War with acts of violence.) Others connect with it the idea of intentional destruction for the sake of destruction because the guerrilla chief cannot aim at any strategic advantages or any regular fruits of victory. Others, again, associate with it the idea of danger with which the spy surrounds us because he that today passes you in the garb and mien of a peaceful citizen may tomorrow, as a guerrilla man, set fire to your house or murder you from behind a hedge. Others connect with the *guerrillero* the idea of necessitated murder because guerrilla bands cannot encumber themselves with prisoners of war. They have, therefore, frequently (perhaps generally) killed their prisoners and of course have been killed in turn when made prisoners, thus introducing a system of barbarity which becomes more intense in its demoralization as it spreads and is prolonged. Others, again, connect the ideas of general and heinous criminality, robbery, and lust with the term because the organization of the party being but slight and the leader being utterly dependent upon the band, little discipline can be enforced. And where no discipline is enforced in war, a state of things results which resembles far more the wars recorded in Froissart or Comines, the Thirty Years' War, or the Religious War in France than the regular wars of modern times. And such a state of things results speedily, too; for all growth, progress, and rearing, moral or material, is slow; and all destruction, relapse, and degeneracy, fearfully rapid.

It does not seem that, in the case of a rising en masse, the absence of a uniform can constitute a difference. There are cases, indeed, in which the absence of a uniform may be taken as very serious prima facie evidence against an armed prowler or marauder, but it must be remembered that a uniform dress is a matter of impossibility in a levy en masse; and in some cases regulars have not had uniforms for at least a considerable time. The Southern prisoners at Fort Donelson had no uniform. They were indeed dressed very much alike, but theirs was the uniform dress of the country-man in that region. Yet they were treated by us as prisoners of war, and well treated, too.

Nor would it be difficult to adopt something of a badge, easily put on and off, and to call it a uniform. It makes a great difference, however, whether the absence of a uniform is used for the purpose of concealment or disguise in order to get by stealth within the lines of the invader for destruction of life and property or for pillage and whether the parties have no organization at all and are so small that they cannot act otherwise than by stealth. Nor can it be maintained in good faith, or with any respect for sound sense and judgment, that an individual—an armed prowler (now frequently called a bushwhacker)—shall be entitled to the protection of the law of war simply because he says that he has taken up his gun in defense of his country or because his government or his chief has issued a proclamation by which he calls upon the people to infest the bushes and commit homicides which every civilized nation will consider murders. Indeed, the importance of writing on this subject is much diminished by the fact that the soldier generally decides these cases for himself. The most disciplined soldiers will execute on the spot an armed and murderous prowler found where he could have no business as a peaceful citizen. Even an enemy in the uniform of the hostile army would stand little chance of protection if found prowling near the opposing army, separate from his own troops at a greater than picket distance and under generally suspicious circumstances. The chance would, of course, be far less if the prowler was in the common dress worn by the countrymen of the district. It may be added here that a person proved to be a regular soldier of the enemy's army and found in citizen's dress within the lines of the captor is universally dealt with as a spy.

It has been stated that the word guerrilla is not only used for individuals engaged in petty war but frequently for an equivalent of the partisan. General Halleck, in his *International Law, or Rules Regulating the Inter-*

*course of States in Peace and War* (San Francisco, 1861), seems to consider partisan troops and guerrilla troops as the same and seems to consider "self-constitution" a characteristic of the partisan. Other legal and military writers define partisan as I have stated—namely, as a soldier belonging to a corps which operates in the manner given above.

If the term "partisan" is used in the sense in which I have defined it, it is not necessary to treat of it specially. The partisan, in this sense, is, of course, answerable for the commission of those acts for which the law of war grants no protection and by which the soldier forfeits being treated as a prisoner of war, if captured.

It is different if we understand by guerrilla parties self-constituted sets of armed men in times of war who form no integral part of the organized army, do not stand on the regular payroll of the army, or are not paid at all, who take up arms and lay them down at intervals and carry on petty war (guerrilla) chiefly by raids, extortion, destruction, and massacre—and who cannot encumber themselves with many prisoners and will therefore generally give no quarter.

They are peculiarly dangerous because they easily evade pursuit and by laying down their arms become insidious enemies. Because they cannot otherwise subsist than by rapine and they almost always degenerate into simple robbers or brigands. The Spanish guerrilla bands against Napoleon proved a scourge to their own countrymen and became efficient for their own cause only in the same degree in which they gradually became disciplined.

But when guerrilla parties aid the main army of a belligerent, it will be difficult for the captor of guerrilla men to decide at once whether they are regular partisans distinctly authorized by their own government. This contention would seem to be borne out by the conduct of the most humane belligerents in recent times and by many of the modern writers if the rule be laid down that guerrilla men, when captured in a fair fight and open warfare, should be treated as the regular partisan is until special crimes such as murder, the killing of prisoners, or the sacking of places are proved upon them, leaving the question of self-constitution unexamined.

The law of war, however, would not extend a similar favor to small bodies of armed country people near the lines whose very smallness shows that they must resort to occasional fighting, the occasional assuming of peaceful habits, and to brigandage. The law of war would still less favor them when they trespass within hostile lines to commit devastation, rapine, or destruction. Every European army has treated such persons and, it seems to me, would continue—even in the improved state of the present usages of war—to treat them as brigands, whatever prudential mercy might be decided upon in single cases. This latter consideration cannot be discussed here because it does not pertain to the law of war.

It has been stated already that the armed prowler, the so-called bush-whacker, is a simple assassin and will thus always be considered by soldier and citizen. We have likewise seen that the armed bands that rise in a district fairly occupied by military force or at the rear of an army are universally considered brigands, if captured, and not prisoners of war. They unite the fourfold character of the spy, brigand, assassin, and rebel, and cannot—indeed, it must be supposed, will not—expect to be treated as a fair enemy of the regular war. They know what a hazardous career they enter upon when they take up arms and that, were the case reversed, they would surely not grant the privileges of regular warfare to persons who should thus rise at their rear.

KARL HRON

# PARTISANS IN THE AUSTRIAN MIRROR

IT WOULD BE UNJUST to accuse present-day writings on military science of a poverty of ideas, but it is certainly fair to say that they are monotonous; they treat only of masses and the use of masses. And not without reason, for with the advent of vast armies military leadership has become not only a duller but also a weightier matter. In the scales of the final outcome, isolated exploits are as light as a feather when balanced against such weight. Furthermore, if one considers the rapid development of those branches of technology such as railways, the telegraph (and, in future, the air-balloon), which military science has appropriated for its own uses and which help shorten wars, then it seems natural that the small war should be disappearing under the shadow of its big brother. Yet it has not entirely withered away, and it may be longer in dying than one might otherwise think.

In times gone by, the small war was a highly respected branch of warfare and the subject of a sizable number of military treatises. There was scarcely a campaign that was not planned in close conjunction with an intensive "small war" waged by one's "light troops" who hung doggedly at the enemy's heels and harried him with needle-pricks and stabs of the dagger until the sword of actual battle was drawn. The tasks carried out nowadays by our autonomous advanced cavalry divisions—reconnoitering, preventing the enemy from gaining information about one's circumstances, and covering areas removed from the main theater of operations—fell at that time to the light troops and was part of the small war. Indeed, they did more; they roved about at the enemy's rear, harassed his communications, threatened his depots, captured his supplies, and overpowered important positions in daring surprise attacks.

The golden age of the small war was in the days when armies were still small but had to cover theaters of operations the same size as those the mighty columns of our armies fill today. To avoid the nucleus of the army, the striking force proper, being dissipated over large areas and to protect it against surprise enemy raids, the general command unleashed the pack of light troops to encircle the enemy on all sides and to ensure that the main force was left in peace.

Nowadays we are presented with a somewhat different picture. A half million soldiers concentrated in a small space sleep peacefully wherever they are. Larger disturbances than pistol shots are needed to wake them up and unsettle them today. The value of the light troops and their activities has therefore suffered some depreciation over the years as far as army movements over large areas are concerned. But as I said, their death knell has not yet sounded, least of all here in Austria, for in the occupied areas and farther south, and likewise in the Tyrol and the Siebenburg Carpathians, we shall never be able to wage anything but a small war. Moreover, our Russian neighbors also set great store by the small war, as is sufficiently proved by the way they arm and train their cavalry. This cavalry is developing into a partisan troop par excellence.

The waging of partisan warfare comprises an infinite variety of tasks. Generally speaking, the partisans are to the main body of the army what the hounds are to the hunter. They smell out the enemy and stick to his trail; whenever possible, they get their teeth into him and tug at him. They drop back if he really shows his teeth, only to move up on him again at the next favorable opportunity. They surround the enemy's troops on every side and watch his every move; they hamper his freedom of movement as much as their strength allows and at the same time conceal their own forces' movements. They never recklessly risk their own necks, and while they do not refuse a fight, they are extremely careful not to deliver themselves into the enemy's hands.

They must pester and unsettle the enemy, wear him down and drive him to distraction with a continuous succession of tricks and ruses so that, without any decisive battle being fought, he is actually weakened for the decisive battle to come. By making a great clamor at a spot far removed from the scene of the main action, they will often be able to lure him into sending off detachments of troops, thus weakening his main striking force. Conversely, because of their mobility, they will be able to slow down the enemy's advance to distant areas of operations and relieve their side's main force of the responsibility for the security of these areas and thus keep that force intact.

The partisans will dog the heels of a defeated enemy and harry him as long as possible until he can be routed completely. In the case of a victorious enemy, on the other hand, they will do everything they can to slow down or halt his advance. They will set traps and threaten him on his flanks or at his rear so that their own defeated forces can gain time to recover. It may well be that at times when the military situation is going against their own forces they will prove themselves most invaluable, for, in Schiller's words: "All around must be night when Friedland's star is shining." The same is true of the partisan's star of honor.

General R.v.L. says in one of his books that when partisan warfare truly lives up to its name, it is the finest flower of all the departments of the small war. In his view, the lot of the partisan is an enviable one, as indeed it is when the partisan stands at the head of fine, courageous troops prepared to undertake anything and when his general bestows upon him a trust that allows him complete freedom and even some latitude for personal caprice. The partisan must be in part a born military genius, and genius needs freedom if it is to stretch its wings to the full.

"That which is exceptional in life acknowledges no rules, submits to no coercion; it knows no law or virtue but its own; it cannot be measured by an earthly measure nor bound by earthly limitations," as Korner says.

---

Karl Hron, *Der Parteigänger-Krieg* (Vienna, 1885).

FRIEDRICH WILHELM RÜSTOW

# PEOPLE'S WAR AND MOBILE WARFARE

L ET US NOW TURN TO THE QUESTION of the particular ways in which those resources characteristic of small war are to be exploited. The paucity of resources available will often lead to the use of naked force customary in large-scale warfare being replaced—or at least supplemented—by *cunning, deception,* and *surprise,* for which small war offers much greater opportunity. As mobile troops enjoy much greater scope for the application of such methods than do stationary troops and as mobility enhances one's strength of arms, small wars will tend to involve more movement than large-scale wars, even when the fighting is restricted to a very small area.

As we might expect, the deliberate confrontation with the enemy characteristic of large wars is more seldom sought here. Should circumstances be especially favorable, then the fighting should take the form of a violent charge, preceded by a surprise attack or ambush. But just as often delaying tactics will be required, particularly in small wars involving security troops which are, after all, primarily intended as preparation for larger engagements and battles. Partly because they always try to turn the particular terrain to their advantage, partly because the fighting in small wars only ever involves small numbers, the troops waging such wars will always seek to engage the enemy in places where they can impose their own character on the fighting.

A troop dispatched to a secondary theater of war to carry out this or that task may, circumstances permitting, regard itself as nothing more than the nucleus of a fighting force to be drawn from among the local population if this secondary theater is located on the troops' own soil or in allied territory. These local reinforcements may be organized in one of two ways. The first alternative is to create by voluntary recruitment or conscription new *mobile* battalions and squadrons from among the local inhabitants which then are welded onto the nucleus of regular troops. The second is to have the local population remain in their homes ready, when the moment arrives, to rise up as a local militia and wreak all manner of destruction on the enemy without, however, remaining continually under arms and without following the movements of the mobile nucleus of troops. This second alternative represents a true people's war, a type of war which has always proven ruinous to conquering armies when they have encountered freedom-loving peoples and which, for this reason, has been so heartily cursed by such armies and their allies who have coined a variety of terms, all equally unpleasant, for this kind of war and those who wage it ...

In general one should create small tactical units, for this enables one to keep a greater number of units in the field at any one time and also to mislead the enemy about the true strength of one's forces. Moreover, untrained officers, without whom it is almost impossible to get by in such circumstances, will not have too great a responsibility thrust upon them. There is a further consideration. It may be possible to supplement one's forces from among the inhabitants of the country in which the small war is to be waged.

If the situation allows, it is a great help if the new recruits can be integrated into already existing units, for there they will develop more rapidly into soldiers than if each time separate new tactical units were to be formed. If the units were very large from the outset, the addition of any new recruits would render them unmanageable.

On occasions, it is true, this policy of integrating local recruits into old units may meet with special difficulties. In 1860, for instance, when Garibaldi was advancing through Sicily and Calabria, there appeared wherever the Neapolitan troops had retreated, individuals of standing in their particular area who—often before a nucleus of Garibaldi's troops had arrived—began to assemble bands of partisans who themselves, however, were only interested in serving under these leaders. These partisans then had to be placed alongside the nucleus as *special* battalions. This arrangement did not benefit the cause as a whole, for as soon as the fighting or the advance had passed beyond their part of the country, these new battalions shrank dramatically. Nor did they, due to the rapidity with which the campaign developed, ever attain the standard of discipline of the old battalions and those from northern Italy, in which ranks the forces which had been recruited (where circumstances allowed) from among the local population quickly became accustomed to military organization and discipline....

---

Friedrich Wilhelm Rüstow, *Die Lehre vom kleinen Krieg*
(Zurich, 1864).

CHARLES CALLWELL

# THE DANGERS OF GUERRILLA WARFARE—1900

IT MAY BE ACCEPTED AS A GENERAL RULE that guerrilla warfare is the most unfavorable shape which a campaign can take for the regular troops. At surprises and ambushes, at petty skirmishes, at attacks on detached parties, and at cutting off stragglers, the enemy is usually adept. Intimate acquaintance with the terrain, natural agility, cunning, and the warlike instinct which is natural in races where security of life and property does not exist, all combine to make antagonists of this kind formidable when hostilities are confined to operations of a guerrilla character. In most small wars the enemy inclines to this mode of carrying on the campaign and shirks more regular engagements. It becomes necessary, therefore, to force him into decisive action. During the French campaigns against Abd el Kader it was found almost impossible to get the wary emir to fight. The British troops have experienced the same difficulty in recent times in Burma, and also in the Kaffir wars. It is a feature of most insurrectionary wars on a small scale, as for instance in Montenegro in 1876-77. The great Circassian leader Schamyl kept the Russians at bay for years with guerrilla tactics; his cause declined when he formed his followers into armies and weighed them down with guns. The Poles in 1863 committed the fatal error of assembling in formed bodies; had they confined themselves to desultory warfare, their overthrow would have been more difficult. But circumstances often are such that the enemy cannot be tempted into battle and adheres entirely to the guerrilla form of making war....

Guerrilla warfare is what the regular armies always have to dread. And when this is directed by a leader with a genius for war, an effective campaign becomes well-nigh impossible. The guerrilla has ever been a thorn in the side of the organized force. It was so in the Peninsular War, where the Spanish partisans proved a formidable foe to the French invaders. Fra Diavolo and his brigand bands were almost a match for the veterans of Massena in Calabria. The Turks before the last Russian intervention in the Balkans found the Montenegrins far more difficult to subdue than the organized Serbian armies. Therefore, it is that the art of combating this method of conducting operations deserves especial attention when small wars are in question. Moreover, even when there have been at the outset armies in the field to beat, the campaign often drifts on in desultory fashion long after these have been overthrown.

The terrain has much to say to effective conduct of partisan warfare. Montenegro and Brittany, Castille, and Trans-Caucasia present theaters of operations eminently suited to operations of this class. New Zealand, the kloofs and bushland of Kaffraria, Burma, and Achin suited to a nicety the guerrilla tactics of opponents designed by nature to pursue this form of war. Hilly and broken ground or districts clothed in jungle growth and thickets are requisite. On the prairie and the steppes guerrilla warfare is confined to mounted men whose mobility compensates for the want of cover.

Surprise is the essence of such operations—surprise, with retreat ere the opponent can recover as a sequel. And in consequence the combinations are of necessity framed on a small scale. Surprises with large forces are difficult to carry out; the withdrawal of these when once committed to action is most risky. Guerrilla warfare therefore means petty annoyance and not operations of a dramatic kind. But such capricious methods are best met by a resolute plan of campaign, and by an organization favoring rapid and energetic counterstrokes. Surprise can to a certain extent be guarded against by measures taken for security. But the escape of the enemy can only be frustrated by having troops ready to follow up at once and to follow up effectively....

The guerrilla mode of war must in fact be met by an abnormal system of strategy and tactics. The great principle which forms the basis of the art of war remains the combination of initiative with energy. But this is applied in a special form. The vigor and decision must be displayed in harassing the enemy and in giving him no rest. The hostile bands may elude the regular detachments, but their villages and flocks remain. The theater of war must be subdivided into sections, each to be dealt with by a given force or by a given aggregate of separate detachments. Defensive posts must be established where supplies can be collected, whither raided cattle can be brought, and which form independent bases. To each such base are attached one or more mobile or "flying" columns, organized to be ready to move out at a moment's notice, and equipped so as to penetrate to any part of the district told of to it and to return, certain of supplies for the task.

This question of flying columns deserves some further notice. The system which General Bugeaud introduced in Algeria was not new. General Hoche had worked on similar lines against the Chouans in Brittany with brilliant success. The principle of flying columns has since been used with great success in the Western States against the Red Indians, in Afghanistan, and recently in Burma.

The troops forming such columns must be thoroughly equipped and must be able to travel light. Mobility is the first essential; for the guerrilla trusts to sudden strokes, and it is of the utmost importance that the marauding party should not have time to disperse, and that it should be attacked before it can withdraw and dissolve. Hoche urged the leaders of mobile columns to accustom their men to fatigue and hardships, and to keep them in condition. The strength of such columns depends upon the circumstances of the case. In Burma they seldom numbered more than three hundred men, with one or two guns. In Algeria where the enemy was brave and resolute, small bodies would have been unsuitable, and General Bugeaud recommended three or four battalions with cavalry and two guns as a proper strength. Practically they should be as small as possible, consistent with safety. Their composition, of course, depends upon the conditions of the campaign and upon the terrain. On open ground a large part of the force would often consist of mounted men. In the bush, infantry alone can be used. In Abd el Kader's days portable artillery scarcely existed, and it was wheeled guns to which General Bugeaud so much objected. Guns on mules are not out of place in a flying column of dismounted troops, and they may be very useful. Where it is proposed to raid livestock some mounted troops are indispensable to bring the booty in.... But, although the columns should be as small as possible they must not be too small. If there is any fear of the enemy combining his forces to attack columns in detail, or of acting on interior lines as it is called, there must be troops enough to deal with whatever hostile forces can be assembled. In the early days of La Vendee separation proved fatal to the republican forces. The peasants assembled from time to time in great force and overwhelmed the detachments of regulars. The system of small columns introduced later by General Hoche was adapted to different conditions, to a more purely guerrilla warfare than when the insurrection was at its height. In Mexico small columns of French and of imperial troops suffered very severely when the troubles first broke out against Maximilian's rule; the enemy was able to bring considerable forces against them. In upper Burma where very small columns were adopted during the prolonged period of pacification no serious disaster occurred. This, considering the great number of columns operating in a vast extent of almost unexplored country for many months, is remarkable. But on one or two occasions it would have been advantageous had they been stronger. Sir F. Roberts' instructions were that "the troops should make their presence felt everywhere." And in view of the enormous area to be overrun, the columns had to be reduced to a minimum strength.... In no class of warfare is a well-organized and well-served intelligence department more essential than in that against guerrillas. Hoche instituted an elaborate system of espionage in Brittany, paying especial attention to this very important subject. Guerrillas trust to secret and to sudden strokes, and if the secret is discovered, their plan miscarries. On the other hand all movements intended against them must be concealed. Guerrilla warfare means that the regular troops are spread about a hostile country where all their movements can be watched by the enemy and where their camps are full of spies. Partisan leaders seldom can be trusted, and in all dealings with them, great circumspection is essential. Hoche discouraged parleying with the rebels by subordinate officers, distrusting their chiefs. *Parle comme si tu avais confiance en tout le monde et agis comme si tu ne pouvais t'en rapporter a personne,* was the motto of General Bugeaud.

---

Charles Callwell, *Small Wars: Their Principles and Practice* (London, 1899).

T. MILLER MAGUIRE

# DIFFERENCES BETWEEN GUERRILLA AND REGULAR WARFARE

## ADVANTAGES OF SAVAGE AND SEMICIVILIZED RACES

The natural man—the dweller in the hills and plains as distinguished from the product of the factory or large towns—has other qualifications besides eyesight and woodcraft which make him an ideal recruit. He can usually do with less food than his more civilized brother; he will exercise greater frugality and economy with regard to what he obtains. He is adept at cooking or preparing an impromptu meal, he knows where and how to obtain food if there is any to be had in the country, and he can usually manage to carry it with him in a small compass. He is comparatively little affected by heat or cold and he can sleep as soundly on the ground as in bed. He is not often ill and, when he has slight ailments *or* has met with minor accidents, knows how to treat himself and requires no medical advice. In a word, he is tougher, harder, more enduring than his more civilized brother, and it is natural that his mode of life should render him so. In everything except discipline and armament he is, as a rule, superior to the man he has to fight.

But now the growth of trade routes and facilities of communication are rapidly taking away from us and the other civilized powers the privileges of better armaments. The possession of the very newest and most perfect weapons is simply a matter of money, and the firms which turn them out will sell as freely to a savage as to the most enlightened of the world's rulers.

Nor have the minor powers and half-civilized, or wholly savage, tribes of the world failed to avail themselves of their chances ...

## WELL-ARMED SAVAGES OR MOSLEMS

An Abyssinian or Afghan war would now mean for us that we should have to face foemen individually superior to the vast majority of our men in all the qualities that go to make a good soldier, and no longer wielding swords and spears, but rifles equal in every respect to our own. In a few years it may well be that a similar state of things will be seen in China, while the distribution of modern weapons all over the globe will make it often probable that when we send an expedition against savages, it will not follow that we shall find primitive weapons in their hands.

If Fuzzy-wuzzy be, as he often is, as good a man as Tommy Atkins, or Fritz, or Jacques, and is even approximately as well armed, numerical superiority, knowledge of the country, and better health will go a long way to redress the balance in our favor, which experience and discipline in these days of loosened fighting may produce. Both sides—nature and civilization—being once more on an equality, the scale must be turned by better generalship in the future, as it has been in the past.

A careful study of the military art and the selection of the most competent men for leaders will become as requisite in the future when a "little war" is undertaken, as when a struggle with a great power is inevitable....

## DIFFERENCES BETWEEN REGULAR
## AND GUERRILLA WARFARE

The mere initiative does not make so much difference as in regular European warfare.

The strategical conditions are not reciprocal, and are against the regular invader, as the savage or irregular is not troubled about his lines of communication.

Observe the swelling or contracting of savage forces, according to failure or success of invader.

Reverses, even at first, must be avoided at all costs. The motto "Don't begin till you are ready," applies even more to these wars than to great wars; as even a stategical defensive must be combined with a tactical offensive for moral reasons.

Prolonged operations are to be avoided; hence, prefer tactics to strategy.

Complete enveloping movements like those of the Germans at Sedan are to be avoided; if driven to bay the savage will, in his fear of massacre, fight á *outrance*.

Leave the enemy an avenue of escape and hit him hard in the flank as he is trying to escape.

The army must be split up into several unconnected columns; the inner line principle is not so effective against invaders as it has been in France, Bohemia, or the United States, as the savage has no idea of strategy.

The situation as to flying columns, and long lines of communications and transport columns, unless very carefully managed, soon becomes hazardous.

It can be a terrible embarrassment if many men are wounded, and they must not be allowed to fall into the hands of the enemy.

Most serious dangers accompany the resort to guerrilla warfare by the enemy. It is therefore necessary to strike them hard and demoralize them.

The subaltern officers were formerly of a higher standard of efficiency relatively than in regular warfare. But this condition is rapidly changing with the growing importance of individual efficiency in all wars.

Still, there is much more freedom and latitude of movement for subordinates. There is a lack of maps and difficulty of obtaining information, while the natives gain information with an almost incredible speed and accuracy.

Savages are masters of surprises, and yet are taken aback by ambuscades and surprises applied to themselves. The individual savage is a far better tactician than the individual European—and his armament is daily improving.

Turning movements surprise savages, but may do more harm than good. Get the irregular to stand and crush him, keep him in his position; don't frighten him away from it. Don't drive him to stand at bay.

Press the pursuit hard; the enemy does not pursue ably and does not understand persistent pursuit.

Reserves are not very much required for battles, but the flanks and rear are in constant danger on the march and in the battle.

Attack early; savages and irregulars are not vigilant at dawn.

When the enemy pushes his attack with fanatic swordsmen, or spearmen, it is sink or swim, and counterstrokes are impossible till the crisis is over; then use them.

Squares and defense works are far more important than in regular warfare. The study of rigid and of elastic squares is needful.

Guns and cavalry produce an enormous moral effect in these wars, lancers are of great moral value.

The outpost systems are quite different. There is danger of isolation of advanced and rear guard, dangers from lateral valleys, from even the semblance of retreat, and from "sniping."

Regulars in small wars must frequently adopt retrograde movements, but these must be very deliberate, as they always encourage the enemy.

Always get close to the enemy and insist on his being roughly handled.

The principles on which outposts, patrols, vedettes, advanced guards, and rear guards are arranged are quite different.

The extraordinary rapidity of movement by savages must be borne in mind.

Races who live in the tropics, and in countries full of jungle and bush, are timid as compared with hill men and the nomad wanderers of the desert.

There is a danger of rushes by day and by night.

The more irregular and desultory the campaign, the more important is the service of security.

As to defensive works: attack and not defense is the first principle for regulars in small and irregular wars. But all isolated forces must be well protected and have clear fields of fire with flanking positions and obstacles.

---

T. Miller Maguire, *Guerrilla or Partisan Warfare*
(London, 1904).

T. H. C. FRANKLAND

# EFFICACY
# AND DIFFICULTIES

## COUNTRY AND CHARACTER

We are told that the objects of a regular army engaged in regular warfare are, firstly, the destruction of the enemy's organized forces, and, secondly (if the terms demanded by the conqueror are not already acceded), the seizure of the capital, chief centers, and therefore the resources of the enemy's country.

In a civilized country the dislocation of trade and government that results brings about inevitable surrender. Sometimes, as was the case in 1871, hastily levied armies of untrained inhabitants are placed between the invader and his second object. But the doom of these is foregone. To prevent the enemy reaching certain objectives, his masses must be opposed by masses, and where masses are contending, organization, trained leaders, and a trained staff are more important than the individual qualities of the rank and file; so that however brave, however patriotic, the untrained levies may be, the very necessity of forming them into large armies dooms them to defeat. It is when fighting in masses that the untrained combatant becomes an amateur indeed.

We have arrived at this, then: that where it is necessary to bar the conqueror's way to a certain objective, untrained men are useless. In other words, in civilized countries, where the loss of capital and chief towns paralyzes all action, the destruction of its organized forces must be followed by surrender.

In less civilized countries, however, where the inhabitants are self-contained and dependent on the soil rather than the town, the loss of capital by no means entails loss of resources, and frequently has no effect on their resisting power. And the very fact of their offering no stationary vitals as an object to the enemy's armies gives them a great advantage. It relieves them of the necessity of opposing the march of the enemy's masses; it relieves them of the necessity of concentrating and it relieves them of the necessity of being beaten. In an only partially civilized country roads are generally bad and railways few, and the movements of large bodies of troops with their cumbrous supply columns is a matter of greater difficulty than in more developed countries.

Where civilization precludes resistance to an invader except by organized forces, the absence of civilization affords great facilities for guerrilla warfare. As regards the nature of terrain most suitable for irregular fighting, one of two conditions is necessary—either a wild surface or great space. In the one the difficulties of transport, of the movement of troops and guns, and of reconnaissance obstruct the path of the invader, while inaccessible fastness and facilities of ambush favor the defenders. In the other, the guerrilla has plenty of room to deliver his blow and get away. The mobility of mounted bands has its full scope, and the number of troops required by the enemy is out of all proportion to the numbers of its adversary. It is natural that countries most suitable to guerrilla fighting should breed the best guerrilla fighters. Where civilization from the point of luxury and comfort is absent, the inhabitants, hardened to exposure and accustomed to irregular and primitive feeding, find in the hardships of campaigning but the ordinary routine of their daily life. Possessing practically no capital, they have generally little to lose and much to gain, for it is more congenial to reap by plunder and capture what others have sown than to toil all day for a bare living. Beyond this the inhabitants of a wild or extended country, where self-reliance, keen eyesight, knowledge of country, and other qualities are daily acquired, become naturally and almost unconsciously excellent scouts and skirmishers.

## DIFFICULTIES OF GUERRILLA WARFARE

Generally speaking, guerrilla warfare has as its object the exhaustion of the invader, for the primary aim of driving him away can only be brought about in this way; unable to bar his progress to any part of their country, or to prevent his occupation of what territory he chooses, the guerrilla can at least dog his steps, delay his progress, and sap his strength until exhaustion or intervention causes the invader to withdraw. As has already been remarked, the guerrillas start with a great advantage, namely, their invulnerability. Only by actually capturing or killing each individual can the prospective conqueror, so long as the patriotism of the inhabitants remains firm, hope to terminate the struggle. The guerrillas have no accessible vitals, and receding like the tide before their organized foe, they close in again behind him unharmed. On the other hand, their "regular" opponent is always open to serious wounds. The necessary appendage of a line of communication, the essential small posts, lie a perpetual prey to the swoop of the moving bands.

Again, the guerrillas derive an advantage from their very want of organization. Untrammeled by detailed orders, they move hither and thither till, each band reported in several places at the same time, the veriest paragon of an intelligence officer is puzzled to distraction. For themselves, served by their friends and families, whom, in hopes of pacification, the invader has left on the land, their intelligence is of the surest. And their scouts are in turn aided in their work by the very organization and methodical movements of their opponents. For the comparatively slow-moving columns of a regular army, with their train of transport and artillery, betrayed by their regularly formed advanced guards, are easily located; the direction of their march is obvious, and their arrival at any particular spot readily calculated. Ambushes are, hence, easily laid for flank or rear guards; and convoys, always moving on the same routes, and protected in the same way, are easily held up.

On the other hand, the want of organization has its disadvantages—in the consequent difficulty of cooperation. For, though a common object and a common instinct, namely, to harm the enemy in every possible way, brings of its own accord some semblance of unity of action, yet cooperation on a large scale has been often proved to be almost impossible, and big results therefore unattainable. ...

## EFFICACY OF THIS CLASS OF WARFARE: A COMPARISON

As to the efficacy of unaided guerrilla warfare, Napier speaks in no uncertain terms: "They (the Spanish *partidas*) never occupied half their own numbers of French at the same time, never absolutely defeated a single division, never prevented any considerable enterprise."

Our experience in South Africa was very different to this, and this difference may be partly traced to the stamp of leader in each case. With a few exceptions, such as Mina, the leaders of the Spanish bands failed to grasp the essentials of guerrilla warfare. Full of arrogance and a false notion of their military abilities, they assumed the dignity of generals, tried to form armies out of their irregular bands, and with their inextinguishable self-confidence constantly sought pitched battles.

Wellington, seeing that their true role was to avoid encounters in large bodies, and to concentrate their attentions on the less glorious but more certain operations of harassing the enemy's communications, was ever trying to persuade his allies so to act. But his advice was constantly rejected, and defeat as constantly followed. The Boer leaders, on the contrary, recognized their true *role* from the beginning, and the almost systematic way in which they worked, each in their own districts, concentrating suddenly on weak points and dispersing as rapidly before relieving columns, ensured such success as is possible in this method of warfare.

But the greater difficulties experienced by the British in South Africa find, perhaps, a better explanation in the modern rifle; in the hands of the Boers it proved a very formidable weapon. The difficulties of reconnaissance in guerrilla warfare, already remarked on, were greatly increased. Rapidity of fire, accuracy, smokeless powder, and long range added to the irregular's power of harassing, while a few guerrillas could easily impose on large columns. In the Peninsula the Spaniards, even when well-armed, could only attack French columns at close ranges, when a charge of the regular troops would always route them, and the escape of the intruders was a matter of difficulty.

In South Africa a few men with rifles could force a column to deploy at fourteen hundred yards, and could withdraw after doing considerable damage, while their opponents were still half a mile distant.

The modern rifle, however, also gave advantages to the invaders. Posts could be held by fewer men, and the blockhouses on the lines of communication could be separated by wider distances. It was on account of the modern rifle that the "drives" in South Africa were possible, for with the Brown Bess of the Peninsula the number of men that would have been necessary to hold the blockhouse lines efficiently would have been prohibitive.

Still, the advantages rest rather with the guerrilla. The fact that, armed and led as they were, the Boers nonetheless succumbed at last to the relentless pressure of a regular army, proves that guerrillas alone, even under the most favorable circumstances, cannot even hope for incessant war as a reward to their exertions.

---

T. H. C. Frankland, "Notes on Guerrilla Warfare,"
in *United Service Magazine,* Vol. 33 (1912).

THOMAS EDWARD LAWRENCE

# THE LESSONS OF ARABIA

## THE ARAB REVOLT OF 1916–18

The Arab revolt began in June 1916, with an attack by the half-armed and inexperienced tribesmen upon the Turkish garrisons in Medina and about Mecca. They met with no success, and after a few days' effort withdrew out of range and began a blockade. This method forced the early surrender of Mecca, the more remote of the two centers. Medina, however, was linked by railway to the Turkish main army in Syria, and the Turks were able to reinforce the garrison there. The Arab forces which had attacked it then fell back gradually and took up a position across the main road to Mecca.

At this point the campaign stood still for many weeks. The Turks prepared to send an expeditionary force to Mecca, to crush the revolt at its source, and accordingly moved an army corps to Medina by rail. Thence they began to advance down the main western road from Medina to Mecca, a distance of about two hundred fifty miles. The first fifty miles were easy, then came a belt of hills twenty miles wide, in which were Feisal's Arab tribesmen standing on the defensive, next come a level stretch for seventy miles along the coastal plain to Rabegh, rather more than halfway. Rabegh is a little port on the Red Sea, with good anchorage for ships, and because of its situation was regarded as the key to Mecca. There lay Sherif Ali, Feisal's eldest brother, with more tribal forces, and the beginning of an Arab regular army, formed from officers and men of Arab blood who had served in the Turkish army. As was almost inevitable in view of the general course of military thinking since Napoleon, the soldiers of all countries looked only to the regulars to win the war. Military opinion was obsessed by the dictum of Foch that the ethic of modern war is to seek for

311

the enemy's army, his center of power, and destroy it in battle. Irregulars would not attack positions and so they were regarded as incapable of forcing a decision.

While these Arab regulars were still being trained, the Turks suddenly began their advance on Mecca. They broke through the hills in twenty-four hours, and so proved the second theorem of irregular war—namely, that irregular troops are as unable to defend a point or line as they are to attack it. This lesson was received without gratitude, for the Turkish success put the Rabegh force in a critical position, and it was not capable of repelling the attack of a single battalion, much less a corps.

In the emergency it occurred to the author that perhaps the virtue of irregulars lay in depth, not in face, and that it had been the threat of attack by them upon the Turkish northern flank which had made the enemy hesitate for so long. The actual Turkish flank ran from their front line to Medina, a distance of about fifty miles; but, if the Arab force moved toward the Hejaz railway behind Medina, it might stretch its threat (and, accordingly, the enemy's flank) as far, potentially, as Damascus, eight hundred miles away to the north. Such a move would force the Turks to the defensive, and the Arab force might regain the initiative. It seemed the only chance, and so, in January, 1917, Feisal's tribesmen turned their backs on Mecca, Rabegh and the Turks, and marched away north two hundred miles to Wejh.

This eccentric movement acted like a charm. The Arabs did nothing concrete, but their march recalled the Turks (who were almost into Rabegh) all the way back to Medina. There, one half of the Turkish force took up the entrenched position about the city, which it held until after the Armistice. The other half was distributed along the railway to defend it against the Arab threat. For the rest of the war the Turks stood on the defensive and the Arab tribesmen won advantage over advantage till, when peace came, they had taken thirty-five thousand prisoners, killed and wounded and worn out about as many, and occupied one hundred square miles of the enemy's territory, at little loss to themselves. However, although Wejh was the turning point, its significance was not yet realized. For the moment the move thither was regarded merely as a preliminary to cutting the railway in order to take Medina, the Turkish headquarters and main garrison.

## STRATEGY AND TACTICS

The author was unfortunately as much in charge of the campaign as he pleased, and lacking a training in command sought to find an immediate equation between past study of military theory and the present movements—as a guide to, and an intellectual basis for, future action. The textbooks gave the aim in war as "the destruction of the organized forces of the enemy" by "the one-process battle." Victory could only be purchased by blood. This was a hard saying, as the Arabs had no organized forces, and so a Turkish Foch would have no aim; and the Arabs would not endure casualties, so that an Arab Clausewitz could not buy his victory. These wise men must be talking metaphors, for the Arabs were indubitably winning their war... and further reflection pointed to the deduction that they had actually won it. They were in occupation of 99 percent of the Hejaz. The Turks were welcome to the other fraction till peace or doomsday showed them the futility of clinging to the windowpane. This part of the war was over, so why bother about Medina? The Turks sat in it on the defensive, immobile, eating for food the transport animals which were to have moved them to Mecca, but for which there was no pasture in their now-restricted lines. They were harmless sitting there; if taken prisoner, they would entail the cost of food and guards in Egypt; if driven out northward into Syria, they would join the main army blocking the British in Sinai. On all counts they were best where they were, and they valued Medina and wanted to keep it. Let them!

This seemed unlike the ritual of war of which Foch had been priest, and so it seemed that there was a difference of kind. Foch called his modern war "absolute." In it two nations professing incompatible philosophies set out to try them in the light of force. A struggle of two immaterial principles would only end when the supporters of one had no more means of resistance. An opinion can be argued with; a conviction is best shot. The logical end of a war of creeds is the final destruction of one, and Salammbo is the classic textbook instance. These were the lines of the struggle between France and Germany, but not, perhaps, between Germany and England, for all efforts to make the British soldier hate the enemy simply made him hate war. Thus, the "absolute war" seemed only a variety of war; and beside it other sorts could be discerned as Clausewitz had numbered them, personal wars for dynastic reasons, expulsive wars for party reasons, and commercial wars for trading reasons.

Now the Arab aim was unmistakably geographical; to occupy all Arabic-speaking lands in Asia. In the doing of it Turks might be killed; yet "killing Turks" would never be an excuse or aim. If they would go quietly, the war would end. If not, they must be driven out—but at the cheapest possible price, since the Arabs were fighting for freedom, a pleasure only to be tasted by a man alive. The next task was to analyze the process, both from the point of view of strategy, the aim in war, the synoptic regard which sees everything by the standard of the whole, and from the point of view called tactics, the means toward the strategic end, the steps of its staircase. In each were found the same elements, one algebraic, one biological, a third psychological. The first seemed a pure science, subject to the laws of mathematics, without humanity. It dealt with known invariables, fixed conditions, space and time, inorganic things such as hills and climates and railways, with mankind in type masses too great for individual variety, with all artificial aids, and the extensions given our faculties by mechanical invention. It was essentially formulable. In the Arab case the algebraic factor would take first account of the area to be conquered. A casual calculation indicated perhaps one hundred forty thousand 140,000 square miles. How would the Turks defend all that? No doubt by a trench line across the bottom, if the Arabs were an army attacking with banners displayed.... But suppose they were an influence, a thing invulnerable, intangible, without front or back, drifting about like a gas? Armies were like plants, immobile as a whole, firm-rooted, nourished through long stems to the head. The Arabs might be a vapor, blowing where they listed. It seemed that a regular soldier might be helpless without a target. He would own the ground he sat on, and what he could poke his rifle at. The next step was to estimate how many posts they would need to contain this attack in depth, sedition putting up her head in every unoccupied one of these one hundred thousand square miles. They would have need of a fortified post every four square miles, and a post could not be less than twenty men. The Turks would need six hundred thousand men to meet the combined ill wills of all the local Arab people. They had one hundred thousand men available. It seemed that the assets in this sphere were with the Arabs, and climate, railways, deserts, and technical weapons could also be attached to their interests. The Turk was stupid and would believe that rebellion was absolute, like war, and deal with it on the analogy of absolute warfare.

## HUMANITY IN BATTLE

So much for the algebraic element. The second factor was biological, the breaking point, life and death; or better, wear and tear. Bionomics seemed a good name for it. The war philosophers had properly made it an art, and had elevated one item in it, "effusion of blood," to the height of a principle. It became humanity in battle, an art touching every side of our corporal being. There was a line of variability (man) running through all its estimates. Its components were sensitive and illogical, and generals guarded themselves by the device of a reserve, the significant medium of their art. Colmar von der Goltz had said that when you know the enemy's strength, and he is fully deployed, then you know enough to dispense with a reserve. But this is never completely so. There is always the possibility of accident, of some flaw in materials, present in the general's mind, and the reserve is unconsciously held to meet it. There is a "felt" element in troops, not expressible in figures, and the greatest commander is he whose intuitions most nearly happen. Nine-tenths of tactics are certain, and taught in books; but the remaining irrational tenth is like the kingfisher flashing across the pool—and that is the test of generals. It can only be ensured by instinct and sharpened by thought—practicing the stroke so often that at the crisis it is as natural as a reflex.

Yet to limit the art to humanity seemed an undue narrowing down. It must apply to materials as much as to organisms. In the Turkish army, materials were scarce and precious, men more plentiful than equipment. Consequently, the cue should be to destroy not the army but the materials. The death of a Turkish bridge or rail, machine or gun, or high explosive was more profitable than the death of a Turk. The Arab army just then was equally chary of men and materials: of men because they being irregulars were not units, but individuals, and an individual casualty is like a pebble dropped in water: each may make only a brief hole, but rings of sorrow widen out from them. The Arab army could not afford casualties. Materials were easier to deal with. Hence its obvious duty to make itself superior in some one branch, guncotton or machine guns, or whatever, could be most decisive. Foch had laid down the maxim, applying it to men, of being superior at the critical point and moment of attack. The Arab army might apply it to materials and be superior in equipment in one dominant moment or respect.

For both men and things it might try to give Foch's doctrine a negative twisted side, for cheapness' sake, and be weaker than the enemy everywhere except in one point or matter. Most wars are wars of contact, both forces striving to keep in touch to avoid tactical surprise. The Arab war should be a war of detachment: to contain the enemy by the silent threat of a vast unknown desert, not disclosing themselves till the moment of attack. This attack need be only nominal, directed not against his men, but against his materials, so it should not seek for his main strength or his weaknesses, but for his most accessible material. In railway cutting this would be usually an empty stretch of rail. This was a tactical success. From this theory came to be developed ultimately an unconscious habit of never engaging the enemy at all. This chimed with the numerical plea of never giving the enemy's soldier a target. Many Turks on the Arab front had no chance all the war to fire a shot, and correspondingly the Arabs were never on the defensive, except by rare accident. The corollary of such a rule was perfect "intelligence," so that plans could be made in complete certainty. The chief agent had to be the general's head (Antoine de Pas de Feuquiere said this first), and his knowledge had to be faultless, leaving no room for chance.

The headquarters of the Arab army probably took more pains in this service than any other staff.

## THE EXACT SCIENCE OF GUERRILLA WARFARE

By careful persistence, kept strictly within its strength and following the spirit of these theories, the Arab army was able eventually to reduce the Turks to helplessness, and complete victory seemed to be almost within sight when General Edmund Allenby by his immense stroke in Palestine threw the enemy's main forces into hopeless confusion and put an immediate end to the Turkish war. He deprived the Arab revolt of the opportunity of following to the end the dictum of Maurice Saxe that a war might be won without fighting battles. But it can at least be said that its leaders worked by his light for two years, and the work stood. This is a pragmatic argument that cannot be wholly derided. The experiment, although not complete, strengthened the belief that irregular war or rebellion could be proved to be an exact science, and an inevitable success, granted certain factors—and if pursued along certain lines.

Here is the thesis: rebellion must have an unassailable base, something guarded not merely from attack, but from the fear of it. Such a base the Arab revolt had in the Red Sea ports, the desert, or in the minds of men converted to its creed. It must have a sophisticated alien enemy, in the form of a disciplined army of occupation too small to fulfill the doctrine of acreage: too few to adjust number to space, in order to dominate the whole area effectively from fortified posts. It must have a friendly population—not actively friendly, but sympathetic to the point of not betraying rebel movements to the enemy. Rebellions can be made by 2 percent active in a striking force, and 98 percent passively sympathetic. The few active rebels must have the qualities of speed and endurance, ubiquity and independence of arteries of supply. They must have the technical equipment to destroy or paralyze the enemy's organized communications, for irregular war is fairly Wilhelm von Willisen's definition of strategy, "the study of communication," in its extreme degree—of attack where the enemy is not. In fifty words: Granted mobility, security (in the form of denying targets to the enemy), time and doctrine (the idea to convert every subject to friendliness), victory will rest with the insurgents, for the algebraic factors are in the end decisive, and against them perfections of means and spirit struggle quite in vain.

---

Reprinted from the *Encyclopaedia Britannica,* 14th ed.
(1929).

B. C. DENING

# GUERRILLAS AND POLITICAL PROPAGANDA

I N STUDYING THE GUERRILLA WARS OF THE PAST, it is remarkable how little the characteristics of this type of fighting have altered with the passage of time. Thus, the cause of such warfare has inevitably been an actual or imaginary suppression of the national aspirations of a smaller race by the force of a larger one. Such wars have always been carried out with the utmost ferocity on both sides. Tactics have varied only in detail from century to century. Mobility, good intelligence, surprise and cunning, and the nature of the country have continued to play their part time after time. What is more—far more so than has been possible in the case of greater wars—with the facts of history available, it has been feasible nearly always to forecast the inevitable result of guerrilla wars. This latter fact being so, it is remarkable how often one side has embarked on the struggle, knowing well what its end was likely to be. While discussing this aspect of the question, it is interesting to go back over the principal guerrilla wars of comparatively modern history and to note the results of these struggles and how such results were obtained.

Ten principal guerrilla wars have taken place since 1792. In five of them, the victory rested with a Great Power, though in two of them only after a most protracted struggle. In two cases the result was indecisive, and in the remaining three the guerrilla forces were victorious. If the causes which led to these results are examined, it is abundantly clear that where a Great Power had the means and the will to exert itself, where it employed the right tactics, unless outside intervention entered as a factor, it invariably won, and that only where the reverse was the case could the guerrillas hope to win.

Where outside factors, such as the remoteness or other entanglements of a Great Power have come in to balance the scales (at least temporarily) in a guerrilla struggle, the decision has rested to some extent upon the tactics employed by the combatants.

For any given Great Power, it has been sound tactics in all cases to employ strong mobile columns. In confined territories these have worked in conjunction with fixed lines intended progressively to envelop the disaffected areas. These methods were employed by Hoche in La Vendee in 1796, and by Kitchener in South Africa in 1901-02. In more extensive or very inaccessible territories, such as Algiers and the Caucasus, successive envelopment of the whole country has been impracticable and results have taken longer to achieve. In such cases it has been necessary to wait for the guerrillas to provide an objective and then to strike with the nearest mobile column.

For the guerrillas, the right tactics have consisted in concentrating for the attack of suitable objectives and dispersing immediately afterward in order not to give the regular forces an objective. Where guerrillas have so often failed is in not adhering to this primary principle. Success in minor actions has led them to believe themselves capable of fighting large battles, and attempts to do so have usually proved disastrous to themselves. This was the case in Spain in 1811. Again in the Caucasus, the Circassians, in the latter part of their long struggle, made the fatal mistake of acquiring artillery and attempting to fight as permanently formed bodies.

It is now for consideration whether the problems of guerrilla warfare have changed, and, if so, whether the principles which have been applied to their solution in the long past still hold good today.

It is certain that the conditions in which guerrilla warfare is likely to be fought today have altered. To begin with, modern methods of communication and publicity, combined with the progress which has been recorded in the civilization of most of the Great Powers, it is inconceivable that the forces of a Great Power will be able to display that ferocity in their conduct of the struggle, whatever the guerrillas may do, which has been such a potent ally in the past in the task of putting down an insurrection. The methods of a Great Power will of necessity, if not by inclination, have to be cleaner and more above board than was the case in bygone years. Otherwise, such an outcry would arise as would be certain to bring about either the fall of the government responsible or the intervention of an interested outside power. This change is definitely a loss to the Great Powers and a gain to the fomenters of guerrilla troubles, for by barbarous acts guerrillas can possibly compel the forces of a Great Power into reprisals and thereby weaken the case of a Great Power. Guerrillas have in fact, today, a new weapon—political propaganda—which draws blood upon the home fronts of the Great Powers.

Further, guerillas' methods of conducting warfare have advanced. In former days, the object of the guerrilla was to incapacitate, permanently, as many of the soldiers of a Great Power as was possible, hoping that the accumulation of pinpricks would cause the Great Power to give way. Today the policy of pinpricks continues, but the nature of the prick has changed. Guerrillas aim, where possible (and today every Great Power, except perhaps the U.S., is sensitive where expenditure is concerned), at draining the financial rather than the military resources of the Great Power. This method may be said to have been started with the Cuban insurrection of 1895, where the guerrillas, realizing that Spain was very greatly dependent upon the revenue obtained from their island, concentrated their strategy and tactics upon the destruction of the chief crop of the island, the sugar crop. In this objective the guerrillas were successful, and it is on record that Spain had given way to them before the threat of American intervention became real. This same object underlay the majority of de Wet's exploits in South Africa where the burning of trains, bridges, and supplies was a feature of the later guerrilla operations. In Ireland in 1921 the republicans were pursuing the same ends and instructions to that effect were issued to their forces and were being carried out up to the time of the truce, as the burning of the Customs House, the main army M.T. workshops, and other government property in Dublin at the time testify. This new line of attack may well again be a source of weakness to all the Great Powers, where vulnerable and valuable property is readily accessible to the civil population, for it is impossible to abandon such property and face the losses that may be entailed. At the same time the protection of a Great Power ties up (in guards) incalculable numbers of troops or police.

In addition, the invention of bombs, automatic pistols, and high explosive mines as effective weapons of attack has increased the difficulties of stopping guerrilla warfare, particularly in large centers of population. These weapons are readily concealed on the person in a crowd or in endless hiding places in a city. They lend themselves to the first principle of guerrilla fighting—the rapid concentration of armed force for an operation, combined with its equally rapid dispersion upon the completion of the task.

Against these advantages which guerrillas now have, the Great Powers have also certain advantages compared to former days. The advent of mechanical transport has added greatly to the mobility of troops in most countries, though in Ireland it was shown what could be done to reduce this mobility by systematic road cutting and destruction. The invention of

wireless enables news to travel very quickly, and in future will greatly facilitate the rapid concentric advance of scattered columns when an objective
has been located. The increased firepower of small arms also enables small
detachments to be more effective than was formerly the case.

On the whole, however, it must be admitted that by modern developments, guerrilla forces have gained more than the forces of the Great Powers. This being so, it behooves the Great Powers to have a clear doctrine as
to the action required if and when guerrilla trouble breaks out.

B. C. Dening, "Modern Problems of Guerrilla Warfare,"
in *Army Quarterly,* Vol. 13, No. 2 (1927).

HAROLD H. UTLEY

# WAR AT A TIME OF PEACE

T HE RULES OF LAND WARFARE for the guidance of the combatants in small wars, or "wars that are not wars," have not been and probably never will be written. When a situation arises not contemplated by the instructions issued, the only sound guide to action is a thorough knowledge of the mission of the whole force coupled with knowledge of the methods that have been used in the past by civilized nations in like situations. These comprise:

- the killing, wounding, or capture of those opposed to us and the destruction of their property;
- the destruction of the property of those who aid or abet those hostile to us;
- the laying waste of entire sections inhabited by people generally supporting those hostile to us; and
- the removal and dispersion of all of the inhabitants of an area of unrest.

The great disadvantage in the application of these measures, excepting the first, lies in the fact that their application will probably exasperate the people as a whole against us, and tend to forfeit their friendship permanently, as well as stir up more or less trouble for us among neighboring nations and at home....

The late Lieutenant Colonel Ellis in his article on the subject lays down this sound doctrine:

"That the friendship of the people of any occupied nation should be forfeited by the adoption of any unnecessarily harsh measures, is avowedly contrary to the policy of the United States."

When Uncle Sam occupies the territory of a small nation he wants to enforce his will, but he does not want any trouble—that is, anything that will cause undue comment among his own or foreign people. Such comments may not only cause countless "investigations" at a more or less later date (there have been seven in Haiti in the fourteen years of occupation), but also—and what is more important from our point of view—such comments in the halls of Congress and in the press of our own and nearby countries are interpreted by the natives as having far greater weight than they really possess (are taken indeed as an indication of strong support for the forces arrayed against us) and thus serve to intensify and prolong the opposition we must overcome. Of course the leaders know better, but they are skilled in the use of propaganda for their own ends. And there will always be found so-called Americans who under one pretext or another will assist in originating and spreading tales of alleged "atrocities" said to have been committed by our troops. If we were at war, if the laws of war applied, we could justly charge them—the originators and the publishers—with giving aid and comfort to the enemy. But in small wars we are at peace no matter how thickly the bullets are flying.

We must never in our zeal for the perfection of plans for a small war, overlook the fact that behind and over us is that force known as "public opinion in the United States...." Measures justifiable in a regular war, tactically sound, and probably the most efficient available, must frequently be eliminated from the plan of campaign as not being in accord with public policy in the existing situation....

Some writers have held that in small wars only a limited number of the principles of war apply. The implication is that the remainder may be disregarded. With such a doctrine we cannot agree, although of course in each situation arising in small wars, as in every other situation, whether in the map problem room or in the field, some of the principles will predominate. It is believed that a careful analysis of those occasions where it is alleged that the principles were disregarded will show that the principles as a whole were not violated with success. The fact that due to difference in weapons, terrain, hostile methods of fighting, etc., the manner of applying the principles—the tactics—will sometimes vary from the accepted doctrine, for major warfare must not be confused with the nonapplication of the principles of war.

---

Harold H. Utley, "An Introduction to the Tactics
and Techniques of Small Wars," *Marine Corps Gazette,*
Vol. 15, No. 5 (1931).

ARTHUR EHRHARDT

# IN PRAISE OF BOLD ATTACK

A TTACK REMAINS THE BEST POLICY IN SMALL WAR, despite the development of automatic weapons. Nor have progressive motorization and mechanization... altered this principle in any way. On the contrary, the increasing use of motorized units, tanks, and aircraft tends to disperse the fighting over much larger areas, thus positively encouraging guerrilla activity. Nowadays, strikes against the enemy's supply lines, the Achilles' heel of every tank army, or on his flanks or even in his own territory are much easier to carry out than they used to be. The transportation of troops and arms by air is no longer a pipe dream, and even tank and motorized units can be used to support the aggressive tactics of the guerrillas. Nor do the thrusts against the enemy's flanks and rear so typical of the new mobile units have to be satisfied with short-lived tactical gains. Provided the terrain in question is suitable for small war, motorized units, by setting down partisans in the vicinity of strategically important points in the enemy hinterland to which they have broken through, not only cut gashes in the body of the enemy's forces but also introduce noxious foreign bodies, so to speak, into the vulnerable tissue of his supply system. With time this partisan presence becomes increasingly annoying and, in critical situations, may even prove highly dangerous. Motorized units on the ground and the aircraft above it break up the rigid lines of the old fronts. One effect of this is to greatly extend the area open to guerrilla warfare. In World War I we got used to advancing deep into the field of battle and seeing coherent firing lines completely disintegrate. In the coming war the fronts will in all probability be entirely dissolved and far deeper battle areas created; the theater of operations will stretch at least as far as motor vehicles can travel—and possibly as far as the effect of propaganda and financial support can reach. This extension of the theater of operations is literally an invitation to guerrilla activity. What this means is a return to the style of campaign not seen for many years and certainly never even dreamed of during the World War I, at least on the western front. ...

The air force is particularly effective in countering partisan activity. The years after the World War I have provided us with several illustrations of how useful a weapon it is for modern troops fighting against partisans and guerrilla bands. There can be no doubt that its use has severely diminished the chances of successful small wars. On the other hand, it is true that there are considerable problems attached to sending out modern fighter- and bomber-squadrons against partisans. One drawback is that high flying-speeds make it almost impossible to observe enemy bands if they are quick and clever at taking cover. It is also hard to distinguish enemy bands from one's own partisans. ...

It follows from the significant role tanks and airplanes have to play in fighting partisans that out-of-date airplanes and motor vehicles are a by no means insignificant parts of an enemy's strength. They can be used to great effect to protect one's hinterland, supply lines, bases, camps, and airfields, thereby freeing more valuable units for operational use.

Such reinforcements in the form of motor vehicles and tanks will be very welcome to the troops guarding the supply lines in the rear, for, as I have already mentioned, the supply lines of a highly motorized army are literally an invitation to ambushes and sudden attacks. To keep the tanks and motorized units on the move and the squadrons of aircraft in the air there must be a continuous stream of fuel flowing down the supply lines. If partisan warfare were to flare up along this highly flammable stream, or even near important depots, this would constitute a grave threat to the efficacy of the decisive weaponry. The deeper the steel prongs of the tank and motorized units thrust their way into the enemy, the longer the supply lines become and the harder it will be to ensure that the huge fuel requirement is satisfied. ...

The most important principle of small war, then, remains unchanged: in partisan and guerrilla warfare, bold attack is the best strategy. From this it follows that the forces fighting against such partisans must themselves be mobile. They should always be looking to attack and always be trying to strike at the opposing forces, even if they occasionally misfire. For a troop to try to fight a group of partisans purely defensively would be like a boxer fighting in the dark, defending himself against his opponent just by parrying his blows: such a troop would suffer one blow after another. As history shows us, surprise attacks and lightning descents upon the enemy are of greater importance than force of arms in such warfare. *Anyone who relies purely upon defensive tactics in a small war is lost.* No advances in weapons technology will alter this fact. ...

Now to the last, but by no means least, principle: it is impossible to wage a protracted small war without either support from a troop of regular soldiers or help from the population. This rule has lost nothing of its validity. To be sure, the development of the motor vehicle has considerably increased the possibility of providing support for partisans. For one thing, partisans may well be able to carry out their exploits from motor vehicles in many cases. One instance would be a sudden declaration of war when the enemy has not had time to take even the most rudimentary defensive measures and poorly guarded frontiers are open to deep forward thrusts by guerrillas. The longer the war goes on, the less chance improvised motorized units will have to score any successes in the hostile environment of the enemy's hinterland. However, in a country where the tolerance and support of the large mass of the population may be reckoned with, the use of motor vehicles can be of inestimable value to guerrilla bands, even in the later stages of a war. Motorized support makes it far easier for them to practice their characteristic methods, namely, sudden appearance, lightning attack, and rapid disappearance. It goes without saying that on their own territory, partisans should make general use of motor vehicles for as long as possible— provided, of course, that they have sufficient fuel.

Small war shock troops in enemy territory, however, will have to forego the advantages of motor vehicles as soon as they meet serious opposition. They can be flown far behind enemy lines to within a short distance of their target and dropped there by parachute; in favorable circumstances, they may possibly be escorted there by tanks that have broken through enemy lines; in each case, the long and dangerous march to their destination is avoided and the area of guerrilla warfare in enemy territory is greatly extended. Necessarily, the regions involved will be sparsely populated and offer sufficient cover. Only seldom, however, will the return to the guerrillas' own lines be facilitated by tanks or planes. After completing their mission, the guerrillas will as in the past have to find their way back to their base without outside help. They must realize that their withdrawal will require a maximum of caution, quick thinking, and toughness. There will always be fighters prepared to court even such dangers as these. However, the commanding officers must be clear in their own minds that even successful operations undertaken deep inside enemy territory frequently end in the obliteration of the shock troops involved. To put it metaphorically, the command fires the supremely valuable missile of the shock troops at the target in the enemy hinterland, and only in a few rare cases will it return, boomerang-like, to the hand of him who launched it. In other words, the "firing" of such commandos is only justified if the results of the under-taking outweigh the sacrifice of such prized troops.

In the case of weak guerrillas, although it is more or less inevitable that they will eventually be destroyed if they make forward thrusts into terri-tory inhabited by a predominantly hostile or ill-disposed populace, their thrusts may be successful if they find support among the population. One of the aims of propaganda, therefore, must be to create and sustain a state of mind among the populace favorable to the guerrillas, assuring them a stratum of sympathy to fall back on. On home ground, one of its aims must be to rouse the people to resistance against enemy guerrilla bands. It will further direct itself toward undermining the will to fight of the inhabitants of the enemy hinterland. Often, a daring raid is all that is needed to spark off a smoldering uprising which will tie down considerable enemy forces, endanger the army's supplies, and even, in a critical situation, present incalculable strategic consequences. We can expect, then, to see partisan warfare and propaganda working hand in glove in areas where the popu-lace is undecided in its loyalties. In many cases, skillful propaganda will be able to create nests of unrest in the enemy's home territory or in the vicinity of his supply lines where the partisans will meet with a favorable attitude among the people. We saw time and time again when we were studying the history of small war how valuable, even vital, such support among the local inhabitants (or groups of them at least) is for partisans. *Small war has always been and will continue to be supported and nurtured from among the ranks of the people. ...*

---

Arthur Ehrhardt, *Kleinkrieg* (Potsdam, 1935).

# Socialism and the Armed Struggle

# INTRODUCTORY NOTE

INSURRECTION AS AN IDEA played a central role in European revolutionary doctrine of the nineteenth century, but insurrection as a technique was largely neglected. It was discussed in the writings of Giuseppe Mazzini and Carlo Bianco, and then there was the preeminent example of Auguste Blanqui (1805-81). Leon Trotsky said of Blanqui that he did not know the difference between revolution and insurrection. This does not do Blanqui justice, but of course Trotsky was not familiar with Blanqui's writings on the subject. *Instructions pour une prise des armes* was published only in the 1930s. Far from being a blind believer in violent action, Blanqui wrote after 1848 that conspiracy, which had been a virtue under the monarchy, was a public offense under the republic.

Marx and Engels wrote much on military affairs, but guerrilla warfare rarely preoccupied them. They thought it had only limited applicability. And Engels doubted whether guerrilla warfare, effective under specific conditions in the preceeding fifty years, had much of a future. This conclusion emerges, for instance, from his writings on the French colonial experience in North Africa. For a few weeks in late 1870 he thought that the spirit of popular resistance had been reawakened in France and that a people's war would keep the Prussians at bay. He would soon conclude sadly, that such fanaticism and enthusiasm were no longer customary among civilized nations, the sentiment apparently having migrated to the realm of Turks and Mexicans. Engels thought that guerrilla warfare in Europe could succeed only in certain mountainous regions and in conjunction with regular army operations. Outside Europe the conditions for it were more propitious. While not belittling the importance of colonial wars, he would have had difficulty accepting that the fate of the world might be decided in the jungles of Asia and Africa. The excerpts published here are from Marx's article in the *New York Tribune* of October 30, 1854 (on Spain) and from Engels's article in the London *Pall Mall Gazette* of October and November, 1870.

Marx and Engels, who showed little enthusiasm about the prospects of guerrilla warfare, became the idols of a subsequent generation of guerrillas. On the other hand, John Most (1846-1906), who first provided an elaborate strategy for "urban guerrillas," has been virtually forgotten. One of the first German Social Democrats to be elected to the Reichstag, he had to leave Germany under Bismarck's antisocialist emergency laws. Having been expelled from the party for anarchist deviations, he settled in the United States where, as editor of *Freiheit,* he had a considerable following for a time. His *Revolutionäre Kriegswissenschajt* was published in German in New York in 1884.

James Connolly (1868–1916), vice-president of the provisional government and commander of the Irish forces in Dublin, was one of the heroes of the Dublin Easter uprising of 1916. A lifelong socialist, he organized many Irish republican clubs and edited left-wing republican journals. He emigrated to the United States in 1903, became a member of the IWW, and returned to Ireland seven years later. A convert to Marxism, he nonetheless remained a Catholic and tried to provide an ideological synthesis of the two belief systems in his writings. Connolly published several articles on the technique of revolutionary warfare; the article presented here was published in the *Workers' Republic* of July 24, 1915.

Lenin, like Trotsky and Marx and Engels, seldom commented on guerrilla warfare. Because he was primarily concerned with European politics, he regarded it as merely one rather unimportant aspect of revolutionary war. Lenin's article on guerrilla warfare in *Proletary,* No. 5 (1906) points to the experiences gained in the abortive Russian revolution of 1905-6. Lenin's late references to guerrilla warfare and "guerrillaism" concern the post-revolutionary situation and are without exception negative in character.

Marshal Mikhail Nikolayevich Tukhachevsky (1893-1937) wrote three articles on how to fight counterrevolutionary guerrillas; these were published in three installments in *Voina i Revolutsia, VII -1X* (1926) and are of particular interest as an early outline of counter-guerrilla operations from unexpected quarters. Tukhachevski was Deputy Minister of War before he was executed as a spy in the great "purge" of the 1930s. He was "rehabilitated" in 1956.

# A BLUEPRINT FOR INSURRECTION

THIS PROGRAM IS PURELY MILITARY, and the political and social question, which is out of place here, is entirely set aside. In any case, it goes without saying that the revolution should [be made for the benefit of labor against the tyranny of capital and] reconstitute society on the basis of justice.

Today, a Parisian insurrection along the mistaken old lines has lost all chance of success. In 1830, the people's impulse alone was enough to overthrow an authority surprised and terrified by a show of armed force, something unheard-of and far from anticipated. It was successful, but only once. The government, which was still monarchic and counterrevolutionary, even though it had sprung from a revolution, profited by the lesson. It embarked upon a study of street warfare and soon recovered the natural superiority of skill and discipline over inexperience and confusion.

Yet, you may say, in 1848 the people gained the upper hand by the methods of 1830. Very well. But have no illusions! The victory of February was only a fluke. If Louis-Philippe had made a stout defense, power would have rested with the uniforms. The days of June are proof of this. On that occasion, it was revealed how fatal were the insurrection's tactics, or rather, how totally wanting were its tactics. Never had its chances been so splendid: the odds were ten to one in its favor. On the one hand, the government was in total disarray and the troops demoralized; on the other, all the workers were roused and almost sure of success. How were they beaten? By their lack of organization. To understand their defeat, we need only analyze their strategy.

The rising erupts. In the working class districts, barricades are at once set up, here and there, randomly, at many points. Five, ten, twenty, thirty, fifty men, assembled by chance, mostly unarmed, begin to overturn carts and carriages and pile up paving stones to bar the road, sometimes in the middle of streets, more often where roads join. Many of these barriers would present little hindrance to the passage of cavalry. Sometimes, after making a rough attempt at an entrenchment, the builders go in search of guns and ammunition.

Over six hundred barricades might have been counted in June; some thirty, at most, bore the brunt of the battle. At the others, nineteen out of every twenty, not a shot was fired. Hence those vainglorious bulletins which rapped out reports of fifty barricades— where not a soul was present—being removed.

While some men are thus taking up paving stones, other small bands go off to disarm the guard rooms or to seize powder and weapons at the gunsmiths. All this is done without concert or direction and at the whim of the individual.

Little by little, however, a certain number of barricades, higher, stronger, better built, prove more attractive to defenders, who concentrate around them. Not calculation, but chance determines the emplacement of these main fortifications. Only a few of them, by some not inconceivable kind of military inspiration, are at major street openings.

During this first stage of the insurrection, the soldiers have assembled. The generals receive and study the police reports. They take care not to imperil their detachments without sure and certain information and not to risk a setback which would demoralize the soldiery. As soon as they are thoroughly familiar with the insurgents' position, they mass their regiments at definite points which are henceforward to constitute the base of operations.

The armies are face to face. Watch their maneuvers. This is where the flaw of the people's tactics will show itself and be the infallible cause of disaster.

There is neither overall control nor general command, nor even agreement between the fighters. (No general command, hence no control.) Each barricade has its particular group which varies in number; it is always isolated. Whether its force is ten men or a hundred, it maintains no communication with the other posts. Often there is no leader to direct the defense, and where there is one, his influence counts for little. The soldiers simply follow their own way. They stay; they leave; they return as the fancy takes them. At night they go to bed.

Because of these continual comings and goings, the number of citizens changes rapidly, now down to one third, now one half, sometimes three-quarters of the total. None can rely on any other. Consequently, there is no confidence in success and so discouragement reigns.

No one knows or cares about what is happening elsewhere. Rumors fly, some gloomy, some cheerful. Drinking at the bar, the men placidly listen to the cannons and rifle fire. There is not the least notion of bringing help to the positions under attack. "Let each man defend his post," say the staunchest, "and all will go well." This peculiar reasoning is based on the fact that most insurgents are fighting in their own district. This is a fatal error with disastrous consequences, notably denunciation by neighbors after the defeat.

With such a system, defeat is a foregone conclusion. In the end, it takes the shape of two or three regiments which fall upon the barricade and crush its few defenders. The entire battle is nothing but the monotonous repetition of this unvarying maneuver. While the insurgents smoke their pipes behind the pile of paving stones, the enemy successively brings all his forces to bear on one point, then on a second, a third, a fourth, and so wipes out the insurrection piecemeal.

The people do nothing to thwart this easy task. Each group philosophically waits its turn and never takes it into its head to go to the help of an imperiled neighbor. No. "He defends his post; he cannot abandon his post."

See how men die of absurdity!

If, owing to such a gross error, the great Paris revolt of 1848 was broken like glass by the paltriest of governments, what a catastrophe might not be apprehended if the same folly were embarked upon again in the face of a cruel army—an army which can now exploit the latest achievements of science and artifice: railways, the electric telegraph, rifled cannon, and the Chassepot rifle.

Take, for example, something which should not be regarded as an advantage to the enemy—the strategic roads now scoring the city in all directions. They are feared, but wrongly so. They should cause no anxiety. Far from having created an additional danger for the insurrection, as is believed, on the contrary they offer mixed drawbacks and advantages to both parties. The soldiers, it is true, can move about them more easily; on the other hand, they are in a very exposed and unprotected position on them.

Such streets are impassable under fire. Moreover, unlike ordinary streets, their windows, balconies, and miniature bastions furnish opportunities for flanking shots. In short, these long, straight avenues are quite properly called bulwarks or boulevards, as they have been named. They really are bulwarks constituting the natural front of a very great force.

The preeminent weapon for street warfare is the gun. The cannon has more bark than bite. The only way in which artillery can be really effective is by starting fires. However, such an atrocity systematically employed on a large scale would soon rebound on its perpetrators and bring about their destruction. The grenade—which people have improperly taken to calling a bomb—is an auxiliary only and, moreover, subject to many disadvantages; it uses a great deal of powder to little effect, is highly dangerous to handle, has a negligible range, and can only be thrown out of windows to be of use. Flagstones do nearly as much damage and are cheaper. Workmen have no money to waste. For the interior of houses, the revolver and side arms, bayonets, swords, sabers, and daggers are useful. In hand-to-hand fighting, a pike or an eight-foot halberd would always master the bayonet.

The army has only two great advantages over the people, the Chassepot rifle and organization. The latter, above all, is an immense and irresistible advantage. Fortunately, the army can be dispossessed of it and then the ascendancy passes over to the insurrection.

In civil conflicts the soldiers, with rare exceptions, march reluctantly and under the influence of constraint and liquor. They wish themselves elsewhere and are readier to look behind than before them. But an iron hand holds them slaves and victims of a ruthless discipline: with no love of authority, they obey only through fear and are incapable of the slightest initiative. A detachment cut off is a detachment lost. Aware of this, their leaders make it their first care to maintain communications between all their corps. The need for this cancels out part of their effective forces.

In the ranks of the people there is nothing like this. There an idea is fought for. There are found only volunteers motivated not by fear but by enthusiasm. Superior to their adversaries in devotion, they are far more so in their intelligence. They rise above them on the moral and even on the physical scale by their conviction, vigor, resourcefulness, and agility of body and mind; both head and heart are theirs. No troops in the world equal these picked men.

---

Auguste Blanqui, *Instructions pour une prise des armes*,
ca. 1850, published posthumously

KARL MARX AND FRIEDRICH ENGELS

# GUERRILLAS IN SPAIN

W HEN THE DISASTERS OF THE STANDING ARMY became regular, the rising of the guerrillas became general, and the body of the people, hardly thinking of the national defeats, exulted in the local success of their heroes. In this point at least the central junta shared the popular delusion. "Fuller accounts were given in the *Gaceta* of an affair of guerrillas than of the battle of Ocana."

As Don Quixote had protested with his lance against gunpowder, so the guerrillas protested against Napoleon, only with different success. "These guerrillas," says the *Austrian Military Journal,* (Vol. 1, 1821), "carried their basis in themselves, as it were, and every operation against them terminated in the disappearance of its object."

There are three periods to be distinguished in the history of the guerrilla warfare. In the first period the population of whole provinces took up arms and made partisan warfare, as in Galicia and Asturias. In the second period, guerrilla bands formed of the wrecks of the Spanish armies, of Spanish deserters from the French armies, of smugglers, etc., carried on the war as their own cause, independently of all foreign influence and agreeable to their immediate interest. Fortunate events and circumstances frequently brought whole districts under their colors. As long as the guerrillas were thus constituted, they made no formidable appearance as a body, but were nevertheless extremely dangerous to the French. They formed the basis of an actual armament of the people. As soon as an opportunity for a capture offered itself, or a combined enterprise was meditated, the most active and daring among the people came out and joined the guerrillas. They rushed with the utmost rapidity upon their booty, or placed themselves in order of battle, according to the object of their undertaking. It was not uncommon to see them standing out a whole day in sight of a vigilant enemy, in order to intercept a courier or to capture supplies. It was in this way that the younger Mina captured the viceroy of Navarra, appointed by Joseph Bonaparte, and that Julian made a prisoner of the commandante of Ciudad Rodrigo. As soon as the enterprise was completed, everybody went his own way, and armed men were soon scattering in all directions. But the associated peasants quietly returned to their common occupation without „as much as their absence having been noticed." Thus, the communication on all the roads was closed. Thousands of enemies were on the spot, though not one could be discovered. No courier could be dispatched without being taken; no supplies could set out without being intercepted. In short, no movement could be effected without being observed by a hundred eyes. At the same time, there existed no means of striking at the root of a combination of this kind. The French were obliged to be constantly armed against an enemy who, continually flying, always reappeared, and was everywhere without being actually seen, the mountains serving as so many curtains. "It was," says the Abbe de Pradt, "neither battles nor engagements which exhausted the French forces, but the incessant molestations of an invisible enemy, who, if pursued, became lost among the people, out of which he reappeared immediately afterward with renewed strength. The lion in the fable tormented to death by a gnat gives a true picture of the French army."

In their third period, the guerrillas aped the regularity of the standing army, swelled their corps from three thousand to six thousand men, ceased to be the concern of whole districts, and fell into the hands of a few leaders, who made such use of them as best suited their own purposes. This change in the system of the guerrillas gave the French, in their contests with them, considerable advantage. Rendered incapable by their great numbers to conceal themselves, and to suddenly disappear without being forced into battle, as they had formerly done, the *guerrilleros* were now frequently overtaken, defeated, dispersed, and disabled for a length of time from offering any further molestation.

By comparing the three periods of guerrilla warfare with the political history of Spain, it is found that they represent the respective degrees into which the counterrevolutionary spirit of the government had succeeded in cooling the spirit of the people. Beginning with the rise of whole populations, the partisan war was next carried on by guerrilla bands, of which whole districts formed the reserve and terminated in *corps francs* (commandos) continually on the point of dwindling into *banditti,* or sinking down to the level of standing regiments.

Estrangement from the supreme government, relaxed discipline, continual disasters, constant formation, decomposition, and recomposition during six years of the *cadrez* must have necessarily stamped upon the body of the Spanish army the character of praetorianism, making them equally ready to become the tools or the scourges of their chiefs. The generals themselves had necessarily participated in, quarreled with, or conspired against the central government, and had always thrown the weight of their sword into the political balance. Thus Cuesta, who afterward seemed to win the confidence of the central junta at the same rate that he lost the battles of the country, had begun by conspiring with the *Consejo Real* (royal council) and by arresting the Leonese deputies to the central junta. General Morla himself, a member of the central junta, went over to the Bonapartist camp, after he had surrendered Madrid to the French. The coxcombical Marquis de las Romerias, also a member of the junta, conspired with the vainglorious Francisco Palafox, the wretch Montijo, and the turbulent junta of Seville against it. The Generals Castaiios, Blake, La Bisbal (an O'Donnell) figured and intrigued successively at the times of the Cortes as regents, and the Captain-General of Valencia, Don Xavier, Elio, surrendered Spain finally to the mercies of Ferdinand VII. The praetorian element was certainly more developed with the generals than with their troops.

On the other hand, the army and *guerrilleros*—which received during the war part of their chiefs, like Porlier, Lacy, Eroles and Villacampa, from the ranks of distinguished officers of the line, while the line in its turn afterward received guerrilla chiefs, like Mina, Empecinado, etc.—were the most revolutionized portion of Spanish society. They were recruited from all ranks, including the whole of the fiery, aspiring, and patriotic youth, inaccessible to the soporific influence of the central government. Some were emancipated from the shackles of the ancient regime; part of them, like Riego, return after some years' captivity in France. We are, then, not to be surprised at the influence exercised by the Spanish army in subsequent commotions; neither when taking the revolutionary initiative, nor when spoiling the revolution by praetorianism.

As to the guerrillas, it is evident that, having for some years figured upon the theater of sanguinary contests, taken to roving habits, freely indulged all their passions of hatred, revenge, and love of plunder, they must, in times of peace, form a most dangerous mob, always ready at a nod in the name of any party or principle, to step forward for him who is able to give them good pay or to afford them a pretext for plundering excursions.

---

Karl Marx and Friedrich Engels, "Revolution in Spain,"
in *New York Tribune* (October 30, 1854).

FRIEDRICH ENGELS

# FRANC-TIREURS 1870

IN THE COURSE OF THE LAST SIX WEEKS, the character of the [Franco-Prussian] war has markedly changed. The regular armies of France have disappeared. The struggle is being carried on by recently mobilized troops whose inexperience makes them more or less irregular. Wherever they attempt to mass and fight in the open, they are easily defeated. But when they fight under the cover of villages and towns equipped with barricades and embrasures, it becomes evident that they are capable of offering serious resistance. They are encouraged to carry on this type of struggle, with night surprise attacks and other methods of guerrilla warfare, by proclamations and orders from the government, which also advises the population of the district in which they operate to give them every possible assistance.

If the enemy possessed sufficient troops to occupy the whole of the country, this resistance could be easily broken. But for this, up to the surrender of Metz, he has not had the strength. The ubiquitous "four Uhlans" are no longer able to ride into a village or town outside their own lines, demanding absolute subjection to their orders, without incurring the risk of captivity or death. Requisitioning detachments have to be accompanied by escorting troops, and single companies or squadrons quartering in a village must guard against night attacks, and also, when they are on the march, against attacks from the rear. The German positions are surrounded by a belt of disputed territory, and it is just here that popular resistance makes itself felt most seriously.

In order to break this popular resistance, the Germans are resorting to a type of martial law that is as obsolete as it is barbaric. They act on the principle that any town or village in the defense of which one or more inhabitants have taken part, have fired on German troops or generally assisted the French—any such town or village is to be burnt down. Further, any man found carrying weapons, and not in their eyes a regular soldier, is to be summarily shot. When there is any suspicion that a considerable section of a town has been guilty of such a misdeed, all men capable of bearing arms are to be massacred forthwith. For the past six weeks this policy has been pitilessly carried out, and is still at this moment in full sway. One cannot open a single German newspaper without coming on half a dozen reports of such military executions. These are made to appear as a matter of course, as a simple process of military justice, carried out with salutary firmness by "honest soldiers against cowardly assassins and robbers." There is, of course, no disorder, no looting, no raping of women, no irregularity. Indeed no. Everything is done systematically, and by order. The condemned village is surrounded, the inhabitants driven out, the provisions confiscated, the houses set alight. The real or imaginary culprits are brought before a court martial, where a brief, final confession and half a dozen bullets are their certain lot.

It is no exaggeration to say that wherever the German flying columns march into the heart of France, their path is all too often marked with fire and blood. It is hardly sufficient, in this year of 1870, to claim others, not immediately recognizable as soldiers are the equivalent of banditry, and must be put down with fire and sword. Such an argument might have been valid in the day of Louis XIV or Frederick II, when there was no kind of fighting other than that of regular armies. But ever since the American War of Independence and up to the American War of Secession, it has been the rule rather than the exception for the people to take part in war. Wherever a people has allowed itself to be subjected for no other reason than that its armies have been incapable of offering resistance, it has earned general contempt as a nation of cowards. And wherever a people has energetically waged such irregular warfare, the invader soon found it impossible to carry through the obsolete law of blood and fire. The English in America, the French under Napoleon in Spain (and in 1848, the Austrians in Italy and Hungary) were very soon compelled to treat popular resistance as an entirely legitimate form of warfare. They were compelled to do so from the fear of reprisals against their own prisoners....

Of all the armies in the world, the Prussian army should have been the last to revive these practices. In 1806 Prussia collapsed solely because nowhere in the country was there any sign of such a national spirit of resistance. After 1807 the reorganizers and the administrators of the army did everything in their power to resurrect this spirit. It was at this time that Spain furnished a glorious example of how a nation can resist an invading army. The military leaders of Prussia all pointed to it as an example worthy of the emulation of their compatriots. Scharnhorst, Gneisenau, Clause-witz—all were of the same opinion. Gneisenau even went to Spain himself to take part in the struggle against Napoleon. The whole military system that was subsequently introduced in Prussia was an attempt to mobilize popular resistance against the enemy, insofar as this was possible at all in an absolute monarchy. Not only had every fit man to join the army and serve in the reserves *(Landwehr)* up to his fortieth year, but boys between seventeen and twenty and men between forty and sixty-five were also in-cluded in the *levee en masse,* or mass conscription, in the final reserves *(Landsturm)* whose function it was to rise at the rear and on the flanks of the enemy, to interfere with his movements, and to cut off his supplies and his couriers. They were expected to use any weapon they could lay their hands on and to employ without distinction all available measures to harry the invader—"the more effective the measure the better." Nor was "any kind of uniform to be worn," so that the men of the *Landsturm* might at any moment resume their character of civilians, thus remaining unrecog-nizable to the enemy.

The Landsturm Order of 1813, as the document in question was called—its author being no other than Scharnhorst, the organizer of the Prussian army—was drawn up in this spirit of irreconcilable national re-sistance, according to which all means are valid, and the most effective the best. At that time, however, all this was to be done by the Prussians against the French. When the French chose to behave in precisely the same man-ner toward the Prussians, it was quite another matter. What had become patriotism in one case became banditry and assassination in the other.

The fact is that the present Prussian government is ashamed of this old semirevolutionary *Landsturm* order, and by its actions in France seeks to erase it from memory. But the deliberate atrocities they themselves have committed in France will, instead, call it all the more to mind. The argu-ment brought forward in favor of so despicable a method of waging war serves only as proof that, if the Prussian army has immeasurably improved since Jena, the Prussian government, on the other hand, is ripening for the conditions that made Jena possible.

---

Friedrich Engels, in *Pall Mall Gazette,*
(November 11, 1870).

JOHN MOST

# THE CASE FOR DYNAMITE

THE IMPORTANCE OF MODERN EXPLOSIVES for social revolution need hardly be stressed nowadays. They are going to be the decisive factor in the next period of world history.

Naturally, therefore, revolutionaries throughout the world are increasingly trying to acquire them and learn how to use them. ...

It is of course out of the question that revolutionaries should try to procure a dynamite gun (cumbersome things over forty feet long), but they can certainly make bombs of the type described above. These bombs either have to be planted or be flung a short distance, for which latter purpose an old-fashioned catapult is quite adequate.

A bomb that can blow a hole in a rock face is bound to do a fair bit of damage at court or at a monopolists' ball. ...

Whenever it proves impossible in the struggle against the private property monster and the government hyenas to pick off by means of explosives or fire bombs those whose elimination is of special importance for the social revolution, then, for good or ill, one or more revolutionaries will have to break their cover and put their lives at risk.

I am using the word "cover" here quite deliberately; the view some simpletons hold that the revolutionary's job is just to depart this life "courageously" when in fact his job is to make sure *others* depart this life, is absolute rubbish.

Any revolutionary who frivolously endangers his own life without making absolutely certain of the success of his undertaking is acting against the interests of the revolutionary cause.

Quite apart from the fact that the bullies of "law and order" are a hundred times more frightened if the man who commits the deed remains undiscovered than if he is caught or gets himself killed, it is one of the

340

basic rules of military tactics that no group of men endangers itself during an operation more than is absolutely necessary. For this reason, two or three must never put themselves at risk when one is enough to carry out the revolutionary act.

If a revolutionary *must* undertake an action endangering his own life because there is no other way of eliminating the enemy in question, then he must make absolutely sure of the success of his mission. ....

"The explosion was like a cannon firing. The stone slab disintegrated into about twenty pieces which were hurled at least ten to fifteen feet into the air. The bomb ripped a hole two feet in diameter and of similar depth in the ground. It took some time to find any remains of the bomb. Only after a considerable search were some jagged fragments the size of revolver bullets found about thirty to forty feet away."

Now, just imagine what a magnificent effect this bomb would have had if it had been placed under the table of some gluttons having a banquet or if it had been thrown through the window onto the table. ...

It is no doubt unnecessary for me to say this, since only too many comrades have fallen into the hands of our opponents after unsuccessful missions and have perished. Knives have not been pushed in far enough and glancing shots have caused only slight wounds—not to mention shots and knives that have missed their mark entirely.

These failures have made people think of poisoning the weapons to be used in assassination attempts, but nothing has come of this idea as yet.

The reason for this is the difficulty in finding and getting hold of suitable poisons. Or to be more precise, it is revolutionaries' poverty that is to blame. ...

Good revolvers, knives, poisons, and fuses are destined to play an important role at the moment of rebellion because it is impossible for the enemy to tell whether those carrying them are armed. He has no reason to avoid them and thus can be cornered and done away within his most private hideouts.

Above all, however, one must never forget modern explosives. To be sure of success, revolutionaries should always have on hand adequate quantities of nitroglycerin, dynamite, hand grenades, and blasting charges—all easily concealed under clothing.

These weapons, the proletariat's artillery, cause surprise, confusion, and panic among the ranks of the enemy. Efforts must therefore be made to ensure that there is a ready supply of these articles. ...

A man or woman intending to carry out a revolutionary act should not discuss it with others; the deed should be kept to oneself until it is done. The only time this does not apply is when the success of the plan absolutely requires more than one person; then, he or she can select the necessary people. Naturally, to make a blunder here is simply to invite treachery!

Anyone planning an action must refrain from consorting in public with people already compromised as revolutionaries, since to do so would immediately attract the attention of spies and lead to police surveillance. From there it is only a short step to being neutralized.

If and when a revolutionary is about to be arrested, it is vital for him to remain calm and collected. Violent resistance or suicide are to be recommended only when there is a chance of destroying the aggressor or when it is already a matter of life and death. If, however, one is certain the arrest is being carried out only on the flimsiest grounds of suspicion, one should submit—with loud protestations—to the inevitable, for it will then be that much easier to save one's neck later.

A revolutionary should speak at a court hearing only if he is in a position (through an alibi, for example) to regain his freedom immediately. Otherwise he should refuse to make a statement of any kind. The lengthier the statements the law manages to wheedle out of a revolutionary, the greater the chances of his undoing.

If it actually comes to the pantomime of a court trial, then the revolutionary should only admit what has really been proven against him.

Finally, when all hope of rescue is gone, the revolutionary has a different duty, the noblest duty, to fulfil: he must defend his actions from the revolutionary-anarchist position and transform the witness stand into a tribune. In other words, one should protect one's person as long as possible so as to be available for further actions. But once it is clear that all is lost, one should use one's remaining time on earth to exploit the propaganda value of one's case as fully as possible. ...

*A tip:* the thorn apple, [aka, jimanweed and hawthorn—ed.] which can frequently be seen on rubbish dumps, in ditches, or growing in gardens as a weed, is a vulgar breed of plant, but it has its uses. Its seeds can be used for truly humanitarian ends. Grind about twenty-five of its seeds (mature black ones, of course) into a flour, then bake them into a biscuit of some kind, like an almond biscuit, and offer them to a spy, denouncer, bailiff, or similar scum. The effects will be seen immediately. Within the next few days, the rat will go raving mad and snuff it. To be highly recommended. ...

To deliver letters of this kind, procure a tin box in the shape of a normal envelope, put into it a half-dozen or more letters (according to requirements), and place it—there is no danger—in your pocket. Go for a walk and empty the tin letter by letter into the letter boxes of various notorious houses. Success is ensured after a quarter of an hour.

Treated letters can be kept in a tightly closed tin for up to eight or ten hours without spontaneous combustion because no air reaches them.

For buildings such as churches and courts, you need a small wooden box that will fit easily into an overcoat pocket. Make a false bottom for it, fill the bottom part with pitch and the top with shavings soaked in phosphorus or similarly treated letters, and add potash to this. Carefully nail on the lid and then bore holes in it with a sharp, finely pointed instrument so as to allow a little air to enter. Place it in a suitable spot (on wood or upholstered seats). The desired effect will follow in three to four hours.

Phosphorus can also be used to trigger explosions. Attach to a container filled with dynamite a small box with a lid, from which the fuse runs to the container. Soak the fuse in phosphorus and close the lid. After placing the whole device in the desired spot, remove the lid so that the fuse is exposed to the air and then calmly walk away. By the time the explosion takes place—and it will—the person responsible is safe and sound. ...

---

John Most, *Revolutionäre Kriegswissenschaft*
(New York, n.d.).

JAMES CONNOLLY

# ON STREET FIGHTING

I N THE MILITARY SENSE OF THE TERM what after all is a *street?* A street is
a defile in a city. A defile is a narrow pass through which troops can
only move by narrowing their front, and therefore making themselves
a good target for the enemy. A defile is also a difficult place for soldiers to
maneuver in, especially if the flanks of the defile are held by the enemy.

A mountain pass is a defile the sides of which are constituted by the
natural slopes of the mountainsides, as at the Scalp. A bridge over a river
is a defile the sides of which are constituted by the river. A street is a defile
the sides of which are constituted by the houses in the street.

To traverse a mountain pass with any degree of safety the sides of the
mountain must be cleared by flanking parties ahead of the main body; to
pass over a bridge the banks of the river on each side must be raked with
gun or rifle fire whilst the bridge is being rushed; to take a street properly
barricaded and held on both sides by forces in the houses, these houses
must be broken into and taken by hand-to-hand fighting. A street barricade placed in position where artillery cannot operate from a distance is
impregnable to frontal attack. To bring artillery within a couple of hundred
yards—the length of the average street—would mean the loss of the artillery if confronted by even imperfectly drilled troops armed with rifles.

The Moscow revolution, where only eighty rifles were in the possession
of the insurgents, would have ended in the annihilation of the artillery had
the number of insurgent rifles been eight hundred.

The insurrection of Paris in June, 1848, reveals how districts of towns,
or villages, should be held. The streets were barricaded at tactical points
*not on the main streets*, but commanding them. The houses were broken
through so that passages were made inside the houses along the whole
length of the streets. The party walls were loopholed, as were also the front

344

walls, the windows were blocked by sandbags, boxes filled with stones and dirt, bricks, chests, and other pieces of furniture with all sorts of odds and ends piled up against them.

Behind such defenses the insurgents poured fire upon the troops through loopholes left or the purpose.

In the attack upon Paris by the allies fighting against Napoleon a village held in this manner repulsed several assaults of the Prussian allies of England. When these Prussians were relieved by the English these latter did not dare attempt a frontal attack but instead broke into an end house on one side of the village street and commenced to take the houses one by one. Thus, all the fighting was inside the houses, and musket fire played but a small part. On one side of the street they captured all the houses, on the other they failed, and when a truce was declared the English were in possession of one side of the village, and their French enemies on the other.

The truce led to a peace. When peace was finally proclaimed, the two sides of the village street were still held by opposing forces.

The defense of a building in a city, town, or village is governed by the same rules. Such a building left unconquered is a serious danger even if its supports are all defeated. If it had been flanked by barricades, and these barricades were destroyed, no troops could afford to push on and leave the building in the hands of the enemy. If they did so, they would be running the danger of perhaps meeting a check farther on, which check would be disastrous if they had left a hostile building manned by an unconquered force to their rear. Therefore, the fortifying of a strong building, as a pivot upon which the defense of a town or village should hinge, forms a principal object of the preparations of any defending force, whether regular army or insurrectionary.

In the Franco-German War of 1870 the chateau, or castle, of Geissberg formed such a position in the French lines on 4 August. The Germans drove in all the supports of the French party occupying this country house and stormed the outer courts, but were driven back by the fire from the windows and loopholed walls. Four batteries of artillery were brought up to within nine hundred yards of the house and battered away at its walls, and battalion after battalion was hurled against it. The advance of the whole German army was delayed until this one house was taken. To take it caused a loss of twenty-three officers and three hundred twenty-nine men, yet it had only a garrison of two hundred.

In the same campaign the village of Bazeilles offered a similar lesson in the tactical strength of a well-defended line of houses. The German army drove the French off the field and entered the village without a struggle.

But it took a whole army corps seven hours to fight its way through to the other end of the village.

A mountainous country has always been held to be difficult for military operations owing to its passes or glens. A city is a huge mass of passes or glens formed by streets and lanes. Every difficulty that exists for the operation of regular troops in mountains is multiplied a hundredfold in a city. And the difficulty of the commissariat, which is likely to be insuperable to an irregular or popular force taking to the mountains, is solved for them by the sympathies of the populace when they take to the streets.

The general principle to be deducted from a study of the examples we have been dealing with is that the defense is of almost overwhelming importance in such warfare as a popular force like the Citizen Army might be called upon to participate in. Not a mere passive defense of a position valueless in itself, but the active defense of a position whose location threatens the supremacy or existence of the enemy. The genius of the commander must find such a position, the skill of his subordinates must prepare and fortify it, and the courage of all must defend it. It is only from this combination of genius, skill, and courage that the flower of military success can grow.

The Citizen Army and the Irish Volunteers are open for all those who wish to qualify for the exercise of these qualities.

---

James Connolly in *Workers' Republic* (July 24, 1915)
from *Revolutionary Warfare* (Dublin, 1968).

## V. I. LENIN

# GUERRILLA WARFARE

THE FORMS OF STRUGGLE IN THE RUSSIAN REVOLUTION are distinguished by their colossal variety compared with the bourgeois revolutions in Europe. Kautsky partly foretold this in 1902 when he said that the future revolution (with the exception *perhaps* of Russia, he added) might be not so much a struggle of the people against the government as a struggle between two sections of the people. In Russia we undoubtedly see a wider development of this latter struggle than in the bourgeoisie revolutions in the West. The enemies of our revolution among the people are few in number, but as the struggle grows more acute they become more and more organized and receive the support of the reactionary strata of the bourgeoisie. It is therefore absolutely natural and inevitable that in such a period, a period of nationwide political strikes, an uprising cannot assume the old form of individual acts restricted to a very short time and to a very small area. It is absolutely natural and inevitable that the uprising should assume the higher and more complex form of a prolonged civil war embracing the whole country, i.e., an armed struggle between two sections of the people. Such a war cannot be conceived otherwise than as a series of a few big engagements at comparatively long intervals and a large number of small encounters during these intervals. That being so—and it is undoubtedly so—the Social Democrats must absolutely make it their duty to create organizations best adapted to lead the masses in these big engagements and, as far as possible, in these small encounters as well. In a period when the class struggle has become accentuated to the point of civil war, Social Democrats must make it their duty not only to participate but also to play the leading role in this civil war. The Social Democrats must train and prepare their organizations to be really able to act as a belligerent side which does not miss a single opportunity of inflicting damage on the enemy's forces.

This is a difficult task, there is no denying. It cannot be accomplished at once. Just as the whole people are being retrained and are learning to fight in the course of the civil war, so our organizations must be trained, and must be reconstructed in conformity with the lessons of experience to be equal to this task.

We have not the slightest intentions of foisting on practical workers any artificial form of struggle, or even of deciding from our armchair what part any particular form of guerrilla warfare should play in the general course of the civil war in Russia. We are far from the thought of regarding a concrete assessment of particular guerrilla actions as indicative of a trend in Social Democracy. But we do regard it as our duty to help as far as possible to arrive at a correct *theoretical* assessment of the new forms of struggle engendered by practical life. We do regard it as our duty relentlessly to combat stereotypes and prejudices which hamper the class-conscious workers in correctly presenting a new and difficult problem and in correctly approaching its solution.

# Guerrilla Doctrine Today

# INTRODUCTORY NOTE

TWENTIETH-CENTURY WRITINGS ON GUERRILLA WARFARE are much better known than earlier ones, but no collection of the classics of guerrilla doctrine would be complete without excerpts from Mao Tse-tung and some other contemporary authors. "On Protracted War" is the text of a series of lectures delivered by Mao at Yenan in May and June 1938. Lin Piao (1907-71) was at one time Mao's closest collaborator. One of the chief commanders in the war against Chiang and the Japanese, he was appointed Minister of Defense in 1959. *Long Live the Victory of People's War,* published in 1965, created a brief sensation because of its emphasis on the encirclement of the "cities of the world" by the "rural areas of the world." Lin Piao died in a plane crash in September 1971, apparently trying to escape to the Soviet Union.

Ernesto (Che) Guevara de la Serna (1928–67) is the most important theoretician of the Cuban Revolution. The eldest son of an upper class Argentinian family, he studied medicine and joined the Castro brothers in their invasion of Cuba in November 1956. "Guerrilla Warfare—A Method," Guevara's last theoretical essay, published in *Cuba Socialista III,* No. 25, deals with the prospects for revolution in other Latin American countries. Guevara's theoretical reflections about the lessons of the Cuban war are of great interest, but they do not pertain to what really happened during the war. Such discrepancies between guerrilla myth and reality can be found in most writings on the subject. In this case, however, the divergence is very pronounced indeed. Guevara, like Castro, was a firm believer in rural guerrilla warfare; the city, as he saw it, was the grave of the guerrilla. The same view was taken by Regis Debray (1941-), the chief interpreter of Castroism-Guevarism. A graduate of the École Normale and a student of Louis Althusser, he went to Cuba in 1961. He was arrested in Bolivia in 1967 and released in 1970. *Revolution in the Revolution* was published in 1967. According to Debray the guerrilla force is the Communist Party in embryo (not vice versa); it should not be subordinated to the party. Insurrectional activity was the commandment of the hour, not political activity. In later years, having parted with his erstwhile comrades and returned to French politics, Debray admitted that his earlier views had been partly mistaken.

The shift from rural to urban guerrilla warfare is reflected in the writings of Abraham Guillen (1913–1993) and, above all, in the works of Carlos Marighella (1911–1969). Guillen, Spanish by origin, emigrated to Latin America after the end of the Spanish Civil War and became one of the chief theoreticians of urban guerrillaism. For a time he had considerable influence upon the Tupamaros, but later on he disapproved of their policy. A leading member of the Brazilian Communist Party, Marighella broke with it in 1967 and set up a terrorist organization, the Action for National Liberation (ALN). While attributing equal importance to rural and urban guerrilla warfare in theory, he concentrated in practice entirely on urban terrorism. His *Minimanual,* published in June 1969, became a guide for terrorists in many countries. Marighella and the other leaders of the ALN lost their lives in a shoot-out with the police.

Although the Vietnamese communists displayed courage, initiative, and great stamina in applying guerrilla warfare within their overall strategy, they were not innovative, and there is little in the theoretical writings of Vo Nguyen Giap and other Vietnamese leaders that was not stated earlier by Mao and his comrades.

Of all the African guerrilla leaders, Amilcar Cabral (1926-1973) of Guinea-Bissau, a nonorthodox Marxist-Leninist, was the most successful, even though Portuguese Guinea-Bissau was anything but the ideal country from a guerrilla point of view.

MAO TSE-TUNG

# THE THREE STAGES OF THE PROTRACTED WAR

SINCE THE SINO-JAPANESE WAR is a protracted one and final victory will belong to China, it can reasonably be assumed that this protracted war will pass through three stages. The first stage covers the period of the enemy's strategic offensive and our strategic defensive. The second stage will be the period of the enemy's strategic consolidation and our preparation of the counteroffensive. The third stage will be the period of our strategic counteroffensive and the enemy's strategic retreat. It is impossible to predict the concrete situation in the three stages, but certain main trends in the war may be pointed out in the light of present conditions. The course of objective events will be exceedingly rich and varied, with many twists and turns, and nobody can cast a "horoscope" for the Sino-Japanese War; nevertheless it is necessary for the strategic direction of the war to make an outline sketch of its trends. Although our sketch may not be in full accord with the subsequent facts and will be amended by them, it is still necessary to make such a sketch in order to give firm and purposeful strategic direction to the protracted war.

The first stage has not yet ended. The enemy's design is to occupy Canton, Wuhan, and Lanchow and link up these three points. To accomplish this aim the enemy will have to use at least fifty divisions, or about one-and-a-half million men, spend from one-and-a-half to two years, and expend more than ten thousand million yen. In penetrating so deeply, the enemy will encounter immense difficulties, with consequences disastrous beyond imagination. As for attempting to occupy the entire length of the Canton-Hankow railway and the Sian-Lanchow highway, he will have to fight perilous battles and, even so, may not fully accomplish his design. But in drawing up our operational plan we should base ourselves on the assumption that the enemy may occupy the three points and even certain additional areas, as well as link them up. We should make dispositions for a protracted war, so that even if the enemy accomplishes all his plans. We shall be able to cope with him. In this stage the form of fighting we should adopt is primarily mobile warfare, to be supplemented by guerrilla and positional warfare. Through the subjective errors of the Kuomintang military authorities, positional warfare was assigned the primary role in the first phase of this stage; nevertheless, it is supplementary from the point of view of the stage as a whole. In this stage, China has already built up a broad united front and achieved unprecedented unity. Although the enemy has used and will continue to use base and shameless means to induce capitulation in the attempt to realize his plan for a quick decision and to conquer the whole of China without much effort, he has failed so far. Nor is he likely to succeed in the future. In this stage, in spite of considerable losses, China has made considerable progress, which will become the main basis for her continued resistance in the second stage. In the present stage the Soviet Union has already given substantial aid to China. On the enemy side, there are already signs of flagging morale, and the momentum of attack of his army is less in the middle phase of this stage than in the initial phase and will diminish still further in the concluding phase. His finances and economy are beginning to show signs of exhaustion. War weariness is beginning to set in among his people and troops, and within the clique that is running the war, "war frustrations" are beginning to manifest themselves and pessimism about the prospects of the war is growing.

The second stage may be termed one of strategic stalemate. At the tail end of the first stage, the enemy will be forced to fix certain terminal points to his strategic offensive owing to his shortage of troops and our firm resistance, and upon reaching them he will stop his strategic offensive and enter the stage of safeguarding his occupied areas. In the second stage, the enemy will attempt to safeguard the occupied areas and to make them his own by the fraudulent method of setting up puppet governments, while plundering the Chinese people to the limit; but again he will be confronted with stubborn guerrilla warfare. Taking advantage of the fact that the enemy's rear is unguarded, our guerrilla warfare will develop extensively in the first stage, and many base areas will be established, seriously threatening the enemy's consolidation of the occupied areas, and so in the second stage there will still be widespread fighting. In this stage, our form of fighting will be primarily guerrilla warfare, supplemented by mobile warfare. China will still retain a large regular army, but she will find it difficult to launch the strategic counteroffensive immediately because, on the one hand, the enemy will adopt a strategically defensive position in the big cities and along the main lines of communication under his occupation and, on the other hand, China will not yet be adequately equipped technically. Except for the troops engaged in frontal defense against the enemy, our forces will be switched in large numbers to the enemy's rear in comparatively dispersed dispositions. Basing themselves on all the areas not actually occupied by the enemy and coordinating with the people's local armed forces, they will launch extensive, fierce guerrilla warfare against enemy-occupied places, keeping the enemy on the move as far as possible in order to destroy him in mobile warfare, as is now being done in Shansi Province. The fighting in the second stage will be ruthless, and the country will suffer serious devastation. But the guerrilla warfare will be successful, and if it is well conducted the enemy may be able to retain only about one-third of his occupied territory, with the remaining two-thirds back in our hands, which will constitute a great defeat for the enemy and a great victory for China. By then the enemy-occupied territory as a whole will fall into three categories: first, the enemy base areas; second, our base areas for guerrilla warfare; and, third, the guerrilla areas contested by both sides. The duration of this stage will depend on the degree of change in the balance of forces between us and the enemy and on the changes in the international situation. Generally speaking, we should be prepared to see this stage last a comparatively long time and to weather its hardships. It will be a very painful period for China; the two big problems will be economic difficulties and the disruptive activities of the traitors. The enemy will go all out to wreck China's united front, and the traitor organizations in all the occupied areas will merge into a so-called unified government. Owing to the loss of big cities and the hardships of war, vacillating elements within our ranks will clamor for compromise, and pessimism will grow to a serious extent. Our tasks will then be to mobilize the whole people to unite as one man and carry on the war with unflinching perseverance, to broaden and consolidate the united front, sweep away all pessimism and ideas of compromise, promote the will to hard struggle and apply new wartime policies, and so to weather the hardships. In the second stage, we will have to call upon the whole country resolutely to maintain a united government, oppose splits, and systematically improve our fighting technique, reform the armed forces, mobilize the entire people, and prepare for the counteroffensive. The international situation will become still more unfavorable to Japan and the main international forces will incline toward giving more help to China, even though there may be talk of "realism" of the Chamberlain type which accommodates itself to *faits accomplis*. Japan's threat to Southeast Asia and Siberia will become greater, and there may even be another war. As regards Japan, scores of her divisions will be inextricably bogged down in China. Widespread guerrilla warfare and the people's anti-Japanese movement will wear down this big Japanese force, greatly reducing it and also disintegrating its morale by stimulating the growth of homesickness, war-wariness, and even antiwar sentiment. Though it would be wrong to say that Japan will achieve no results at all in her plunder of China, yet, being short of capital and harassed by guerrilla warfare, she cannot possibly achieve rapid or substantial results. This second stage will be the transitional stage of the entire war; it will be the most trying period but also the pivotal one. Whether China becomes an independent country or is reduced to a colony will be determined not by the retention or loss of the big cities in the first stage but by the extent to which the whole nation exerts itself in the second. If we can persevere in the War of Resistance, in the united front and in the protracted war, China will in that stage gain the power to change from weak to strong. It will be the second act in the three-act drama of China's War of Resistance. And through the efforts of the entire cast it will be possible to perform a most brilliant last act.

The third stage will be the stage of the counteroffensive to recover our lost territories. Their recovery will depend mainly upon the strength which China has built up in the preceding stage and which will continue to grow in the third stage. But China's strength alone will not be sufficient, and we shall also have to rely on the support of international forces and on the changes that will take place inside Japan, or otherwise we shall not be able to win. This adds to China's tasks in international propaganda and diplomacy. In the third stage, our war will no longer be one of strategic defensive, but will turn into a strategic counteroffensive manifesting itself in strategic offensives. And it will no longer be fought on strategically interior lines, but will shift gradually to strategically exterior lines. Not until we fight our way to the Yalu River can this war be considered over. The third stage will be the last in the protracted war, and when we talk of persevering in the war to the end, we mean going all the way through this stage. Our primary form of fighting will still be mobile warfare, but positional warfare will rise to importance. While positional defence cannot be regarded as important in the first stage because of the prevailing circumstances, positional attack will become quite important in the third stage because of the changed conditions and the requirements of the task. In the third stage guerrilla warfare will still provide strategic support by supplementing mobile and positional warfare, but it will not be the primary form as in the second stage.

It is thus obvious that the war is protracted and consequently ruthless in nature. The enemy will not be able to gobble up the whole of China but will be able to occupy many places for a considerable time. China will not be able to oust the Japanese quickly, but the greater part of her territory will remain in her hands. Ultimately the enemy will lose and we will win, but we shall have a hard stretch of road to travel.

The Chinese people will become tempered in the course of this long and ruthless war. The political parties taking part in the war will also be steeled and tested. The united front must be persevered in. Only by persevering in the united front can we persevere in the war, and only by persevering in the united front and in the war can we win final victory. Only thus can all difficulties be overcome. After traveling the hard stretch of road we shall reach the highway to victory. This is the natural logic of the war.

Mao Tse-tung, *On Protracted War* (1938).

LIN PIAO

# ENCIRCLING THE CITIES OF THE WORLD

WHAT SHOULD THE OPPRESSED NATIONS and the oppressed people do in the face of wars of aggression and armed suppression by the imperialists and their lackeys? Should they submit and remain slaves in perpetuity? Or should they rise in resistance and fight for their liberation?

Comrade Mao Tse-tung answered this question in vivid terms. He said that after long investigation and study the Chinese people discovered that all the imperialists and their lackeys "have swords in their hands and are out to kill. The people have come to understand this and so act after the same fashion." This is called doing unto them what they do unto us.

In the last analysis, whether one dares to wage a tit-for-tat struggle against armed aggression and suppression by the imperialists and their lackeys whether one dares to fight a people's war against them means whether one dares to embark on revolution. This is the most effective touchstone for distinguishing genuine from fake revolutionaries and Marxist-Leninists. *terrorism a matter of revolution*

In view of the fact that some people were afflicted with the fear of the imperialists and reactionaries, Comrade Mao put forward his famous thesis that "the imperialists and all reactionaries are paper tigers." He said that all reactionaries are paper tigers. In appearance, the reactionaries are terrifying, but in reality they are not so powerful. From a long-term point of view, it is not the reactionaries but the people who are really powerful.

The history of the people's war in China and other countries provides conclusive evidence that the growth of the people's revolutionary forces from weak and small beginnings into strong and large forces is a universal law of development of class struggle, a universal law of development of a

357

people's war. A people's war inevitably meets with many difficulties, with ups and downs and setbacks in the course of its development, but no force can alter its general trend toward inevitable triumph.

Comrade Mao points out that we must despise the enemy strategically and take full account of him tactically.

To despise the enemy strategically is an elementary requirement for a revolutionary. Without the courage to despise the enemy and without daring to win, it will be simply impossible to make revolution and wage a people's war, let alone to achieve victory.

It is also very important for revolutionaries to take full account of the enemy tactically. It is likewise impossible to win victory in a people's war without taking full account of the enemy tactically and without examining the concrete conditions, without being prudent and giving great attention to the study of the art of struggle and without adopting appropriate forms of struggle in the concrete practice of the revolution in each country and with regard to each concrete problem of struggle.

Dialectical and historical materialism teaches us that what is important primarily is not that which at the given moment seems to be durable and yet is already beginning to die away, but that which is arising and developing, even though at the given moment it may not appear to be durable, for only that which is arising and developing is invincible.

Why can the apparently weak newborn forces always triumph over the decadent forces which appear so powerful? The reason is that truth is on their side and that the masses are on their side, while the reactionary classes are always divorced from the masses and set themselves against the masses.

This has been borne out by the victory of the Chinese revolution, by the history of all revolutions, the whole history of class struggle and the entire history of mankind.

The imperialists are extremely afraid of Comrade Mao's thesis that "imperialism and all reactionaries are paper tigers," and the revisionists are extremely hostile to it. They all oppose and attack this thesis and the philistines follow suit by ridiculing it. But all this cannot in the least diminish its importance. The light of truth cannot be dimmed by anybody.

Comrade Mao's theory of a people's war solves not only the problem of daring to fight a people's war, but also that of how to wage it.

Comrade Mao is a great statesman and military scientist, proficient at directing war in accordance with its laws. By the line and policies, the strategy and tactics he formulated for the people's war, he led the Chinese people in steering the ship of the people's war past all hidden reefs to the shores of victory in most complicated and difficult conditions.

It must be emphasized that Comrade Mao's theory of the establishment of rural revolutionary base areas and the encirclement of the cities from the countryside is of outstanding and universal practical importance for the present revolutionary struggles of all the oppressed nations and peoples, and particularly for the revolutionary struggles of the oppressed nations and peoples in Asia, Africa, and Latin America against imperialism and its lackeys.

Many countries and peoples in Asia, Africa, and Latin America are now being subjected to aggression and enslavement on a serious scale by the imperialists headed by the United States and their lackeys. The basic political and economic conditions in many of these countries have many similarities to those that prevailed in old China. As in China, the peasant question is extremely important in these regions. The peasants constitute the main force of the national democratic revolution against the imperialists and their lackeys. In committing aggression against these countries, the imperialists usually begin by seizing the big cities and the main lines of communication, but they are unable to bring the vast countryside completely under their control. The countryside, and the countryside alone, can provide the broad areas in which the revolutionaries can maneuver freely. The countryside, and the countryside alone, can provide the revolutionary bases from which the revolutionairies can go forward to final victory. Precisely for this reason, Comrade Mao's theory of establishing revolutionary base areas in the rural districts and encircling the cities from the countryside is attracting more and more attention among the people in these regions.

Taking the entire globe, if North America and western Europe can be called "the cities of the world," then Asia, Africa, and Latin America constitute the "rural areas of the world." Since World War II, the proletarian revolutionary movement has for various reasons been temporarily held back in the North American and western European capitalist countries, while the people's revolutionary movement in Asia, Africa, and Latin America has been growing vigorously. In a sense, the contemporary world revolution also presents a picture of the encirclement of cities by the rural areas. In the final analysis, the whole cause of world revolution hinges on the revolutionary struggles of the Asian, African, and Latin American peoples who make up the overwhelming majority of the world's population. The socialist countries should regard it as their internationalist duty to support the people's revolutionary struggles in Asia, Africa, and Latin America.

---

Lin Piao, *Long Live the Victory of People's War*
(Peking, 1965).

CHE GUEVARA

# GUERRILLA WARFARE—
# A METHOD

URING THE WAGING OF THE ARMED STRUGGLE, two moments of extreme danger for the future of the revolution appear. The first arises during the preparatory stage, and the manner in which it is resolves determines the decision to struggle and the clear understanding that the popular forces have of the ends. When the bourgeois state advances against the positions of the people, obviously a defensive process against the enemy must be created which, once it achieves superiority, attacks. If minimum objective and subjective conditions have already developed, the defense should be armed, but in such a way that the popular forces are not converted into mere recipients of the blows of enemies. Nor should the stage for armed defense simply be a last refuge for the persecuted. The guerrilla, the people's defensive movement at a given moment, has in itself, and constantly should develop, its ability to attack the enemy. In time, this ability is what will determine its nature as a catalyst of the popular forces. It merits being said that guerrilla activity is not passive self-defense; it is defense with attack, and from the moment it establishes itself as such, its final goal is the conquest of political power.

This moment is important. In the social processes, the difference between violence and nonviolence cannot be measured by the number of shots that are exchanged; it yields to concrete and fluctuating situations. And it is necessary to be able to see the instant in which the popular forces, aware of their relative weakness, but, at the same time, of their strategic strength, must force the enemy to take the necessary steps so that the situation does not retrocede. The balance between the oligarchic dictatorship and popular pressure must be upset. The dictatorship constantly tries to operate without the showy use of force. Forcing the dictatorship to ap-

*unveiling the repressive nature of govt*

pear undisguised—that is, in its true aspect of violent dictatorship of the reactionary classes— will contribute to its unmasking, which will intensify the struggle to such extremes that there is no turning back. The manner in which the people's forces—dedicated to the task of making the dictatorship define itself, holding back or unleashing the battle—carry out their function depends on the firm beginning of a long-range armed action.

Escape from the other dangerous moment depends on the power of growing development which the popular forces possess. Marx always maintained that once the revolutionary process had begun, the proletariat had to strike and strike unceasingly. Revolution that does not constantly become more profound is a regressive revolution. Tired soldiers begin to lose faith and then some of the maneuvers to which the bourgeoisie has so accustomed us may appear. These can be elections with the transfer of power to another gentleman with a more mellifluous voice and a more angelic countenance than the current dictator, or a coup by reactionaries generally led by the army and directly or indirectly supported by progressive forces. There are others, but we do not intend to analyze tactical stratagems.

Principally, we are calling attention to the maneuvers of the military coup that was previously mentioned. What can the military give to the true democracy? What loyalty can one ask of them if they are mere tools of the domination of the reactionary classes and of the imperialist monopolies, and, as a caste, whose value depends upon the weapons it possesses, aspire merely to maintain their privileges?

In situations difficult for oppressors, when the military plot and oust a dictator who, de facto has already been beaten, it must be supposed that they do it because the dictator is not capable of preserving their class privileges without extreme violence, which, in general, now does not suit the interest of oligarchies.

This in no way means rejecting the use of the military as individual fighters, separated from the social milieu in which they have operated and, in fact, rebelled against. But this use must be made in the framework of the revolutionary course to which they will belong as fighters and not as representatives of a caste.

In the preface to the third edition of *The Civil War in France,* Engels said, "After each revolution, the workers were armed; for that reason, the disarmament of the workers was the first order of the bourgeoisie who headed the State. Hence, after each revolution won by the workers, a new struggle developed that culminated with their overthrow…" (Lenin, *The State and the Revolution*).

This game of continual struggles, in which formal changes of any type are attained (only to strategically regress) has been repeated for decades in the capitalist world. But still, permanent deception of the proletariat in this aspect has been going on periodically for more than a century.

It is also dangerous that, moved by the desire to maintain for some time the conditions most favorable for revolutionary action by means of the use of certain aspects of bourgeois legality, the leaders of the progressive party confuse the terms—which is very common during the course of the action—and forget the final strategic objective: seizure of power.

These two difficult moments of the revolution, which we have briefly analyzed, are obviated when the leading Marxist-Leninist parties are able to see clearly the implications of the moment and to mobilize the masses, to the greatest extent, by correctly leading them to resolve fundamental contradictions.

In discussing the subject, we have assumed that, eventually, the idea of armed struggle and also the formula of guerrilla warfare as a method of combat will be accepted. Why do we estimate that guerrilla warfare is the correct method under the present conditions in America? There are basic arguments which, to our mind, determine the necessity of guerrilla action in America as the central axis of the struggle.

First: Accepting as truth the fact that the enemy will struggle to keep himself in power, it is necessary to consider the destruction of the op- pressing army. But to destroy it, it is necessary to oppose it with a popular army. This army is not created spontaneously but must arm itself from its enemy's arsenal, and this causes a hard and very long struggle in which the popular forces and their leaders would be continually exposed to attack from superior forces without suitable conditions for defense and maneu- verability.

On the other hand, the guerrilla nucleus, settled in terrain favorable to the struggle, guarantees the security and permanence of the revolutionary command. The urban forces, directed from the general staff of the army of the people, can carry out actions of incalculable importance. The possible destruction of these groups would not kill the soul of the revolution. Its leadership, from its rural fortress, would continue to catalyze the revolu- tionary spirit of the masses and organize new forces for other battles.

Furthermore, the organization of the future state apparatus begins in this zone. It is in charge of efficiently guiding the class dictatorship during the entire transition period. The longer the battle, the greater and more complex will be the administrative problems, and in solving them, cadres will be trained for the difficult task of consolidating power and economic development in a future stage.

Second: We have to look at the general situation of the Latin American peasants and the progressively more explosive nature of their struggle against feudal structures in the framework of a social situation of alliance between local and foreign exploiters.

Returning to the Second Declaration of Havana: "The peoples of America freed themselves from Spanish colonialism at the beginning of the last century, but they did not free themselves from exploitation. The feudal landlords took over the authority of the Spanish governors, the Indians continued in grinding slavery, the Latin American man in one form or another followed in the steps of the slave, and the slightest hopes of the people crumbled under the power of oligarchies and the yoke of foreign capital. This has been the situation in [Latin] America, in one form or another. Today Latin America is under an even more ferocious imperialism, far more powerful and ruthless than Spanish colonial imperialism.

"And faced with the objective and historically inexorable reality of the Latin American revolution, what is the attitude of Yankee imperialism? To prepare to begin a colonial war with the peoples of Latin America; to create an apparatus of force, political pretexts, and pseudo-legal instruments signed with the representatives of reactionary oligarchies and to repress by blood and fire the struggle of the Latin American peoples."

This objective situation demonstrates the force that slumbers, unproductive, in our peasants and the need for using it for the liberation of America.

Third: The continental character of the struggle. Could this new stage of the emancipation of America be conceived as the meeting of two local forces struggling for power in a given territory? Only with difficulty. The struggle will be to the death between all the popular forces and all the forces of repression. The paragraphs quoted above also predict it.

The Yankees will intervene out of solidarity of interests and because the struggle in America is a decisive one. In fact, they are already intervening in the preparation of repressive forces and in the organization of a continental fighting apparatus. But, from now on, they will do it with all their energies. They will punish the popular forces with all the destructive weapons at their disposal; they will not permit the revolutionary power to consolidate, and if anyone should do so, they will again attack, they will not recognize it, they will try to divide the revolutionary forces, they will introduce saboteurs of every kind, they will create border problems, they will turn other reactionary states against them, they will try to smother the economy of the new state; in one word, to annihilate it.

With this American panorama, it is difficult to achieve and consolidate victory in an isolated country. The unity of repressive forces must be answered with the unity of popular forces. In all countries where oppression reaches unbearable levels, the banner of rebellion must be raised, and this banner will have, because of historical need, continental features. The Andes Cordillera is called on to be the Sierra Maestra of America, as Fidel has said, and all the vast territories of the continent are called to be the scene of the struggle to the death against the imperialist power.

Che Guevara, "Guerrilla Warfare—A Method,"
in *Cuba Socialista,* III, No. 25.

REGIS DEBRAY

# THE GUERRILLA AS THE POLITICAL VANGUARD

IN CUBA, MILITARY (OPERATIONAL) and political leadership have been combined in one man: Fidel Castro. Is this the result of mere chance, without significance; or is it an indication of a historically different situation? Is it an exception or does it foreshadow something fundamental? What light does it throw on the current Latin American experience? We must decipher this experience in time, and we must not rush to condemn history in the making because it does not conform to received principles. Fidel Castro said recently, "I am accused of heresy. It is said that I am a heretic within the camp of Marxism-Leninism. Hmm! It is amusing that so-called Marxist organizations, which fight like cats and dogs in their dispute over possession of revolutionary truth, accuse us of wanting to apply the Cuban formula mechanically. They reproach us with a lack of understanding of the party's role; they reproach us as heretics within the camp of Marxism-Leninism."

The fact is that those who want mechanically to apply formulas to the Latin American reality are precisely these same "Marxists," since it is always in the interest of the man who commits a robbery to be the first to cry thief. But what does Fidel Castro say that causes him to be characterized as "a heretic," "subjective," and "petty bourgeois"? What explosive message of his causes people in the capitals of America and of the socialist countries of Europe and Asia, all those who "want to wage revolutionary war by telepathy," "the unprincipled ones," to join in the chorus against the Cuban Revolution?

"Who will make the revolution in Latin America? Who?" asks Castro "The people, the revolutionaries, with or without a party."

Fidel Castro says simply that there is no revolution without a vanguard;

365

that this vanguard is not necessarily the Marxist-Leninist party; and that those who want to make the revolution have the right and the duty to constitute themselves a vanguard, independent of these parties.

It takes courage to state the facts out loud when these facts contradict a tradition. There is, then, no metaphysical equation in which vanguard = Marxist-Leninist party, there are merely dialectical conjunctions between a given function (that of the vanguard in history) and a given form of organization (that of the Marxist-Leninist party). These conjunctions arise out of prior history and depend on it. Parties exist here on earth and are subject to the rigors of terrestrial dialectics. If they have been born, they can die and be reborn in other forms. How does this rebirth come about? Under what form can the historic vanguard reappear?

Let us proceed systematically, posing a series of question and issues.

*Question 1:* How can we think or state that under the present circumstances there can be a revolution "with or without a party"? This question must be asked, not in order to revive useless and sterile animosities (of which the chief beneficiary is the counterrevolution everywhere), but because the answer to the second question is contingent on it.

*Question 2:* In what form can the historic vanguard appear?

What is depends on what was, what will be on what is. The question of parties, as they are today, is a question of history. To answer it we must look to the past.

A party is marked by its conditions of birth, its development, the class or alliance of classes that it represents, and the social milieu in which it has developed. Let us take the same counter-examples in order to discover what historic conditions permit the application of the traditional formula for party and guerrilla relationships: China and Vietnam.

The Chinese and Vietnamese parties were involved from the beginning with the problem of establishing revolutionary power. This link was not theoretical but practical and manifested itself very early, in the form of a grievous experience. The Chinese party was born in 1921, when Sun Yat-sen's bourgeois revolution—in which it participated by reason of its affiliation with the Kuomintang—was in ascendancy. From its inception it received direct aid from the Soviet mission, including military advisers led by Joffe and later by Borodin. The latter, on his arrival, organized the training of Chinese Communist officers at the Whampoa Military Academy, which soon permitted the Chinese party, as Mao Tse-tung said in 1938, "to recognize the importance of military matters." Three years after it was organized it underwent the disastrous experience of the first revolutionary civil war (1924–7), the urban insurrection, and the Canton strike in which it took a leading role. It assimilated this experience and, under the aegis of Mao Tse-tung, transmuted it into self-critical understanding, which led to the adoption of an antithetical line, contrary even to the advice of the Third International, i.e., the withdrawal to the countryside and the split with the Kuomintang.

The Vietnamese party came into being in 1930, immediately organized peasant insurrections in the hinterland which were quickly repressed, and two years later defined its line, under the aegis of Ho Chi Minh, in its first program of action: "The only path to liberation is that of armed mass struggle." "Our party," wrote Giap, "came into being when the Vietnamese revolutionary movement was at its peak. From the beginning it led the peasants, encouraged them to rise up and establish Soviet power. Thus, at an early stage, it became aware of the problems of revolutionary power and of armed struggle." In brief, these parties transformed themselves, within a few years of their founding, into vanguard parties, each one with its own political line, elaborated independently of international social forces, and each profoundly linked to its people.

In the course of their subsequent development, international contradictions were to place these parties—like the Bolshevik party some years earlier—at the head of popular resistance to foreign imperialism: in China, against the Japanese invasion in 1937; in Vietnam also, against the Japanese in 1939; and against the French colonialists in 1945. The antifeudal revolt was thus transformed into an anti-imperialist revolt, the latter giving impetus to the former. The class struggle took the form of a patriotic war, and the establishment of socialism corresponded to the restoration of national independence; the two are linked. These parties, spearheading the war of the people against the foreigners, consolidated themselves as the standard-bearers of the fatherland. They became an integral part of it.

The circumstances of this same war of liberation led certain parties, originally composed of students and of the best of the workers' elite, to withdraw to the countryside to carry on a guerrilla war against the occupying forces. They then merged with the agricultural workers and small farmers, and the Red Army and the Liberation Forces (Vietminh) were transformed into peasant armies under the leadership of the party of the working class. They achieved *in practice* the alliance of the majority class and the vanguard class: the worker-peasant alliance. The Communist Party, in this case, was the result and the generative force of this alliance. So were its leaders, not artificially appointed by a congress or co-opted in traditional fashion, but tested, molded, and tempered by this terrible struggle which they led to victory. Function makes the functionary, but paradoxically only historic individuals "make history."

367

Without going into detail, historic circumstances have not permitted Latin American Communist parties, for the most part, to take root or develop in the same way. The conditions of their founding, their growth, their link with the exploited classes are obviously different. Each one may have its own history, but they are alike in that they have not, since their founding, lived through the experience of winning power in the way the Chinese and Vietnamese parties have. They have not had the opportunity, existing as they do in countries possessing formal political independence, of leading a war of national liberation. They have therefore not been able to achieve the worker-peasant alliance—an interrelated aggregation of limitations arising from shared historical conditions.

The natural result of this history is a certain structure of directive bodies and of the parties themselves, adopted to the circumstances in which they were born and grew. But, by definition, historic situations are not immutable. The Cuban Revolution and the processes it has set in motion throughout Latin America have upset the old perspectives. A revolutionary armed struggle, wherever it exists or is in preparation, requires a thoroughgoing transformation of peacetime practices. War, as we know, is an extension of politics, but with specific procedures and methods. The effective leadership of an armed revolutionary struggle requires a new style of leadership, a new method of organization, and new physical and ideological responses on the part of leaders and militants.

A new style of leadership: It has been widely demonstrated that guerrilla warfare is directed not from outside but from within, with the leadership accepting its full share of the risks involved. In a country where such a war is developing, most of the organization's leaders must leave the cities and join the guerrilla army. This is, first of all, a security measure, assuring the survival of the political leaders. One Latin American party has already made this decision. This same party has likewise transformed its central committee, replacing most of the old leaders with young men directly involved in the war or in the underground struggle in the cities. The reconstitution of the party thus goes hand in hand with its rejuvenation.

In Latin America, wherever armed struggle is the order of the day, there is a close tie between biology and ideology. However absurd or shocking this relationship may seem, it is nonetheless a decisive one. An elderly man, accustomed to city living, molded by other circumstances and goals, will not easily adjust himself to the mountain nor, though this is less so, to underground activity in the cities. In addition to the moral factor (conviction), physical fitness is the most basic of all skills needed for waging guerrilla war; the two factors go hand in hand. A perfect Marxist education is not, at the outset, an imperative condition. That an elderly man should be a proven militant—and possess a revolutionary training—is not, alas, sufficient for coping with guerrilla existence, especially in the early stages. Physical aptitude is the prerequisite for all other aptitudes; a minor point of limited theoretical appeal, but the armed struggle appears to have a rationale of which theory knows nothing.

*A New Organization:* The reconstitution of the party into an effective directive organism, equal to the historic task, requires that an end be put to the plethora of commissions, secretariats, congresses, conferences, plenary sessions, meetings, and assemblies at all levels—national, provincial, regional, and local. Faced with a state of emergency and a militarily organized enemy such a mechanism is paralyzing at best, catastrophic at worst. It is the cause of the vice of excessive deliberation which Fidel has spoken of and which hampers executive, centralized, and vertical methods, combined with the large measure of tactical independence of subordinate groups which is demanded in the conduct of military operations....

Regis Debray, *Revolution in the Revolution*
(New York, 1967).

CARLOS MARIGHELLA

# FROM THE "MINIMANUAL"

## A DEFINITION OF THE URBAN GUERRILLA

The chronic structural crisis characteristic of Brazil today, and its resultant political instability, are what have brought about the upsurge of revolutionary war in the country. The revolutionary war manifests itself in the form of urban guerrilla warfare, psychological warfare, or rural guerrilla warfare. Urban guerrilla warfare or psychological warfare in the city depends on the urban guerrilla.

The urban guerrilla is a man who fights the military dictatorship with arms, using unconventional methods. A political revolutionary and an ardent patriot, he is a fighter for his country's liberation, a friend of the people and of freedom. The urban guerrilla operates in the large Brazilian cities. There are also bandits, commonly known as outlaws, who work in the big cities. Many times assaults by outlaws are taken as actions by urban guerrillas.

The urban guerrilla, however, differs radically from the outlaw. The outlaw benefits personally from the action, and attacks indiscriminately without distinguishing between the exploited and the exploiters, which is why there are so many ordinary men and women among his victims. The urban guerrilla follows a political goal and only attacks the government, the big capitalists, and the foreign imperialists, particularly North Americans.

Another element just as prejudicial as the outlaw and also operating in the urban area is the right-wing counterrevolutionary who creates confusion, assaults banks, hurls bombs, kidnaps, assassinates, and commits the worst imaginable crimes against urban guerrillas, revolutionary priests, students, and citizens who oppose fascism and seek liberty.

The urban guerrilla is an implacable enemy of the government and systematically inflicts damage on the authorities and on the men who

370

dominate the country and exercise power. The principal task of the urban guerrilla is to distract, to wear out, to demoralize the militarists, the military dictatorship and its repressive forces, and also to attack and destroy the wealth and property of the North Americans, the foreign managers, and the Brazilian upper class.

The urban guerrilla is not afraid of dismantling and destroying the present Brazilian economic, political, and social system, for his aim is to help the rural guerrilla and to collaborate in the creation of a totally new and revolutionary social and political structure, with the armed people in power....

## PERSONAL QUALITIES OF THE URBAN GUERRILLA AND HOW HE SUBSISTS

The urban guerrilla is characterized by his bravery and decisive nature. He must be a good tactician and a good shot. The urban guerrilla must be a person of great astuteness to compensate for the fact that he is not sufficiently strong in arms, ammunition, and equipment.

The career militarists or the government police have modern arms and transport, and can go about anywhere freely, using the force of their power. The urban guerrilla does not have such resources at his disposal and leads a clandestine existence. Sometimes he is a convicted person or is out on parole, and is obliged to use false documents.

Nevertheless, the urban guerrilla has a certain advantage over the conventional military or the police. It is that, while the military and the police act on behalf of the enemy, whom the people hate, the urban guerrilla defends a just cause, which is the people's cause.

The urban guerrilla's arms are inferior to the enemy's, but from a moral point of view, the urban guerrilla has an undeniable superiority.

This moral superiority is what sustains the urban guerrilla. Thanks to it, the urban guerrilla can accomplish his principal duty, which is to attack and to survive.

The urban guerrilla has to capture or divert arms from the enemy to be able to fight. Because his arms are not uniform, since what he has are expropriated or have fallen into his hands in different ways, the urban guerrilla faces the problem of a variety of arms and a shortage of ammunition. Moreover, he has no place to practice shooting and marksmanship.

These difficulties have to be surmounted, forcing the urban guerrilla to be imaginative and creative, qualities without which it would be impossible for him to carry out his role as a revolutionary.

The urban guerrilla must possess initiative, mobility, and flexibility, as

371

well as versatility and a command of any situation. Initiative especially is an indispensable quality. It is not always possible to foresee everything, and the urban guerrilla cannot let himself become confused, or wait for orders. His duty is to act, to find adequate solutions for each problem he faces, and not to retreat. It is better to err acting than to do nothing for fear of erring. Without initiative there is no urban guerrilla warfare.

Other important qualities in the urban guerrilla are: to be a good walker, to be able to stand up against fatigue, hunger, rain, heat. To know how to hide and to be vigilant. To conquer the art of dissembling. Never to fear danger. To behave the same by day as by night. Not to act impetuously. To have unlimited patience. To remain calm and cool in the worst conditions and situations. Never to leave a track or trail. Not to get discouraged.

In the face of the almost insurmountable difficulties of urban warfare, sometimes comrades weaken, leave, give up the work.

The urban guerrilla is not a businessman in a commercial firm nor is he a character in a play. Urban guerrilla warfare, like rural guerrilla warfare, is a pledge the guerrilla makes to himself. When he cannot face the difficulties, or knows that he lacks the patience to wait, then it is better to relinquish his role before he betrays his pledge, for he clearly lacks the basic qualities necessary to be a guerrilla.

The urban guerrilla must know how to live among the people and must be careful not to appear strange and separated from ordinary city life.

He should not wear clothes that are different from those that other people wear. Elaborate and high fashion clothing for men or women may often be a handicap if the urban guerrilla's mission takes him into working-class neighborhoods or sections where such dress is uncommon. The same care has to be taken if the urban guerrilla moves from the south to the north or vice versa.

The urban guerrilla must live by his work or professional activity. If he is known and sought by the police, if he is convicted or is on parole, he must go underground and sometimes must live hidden. Under such circumstances, the urban guerrilla cannot reveal his activity to anyone, since that is always and only the responsibility of the revolutionary organization in which he is participating.

The urban guerrilla must have a great capacity for observation, must be well informed about everything, principally about the enemy's movements, and must be very knowledgeable about the area in which he lives, operates, or through which he moves.

But the fundamental and decisive characteristic of the urban guerrilla is that he is a man who fights with arms. Given this condition, there is very little likelihood that he will be able to follow his normal profession for long without being identified. The role of expropriation thus looms as clear as high noon. It is impossible for the urban guerrilla to exist and survive without fighting to expropriate.

Thus, within the framework of the class struggle, as it inevitably and necessarily sharpens, the armed struggle of the urban guerrilla points toward two essential objectives:

1. the physical liquidation of the chiefs and assistants of the armed forces and of the police; and,
2. the expropriation of government resources and those belonging to the big capitalists, latifundists, and imperialists, with small expropriations used for the maintenance of individual urban guerrillas and large ones for the sustenance of the revolution itself.

It is clear that the armed struggle of the urban guerrilla also has other objectives. But here we are referring to the two basic objectives, and above all expropriation. It is necessary for every urban guerrilla to keep in mind always that he can only maintain his existence if he is disposed to kill the police and those dedicated to repression, and if he is determined—truly determined—to expropriate the wealth of the big capitalists, the latifundists, and the imperialists.

One of the fundamental characteristics of the Brazilian revolution is that from the beginning it developed around the expropriation of the wealth of the major bourgeois, imperialist, and latifundist interests, without excluding the richest and most powerful commercial elements engaged in the import-export business.

And by expropriating the wealth of the principal enemies of the people, the Brazilian revolution was able to hit them at their vital center, with preferential and systematic attacks on the banking network—that is to say, the most telling blows were leveled against capitalism's nerve system.

The bank robberies carried out by the Brazilian urban guerrillas hurt such big capitalists as Moreira Salles and others, the foreign firms which insure and reinsure the banking capital, the imperialist companies, the federal and state governments—all of them systematically expropriated as of now.

The fruit of these expropriations has been devoted to the work of learning and perfecting urban guerrilla techniques; the purchase, the production, and the transportation of arms and ammunition for the rural areas; the security apparatus of the revolutionaries, the daily maintenance of the fighters of (those who have been liberated from prison by armed force and those who are wounded or persecuted by the police); or to any kind of problem concerning comrades liberated from jail, or assassinated by the police and the military dictatorship.

The tremendous costs of the revolutionary war must fall on the big capitalists, on imperialism, and the latifundists and on the government, too—both federal and state—since they are all exploiters and oppressors of the people.

Men of the government, agents of the dictatorship and of North American imperialism principally, must pay with their lives for the crimes committed against the Brazilian people.

In Brazil, the number of violent actions carried out by urban guerrillas, including deaths, explosions, seizures of arms, ammunition, and explosives, assaults on banks and prisons, etc., is significant enough to leave no room for doubt as to the actual aims of the revolutionaries. The execution of the CIA spy Charles Chandler, a member of the U.S. Army who came from the war in Vietnam to infiltrate the Brazilian student movement, the military henchmen killed in bloody encounters with urban guerrillas, are witness to the fact that we are in full revolutionary war and that the war can be waged only by violent means.

This is the reason why the urban guerrilla uses armed struggle and why he continues to concentrate his activity on the physical extermination of the agents of repression, and to dedicate twenty-four hours a day to expropriation from the people's exploiters.

## TECHNICAL PREPARATION OF THE URBAN GUERRILLA

No one can become an urban guerrilla without paying special attention to technical preparation.

The technical preparation of the urban guerrilla runs from the concern for his physical preparedness to knowledge of and apprenticeship in professions and skills of all kinds, particularly manual skills.

The urban guerrilla can have strong physical resistance only if he trains systematically. He cannot be a good fighter if he has not learned the art of fighting. For that reason the urban guerrilla must learn and practice various kinds of fighting, of attack, and of personal defense.

Other useful forms of physical preparation are hiking, camping, and practice in survival in the woods, mountain climbing, rowing, swimming, skin diving, training as a frogman, fishing, harpooning, and the hunting of birds, small and big game.

It is very important to learn how to drive, pilot a plane, handle a motorboat and a sailboat, understand mechanics, radio, telephone, electricity, and have some knowledge of electronic techniques.

It is also important to have a knowledge of topographical information, to be able to locate one's position by instruments or other available resources, to calculate distances, make maps and plans, draw to scale, make timings, work with an angle protractor, a compass, etc.

A knowledge of chemistry and of color combination, of stamp-making, the domination of the technique of calligraphy and the copying of letters and other skills are part of the technical preparation of the urban guerrilla, who is obliged to falsify documents in order to live within a society that he seeks to destroy.

In the area of auxiliary medicine he has the special role of being a doctor or understanding medicine, nursing, pharmacology, drugs, elementary surgery, and emergency first aid.

The basic question in the technical preparation of the urban guerrilla is nevertheless to know how to handle arms such as the machine gun, revolver, automatic, various types of shotguns, carbines, mortars, bazookas, etc.

A knowledge of various types of ammunition and explosives is another aspect to consider. Among the explosives, dynamite must be well understood. The use of incendiary bombs, of smoke bombs, and other types is indispensable prior knowledge.

To know how to make and repair arms, prepare Molotov cocktails, grenades, mines, home-made destructive devices, how to blow up bridges, tear up and put out of service rails and sleepers, these are requisites in the technical preparation of the urban guerrilla that can never be considered unimportant.

The highest level of preparation or the urban guerrilla is the center for technical training. But only the guerrilla who has already passed the preliminary examination can go on to this school—that is to say, one who has passed the proof of fire in revolutionary action, in actual combat against the enemy. ...

## THE SEVEN SINS OF THE URBAN GUERRILLA

Even when the urban guerrilla applies his revolutionary technique with precision and rigorously abides by security rules, he can still be vulnerable to errors. There is no perfect urban guerrilla. The most he can do is to make every effort to diminish the margin of error since he cannot be perfect.

One of the methods we should use to diminish the margin of error is to know thoroughly the seven sins of the urban guerrilla and try to fight them.

The first sin of the urban guerrilla is inexperience. The urban guerrilla, blinded by this sin, thinks the enemy is stupid, underestimates his intelligence, believes everything is easy and, as a result, leaves clues that can lead to his disaster.

Because of his inexperience, the urban guerrilla can also overestimate the forces of the enemy, believing them to be stronger than they really are. Allowing himself to be fooled by this presumption, the urban guerrilla becomes intimidated, and remains insecure and indecisive, paralyzed and lacking in audacity.

The second sin of the urban guerrilla is to boast about the actions he has completed and broadcast them to the four winds.

The third sin of the urban guerrilla is vanity. The urban guerrilla who suffers from this sin tries to solve the problems of the revolution by actions erupting in the city, but without bothering about the beginnings and the survival of the guerrilla in rural areas. Blinded by success, he winds up organizing an action that he considers decisive and that puts into play all the forces and resources of the organization. Since the city is the area of the strategic circle which we cannot avoid or break (while rural guerrilla warfare has not yet erupted and is not at the point of triumph), we always run the fatal error of permitting the enemy to attack us with decisive blows.

The fourth sin of the urban guerrilla is to exaggerate his strength and to undertake projects for which he lacks forces and, as yet, does not have the required infrastructure.

The fifth sin of the urban guerrilla is precipitous action. The urban guerrilla who commits this sin loses patience, suffers an attack of nerves, does not wait for anything, and impetuously throws himself into action, suffering untold reverses.

The sixth sin of the urban guerrilla is to attack the enemy when he is most angry.

The seventh sin of the urban guerrilla is to fail to plan things, and to act out of improvisation.

---

Carlos Marighella, *Minimanual of the Urban Guerrilla*
(London, n.d.)

ABRAHAM GUILLEN

# URBAN GUERRILLA STRATEGY

I F SEVENTY PERCENT OF A COUNTRY'S POPULATION is urban, the demography and the economy must dictate the specific rules of the strategy of revolutionary combat. The center of operations should never be in the mountains or in the villages, but in the largest cities where the population suffices to form the army of the revolution. In such cases, the countryside must support the actions of urban guerrillas through its clandestine local militias (groups of self-defense), who work during the day and fight at night, encouraged by a program of agrarian reform that gives the land to those who cultivate it.

In underdeveloped countries some of the urban centers are home to the majority of the country's total population. For example, Buenos Aires and Montevideo have, respectively, more than 30 percent and 50 percent of the total population of the country. The capitals of these countries, including their suburban zones, constitute a sea of houses which extends for miles. But in the interior of the country the population of the ranches consists more of animals than men. There are fewer inhabitants per square mile than there were in the Middle Ages in Europe. The great cattle ranges have contributed to transferring population from the countryside to the slums of the city. At the same time, capitalist monopoly concentrates the workers in the cities, extracting them from the marginal population of the countryside. Strategically, in the case of a popular revolution in a country in which the highest percentage of the population is urban, the center of operations of the revolutionary war should be in the city. Operations should consist of scattered surprise attacks by quick and mobile units superior in arms and numbers at designated points, but avoiding barricades in order not to attract the enemy's attention at one place. The units will then attack with the greatest part of their strength the enemy's least fortified or weakest links in the city.

377

In those countries with more than 50 percent urban population (72 percent in Argentina and 84 percent in Uruguay), the revolutionary battle should preferably be not in the mountains and countrysides but in the urban areas. For the revolution's potential is where the population is. In the provinces without a dense population there are possibilities of creating hundreds of incidents in order to attract a part of the enemy troops (the more the better) through hundreds of separate guerrilla actions. Thus, when the enemy is dispersed throughout the country, it is conquered by the concentration of the revolutionary army upon the cities, the rear guard of the revolution. To achieve victory over a powerful army that is hated by the population, it is necessary to scatter it, attracting it here and there, defeating it in small battles in a suitable field for the urban guerrillas, until the population turns against it and more and more people join the army of liberation, regional echelons, and groups of self-defense (local guerrillas).

Each system of production contains its law of the social division of labor, which allocates in time and space the means of production and the population. The city regularly produces machinery and other goods for the countryside, receiving food and raw materials in return. If the rural guerrillas interrupt the communication between city and countryside by means of nocturnal sabotage, food and raw materials will not flow normally into the city. It is the purpose of this strategy to shatter the functioning of the law of the division of labor, the exchange between countryside and city. The city without food is a disintegrating world. The countryside, however, can subsist for a longer period of time without manufactured goods from the cities. Consequently, not even in those countries with a high percentage of urban population is an effective strategy possible without including the countryside. Cooperation between the laborer and the peasant is essential to the revolution.

In those countries with a high percentage of urban population in which the economic system is concentrated upon one, two, or three cities, revolutionary warfare must preferably be urban, without excluding the cooperation of the rural militias, whose job is to attract part of the urban military forces in order to preserve the initiative of the army of liberation....

Buenos Aires represents approximately 70 percent of the wealth, the consumption of energy, the transportation, the industry, the commerce, and in general the greater part of the Argentine economy. Santiago de Chile, Lima, Rio de Janeiro, Mexico City, Bogota, and other Latin American capitals do not have the concentrated economic power of Buenos Aires and Montevideo.... Revolutionary warfare is preferably rural in Brazil, although it has its center of operations in the cities of the Rio de Plata. Brazil is a country in which the war must be conducted against an enormous mass of counterrevolutionary troops, while Uruguay and Argentina must undertake prolonged urban warfare based on many small military victories which together will render the final victory.

## ASSESSMENT OF THE URUGUAYAN TUPAMAROS

To the credit of the Uruguayan guerrillas, they were the first to operate in the cement jungles of a capitalist metropolis, to endure during the first phase of a revolutionary war thanks to an efficient organization and tactics, and to confound the police and armed forces for a considerable period.... With its failures as well as successes, the Movement of National Liberation (*Tupamaros*) has contributed a model of urban guerrilla warfare that has already made a mark on contemporary history—the scene of a struggle between capitalism and socialism with its epicenter in the great cities. The lessons that can be learned from the Tupamaros can be summarized in the following six points.

1. *Fixed or Mobile Front?* When urban guerrillas lack widespread support because of revolutionary impatience or because their actions do not directly represent popular demands, they have to provide their own clandestine infrastructure by renting houses and apartments. By tying themselves to a fixed terrain in this way, the Tupamaros have lost both mobility and security—two prerequisites of guerrilla strategy. In order to avoid encirclement and annihilation through house-to-house searches, the guerrillas can best survive not by establishing fixed urban bases, but by living apart and fighting together.

2. *Mobility and Security.* If urban guerrillas rent houses for their commandos, they are in danger of leaving a trail that may be followed by the police who review monthly all registered rentals. Should most of their houses be loaned instead of leased, then the guerrillas should refrain as a general rule from building underground vaults or hideouts which would increase their dependence on the terrain. To retain their mobility and a high margin of security they must spread out among a favorable population. Guerrillas who fight together and then disperse throughout a great city are not easily detected by the police. When dragnets are applied to one neighborhood or zone, guerrillas without a fixed base can shift to another neighborhood. Such mobility is precluded by a reliance on rented houses or hideouts in the homes of sympathizers, heretofore a major strategical error of the Tupamaros.

3. *Heavy or Light Rear Guard?* Urban guerrillas who develop a heavy infrastructure in many rented houses commit not only a military er-

379

ror, but also an economic and logistical one. For a heavy rear guard requires a comparatively large monthly budget in which economic and financial motives tend to overshadow political considerations. Lacking enough houses, the guerrillas tend to upgrade to positions of command those willing to lend their own. Among the Tupamaros detained in 1972 was the owner of the hacienda "Spartacus," which housed an armory in an underground vault. At about the same time the president of the frigorific plant of Cerro Largo was detained and sentenced for aiding the Tupamaros. He may well have embraced the cause of the Tupamaros with loyalty and sincerity, but as a businessman he responded as any other bourgeois would to his workers' demands for higher wages. Thus, when promotion through the ranks is facilitated by owning a big house, a large farm or enterprise, the guerrillas become open to bourgeois tendencies. When guerrillas rely for cover not on a people in arms but on people of property, then urban guerrilla warfare becomes the business of an armed minority,
· which will never succeed in mobilizing in this manner the majority of the population.

4. *Logistical Infrastructure.* Although a mobile front is preferable to a fixed one, there are circumstances in which a fixed front is unavoidable, e.g., in the assembly, adjustment, and adaptation of arms. These fixed fronts, few and far between, must be concealed from the guerrillas themselves. They should be known only to the few who work there, preferably one person in each, in order to avoid discovery by the repressive forces. In the interest of security it is advisable not to manufacture arms, but to have the parts made separately by various legal establishments, after which they can be assembled in the secret workshops of the guerrillas.

It is dangerous to rely on a fixed front for housing, food, medical supplies, and armaments. If the guerrillas are regularly employed, they should live as everybody else and they should come together only at designated times and places. Houses that serve as barracks or hideouts tend to immobilize the guerrillas and to expose them to the possibility of encirclement and annihilation. Because the Tupamaros immobilized many of their commandos in fixed quarters, they were exposed in 1972 to mass detentions. They lost a large part of their armaments and related equipment and were compelled to transfer military supplies to the countryside for hiding.

In abusing control over their sympathizers and keeping them under strict military discipline, the Tupamaros had to house them together. But they were seldom used in military operations at a single

place or in several simultaneously, indicating the absence of strategical preparation. If urban guerrillas cannot continually disappear and
reappear among the population of a great city, then they lack the
political prerequisites for making a revolution, for creating the conditions of a social crisis through the breakdown of "law and order."
Despite their proficiency during the first hit-and-run phase of a revolutionary war, the Tupamaros have failed to escalate their operations
by using larger units at more frequent intervals for the purpose of
paralyzing the existing regime.

5. *Heroes, Martyrs, and Avengers.* In revolutionary war any guerrilla action that needs explaining to the people is politically useles, it should
be meaningful and convincing by itself. To kill an ordinary soldier in
reprisal for the assassination of a guerrilla is to descend to the same
political level as a reactionary army. Far better to create a martyr
and thereby attract mass sympathy than to lose or neutralize popular
support by senseless killings without an evident political goal. To be
victorious in a people's war one has to act in conformity with the
interests, sentiments, and will of the people. A military victory is
worthless if it fails to be politically convincing.

In a country where the bourgeoisie has abolished the death penalty, it is self-defeating to condemn to death even the most hated
enemies of the people. Oppressors, traitors, and informers have
condemned themselves before the guerrillas. It is impolitic to make
a public show of their crimes for the purpose of creating a climate
of terror, insecurity, and disregard for basic human rights. A popular
army that resorts to unnecessary violence, that is not a symbol of justice, equity, liberty, and security, cannot win popular support in the
struggle against a dehumanized tyranny.

The Tupamaros' "prisons of the people" do more harm than benefit to the cause of national liberation. Taking hostages for the purpose
of exchanging them for political prisoners has an immediate popular
appeal; but informing the world of the existence of "people's prisons" is to focus unnecessarily on a parallel system of repression. No
useful purpose can be served by such politically alienating language.
Moreover, it is intolerable to keep anyone hostage for a long time. To
achieve a political or propaganda victory through this kind of tactic,
the ransom terms must be moderate and capable of being met. In
no event should the guerrillas be pressed into executing a prisoner
because their demands are excessive and accordingly rejected. A
hostage may be usefully executed only when a government refuses
to negotiate on any terms after popular pressure has been applied,

for then it is evident to everyone that the government is ultimately responsible for the outcome.

So-called people's prisons are harmful for other reasons. They require several men to stand guard and care for the prisoners; they distract guerrillas from carrying out alternative actions more directly useful to the population; and they presuppose a fixed front and corresponding loss of mobility. At most it is convenient to have a secure place to detain for short periods a single hostage.

To establish people's prisons, to condemn to death various enemies of the people, to house the guerrillas in secret barracks or underground hideouts is to create an infrastructure supporting a miniature state rather than a revolutionary army. To win the support of the population, arms must be used directly on its behalf. Whoever uses violence against subordinates in the course of building a miniature counterstate should be removed from his command. Surely, there is little point in defeating one despotism only to erect another in its place!

*guerrillas don't kill innocents*

6. *Delegated Commands.* In a professional army the leadership is recruited from the military academies within a hierarchical order of command. In a guerrilla organization the leaders emerge in actual revolutionary struggles, elected because of their capacity, responsibility, combativity, initiative, political understanding and deeds rather than words. However, at pain of forfeiting the democratic character of a revolutionary army and the function of authority as a delegated power, not even the best guerrilla commander can be allowed to remain long at the helm. A rotating leadership is necessary to avoid the "cult of personality." Power should be alternately exercised by those commanders with the most victories, by those most popular with their soldiers and most respected by the people. Inasmuch as guerrilla warfare takes the form of self-defense, its success depends on the exercise of direct democracy, on guerrilla self-management and self-discipline—a far cry from the barracks discipline typical of a bureaucratic or professional army....

The people have more need of many revolutionary heroes than of a single outstanding leader like Julius Caesar or Napoleon Bonaparte. Epaminondas, the Theban general who defeated the Spartans, held a command that lasted only two years. Although the greatest strategist of his time, he became an ordinary soldier when his command expired. Only because of his extraordinary skill was he made a military adviser to the new commander-in-chief. Guerrillas can benefit by his example.

A delegated command is unlimited except for the time determining its delegation. The responsibility of subordinates is to discuss in advance each operation, to make recommendations, etc. But the discussion ends when the supreme command assumes responsibility for the outcome of a particular battle or engagement. If the commander is mistaken in his judgment, if the result is defeat rather than victory, his duty is to resign. Should he succeed in a vote of confidence he may retain his command; but two successive defeats should make his resignation irrevocable.

One of the most common errors of Latin American guerrillas is to make legends of their leaders as they did of Fidel Castro and Che Guevara. The resulting messianism conceals the incapacity of many guerrilla commanders who take their troops into the countryside— like the Tupamaros in 1972—without revising mistaken strategies. Perhaps the leaders of the Uruguayan guerrillas have come to believe in their providential powers, thereby reducing the ordinary guerrilla to a political and military zero, to the status of a soldier in a conventional army.

---

Abraham Guillen, *Estrategia de la guerrilla urbana*
(c. 1971), translated in Donald C. Hodges (ed.),
*Philosophy of the Urban Guerrilla* (New York, 1973).

# PART THREE

# THE ORIGINS OF TWENTY-FIRST CENTURY TERRORISM

# Terrorism in the Muslim World

# INTRODUCTORY NOTE

O F THE TERRORIST GROUPS DOCUMENTED when the first edition of *The Guerrilla and Terrorist Readers* appeared (1977) only a few are still active. Islamist terrorism was not an important factor on the global terrorist scene at the time and there seemed to be no necessity to include documents or comments on its specific character. There had been acts of terror in Muslim countries and also guerrilla warfare after World War II (and even before) notably in Algeria, Egypt, the Sudan, and Palestine. No Middle Eastern or North African country was entirely free of it, but the great upsurge of radical Islamism with its emphasis on Holy War (jihad) took place only in later years; hence, the necessity of this section which looks at the doctrinal origins and the present day practice of jihad in some detail.

The main inspiration for today's jihadist ideologues came from a medieval theologian named Ibn Taymiyyah whose works are quoted in virtually every statement of radical Islamism to this very day. Born in Damascus in 1268, he also lived in Baghdad and Cairo. He represented a fundamentalist approach to Islam at a time when the Near East was invaded by the Mongols from the North and East and the Abbasid dynasty was defeated. Since the Mongols had converted to Islam, Ibn Taymiyyah's call for armed resistance may at first seem surprising. But as he saw it, these new coreligionists did not embrace Islam wholeheartedly but rather stuck to a certain extent to their old laws and customs and constituted, therefore, a threat to pure, traditional Islam which he felt needed to be restored in its pristine glory.

Ibn Taymiyyah's opinions were controversial even in his own lifetime and they did not become official doctrine after his death. But they have remained the guideposts of Muslim radicals ever since.

Sayed Qutb (1906-66) and Sayed Abu ala Maududi (1903-1979) are the leading radical Islamic interpreters of the twentieth century. The Egyptian Sayed Qutb was originally a school teacher and inspector of the Egyptian ministry of education as well as a literary critic. Following a visit to the United States in 1948 he underwent a conversion to radical Islamism and joined the Muslim Brotherhood and became one of the leading ideologues. Arrested under Nasser (and eventually executed for sedition) he wrote many volumes in prison all of them purporting to demonstrate why a holy war had to be declared not only against the outside enemy but also the rulers of the Muslim countries whom (he claimed) without exception were traitors to the true faith. Though Qutb was not among the leading Islamic authorities of his day, the very radicalism of his message made it very popular at a time of crisis, and millions of copies of his writings circulated throughout the Muslim world.

Maududi, an Indian Muslim (later a Pakistani) was, like Qutb, self-taught, so he was not a recognized scholar; but he gained wider recognition among the higher Muslim clergy. He actively participated in Indian and Pakistani politics and was at one time sentenced to death. But by and large his message was slightly less extremist than Qutb's even though jihad was the subject of his first major work. Maududi was the author of some one hundred twenty books and booklets. His influence was limited, however, by and large to Muslims in South and Southeast Asia.

"Absent Obligation" (meaning jihad) by Abdus Salam Faraj was the manifesto by a leader of one of the terrorist groups in Egypt at the time of Anwar al Sadat, as a group which prepared and carried out his assassination. The author, an electrician and lay preacher had no formal religious education. Only fifty copies of his booklet were originally published and it consisted mainly of quotations from other authors. But as in the case of Qutb, the radicalism of the message more than compensated for the lack of religious learning and sophistication.

Abdullah Azzam played an important historical role as the precursor and mentor of contemporary jihadism. He was in most respects the teacher of Osama bin Laden whose declaration of war against crusaders and Jews was published in February, 1998 by *Al Quds al Arabi,* a London-based newspaper allegedly supported by the Iraqis at the time. (There had been an earlier appeal for jihad published in the same newspaper in August 1996, initiated apparently only by bin Laden and his followers). The sponsors of the declaration of 1998 were several jihadist groups convened in Afghanistan by bin Laden, among them Al-Qaeda.

Ayman al Zawahiri, originally the leader of the Egyptian jihad, was bin Laden's deputy. Born in 1951, he trained as a physician. His family was well established in Egypt—one grandfather was an important Muslim dignitary in the country. Another close relation was the first secretary general of the Arab League. An uncle served as an ambassador whose memoirs appeared in many installments in a London Arab newspaper.

The Palestinian organization, known as Hamas, originally an offshoot of the Muslim Brotherhood, is of interest because it reveals the impact of the European extreme right, hence the references to the "Protocols of the

Elders of Zion," the attacks against free masons, and liberal thinking in general.

*Khilafah* is the organ of various radical Islamist groups in Europe; their main aim is the restitution of the Khalifat, the return of Islam on the global scene as a political power, which formally came to an end with the abdication of the last Turkish Sultan after World War I.

Following ten years of civil war, Algeria has been immunized to a considerable extent against extremist Islamic groups—in contrast to metropolitan France where these groups continue to play an important role. Redha Malek is a former prime minister and foreign minister of Algeria. Boudjemaa is a political commentator for the Algerian media.

In the absence of journalists and television cameras, the war for Kashmir has frequently been ignored in the Western media.

Sumantra Bose, author of *Kashmir, Roots of Conflict, Path to Peace* (from which these excerpts are taken) teaches at the London School of Economics. Yogindar Sikand is a well-known Indian author and editor specializing in Hindu-Muslim relations.

The interview with Pirabakaran, guru and commander of the Tamil Tigers, is of special significance in view of the pioneering role this group has had in the field of suicide terrorism. Junius Jayawardena (d. 1996), mentioned in this interview, was president of Sri Lanka from 1978 to 1989. Indian President Rajiv Gandhi was killed by a group of Tamil Tigers in Madras in May, 1991. Terrorism in Sri Lanka was not motivated by religious feeling, that is unless ethnic nationalism can be interpreted as a political religion. Terrorism in the Caucasus was not originally motivated by religion either, and if Muslim radicalism has grown during the last decade, it is doubtful whether even now it is the decisive factor.

Terrorism of the extreme left has decreased in intensity since the 1970s when it played an important role in Europe and Latin America. Colombian terrorism is a mixture of a variety of motive forces including ideology but also the drug trade and abductions-for-profit. The doctrine of Basque terrorism was originally Marxist-Leninist or even more extreme in its phraseology, but, has shed much of this ideological ballast over the years, becoming openly (and exclusively) nationalist.

Nor has terrorism of the extreme right been very much in appearance during the last decade. Of course, these groups continue to exist in the United States as well as in Europe and may return to action in future. Like factions of the extreme left they have welcomed the attacks by bin Laden and other radical Muslim groups. "Neither Left nor Right" points to attempts made by radical right- and left-wing groups to cooperate within the framework of a "third way."

TAQI-UD-DEEN AHMAD IBN TAYMIYYAH

# THE RELIGIOUS AND MORAL DOCTRINE OF JIHAD

## AL-SIYAASA AL-SHAR'IYYA FEE ISLAAH AL-RAA'EE WA AL-RAA'IYYA

*(Governance according to Allah's Law in reforming both the ruler and his flock)*

THE PENALTIES THAT THE SHAREE'AH has introduced for those who disobey Allah and His Messengers are of two kinds:

1. The punishment of those who are under the sway [of the Imam], both individuals and collectivities, as has been mentioned before [in the chapter on criminal law]; and,
2. The punishment of recalcitrant groups, such as those that can only be brought under the sway of the Imam by a decisive fight.

That then is the jihad against the unbelievers (*kufaar*), the enemies of Allah and His Messenger. For whoever has heard the summons of the Messenger of Allah, and has not responded to it, must be fought, "until there is no persecution and the religion is Allah's entirely." [*Qur'an. 2:193, 8:39*]

When Allah sent His Prophet and ordered him to summon the people to His religion, He did not permit him to kill or fight anyone for that reason before the Prophet emigrated to Medina.

Thereafter, He gave him and the Muslims permission with the words:

"Leave is given to those who are fought because they were wronged—surely Allah is able to help them—who were expelled from their habitations without right, except that they say 'Our Lord is Allah.' Had Allah not driven back the people, some by the means of others, there would had been destroyed cloisters and churches, oratories and masjids, wherein Allah's name is much mentioned. Assuredly Allah will help him who helps Him—surely Allah is all-strong, all-mighty—who, if We establish them in the land, perform the prayer, and pay the alms, and bid to honour, and forbid dishonour; and unto Allah belongs the issue of all affairs." [Qur'an, 22:39-41]

Then, after that, He imposed fighting on them with the following words:

"Prescribed for you is fighting, though it be hateful to you. Yet it may happen that you will hate a thing which is better for you; and it may happen that you love a thing which is worse for you. Allah knows and you know not." [Qur'an. 2:216]

He has emphasized this command and glorified jihad in many of the Medinese suras. He has criticized those who fail to participate in it and called them hypocrites (munaafiq) and sick in their hearts.

The command to participate in jihad and the mention of its merits occur innumerable times in the Qur'an and the Sunnah.

Therefore, it is the best voluntary [religious] act that man can perform. All scholars agree that it is better than the hajj (greater pilgrimage) and the 'umrah (lesser pilgrimage), than voluntary salaat and voluntary fasting, as the Qur'an and the Sunnah indicate.

In the Saheeh of al-Bukhaari as well as the Saheeh of Muslim we find:

"A man said: 'O Messenger of Allah, tell me of an act that equals jihad in the way of Allah.' He answered:'You will not be capable of it.' The man said: 'Tell me anyway.' The Messenger of Allah said: 'Can you, when a jihad warrior has gone out on expedition, fast without interruption and spend the night in continuous prayer?' The man said: 'No.' Then the Messenger of Allah said: 'This then is what equals jihad.'"

In the Sunan we find that Muhammed, has said: "Every community has its devotional journeys and the devotional journey of my community is jihad in the way of Allah."

This is a vast subject, unequalled by other subjects as far as the reward and merit of human deeds is concerned. This is evident upon closer examination. The [first] reason is that the benefit of jihad is general, extending not only to the person who participates in it but also to others, both in a religious and a temporal sense.

[Secondly,] jihad implies all kinds of worship, both in its inner and outer forms. More than any other act it implies love and devotion for Allah, Who is exalted, trust in Him, the surrender of one's life and property to Him, patience, asceticism, remembrance of Allah and all kinds of other acts [of worship]. And the individual or community that participates in it, finds itself between two blissful outcomes: either victory and triumph or martyrdom and Paradise.

[Thirdly,] all creatures must live and die. Now, it is in jihad that one can live and die in ultimate happiness, both in this world and in the hereafter. Abandoning it means losing entirely or partially both kinds of happiness. There are people who want to perform religious and temporal deeds full of hardship in spite of their lack of benefit, whereas jihad is religiously and temporally more beneficial than any other deed full of hardship. Other people [participate in it] out of a desire to make things easy for themselves when death meets them, for the death of a martyr is easier than any other form of death. In fact, it is the best of all manners of dying.

Since lawful warfare is essentially jihad and since its aim is that the religion is Allah's entirely [2:189, 8:39] and Allah's word is uppermost [9:40], therefore, according to all Muslims, those who stand in the way of this aim must be fought.

As for those who cannot offer resistance or cannot fight, such as women, children, monks, old people, the blind, handicapped and the like, they shall not be killed, unless they actually fight with words [e.g. by propaganda] and acts [e.g., by spying or otherwise assisting in the warfare].

Some [jurists] are of the opinion that all of them may be killed, on the mere ground that they are unbelievers, but they make an exception for women and children since they constitute property for Muslims.

However, the first opinion is the correct one, because we may only fight those who fight us when we want to make Allah's religion victorious. Allah, Who is exalted, has said in this respect:

"And fight in the way of Allah those who fight you, but transgress not: Allah loves not the transgressors." [The Qur'an, 2:190]

---

*www.sullivan-county.com/z/tay.htm*

SAYED QUTB

# JIHAD IN THE CAUSE OF GOD

I F WE INSIST ON CALLING ISLAMIC JIHAD a defensive movement, then we
must change the meaning of the word "defense" and mean by it "the
defense of man" against all those elements which limit his freedom.
These elements take the form of beliefs and concepts, as well as of political
systems, based on economic, racial, or class distinctions. When Islam first
came into existence, the world was full of such systems, and the present-
day Jahiliyyah also has various kinds of such systems.

When we take this broad meaning of the word "defense," we understand the true character of Islam, and that it is a universal proclamation of
the freedom of man from servitude to other men, the establishment of the
sovereignty of God and His Lordship throughout the world, the end of
man's arrogance and selfishness, and the implementation of the rule of the
Divine Shari'ah in human affairs.

As to persons who attempt to defend the concept of Islamic jihad by
interpreting it in the narrow sense of the current concept of defensive war,
and who do research to prove that the battles fought in Islamic jihad were
all for the defense of the homeland of Islam—some of them considering
the homeland of Islam to be just the Arabian peninsula—against the aggression of neighboring powers, they lack understanding of the nature of
Islam and its primary aim. Such an attempt is nothing but a product of a
mind defeated by the present difficult conditions and by the attacks of the
treacherous orientalists on the Islamic jihad.

Can anyone say that if Abu Bakr, 'Umar or 'Othman had been satisfied
that the Roman and Persian powers were not going to attack the Arabian
peninsula, they would not have striven to spread the message of Islam
throughout the world? How could the message of Islam have spread when

394

it faced such material obstacles as the political system of the state, the socio-economic system based on races and classes, and behind all these, the military power of the government?

It would be naive to assume that a call is raised to free the whole of humankind throughout the earth, and it is confined to preaching and exposition. Indeed, it strives through preaching and exposition when there is freedom of communication and when people are free from all these influences, as "There is no compulsion in religion; but when the above-mentioned obstacles and practical difficulties are put in its way, it has no recourse but to remove them by force so that when it is addressed to people's hearts and minds they are free to accept or reject it with an open mind."

Since the objective of the message of Islam is a decisive declaration of man's freedom, not merely on the philosophical plane but also in the actual conditions of life, it must employ jihad. It is immaterial whether the homeland of Islam—in the true Islamic sense, Dar ul-Islam—is in a condition of peace or whether it is threatened by its neighbors. When Islam strives for peace, its objective is not that superficial peace which requires that only that part of the earth where the followers of Islam are residing remain secure. The peace which Islam desires is that the religion (i.e., the law of the society) be purified for God, that the obedience of all people be for God alone, and that some people should not be lords over others. After the period of the Prophet—peace be on him—only the final stages of the movement of jihad are to be followed; the initial or middle stages are not applicable. They have ended, and as Ibn Qayyim states, "Thus, after the revelation of the chapter 'Bratt,' the unbelievers were of three kinds: adversaries in war, people with treaties, and Dhimmies. The people with treaties eventually became Muslims, so there were only two kinds left: people at war and Dhimmies. The people at war were always afraid of him. Now the people of the whole world were of three kinds: one, the Muslims who believed in him: two, those with whom he had peace (and from the previous sentence, we understand that they were Dhimmies); and three, the opponents who kept fighting him."

These are the logical positions consonant with the character and purposes of this religion, and not what is understood by the people who are defeated by present conditions and by the attacks of the treacherous orientalists.

God held back Muslims from fighting in Mecca and in the early period of their migration to Medina, and told them, "Restrain your hands, and establish regular prayers, and pay Zakat." Next, they were permitted to fight: "Permission to fight is given to those against whom war is made, because they are oppressed, and God is able to help them. These are the people who were expelled from their homes without cause." The next stage came when the Muslims were commanded to fight those who fight them: "Fight in the cause of God against those who fight you." And finally, war was declared against all the polytheists: "And fight against all the polytheists, as they all fight against you"; "Fight against those among the people of the book who do not believe in God and the Last Day, who do not forbid what God and His Messenger have forbidden, and who do not consider the true religion as their religion, until they are subdued and pay Jizyah." Thus, according to the explanation by Imam Ibn Qayyim, the Muslims were first restrained from fighting; then they were permitted to fight; then they were commanded to fight against the aggressors; and finally they were commanded to fight against all the polytheists.

With these verses from the Qur'an and with many traditions of the Prophet—peace be on him—in praise of jihad, and with the entire history of Islam, which is full of jihad, the heart of every Muslim rejects that explanation of jihad invented by those people whose minds have accepted defeat under unfavorable conditions and under the attacks on Islamic jihad by the shrewd orientalists.

What kind of a man is it who, after listening to the commandment of God and the Traditions of the Prophet—peace be on him—and after reading about the events which occurred during the Islamic jihad, still thinks that it is a temporary injunction related to transient conditions and that it is concerned only with the defense of the borders?

In the verse giving permission to fight, God has informed the believers that the life of this world is such that checking one group of people by another is the law of God, so that the earth may be cleansed of corruption. "Permission to fight is given to those against whom war is made, because they are oppressed, and God is able to help them. These are the people who were expelled from their homes without cause, except that they said that our Lord is God. Had God not checked one people by another, then surely synagogues and churches and mosques would have been pulled down, where the name of God is remembered often." Thus, this struggle is not a temporary phase but an eternal state—an eternal state, as truth and falsehood cannot co-exist on this earth. Whenever Islam stood up with the universal declaration that God's lordship should be established over the entire earth and that men should become free from servitude to other men, the usurpers of God's authority on earth have struck out against it fiercely and have never tolerated it. It became incumbent upon Islam to strike back and release man throughout the earth from the grip of these usurpers. The eternal struggle for the freedom of man will continue until the religion is purified for God.

The command to refrain from fighting during the Meccan period was a temporary stage in a long journey. The same reason was operative during the early days of Hijira, but after these early stages, the reason for jihad was not merely to defend Medina. Indeed, its defense was necessary, but this was not the ultimate aim. The aim was to protect the resources and the center of the movement—the movement for freeing mankind and demolishing the obstacles which prevented mankind from attaining this freedom.

SYED ABUL ALA MAUDUDI

# JIHAD IN ISLAM

## A WORLD REVOLUTION

It must be evident to you from this discussion that the objective of the Islamic jihad is to eliminate the rule of a non-Islamic system and establish in its stead an Islamic system of state rule. Islam does not intend to confine this revolution to a single State or a few countries; the aim of Islam is to bring about a universal revolution. Although in the initial stages it is incumbent upon members of the party of Islam to carry out a revolution in the state system of the countries to which they belong, but their ultimate objective is no other than to effect a world revolution. No revolutionary ideology which champions the principles of the welfare of humanity as a whole instead of upholding national interests can restrict its aims and objectives to the limits of a country or a nation. The goal of such an all-embracing doctrine is naturally bound to be world revolution. Truth cannot be confined within geographical borders. Truth demands that whatever is right on this side of the river or the mountain is also right on the other side of the river or mountain; no portion of mankind should be deprived of the Truth; wherever mankind is being subjected to repression, discrimination, and exploitation, it is the duty of the righteous to go to their succor. The same concept has been enunciated by the Holy Qur'an in the following words:

"What has happened to you? Why don't you fight in the way of God in support of men, women and children, whom finding helpless, they have repressed; and who pray, "O, God! Liberate us from this habitation which is ruled by tyrants." (4: 75)

Moreover, notwithstanding the national divisions of mankind, human relations and connections have a universal significance so that no state can put her ideology into full operation until the same ideology comes into force in the neighboring states. Hence, it is imperative for the Muslim Party for reasons of both general welfare of humanity and self-defense that it should not rest content with establishing the Islamic system of government in one territory alone, but to extend the sway of the Islamic system all around as far as its resources can carry it. The Muslim Party will inevitably extend invitations to the citizens of other countries to embrace the faith which holds promise of true salvation and genuine welfare for them. If the Muslim Party commands adequate resources it will eliminate non-Islamic governments and establish the power of Islamic government in their stead. It is the same policy which was executed by the Holy Prophet—peace of Allah be upon him—and his successor, illustrious Caliphs—may Allah be pleased with them. Arabia, where the Muslim Party was founded, was the first country which was subjugated and brought under the rule of Islam. Later the Holy Prophet—peace of Allah be upon him—sent invitations to other surrounding states to accept the faith and ideology of Islam. Where the ruling classes of those countries declined to accept this invitation to adopt the true faith, the Prophet—peace of Allah be upon him—resolved to take military action against them. The war of Tubuk was the first in the series of military actions. When Hadrat Abu Bakr—may Allah be pleased with him—assumed leadership of the Muslim Party after the Prophet— peace of Allah be upon him—have had left for his heavenly homes he launched an invasion of Rome and Iran, which were under the dominance of non-Islamic governments. Later, Hadrat 'Umar—may Allah be pleased with him—carried the war to a victorious end. The citizens of Egypt, Syria, Rome, and Iran initially took these military actions as evidence of the imperialist policy of the Arab nation. They believed that, like other nations, this nation had also set out on a course of enslaving other nations under the yoke of imperialism. It was owing to this misconception that they advanced under the banners of Caesar and Khosros to give battle to the Muslims. But when they discovered the revolutionary ideology of the Muslim Party—when it dawned on them that Muslin armies were not the champions of aggressive nationalism, that they had no nationalistic objectives, that they had come with the sole object of instituting a just system, that their real purpose was to annihilate the tyrannical classes which had assumed divine powers and were trampling down their subjects under the patronage of despotic Caesars and kings—the moral sympathies of those downtrodden people turned towards the party of Islam. They began to forsake their allegiance to the flags of their own monarchs, and when they were conscripted by force and driven to fight against the Muslims, they had no heart in the fight. This is the main cause of those astounding victories won by the Muslims in the early period. It is on this account also that after the establishment of Islamic governments in their countries, when they saw the social system of Islam in action, they willingly joined this international party and became the upholders of its ideology and set out to other countries to spread its message.

## THE TERMS "OFFENSIVE" AND "DEFENSIVE"
## ARE IRRELEVANT

If you carefully consider the explanation given above, you will readily understand that the two terms "offensive"and "defensive," by which the nature of welfare is differentiated, are not at all applicable to Islamic jihad. These terms are relevant only in the context of wars between nations and countries, for technically the terms "attack" and "defense" can only be used with reference to a country or a nation. But when an international party rises with a universal faith and ideology and invites all peoples as human beings to embrace this faith and ideology and admits into its fold as equal members men of all nationalities and strives only to dismantle the rule of an opposing ideology and set up in its place a system of government based on its own ideology, then in this case the use of the technical terms like "offence" and "defense" is not germane. Even if we stop thinking about these technical terms, the division of Islamic jihad into offensive and defensive is not admissible. Islamic jihad is both offensive and defensive at one and the same time. It is offensive because the Muslim Party assaults the rule of an opposing ideology and it is defensive because the Muslim Party is constrained to capture state power in order to arrest the principles of Islam in space-time forces. As a party, it has no home to defend; it upholds certain principles which it must protect. Similarly, this party does not attack the home of the opposing party, but launches an assault on the principles of the opponent. The objective of this attack, moreover, is not to coerce the opponent to relinquish his principles but to abolish the government which sustains these principles.

---

Lecture given in Lahore April 13, 1939.
(This address was delivered on Iqbal Day, April 13, 1939,
at the Town Hall, Lahore)

# JIHAD, THE ABSENT OBLIGATION

IT IS CLEAR THAT JIHAD IS NOW OBLIGATORY upon every Muslim, yet there is the one who protests that he is in need of educationg himself, that jihad is divided into stages, and that he is still in the stage of struggling against his *nafs* (inner self), proving this by the classification of jihad made by Imaam al-Qayyaim al-Jawziyyah:

1. jihad of the *nafs* (inner self);
2. jihad of the *shaytan* (the Devil); and
3. jihad against the disbelievers and hypocrites.

Using this as evidence notifies us of either the ignorance or the evil cowardice of the one who is behind it, because Ibn al-Qayyim classified jihadi into categories and not stages. Otherwise we would have to stop struggling against the *shaytan* until we are finished with the stage of struggling against the inner self.

But the truth is that these three categories proceed on a straight line. However, we do not deny that the person who has a stronger iman and practices more jihad of the nafs among us will be firmer in jihad). But he who studies the *seerah* (life of the Messenger) will find that when Jihad was called for, all people used to march forth in the cause of Allah, even those who committed *al-Kabaa'ir* (major sins) as well as those who were new in Islam. A story is told of a man who embraced Islam during a battle, partook in the battle, and was martyred. So the Messenger of Allah said of him: "A small amount of deeds but a great reward."

Also there is story of Abu Mahjan ath-Thaqafi who drank alcohol, but his jihad against the Persians was so famous.

Ibn al-Qayyim mentioned that the *hadeeth* saying: "We have come back from the minor jihad to the major one and someone asked : 'What is the major jihad, O Messenger of Allah?' He replied: "Jihad of the nafs."

It is a fabrication. The reason behind the fabrication (of the *hadeeth*) is to belittle the value of fighting by the sword so as to divert Muslims from fighting the disbelievers and hypocrites.

## THE SUITABLE METHOD OF FIGHTING

As the time advances and mankind develops, a question seems to be raised. There is no doubt that the modern methods of fighting are somewhat different from the methods used in the time of the Prophet. So what is the suitable method of fighting that the Muslims should use in our age? And is it permissible for him to use his brain and opinion?

## ONE OF THE ARTS OF FIGHTING IN ISLAM

The Prophet said: "War is deceit."

Explaining this *hadeeth* Imaam Nawawi said, "The scholars are agreed that it is permissible to deceive the kuffaar in war, unless that breaks a covenant or a promise of protection [in this case] it is not permitted."

It is known that there is no covenant between us and them (i.e., the present rulers of the Muslims), because they are at war with the religion of Islam. So the Muslims are free to choose the suitable (permitted) method of fighting which will enable them to deceive the enemy and achieve the victory with the least damage and in the easiest way.

# AL-QA'EDA MANUAL

In the name of Allah, the merciful and compassionate

## PRESENTATION

To those champions who avowed the truth day and night. . . [And wrote with their blood and sufferings these phrases...] *implies that people acted*

The confrontation that we are calling for with the apostate regimes does not know Socratic debates… Platonic ideals…nor Aristotelian diplomacy. But it knows the dialogue of bullets, the ideals of assassination, bombing, and destruction, and the diplomacy of the cannon and machine gun.

..[Islamic governments have never and will never be established through peaceful solutions and cooperative councils. They are established as they [always] have been:

by pen and gun;

by word and bullet; and

by tongue and teeth[

*Eleventh Lesson*
*Espionage*
*(1) Information-gathering using open methods*

## UK/BM-76 TRANSLATION

Definition of Espionage*: It is the covert search for and examination of the enemy's news and information for the purpose of using them when a plan is devised. In [the book titled] "Nile AI-Aoutar wa Fath Al-Bari," [it is said that] the spy is called an eye because his work is through his eyes, or because of his excessive and preoccupation with observation, as if all his being is an eye.

Espionage in the era of the prophet—Allah bless and keep him—and his honored companions. The prophet—Allah bless and keep him—used informants in most of his attacks. As Abou Soufian's caravan, that was coming from Damascus, was approaching, the prophet—Allah bless and keep him—wanted to know the caravan's destination. While the prophet was in Medina, he sent Talha Ibn Obaidallah and Said Ibn Zeid on the Damascus route to gather information about the caravan. On their way back to Medina, and at the conclusion of the Badr battle, they met the prophet—Allah bless and keep him—in Terban, as he was descending from Badr to take Madina. [Though] they did not participate in the battle, they nevertheless got their share of the [spoils].

In his attacks, the prophet—Allah bless and keep him—would find out the enemy's intention. In the Hodaibiya [battle] days, though he did not want war, he exercised caution by sending a special forty-man reconnaissance group, headed by A'kkasha Ibn Mohsen Al-Azda. One of that group's forerunners found a man who led them to the enemy's livestock. They captured two hundred camels from that livestock and brought them to Medina.

The prophet—Allah bless and keep him—had local informants in Mecca who told him everything, big and small, that might harm the Muslims' welfare. Among those [enemies] were his uncle Al-Abbas Ibn Abd Al-Mutlib, and Bashir Ibn Soufian Al-Atki. Al-Khulafa Arrashidun [Mohammed's successors] advised their commanders about the importance of using scouts and informants to learn the enemy's secrets. Abou Bakr Al-Siddik—may Allah be pleased with him—said to his commander Amro Ibn AI-A'ss—may Allah be pleased with him—"Send your informants to bring you Abou Obeida's news. If he is victorious over his enemy, then you

---

* For details, refer to *The Spying Journal* "Religious Duty and Human Necessity."

fight those that are in Palestine. If he needs soldiers, then dispatch one battalion after another for him."

Omar Ibn Al-Khattab—may Allah be pleased with him—advised his commander Saad Ibn Abou Wakkas—may Allah be pleased with him—saying, "If you step foot on your enemies' land, get spies for them. Choose those whom you count on for their truthfulness and advice, whether Arabs or inhabitants of that land. Liars' accounts would not benefit you, even if some of them were true; the deceiver is a spy against you and not for you." Khaled Ibn Al-Walid—may Allah be pleased with him—used to take informants and spies with him in each of his wars against the Christian Orthodox. He chose them carefully and treated them well.

Principle of Moslems Spying on their Enemies: Spying on the enemy is permitted and it may even be a duty in the case of war between Moslems and others. Winning the battle is dependent on knowing the enemy's secrets, movements, and plans. The prophet—Allah bless and keep him—used that method. He would send spies and informants. Perhaps, he—Allah bless and keep him—even went himself as in the major Badr attack. Ai-Khulafa Arrashidun [Mohammed's successors] also ordered it [spying]. Since Islam is superior to all human conditions and earthly religions, it permits spying for itself but not for others. Majestic Allah says, "Not equal are the companions of the fire and the companions of the garden," and the prophet says, "Islam is supreme and there is nothing above it." Islam, therefore, fights so the word of Allah can become supreme. Others fight for worldly gains and lowly and inferior goals.

How can a Muslim spy live among enemies if he maintains his Islamic characteristics? How can he perform his duties to Allah and not want to appear Muslim?

Concerning the issue of clothing and appearance (appearance of true religion), Ibn Taimia—may Allah have mercy on him—said, "If a Muslim is in a combat or godless area, he is not obligated to have a different appearance from [those around him]. The [Muslim] man may prefer or even be obligated to look like them, provided his action brings a religious benefit of preaching to them, learning their secrets and informing Muslims, preventing their harm, or some other beneficial goal."

Resembling the polytheist in religious appearance is a kind of "necessity permits the forbidden" even though they [forbidden acts] are basically prohibited. As for the visible duties, like fasting and praying, he can fast by using any justification not to eat with them [polytheist]. As for prayer, the book (Al-Manhaj Al-Haraki Lissira Al-Nabawiya) quotes Al-Bakhari: "he [the Moslem] may combine the noon and afternoon [prayers], sunset and evening [prayers]. That is based on the fact that the prophet—Allah

bless and keep him—combined [prayers] in Medina without fear or hesitation."

Though scholars have disagreed about the interpretation of that tradition,
it is possible—though Allah knows best—that the Moslem spy may combine [prayers]. It is noted, however, that it is forbidden to do the unlawful,
such as drinking wine or fornicating. There is nothing that permits those*

## Guidelines for Beating and Killing Hostages

Religious scholars have permitted beating. They use a tradition explained
in Imam Mosallem's manuscript, who quotes Thabit Ibn Ans that Allah's
prophet—Allah bless and keep him—sought counsel when he was informed about Abou Soufian's arrival. Abou Bakr and Omar spoke, yet
he [the prophet] did not listen. Saad Ibn Ibada said, "Do you want us, O
Allah's prophet, who controls my life?"

If you order us to subdue the camel we would do it, or beat and follow them to Al-Ghimad lakes (five-day trip beyond Mecca), we would do
it, too." The prophet—Allah bless and keep him—called on the people,
who then descended on Badr. They were met by Kureish camels carrying
water. Among their takers was a young black [slave] man belonging to the
Al-Hajjaj clan. They took him [as hostage]. The companions of the prophet—Allah bless and keep him—started asking him about Abou Sofian and
his companions. He first said, "I know nothing about Abou Soufian, but I
know about Abou Jahl, Atba, Sheiba, and Omaya Ibn Khalaf." But when
they beat him he said, "O, yes, I will tell you. This is the news of Abou
Soufian..." Meanwhile, the prophet—Allah bless and keep him—who was
praying, started to depart saying, "Strike him if he tells you the truth and
release him if he lies." Then he said, "That is the death of someone [the
hostage]." He said that in the presence of his companions and while moving his hand on the ground.

In this tradition, we find permission to interrogate the hostage for the
purpose of obtaining information. It is permitted to strike the nonbeliever
who has no covenant until he reveals the news, information, and secrets of
his people.

The religious scholars have also permitted the killing of a hostage if he
insists on withholding information from Moslems. They permitted his killing
so that he would not inform his people of what he learned about the Muslim
condition, number, and secrets. In the Honein attack, after one of the spies

*Al-Morabitoun Magazine*, Issue No. 6

learned about the Muslims' kindness and weakness, then fled, the prophet—Allah bless and keep him—permitted [shedding] his blood and said, "Find and kill him." Salma Ibn Al-Akwaa followed, caught, and killed him.

The scholars have also permitted the exchange of hostages for money, services, and expertise, as well as for secrets of the enemy's army, plans, and numbers. After the Badr attack, the prophet—Allah bless and keep him—showed favor to some hostages, like the poet Abou Izza, by exchanging most of them for money. The rest were released for providing services and expertise to the Muslims.

## Importance of Information

1. Based on the enemy's up-to-date information, his capabilities, and plans, the organization's command can design good-quality and secure plans.
2. Information about the enemy's intention provides early warning signs for the command, which in turn makes appropriate preparation and thwarts the enemy's opportunity.
3. Information benefits the organization's command by providing information about the enemy's strengths and weaknesses.
4. Information benefits the organization's command by providing information about movements of the enemy and his members.

Information requirements include: newness, trustworthiness, forthcoming, security, and confirmation. General Mahmoud Sheet Khattab said, "The nation that wants to achieve victory over its enemy must know that enemy very well. It also must know the site of the battle in detail. Those who fight an enemy that they do not know, do not win because a successful military plan must be built on clear and trustworthy information. The commander who fights an enemy and does not know his strength (number and materiel) is blind and destined to fail and fall."

## Information Sources

Any organization that desires to raise the flag of Islam high and proud must gather as much information as possible about the enemy. Information has two sources:

I. Public Sources: Using public sources openly and without resorting to illegal means, it is possible to gather at least 80 percent of the information available about the enemy. The percentage varies depending on the government's policy on freedom of the press and publication. It is possible to gather information through newspapers, magazines, books, periodicals, official publications, and enemy broadcasts. Attention should also be given to the opinion, comments, and jokes of common people. Truman, a past American President, said, "We attribute our great advance to our press, because it gives America's enemies the capability of learning what we have not officially publicized about our plans and even our establishments."

In 1954, Allan Dulles,Director of American Intelligence [CIA], said, "I am ready to pay any amount of money to obtain information about the Soviet Union, even as little as what the Soviet Union obtains by simply reading American newspapers."

The one gathering public information should be a regular person (trained college graduate) who examines primary sources of information published by the enemy (newspapers, magazines, radio, TV, etc.). He should search for information directly related to the topic in question.

The one gathering information with this public method is not exposed to any danger whatsoever. Any brother can gather information from those aforementioned sources. We cannot label that brother a "Moslem Spy" because he does not make any effort to obtain unpublished and covert information.

The most important sources for gathering information using public means are:

A. Newspapers, magazines, and official and party publications.

In order to gather enemy information, the military organization can use means such as magazines, periodicals, other periodicals, and official printed matter. Through these means, it is possible to learn about major government events and about the news, meetings, and travel of presidents, ministers, and commanders. Information may be:

1. names and photographs of important government personalities, police commanders, and security leaders;
2. published meetings (through these, one can learn about major decisions and topics being discussed);
3. future meeting plans;
4. present and future enemy capabilities through current photographs of projects and strategic sites or through meetings with top officials;
5. beneficial news about the enemy's diplomacy and its present and future plans;
6. tourism news and the arrival times of foreign tourist groups;
7. advertisements about apartments for rent, vacant positions, or anything else that is useful;

8. advertisements about new and used car lots (these may be used in assassination, kidnapping, and overthrowing the government);
9. learning the enemy position on current Islamic issues (veil, beard, dedication, jihad, etc.).

B. Radio and television (the military organization can use these important public sources to gather information all day and night; the importance of these means is explained below.)

1. visual and audio news help the organization to determine its present and future plans.
2. interviews may help to identify the government policy and its general directives.
3. visual and audio media may help spot the appearance of those who occupy high positions.
4. visual and audio media may help reveal the prevailing information diplomacy and its position on contemporary issues.
5. visual and audio media may be a source for learning about the interior of important government places and establishments during their opening ceremonies or through advertisements.

In addition to the aforementioned, [attention should be given] to newspapers, magazines, and the public's comments and jokes.

II. Secret Sources. It is possible, through these secret and dangerous methods, to obtain the 20 percent of information that is considered secret. The most important of these sources are:
A. individuals who are recruited as either volunteers or because of other motives;
B. recording and monitoring;
C. photography;
D. interrogation;
E. documents (by burglary or recruitment of personnel);
F. drugging; and
G. surveillance, spying, and observation.

OSAMA BIN LADEN

# JIHAD AGAINST JEWS AND CRUSADERS

## WORLD ISLAMIC FRONT STATEMENT

23 February 1998
Shaykh Usamah Bin-Muhammad Bin-Ladin
Ayman al-Zawahiri, emir of the Jihad Group in Egypt
Abu-Yasir Rifa'i Ahmad Taha, Egyptian Islamic Group
Shaykh Mir Hamzah, secretary of the Jamiat-ul-Ulema-e-Pakistan
Fazlur Rahman, amir of the Jihad Movement in Bangladesh

Praise be to Allah, who revealed the Book, controls the clouds, defeats factionalism, and says in his book, "But when the forbidden months are past, then fight and slay the pagans wherever ye find them, seize them, beleaguer them, and lie in wait for them in every stratagem (of war)." Peace be upon our Prophet, Muhammad Bin-'Abdallah, who said, "I have been sent with the sword between my hands to ensure that no one but Allah is worshipped, Allah who put my livelihood under the shadow of my spear and who inflicts humiliation and scorn on those who disobey my orders."

The Arabian peninsula has never—since Allah made it flat, created its desert, and encircled it with seas—been stormed by any forces like the crusader armies spreading in it like locusts, eating its riches, and wiping out its plantations. All this is happening at a time in which nations are attacking Muslims like people fighting over a plate of food. In the light of grave situation and the lack of support, we and you are obliged to discuss current events, and we should all agree on how to settle the matter.

No one argues today about three facts that are known to everyone. We will list them, in order to remind everyone:

First, for over seven years the United States has been occupying the lands of Islam in the holiest of places, the Arabian peninsula, plundering its riches, dictating to its rulers, humiliating its people, terrorizing its neighbors, and turning its bases in the peninsula into a spearhead through which to fight the neighboring Muslim peoples.

If some people have in the past argued about the fact of the occupation, all the people of the peninsula have now acknowledged it. The best proof of this is the Americans' continuing aggression against the Iraqi people using the peninsula as a staging post, even though all its rulers are against their territories being used to that end, but they are helpless.

Second, despite the great devastation inflicted on the Iraqi people by the crusader-Zionist alliance, and despite the huge number of those killed, which has exceeded one million... despite all this, the Americans are once against trying to repeat the horrific massacres, as though they are not content with the protracted blockade imposed after the ferocious war or the fragmentation and devastation.

So here they come to annihilate what is left of this people and to humiliate their Muslim neighbors.

Third, if the Americans' aims behind these wars are religious and economic, the aim is also to serve the Jews' petty state and divert attention from its occupation of Jerusalem and murder of Muslims there. The best proof of this is their eagerness to destroy Iraq, the strongest neighboring Arab state, and their endeavor to fragment all the states of the region such as Iraq, Saudi Arabia, Egypt, and Sudan into paper statelets and through their disunion and weakness to guarantee Israel's survival and the continuation of the brutal crusade occupation of the peninsula.

All these crimes and sins committed by the Americans are a clear declaration of war on Allah, his Messenger, and Muslims. And ulema have throughout Islamic history unanimously agreed that the jihad is an individual duty if the enemy destroys the Muslim countries. This was revealed by Imam Bin-Qadamah in "Al-Mughni," Imam al-Kisa'i in "Al-Bada'i," al-Qurtubi in his interpretation, and the shaykh of al-Islam in his books, where he said, "As for the fighting to repulse [an enemy], it is aimed at defending sanctity and religion, and it is a duty as agreed [by the ulema]. Nothing is more sacred than belief except repulsing an enemy who is attacking religion and life."

On that basis, and in compliance with Allah's order, we issue the following fatwa to all Muslims:

The ruling to kill the Americans and their allies—civilians and military—is an individual duty for every Muslim who can do it in any country in which it is possible to do it, in order to liberate the al-Aqsa Mosque and the holy mosque [Mecca] from their grip, and in order for their armies to move out of all the lands of Islam, defeated and unable to threaten any Muslim. This is in accordance with the words of Almighty Allah, "and fight the pagans all together as they fight you all together," and "fight them until there is no more tumult or oppression, and there prevail justice and faith in Allah."

This is in addition to the words of Almighty Allah: "And why should ye not fight in the cause of Allah and of those who, being weak, are ill-treated (and oppressed)?—women and children—whose cry is: 'Our Lord, rescue us from this town, whose people are oppressors; and raise for us from thee one who will help!'"

We—with Allah's help—call on every Muslim who believes in Allah and wishes to be rewarded to comply with Allah's order to kill the Americans and plunder their money wherever and whenever they find it. We also call on Muslim ulema, leaders, youths, and soldiers to launch the raid on Satan's U.S. troops and the devil's supporters allying with them, and to displace those who are behind them so that they may learn a lesson.

Almighty Allah said: "O, ye who believe, give your response to Allah and His Apostle, when He calleth you to that which will give you life. And know that Allah cometh between a man and his heart, and that it is He to whom ye shall all be gathered."

Almighty Allah also says: "O, ye who believe, what is the matter with you, that when ye are asked to go forth in the cause of Allah, ye cling so heavily to the earth! Do ye prefer the life of this world to the hereafter? But little is the comfort of this life, as compared with the hereafter. Unless ye go forth, he will punish you with a grievous penalty, and put others in your place; but him ye would not harm in the least. For Allah hath power over all things."

Almighty Allah also says: "So lose no heart, nor fall into despair. For ye must gain mastery if ye are true in faith."

# THE LETTER LEFT BEHIND

## THE LAST NIGHT

1. Pledge of allegiance for death and renewal of intent
2. To be perfect with the plan very well of all its aspects and expecting the reaction or resistance from the enemy.
3. Reading and understanding well the chapters Al-Anfaal and At-Tawbah [or chapter eight, "The Spoils of War" and chapter nine "Repentance of the Holy Koran" and understanding their meanings very well and what Allah has prepared for the believers or the permanent bliss for the martyrs.
4. Reminding one's self of listening well and obeying that night for you are going to face critical situations which require strict abiding and obeying (one hundred percent). So you should tame yourself and make it apprehend and convince it and incite it for that.

   The Most High says, "Obey Allah and his Messenger and dispute not amongst yourselves, and be not divided amongst yourselves; otherwise you will fail and your power will vanish, and be patient for Allah is with those who are patient.
5. Praying in the middle of the night and asking Allah many times for victory and to overpower and a clear opening and ask for facilitating matters and covering us.
6. Mention God many times and be learned that the best of mentioning God is reciting or reading the Holy Koran, and this is what the scholars have agreed upon unanimously as much as I know. And it is sufficient for us that it is the Word of the Lord of the skies and the earth who you are going to meet.

7. Clean your heart and purify it from mishaps and forget completely a thing which is called worldly life for the time for playing has past and the true promise has come. How much did we waste from our years of time? Shouldn't we utilize these hours to offer obedience and closeness?

8. You should be cheerful for the time between you and your marriage is only a few moments with which you begin the happy, satisfactory life and the eternal bliss with the prophets and the true believers and the martyrs and the good people. What a great company to be among.

    We ask God from his grace and be optimistic because the prophet—peace be upon him—(used to like optimism in all his affairs).

9. Then remember very well that if you have been put into dilemma how to behave and how to be firm. And remember and know that what has befallen upon you should befall upon for sure. And what has not fallen upon you shouldn't fall upon you. And this dilemma from God, the most high and most exalted, to raise your status and forgive your sins, then know that it's a matter of moments then it will be clear with the permission of God. Congratulations for he who won with the great reward from God, the Almighty, who says, "Do you expect to enter paradise without Allah knowing those who struggled from you and know the patient ones?"

10. Then remember the saying of God, the Almighty, "And you were hoping for death before it comes to you that you have seen it while you are looking..."; And after that remember, "Indeed many small groups would defeat a big one with the permission of God"; and his saying, "If God makes you victorious, no one else can conquer you. And if God makes you fail, then who is he that can make you victorious beyond God? And upon God, the believers depend."

11. Remind yourself with supplications and your brothers and comprehend their meanings. (Supplications of the morning and the evening, supplications of the country, supplications of the place, supplications of meeting the enemy, etc.)

12. Pray for your soul, the bag, the clothes, the knife, your stuff—whatever that stuff is—your ID, *tith* [the author does not complete this word: therefore the translators decided to merely transliterate the Arabic here], your passport, and all of your papers.

13. Check your weapons, before departure, and before you leave; and "let every one of you sharpen his knife and kill his animal and bring about comfort and relief of his slaughter" before the journey.

14. Tighten up your clothes and this is the medal of the righteous predecessors. May God be content with them all. They used to tighten up their clothes before the battle, then tighten up your shoes well and put your feet in your socks and hold on in your shoes and do not slip out of it. And these are all causes that we are ordered to undertake. And God is our protector and He is the best deputy.

15. Perform the morning prayers in congregation and think of its reward while you are [reciting] the supplications. And don't get out of your apartment except with [having performed the] ablutions.

For the angels are asking for happiness for you as long as you have ablutions. And they make supplication for you. And read God the Almighty's sayings, "Do you think that We have created you in vain" (chapter of the believer [chapter 23 in the Koran]).

The text of the mentioned *hadith* is reported by An-Nawwawi in his book *The Chosen from the Supplicants*. [The following sentence is squeezed on the bottom of this page and continues at the top of the same page as indicated by an arrow] One of the companions said the Messenger of God ordered us to read it before the conquest. So we read it and we won and we were safe. [The following two short sentences begin with an asterisk and are found at the very top of the page adjacent to sentence following number 1.]

*Depleting the excess hair from the body and perfuming.

*Taking a complete shower.

## THE SECOND STAGE

When the taxi takes you to (M) [airport—*matar* in Arabic] then mention and remember God much in the car (supplication of riding, supplication of town, supplication of place, [and] the other supplications).

When you arrive and see (M) and get out of the taxi, then say the supplication of the place and every place you go to say in it the supplication of place and smile, and be comforted for God is with the believers, and the angels guard you and you do not feel them. Then say the supplication "God is more mightier than all His creation..." and say "O, God, suffice us them with what you willed" and say "O, God, we attack with you into their throats and we take you our shelter against their evil"; and say "O, God, make a dam for us between their fronts and their backs and He made them blind that they could not see"; and say "Our protector is God and he is the best deputy" remembering the Almighty's saying, "Those whom the people said that the people gathered and prepared against you so fear them that increased their faith and said our protector is God and he is the best deputy." That after saying it you will find some matters and companions around you because God has promised his slaves who say this supplication as follows:

1. Winning God's grace and bliss
2. No evil touches them
3. Following God's content

The Almighty said, "They won God's grace and bliss, no evil touched them and they followed God's content and God is the Greatest Benevolent" for their devices and doors and technology—all of it has no benefit in slaughter except with the permission of God. And the believers do not get afraid of, it but those who get afraid of it are the agents of the devil—those in fact are afraid of the devil and have become his agents. Fear is a great worship, which should not be paid except to God alone the Almighty—and he is worthy of it. The Almighty said, commenting on those verses: "That is the devil makes his agents afraid" those who admire civilization of the West those who drink their love and their worship with cold water and were afraid of their equipment which are weak and trivial "That do not be afraid of them and be afraid of me if you are true believers" that fear is a great worship, the angels of God and the believers do not perform it except for God alone, the only one who owns everything and are very sure that God will fail the tricks of the disbelievers that the Almighty said "That God is weakening the tricks of the disbelievers."

Then you must remember what I think is the most important supplication; and especially you must not let it be seen that you say the saying "There is no God except Allah." For if you repeat it a thousand times nobody could tell whether your silent mentioning God and his greatness, his saying peace be upon him [the reference is to Muhammad here] "Whoever says there is no God except Allah, believing in it with all his heart, he enters paradise"; or as [Muhammad] said, "peace be upon him," in that which means, "If the seven earths and skies are placed on one scale and there is no God except Allah on the other scale, then the scale of there is no God except Allah weighs the other down." And you can smile while saying it, and this is of the greatness of this word and that he who thinks deeply in it he finds that its letters have not dots on them and this is of its greatness that the dotted words or letters are less from it, and it is sufficient that it is the word of monotheism which you need most in the battlefield as the Messenger did—peace be upon him and his companions and those who followed them as well until the Day of Judgment.

And also do not let perplexing confusion and nervous tension appear upon you. Be cheerful, happy, serene, and comforted because you are doing a job which God loves and accepts, hence it will be a day with God's permission. You will spend it with the most beautiful women in paradise.

Smile in the face of death, young man for you are on your way to everlasting paradise!

Any place you go to or any action you do, you should supplicate and God is with His slaves the believers with support and guard and facilitation and success and conquest and victory and everything.

## THE THIRD STAGE

When you ride the (T) [plane—*Ta'irah* in Arabic] the moment you put in your leg and before you enter it, make supplications and remember it is an expedition for the way, and as upon him is peace and praying has said [referring to Muhammad] "that a coming or a going for the way of God is better than the worldly life and of all in it." Or as upon him is peace and praying has said, "And when you put your leg into (T) and sit on your seat, say the supplications and remember the well-known supplications which we mentioned earlier, then be busy with mentioning God and be industrious in that God the Almighty said, "Oh, you believers! If you met a group, then be firm and serene and mention God much so as to be successful." Then when (T) moves slowly and heads to (Q) [probably taking off—*Iqla'* in Arabic] say the supplication of travel for you are travelling to God the Almighty, "Enjoy the travel." You will find it stopping then going forth and that is the hour of meeting the attributes; then ask God the Almighty as the Almighty mentioned in His Book "Oh God pour patience upon us and make our feet firm and make us victorious over the disbelieving people"; and His Almighty's saying "And what was their saying except that they said Oh our God forgive our sins and our extravagance in our affair and make our feet firm and make us victorious over the disbelieving people" and His prophet's saying peace be upon him "Oh God, you who has revealed your Book and moved the clouds and defeated the parties defeat them and make us victorious over them oh God defeat them and earthquake them" pray for yourself and for all your companions for conquer and victory and hitting the target and weakening the enemy and ask God to grant you martyrdom going forward not backward being patient and expecting a reward in the hereafter.

Then each one of you should be ready to do his job on the manner which pleases God the Almighty and then press your teeth together as the predecessors used to do—may God have mercy on them—before getting into a fight in the battlefield.

In combat hit firmly and strongly as the heroes do who do not wish to come back to the worldly life and say aloud, "God is great for saying that [causes] horror and terror to enter into the hearts of the disbelievers. God the Almighty said, "Hit over the necks and hit every finger of them." And know that paradise has been decorated for you with the best of its decorations and ornaments and the most beautiful women are calling upon you come oh you the commander with the order of God and they have dressed in the best of their attire.

And if God gave anyone of you a sacrifice of an animal, he should intend it for his father and his mother, for they have a right over you and do not dispute among yourselves and listen and obey. And if you slaughter, then you take the booty of whom you killed for this is a tradition of the selected (chosen Prophet)—peace be upon him—but on the condition that you do not be occupied with taking booties and leaves (neglects), what is more important of paying attention to the enemy and his trickery or attack for this is more harmful, and if it was so.

That giving priority of work and community interest over doing these because work is an individual duty and this is a tradition; and the duty is given priority over the tradition; and do not revenge for yourself, but make you hit everything for God the Almighty. Ali ibn Abi Talib—may God be pleased with him—fought with one of the disbelievers and the disbelievers stood up (and spat) upon Ali—may God be pleased with him. He put down his sword and did not hit him; then the hit him. After the battle had finished, one of the companions asked him about his doing so and why he did not hit that disbeliever when he hit him. Ali—may God be pleased with him—said, "When he spat upon me I thought I would hit him in revenge for myself. I raised my sword (or as he said then) when I remembered the intent. He stood up and he killed him and this all means in a short time one should settle down his soul before all his actions and doings are for God.

"Then apply the tradition of captivity and capture among them and kill them," as God the Almighty said. "No prophet must have prisoners of war until he weakens (the enemy) on the land. Do you want to have the best of the worldly life? God wants the hereafter and God is the most mighty and the most wise."

If everything is done perfectly, then everyone of you pats his brother on the shoulder at (M) and at (T) and at (K), reminding him that this work is for the sake of God the Almighty and the Exalted. And he does not perplex his brothers (companions) even if with any time thing but he makes them hopeful and comforts them and reminds them and encourages them. What a beauty if one repeats verses from the Koran such as God's saying, "That he fights for the way of God those who buy the worldly life for the hereafter..."

And God's saying, "Do not count those who were killed for the way of God dead...." Etc., or sings to them as did the predecessors during the battles. He should comfort his companions and make them serene and cheerful.

And do not forget to take some of the booty (even a cup or a glass of water to gratify yourself and your companions if it was possible); then if the true promise approached and the zero hour, came open up your jacket and open up your chest welcoming death for the way of God and always be remembering and if you can end with praying if it is possible start it a few seconds before the target in The last of your speech is should be "there is no God except Allah and Muhammad is His Messenger. And af-ter that—God willing—will be the meeting in the highest rank of paradise with God's mercy.

God, Pray upon our Prophet Muhammad.

*www.ict.org.il/articles*

---

*If you see the gatherings of disbelief; remember the parties whose numbers were close to ten thou-sand fighters and how God make his slaves the believers victorious over them. God the Almighty says: "And when the believers saw the parties; they said that that which God promised us and God and His Messenger are true; and that increased their belief and faith and submission to God."

# A SHORT BIOGRAPHY

### DR. SHEIKH ABDULLAH YUSUF AZZAM. PALESTINIAN. ASSASSINATED ON 24 NOVEMBER 1989, IN PESHAWAR, PAKISTAN, AGED 48. [...]

*Time Magazine wrote about him that*
*"he was the reviver of Jihad in the 20th Century."*

Abdullah Yusuf Azzam was born in the village of Ass-ba'ah Al-Hartiyeh, province of Jineen in the occupied sacred land of Palestine in 1941. He was brought up in a humble house where he was taught Islam, and was fed with the love of Allah, His Messenger, those striving in the way of Allah, the righteous people and the desire for the hereafter.

Abdullah Azzam [...] started propagating Islam at an early age. His peers knew him as a pious child. He showed signs of excellence at an early age. His teachers recognized this while he was still in elementary school.

Sheikh Abdullah Azzam was known for his perseverance and serious nature ever since he was a small boy. He received his early elementary and secondary education in his village, and continued his education at the agricultural Khadorri College where he obtained a diploma. Although he was the youngest of his colleagues, he was the cleverest and the smartest. After he graduated from college, he worked as a teacher in a village called Adder in south Jordan. Later he joined Sharia College in Damascus University where he obtained a B.A. degree in shariah (Islamic law) in 1966. After the Jews captured the West Bank in 1967, Sheikh Abdullah Azzam decided to migrate to Jordan, because he could not live under the Jews' occupation of Palestine. The sin of the Israeli tanks rolling into the West Bank without any resistance made him even more determined to migrate in order to learn the skills necessary to fight.

In the late 1960s he joined the jihad against the Israeli occupation of Palestine from Jordan. Soon after that, he emigrated to Egypt and graduated with a masters degree in shariah from the University of Al-Azhar. In 1970 and after jihad came to a halt by forcing PLO forces out of Jordan, he assumed the position of teaching in the Jordanian University in Amman. In 1971 he was awarded a scholarship to Al-Azhar University in Cairo from which he obtained a Ph.D degree in principles of Islamic jurisprudence (Usool-ul-Fiqh) in 1973. During his stay in Egypt he came to know the family of Shaheed Sayyed Qutb.

Sheikh Abdullah Azzam spent a long time participating in the jihad in Palestine. However, matters there were not to his liking, for the people involved in the jihad were far removed from Islam. He told of how these people used to spend the nights playing cards and listening to music, under the illusion that they were performing jihad to liberate Palestine. Sheikh Abdullah Azzam mentioned that, out of the thousands in the camp he was in, the number of people who offered their *salah* in congregation were so few that they could be counted on one hand. He tried to steer them towards Islam, but they resisted his attempts. One day he rhetorically asked one of the *Mujahideen* what the religion behind the Palestinian revolution was, to which the man replied, quite clearly and bluntly, "This revolution has no religion behind it."

This was the last straw for Sheikh Abdullah Azzam. He left Palestine, and went to Saudi Arabia to teach in the universities there.

When Sheikh Azzam realized that only by means of an organized force would the *ummah* ever be able to gain victory, then jihad and the gun became his preoccupation and recreation. "Jihad and the rifle alone: no negotiations, no conferences, and no dialogues," he would say. By practicing what he was preaching, Sheikh Abdullah Azzam was one of the first Arabs to join the Afghan jihad against the communist USSR.

In 1979, when he learned about the Afghan jihad, he left his teaching position at King Abdul-Aziz University in Jeddah, Saudi Arabia, and went to Islamabad, Pakistan, in order to be able to participate in the jihad. He moved to Pakistan to be close to the Afghan jihad, and there he got to know its leaders. During the early time of his stay in Pakistan, he was appointed a lecturer in the International Islamic University in Islamabad. After a while he had to quit the University to devote his full time and energy to the jihad in Afghanistan.

In the early 1980s, Sheikh Abdullah Azzam came to experience the jihad in Afghanistan. In this jihad he found satisfaction of his longing and untold love to fight in the path of Allah, just as Allah's Messenger (SAW) once said, "One hour spent fighting in the Path of Allah is worth more than seventy years spent in praying at home." [Authentic, At-Tirmithi and Al-Hakem].

Inspired by this hadith, Sheikh Abdullah Azzam immigrated with his family to Pakistan in order to be closer to the field of jihad. Soon after, he then moved from Islamabad to Peshawar to be even closer to the field of jihad and martyrdom.

In Peshawar, Sheikh Abdullah Azzam founded the Bait-ul-Ansar (Mujahideen Services Bureau) with the aim of offering all possible assistance to the Afghani jihad and the mujahideen through establishing and managing projects that supported the cause. The bureau also received and trained volunteers pouring into Pakistan to participate in jihad and allocating them to the front lines.

Unsurprisingly, this was not enough to satisfy Sheikh Azzam's burning desire for jihad. That desire drove him finally to go to the front line. On the battlefield, the Sheikh gracefully played his destined role in that generous epic of heroism.

In Afghanistan he hardly ever settled in one place. He travelled throughout the country, visiting most of its provinces and states such as Lujer, Qandahar, Hindukush Heights, the Valley of Binjistr, Kabul, and Jalalabad. These travels allowed Sheikh Abdullah Azzam to witness first hand the heroic deeds of these ordinary people who had sacrificed all that they possessed—including their own lives—for the supremacy of the Deen of Islam.

In Peshawar, upon his return from these travels, Sheikh Azzam spoke about jihad constantly. He prayed to restore the unity among the divided mujahideen commanders; called upon those who had not yet joined the fighting to take up arms and to follow him to the front before it would be too late.

Abdullah Azzam was greatly influenced by the jihad in Afghanistan and the jihad was greatly influenced by him since he devoted his full time to its cause. He became the most prominent figure in the Afghani jihad aside from the Afghan leaders. He spared no effort to promote the Afghan cause to the whole world, especially through the Muslim Ummah. He traveled all over the world, calling on Muslims to rally to the defence of their religion and lands. He wrote a number of books on jihad, such as *Join the Caravan* and *Defense of Muslim Lands*. Moreover, he himself participated physically in the Afghan jihad, despite the fact that he was in his forties. He traversed Afghanistan, from north to south, east to west, in snow, through the mountains, in heat and in cold, riding donkeys and on foot. Young men with him used to tire from such exertions, but not Sheikh Abdullah Azzam.

He changed the minds of Muslims about the jihad in Afghanistan and presented the jihad as an Islamic cause which concerned all Muslims around the world. Due to his efforts, the Afghani jihad became universal in that Muslims from every part of the world participated. Soon, volunteer Islamic fighters began to travel to Afghanistan from the four corners of the earth, to fulfil their obligation of jihad and in defence of their oppressed Muslim brothers and sisters.

The Sheikh's life revolved around a single goal, namely the establishment of Allah's rule on earth, this being the clear responsibility of each and every Muslim. So in order to accomplish his life's noble mission of restoring the khilafah (Islamic rule), the Sheikh focused on jihad (the armed struggle to establish Islam). He believed jihad must be carried out until the Khilafah is established so the light of Islam may shine on the whole world.

Sheikh Abdullah Azzam made jihad in every possible way, responding to the call of Allah [...]

He reared his family in the same spirit also, so that his wife, for example, engaged in orphan care and other humanitarian work in Afghanistan. He refused teaching positions at a number of universities, declaring that he would not quit jihad until he was either martyred or assassinated. He used to reiterate that his ultimate goal was still to liberate Palestine. He was once quoted as saying, *"Never shall I leave the Land of Jihad, except in three circumstances. I shall be killed in Afghanistan. Or I shall be killed in Peshawar. Or I shall be handcuffed and expelled from Pakistan."*

Jihad in Afghanistan had made Abdullah Azzam the main pillar of the jihad movement in the modern times. Through taking part in this jihad, and through promoting and clarifying the obstacles which have been erected in the path of jihad, he played a significant role in changing the minds of Muslims about jihad and the need for it. He was a role model for the young generation that responded to the call of jihad. He had a great appreciation for jihad and the need for it. Once he said, "I feel that I am nine years old: seven-and-a-half years in the Afghan jihad, one-and-a-half years in the jihad in Palestine, and the rest of the years have no value."

From his pulpit Sheikh Azzam was always reiterating his conviction that:

*"Jihad must not be abandoned until Allah [...] alone is worshipped. Jihad continues until Allah's word is raised high. Jihad until all the oppressed peoples are freed. Jihad to protect our dignity and restore our occupied lands. Jihad is the way of everlasting glory."*

History, as well as anyone who knew Sheikh Abdullah Azzam closely, all testify to his courage in speaking the truth, regardless of the consequences. He always bore in mind the command of Allah to "Proclaim openly that which you were commanded, and turn away from the polytheists ( mushrikeen)." [Qur'an, 15:94].

On every occasion Sheikh Abdullah Azzam reminded all Muslims that "Muslims cannot be defeated by others. We Muslims are not defeated by our enemies, but instead, we are defeated by our own selves."

He was a fine example of Islamic manners, in his piety, his devotion to Allah and his modesty in all things. He would never adulate in his relations with others. Sheikh Azzam always listened to the youth, he was dignified and did not allow fear to have access to his brave heart. He practised continual fasting especially the alternate daily fasting routine of Prophet Dawud [...]. He strongly counselled others to practice fasting on Mondays and Thursdays. The Sheikh was a man of uprightness, honesty and virtue, and was never heard to slander others or to talk unpleasantly about an individual Muslim.

As the jihad in Afghanistan went on, he was succeeding in uniting together all the various fighting groups in the Afghani jihad. Naturally, such a pride to Islam caused great distress to the enemies of this religion, and they plotted to eliminate him. In 1989, a lethal amount of TNT explosive was placed beneath the pulpit from which he delivered the sermon every Friday. It was such a formidable quantity that if it had exploded, it would have destroyed the mosque, together with everything and everybody in it. Hundreds of Muslims would have been killed, but Allah provided protection and the bomb did not explode.

In the same year, his enemies, determined to accomplish their ugly task, tried another plot in Peshawar, shortly after the first attempt on his life. When Allah [...] willed that Sheikh Abdullah Azzam should leave this world to be in his closest company (we hope that it is so), the Sheikh departed in a glorious manner. The day was Friday, November 24, 1989.

The enemies of Allah planted three bombs on a road so narrow only a single car could travel on it. It was the road Sheikh Abdullah Azzam would use to drive to the Friday Prayer. That Friday, the Sheikh, together with two of his own sons, Ibrahim and Muhammad, and with one of the sons of the late Sheikh Tameem Adnani (another hero of the Afghan jihad), drove along the road. The car stopped at the position of the first bomb, and the Sheikh alighted to walk the remainder of the way. The enemies, lying in wait, then exploded the bomb. A loud explosion and a great thundering were heard all over the city.

People emerged from the mosque, and beheld a terrible scene. Only a small fragment of the car remained. The young son Ibrahim flew 100 metres into the air; the other two youths were thrown a similar distance away, and their remains were scattered among the trees and power lines. As for Sheikh Abdullah Azzam himself, his body was found resting against a wall, totally intact and not at all disfigured, except that some blood was seen issuing from his mouth.

That fateful blast indeed ended the worldly journey of Sheikh Abdullah Azzam which had been spent well in struggling, striving, and fighting in the path of Allah [...]. It also secured his more real and eternal life in the gardens of paradise—we ask Allah that it is so—that he will enjoy along with the illustrious company of "those on whom is the Grace of Allah, the Prophets, the Sincere ones, the Martyrs and the Righteous. The Best of company are they." [Qur'an, 4:69].

It was in this way that this great hero and reformer of Islam departed from the arena of jihad [...].

*www.azzan.com*

AYMAN AL ZAWAHIRI

# KNIGHTS UNDER THE PROPHET'S BANNER

*(Excerpts)*

Al-Zawahiri urges members of the fundamentalist movements to cause the greatest damage and inflict the maximum casualties on the opponent, no matter how much time and effort these operations take, because this is the language understood by the west. In general, Al-Zawahiri calls for moving the battle to the enemy's ground, which he considers the main target of the fundamentalist movement. He adds:

"The struggle for the establishment of the Muslim state cannot be considered a regional struggle, certainly not after it had been ascertained that what he describes as the 'crusader alliance led by the United States' will not allow any Muslim force to reach power in the Arab countries."

He notes that confining the battle to the domestic enemy, meaning within the Arab states, will not be feasible in this stage of the battle, which he considers the battle of every Muslim.

Al-Zawahiri adds: "Victory by the armies cannot be achieved unless the infantry occupies the territory."

Likewise, victory for the Islamic movements against the world alliance cannot be attained unless these movements possess an Islamic base in the heart of the Arab region. He notes that mobilizing and arming the nation will be up in the air, without any tangible results, until a fundamentalist state is established in the region. Bin Ladin's chief ally admits that the establishment of a Muslim state in the heart of the Islamic world is not an easy or close target. However, it is the hope of the Muslim nation to restore its fallen caliphate and regain its lost glory. He advises members of the fundamentalist movement not to precipitate collision and to be patient about victory. [...]

426

We must not despair of the repeated strikes and calamities. We must never lay down our arms no matter how much losses or sacrifices we endure. Let us start again after every strike, even if we had to begin from scratch.

He answers an important question about the fundamentalist movements if their plans are exposed, their members are arrested, and their existence is threatened. "It is better for the movement to pull out whoever it could pull out quietly, without reluctance, hesitation, or reliance on illusions."

Al-Zawahiri refers to the experience of captivity, as if he was looking at the future in an open book and reviewing the investigations conducted with his Egyptian fundamentalist colleagues held in London and New York in connection with the bombing of the U.S. embassies in Africa. These investigations revealed many of the Al-Qaeda secrets. He adds:

"Once the door of the cell is closed, the prisoner will wish that he had spent his entire life without a shelter rather than endure the humiliation of captivity. The toughest thing about captivity is forcing the mujahid, under the force of torture, to confess about his colleagues, destroy his movement with his own hands, and offer his and his colleagues' secrets to his enemies."

Following are excerpts:

And those who disbelieved said unto their messengers: "Verily we will drive you out from our land, unless ye return to our religion. Then their lord inspired them, saying verily We shall destroy the wrongdoers. And verily We shall make you to swell in the land after them. This is for him who feareth My Majesty and feareth My threats."

It is now time to explore the future of the jihad movement in Egypt in particular and the world in general.

## EMERGING PHENOMENA

Any neutral observer could discern a number of phenomena in our Islamic world in general and Egypt in particular:

### The Universality of the Battle

The western forces that are hostile to Islam have clearly identified their enemy. They refer to it as Islamic fundamentalism. They are joined in this by their old enemy, Russia. They have adopted a number of tools to fight Islam, including:

1. The United Nations
2. The friendly rulers of the Muslim peoples

3. The multinational corporations
4. The international communications and data exchange systems
5. The international news agencies and satellite media channels
6. The international relief agencies, which are being used as a cover for espionage, proselytizing, coup planning, and the transfer of weapons.

In the face of this alliance, a fundamentalist coalition is taking shape. It is made up of the jihad movements in the various lands of Islam as well as the two countries (Afghanistan and Chechnya) that have been liberated in the name of jihad for the sake of God.

If this coalition is still at an early stage, its growth is increasingly and steadily accelerating.

It represents a growing power that is rallying under the banner of jihad for the sake of God and operating outside the scope of the new world order. It is free of the servitude of the dominating western empire. It promises destruction and ruin for the new crusades against the lands of Islam. It is ready for revenge against the heads of the world's gathering of infidels, the United States, Russia, and Israel. It is anxious to seek retribution for the blood of the martyrs, the grief of the mothers, the deprivation of the orphans, the suffering of the detainees, and the sores of the tortured people throughout the land of Islam, from Eastern Turkestan to Andalusia.

This age is witnessing a new phenomenon that continues to gain ground. It is the phenomenon of the mujahid youths who have abandoned their families, country, wealth, studies, and jobs in search of jihad arenas for the sake of God.

## THERE IS NO SOLUTION WITHOUT JIHAD

With the emergence of this new batch of Islamists, who have been missing from the nation for a long time, a new awareness is increasingly developing among the sons of Islam, who are eager to uphold it: namely, that there is no solution without jihad.

The spread of this awareness has been augmented by the failure of all other methods that tried to evade assuming the burdens of jihad. The Algerian experience has provided a harsh lesson in this regard. It proved to Muslims that the west is not only an infidel but also a hypocrite and a liar. The principles that it brags about are exclusive to, and the personal property of, its people alone. They are not to be shared by the peoples of Islam, at least nothing more than what a master leaves his slave in terms of food crumbs.

The Islamic Salvation Front in Algeria has overlooked the tenets of the creed, the facts of history and politics, the balance of power, and the laws of control. It rushed to the ballot boxes in a bid to reach the presidential palaces and the ministries, only to find at the gates tanks loaded with French ammunition, with their barrels pointing at the chests of those who forgot the rules of confrontation between justice and falsehood. The guns of the French officers brought them down to the land of reality from the skies of illusions.

The men of the Islamic Salvation thought that the gates of rule had been opened for them, but they were surprised to see themselves pushed toward the gates of detention camps and prisons and into the cells of the new world order.

Particularly helpful in reaching the conclusion that there is no solution without jihad were the brutality and arbitrary nature of the new Jewish crusade that treats the Islamic nation with extreme contempt. As a result, the Muslims in general and the Arabs in particular are left with nothing that is dear to them. We have become like orphans in a banquet for the villains.

Someone may ask, "Don't you think that you are contradicting yourself? A short while ago you talked about the spread of despair in the hearts of some leaders of the jihad movement and now you are talking about a widespread jihad awakening?"

The answer is simple. All movements go through a cycle of erosion and renewal, but it is the ultimate result that determines the fate of a movement: Either extinction or growth.

Confirmed duties:

The Islamic movement in general, and the jihad movements in particular, must train themselves and their members in perseverance, patience, steadfastness, and adherence to firm principles. The leadership must set an example for the members to follow. This is the key to victory. "O, ye who believe, endure, outdo all others in endurance, be ready, and observe your duty to Allah, in order that ye may succeed."

If signs of relaxation and retreat start in show on the leadership, the movement must find ways to straighten out its leadership and not permit it to deviate from the line of jihad.

The loyalty to the leadership and the acknowledgement of its precedence and merit represent a duty that must be emphasized and a value that must be consolidated. But if loyalty to the leadership reaches the point of declaring it holy and if the acknowledgement of its precedence and merit leads to infallibility, the movement will suffer from methodological blindness. Any leadership flaw could lead to a historic catastrophe, not only for the movement but also for the entire nation.

Hence comes the importance of the issue of leadership in Islamic action in general and jihad action in particular and the nation's need for a scientific, struggling, and rational leadership that could guide the nation amidst the mighty storms and hurricanes toward its goal with awareness and prudence, without losing sight of its path, stumbling aimlessly, or reversing its course.

## MOBILIZING THE FUNDAMENTALIST MOVEMENT

The mobilization [*tajyyish*] of the nation, its participation in the struggle, and caution against the struggle of the elite with the authority:

The jihad movement must come closer to the masses, defend their honor, fend off injustice, and lead them to the path of guidance and victory. It must step forward in the arena of sacrifice and excel to get its message across in a way that makes the right accessible to all seekers and makes access to the origin and facts of religion simple and free of the complexities of terminology and the intricacies of composition.

The jihad movement must dedicate one of its wings to work with the masses, preach, provide services for the Muslim people, and share their concerns through all available avenues for charity and educational work.

We must not leave a single area unoccupied. We must win the people's confidence, respect, and affection. The people will not love us unless they felt that we love them, care about them, and are ready to defend them.

In short, in waging the battle the jihad movement must be in the middle, or ahead, of the nation. It must be extremely careful not to get isolated from its nation or engage the government in the battle of the elite against the authority.

We must not blame the nation for not responding to or not living up to the task. Instead, we must blame ourselves for failing to deliver the message, not showing compassion, and not making sacrifice.

The jihad movement must be eager to make room for the Muslim nation to participate with it in the jihad for the sake of empowerment [*al-tamkin*]. The Muslim nation will not participate with it unless the slogans of the mujahidin are understood by the masses of the Muslim nation.

The one slogan that has been well understood by the nation and to which it has been responding for the past fifty years is the call for the jihad against Israel. In addition to this slogan, the nation in this decade is geared against the U.S. presence. It has responded favorably to the call for the jihad against the Americans.

A single look at the history of the mujahidin in Afghanistan, Palestine, and Chechnya will show that the jihad movement has moved to the center of the leadership of the nation when it adopted the slogan of liberating the nation from its external enemies and when it portrayed it as a battle of Islam against infidelity and infidels.

The strange thing is that secularists, who brought disasters to the Muslim nation, particularly on the arena of the Arab-Israeli conflict; and who started the march of treason by recognizing Israel beginning with the Armistice Agreement of 1949, as we explained earlier, are the ones who talk the most about the issue of Palestine.

Stranger still is the fact that the Muslims, who have sacrificed the most for Jerusalem, whose doctrine and *shari'ah* prevent them from abandoning any part of Palestine or recognizing Israel, as we explained earlier; and who are the most capable of leading the nation in its jihad against Israel are the least active in championing the issue of Palestine and raising its slogans among the masses.

The jihad movement's opportunity to lead the nation toward jihad to liberate Palestine is now doubled. All the secular currents that paid lip service to the issue of Palestine and competed with the Islamic movement to lead the nation in this regard are now exposed before the Muslim nation following their recognition of Israel's existence and adoption of negotiations and compliance with the international resolutions to liberate what is left, or permitted by Israel, of Palestine. These currents differ among themselves on the amount of crumbs thrown by Israel to the Muslim and the Arabs.

The fact that must be acknowledged is that the issue of Palestine is the cause that has been firing up the feelings of the Muslim nation from Morocco to Indonesia for the past fifty years. In addition, it is a rallying point for all the Arabs, be they believers or nonbelievers, good or evil.

## SMALL GROUPS COULD FRIGHTEN THE AMERICANS

Through this jihad the stances of the rulers, their henchmen of ulema of the sultan [reference to pro-government clerics], writers, and judges, and the security agencies will be exposed. By so doing, the Islamic movement will prove their treason before the masses of the Muslim nation and demonstrate that the reason for their treason is a flaw in their faith. They have allied themselves with the enemies of God against His supporters and antagonized the *mujahidin*, because of their Islam and jihad, in favor of the Jewish and Christian enemies of the nation. They have committed a violation of monotheism by supporting the infidels against the Muslims.

431

Tracking down the Americans and the Jews is not impossible. Killing them with a single bullet, a stab, or a device made up of a popular mix of explosives or hitting them with an iron rod is not impossible. Burning down their property with Molotov cocktails is not difficult. With the available means, small groups could prove to be a frightening horror for the Americans and the Jews.

The Islamic movement in general and the jihad movement in particular must launch a battle for orienting the nation by:

- exposing the rulers who are fighting Islam;
- highlighting the importance of loyalty to the faithful and relinquishment of the infidels in the Muslim creed;
- holding every Muslim responsible for defending Islam, its sanctities, nation, and homeland;
- cautioning against the ulema of the sultan and reminding the nation of the virtues of the ulema of jihad and the imams of sacrifice and the need for the nation to defend, protect, honor, and follow them; and
- exposing the extent of aggression against our creed and sanctities and the plundering of our wealth.

Adherence to the goal of establishing the Muslim state in the heart of the Islamic world:

The jihad movement must adopt its plan on the basis of controlling a piece of land in the heart of the Islamic world on which it could establish and protect the state of Islam and launch its battle to restore the rational caliphate based on the traditions of the prophet.

## TOWARD A FUNDAMENTALIST BASE IN THE HEART OF THE ISLAMIC WORLD

Armies achieve victory only when the infantry takes hold of land. Likewise, the mujahid Islamic movement will not triumph against the world coalition unless it possesses a fundamentalist base in the heart of the Islamic world. All the means and plans that we have reviewed for mobilizing the nation will remain up in the air without a tangible gain or benefit unless they lead to the establishment of the state of caliphate in the heart of the Islamic world.

Nur-al-Din Zanki, and Salah-al-Din al-Ayyubi [Saladin] after him—may God bless their souls—have fought scores of battles until Nur-al-Din managed to wrestle Damascus from of the hands of the hypocrites and unified greater Syria under his command. He sent Salah-al-Din to Egypt, where he fought one battle after another until he brought Egypt under his control. When Egypt and Syria were unified after the death of Nur-al-Din, the mujahid Sultan Salah-al-Din managed to win the battle of Hittin and conquered Bayt al-Maqdis [Islamic name for Jerusalem]. Only then did the cycle of history turn against the crusaders.

If the successful operations against Islam's enemies and the severe damage inflicted on them do not serve the ultimate goal of establishing the Muslim nation in the heart of the Islamic world, they will be nothing more than disturbing acts, regardless of their magnitude, that could be absorbed and endured, even if after some time and with some losses.

The establishment of a Muslim state in the heart of the Islamic world is not an easy goal or an objective that is close at hand. But it constitutes the hope of the Muslim nation to reinstate its fallen caliphate and regain its lost glory.

London *Al-Sharq al-Awsat in Arabic* 12 Dec 2001
Translation from: Foreign Broadcast Information Service,
Document Number: FBIS-NES-2001-1212

# THE COVENANT

### *Article Seven*

By virtue of the distribution of Muslims, who pursue the cause of the Hamas, all over the globe, and strive for its victory, for the reinforcement of its positions and for the encouragement of its jihad, the movement is a universal one. This universally of the movement may be due to the clarity of its thinking, the nobility of its purpose, and the loftiness of its objectives.

It is in this light that the movement has to be regarded, evaluated and acknowledged. Whoever denigrates its worth, or avoids supporting it, or is so blind as to dismiss its role, is challenging fate itself. Whoever closes his eyes from seeing the facts, whether intentionally or not, will wake up to find himself overtaken by events, and will find no excuses to justify his position. Priority is reserved to the early comers.

Oppressing those who are closest to you, is more of an agony to the soul than the impact of an Indian sword.

"And unto thee have we revealed the Scripture with the truth, confirming whatever scripture was before it, and a watcher over it. So judge between them by that which Allah hath revealed, and follow not their desires away from the truth which has come unto thee. For each we have appointed a divine law and a traced-out way. Had Allah willed, He could have made you one community. But that He may try you by that which he has given you [He has made you as you are]. So vie with one another in good works. Unto Allah, you will all return. He will then inform you of that wherein you differ." *Sura V* (the Table), verse 48.

Hamas is one of the links in the Chain of Jihad in the confrontation with the Zionist invasion. It links up with the setting out of the Martyr Izz a-din al-Qassam and his brothers in the Muslim Brotherhood who fought the Holy War in 1936; it further relates to another link of the Palestinian Jihad and the Jihad and efforts of the Muslim Brothers during the 1948 War, and to the Jihad operations of the Muslim Brothers in 1968 and thereafter.

But even if the links have become distant from each other, and even if the obstacles erected by those who revolve in the Zionist orbit, aiming at obstructing the road before the Jihad fighters, have rendered the pursuance of Jihad impossible; nevertheless, the Hamas has been looking forward to implement Allah's promise whatever time it might take. The prophet, prayer and peace be upon him, said:

The time will not come until Muslims will fight the Jews (and kill them); until the Jews hide behind rocks and trees, which will cry: O Muslim! there is a Jew hiding behind me, come on and kill him! This will not apply to the Gharqad, which is a Jewish tree (cited by Bukhari and Muslim).

[...]

## HAMAS IN PALESTINE: ITS VIEWS ON HOMELAND AND NATIONALISM

### *Article Twelve*

Hamas regards nationalism (*wataniyya*) as part and parcel of the religious faith. Nothing is loftier or deeper in Nationalism than waging jihad against the enemy and confronting him when he sets foot on the land of the Muslims. And this becomes an individual duty binding on every Muslim man and woman; a woman must go out and fight the enemy even without her husband's authorization, and a slave without his masters' permission.

This [principle] does not exist under any other regime, and it is a truth not to be questioned. While other nationalisms consist of material, human and territorial considerations, the nationality of Hamas also carries, in addition to all those, the all important divine factors which lend to it its spirit and life; so much so that it connects with the origin of the spirit and the source of life and raises in the skies of the Homeland the Banner of the Lord, thus inexorably connecting earth with Heaven.

When Moses came and threw his baton, sorcery and sorcerers became futile.

"The right direction is henceforth distinct from error., And he who rejects false deities and believes in Allah has grasped a firm handhold which will never break. Allah is Hearer, Knower." *Sura II (the Cow)*, verse 256.

## PEACEFUL SOLUTIONS [PEACE] INITIATIVES
## AND INTERNATIONAL CONFERENCES

*Article Thirteen*

[Peace] initiatives, the so-called peaceful solutions, and the international conferences to resolve the Palestinian problem, are all contrary to the beliefs of the Islamic Resistance Movement. For renouncing any part of Palestine means renouncing part of the religion; the nationalism of the Islamic Resistance Movement is part of its faith, the movement educates its members to adhere to its principles and to raise the banner of Allah over their homeland as they fight their Jihad: "Allah is the all-powerful, but most people are not aware."

From time to time a clamouring is voiced, to hold an International Conference in search for a solution to the problem. Some accept the idea, others reject it, for one reason or another, demanding the implementation of this or that conditions, as a prerequisite for agreeing to convene the Conference or for participating in it. But the Islamic Resistance Movement, which is aware of the [prospective] parties to this conference, and of their past and present positions towards the problems of the Muslims, does not believe that those conferences are capable of responding to demands, or of restoring rights or doing justice to the oppressed. Those conferences are no more than a means to appoint the nonbelievers as arbitrators in the lands of Islam. Since when did the Unbelievers do justice to the Believers?

And the Jews will not be pleased with thee, nor will the Christians, till thou follow their creed. 'Say: Lo! the guidance of Allah [himself] is the Guidance. And if you should follow their desires after the knowledge which has come unto thee, then you would have from Allah no protecting friend nor helper." Sura 2 (the Cow) verse 120.

There is no solution to the Palestinian problem except by Jihad. The initiatives, proposals and International Conferences are but a waste of time, an exercise in futility. The Palestinian people are too noble to have their future, their right and their destiny submitted to a vain game. As the Hadith has it:

"The people of Syria are Allah's whip on this land; He takes revenge by their intermediary from whoever he wishes among his worshippers. The Hypocrites among them are forbidden from vanquishing the true believers, and they will die in anxiety and sorrow." (Told by Tabarani, who is traceable in ascending order of traditionaries to Muhammed, and by Ahmed whose chain of transmission is incomplete. But it is bound to be a true *hadith*, for both story tellers are reliable. Allah knows best.)

[...]

*Article Twenty-two*

The enemies have been scheming for a long time, and they have consolidated their schemes, in order to achieve what they they have achieved. They took advantage of key-elements in unfolding events, and accumulated a huge and influential material wealth which they put to the service of implementing their dream. This wealth [permitted them to] take over control of the world media such as news agencies, the press, publication houses, broadcasting and the like. [They also used this] wealth to stir revolutions in various parts of the globe in order to fulfill their interests and pick the fruits. They stood behind the French and the Communist Revolutions and behind most of the revolutions we hear about here and there. They also used the money to establish clandestine organizations which are spreading around the world, in order to destroy societies and carry out Zionist interests. Such organizations are: the Free Masons, Rotary Clubs, Lions Clubs, B'nai B'rith and the like. All of them are destructive spying organizations. They also used the money to take over control of the Imperialist states and made them colonize many countries in order to exploit the wealth of those countries and spread their corruption therein.

As regards local and world wars, it has come to pass and no one objects, that they stood behind World War I, so as to wipe out the Islamic Caliphate. They collected material gains and took control of many sources of wealth. They obtained the Balfour Declaration and established the League of Nations in order to rule the world by means of that organization. They also stood behind World War II, where they collected immense benefits from trading with war materials, and prepared for the establishment of their state. They inspired the establishment of the United Nations and the Security Council to replace the League of Nations, in order to rule the world by their intermediary. There was no war that broke out anywhere without their fingerprints on it.

*Article Thirty Two*

World Zionism and Imperialist forces have been attempting, with smart moves and considered planning, to push the Arab countries, one after another, out of the circle of conflict with Zionism, in order, ultimately, to isolate the Palestinian people. Egypt has already been cast out of the conflict, to a very great extent through the treacherous Camp David Accords, and she has been trying to drag other countries into similar agreements in order to push them out of the circle of conflict.

Hamas is calling upon the Arab and Islamic peoples to act seriously and tirelessly in order to frustrate that dreadful scheme and to make the masses aware of the danger of copping out of the circle of struggle with Zionism. Today it is Palestine and tomorrow it may be another country or other countries. For Zionist scheming has no end, and after Palestine they will covet expansion from the Nile to the Euphrates. Only when they have completed digesting the area on which they will have laid their hand, they will look forward to more expansion, etc. Their scheme has been laid out in the Protocols of the Elders of Zion, and their present [conduct] is the the best proof of what is said there.

RÉDHA MALEK

# ISLAMIST TERRORISM IN ALGERIA: AN EXPERIENCE TO PONDER

T HE TIME HAS COME FOR THIS CONFERENCE, devoted to Islamic terrorism, to see through the lens of the Algerian experience. The issues to be addressed merit serious attention. They emerge from clichés and platitudes that have long masked harsh realities with the intention of justifying them and to blur their meaning. Thus Islamic terrorism was both legitimized as an armed opposition, civil war, and cynically exonerated of the most atrocious crimes under the guise of "who kills whom?". Official discourse itself took time to call the phenomenon by its real name: terrorism, and took even longer to attribute the ideological qualifier: Islamist.

Thus, three questions arise:

1. Why terrorism in Algeria?
2. Why does it have such an exceptional scope and virulence?
3. Why was it so often downplayed internationally, if not completely concealed?

These three questions will clarify the nature and shape of this politico-religious phenomenon of extraordinary violence, which failed to support the nation-state. Islamic terrorism in Algeria has two roots, one internal and the other external, but the two constitute a fundamentally inseparable pair. On the internal level, there was, in the beginning, a traditional religious dispute, based on the tenets of "praise of the good and punishment of the evil." A small group, Al-Qiyyam—*the values*—set the tone since 1964. Ethical motives, deploring the breakdown of barriers and the neglect of Koranic teachings, initially criticized the regime in a soft and allusive way, to then branch out into a decisive and determined attack. This is the case of the teachings of one Sheik Sahnoune, who did not hesitate to attack, at the end of the 1960s and beginning of the 1970s, the policies of President Boumediene. A rapid industrialization, and especially the agrarian revolution, awakened the latent hostility of traditional circles to which certain personalities of the old association of the Algerian ulemas belonged. The calling into question of socialism could thus give rise to an inclusive mix until certain groups joined the war of independence. Sheik Abdelatif Soltani questioned, for example, the quality of hahid, usurped, according to him, because it should strictly relate to only those who fell for their Islamic faith. Literal conception in the straight line of wahhabism and of the ideologized Islam of the Muslim Brotherhood. In the eyes of conservative Arab regimes, such as Saudi Arabia, Boumediene, following the example of Gamal Abdel-Nasser, embodied a policy which was not to their liking. In spite of personal affinities between King Fayal and President Boumediène, unspoken reservations surrounded the relations between the two countries. A declaration like that of Boumediène to the conference of the Islamic states in Lahore: "We do not want to go to paradise hungry" did not fail to cause a scandal.

The opposition to progressive regimes by the bias of the religious elite grew under the effect of the international economic situation. 1979 was the key year when Islamic politics made a spectacular entry. In February, the Islamic Revolution of Khomeini triumphed in Iran. In March, the signing of the Camp David accords raised a storm against President Sadat. Fundamentalist Egyptians, whom Sadat had largely restored to favor, were not the least fierce against him. He would die two years later at the hand of one of them: Islambouli. But the most relevant historic event and the most dangerous for international security was the entry of the Red Army into Kabul in December. At the same time, two events heated up the already extremely tense climate towards the end of 1979: the capture of fifty-two American hostages in Teheran and the occupation of the Grande Mosque of Mecca by radical Islamists, of which one of the ring-leaders, Mohamed Amer, would be found in Peshawar. The invasion of Afghanistan by the Soviet Union had as a consequence the important decision by the United States to fight this occupation by co-opting Islamists. This was the ultimate trial of strength of the cold war which would make Afghanistan the global trigger of Islamic terrorism.

By opportunistically exploiting the resistance of a people known for their fierce attachment to independence, the United States was not content to offer discrete support to them on the bilateral level. But they also called upon volunteer Islamists from everywhere in the world to give this resistance the breadth of a multinational Jihad. With this broadening, nebulous Islamists could only answer favorably, finding an occasion to distinguish themselves within a global conflict. If, for Washington, the Islamists were only auxiliaries, not to say mercenaries whom they paid by providing them a strategy that was beyond them, for the Islamists, Afghanistan was only one testing ground, a general trial of future combats which they intended to carry out against regimes in their home countries.

The Algerian case illustrates this approach perfectly. With Mustapha Bouyali and his armed Islamic Movement (MIA), founded in 1982, terrorism crossed the line. Thus, the cores of the future AIS and GIA were formed. These groups would be heard from in the beginning of the 1990s. Meanwhile, Islamic agitation developed a crescendo in the form of teachings in the mosques, propaganda in the universities and in the streets, with recourse to intimidation, assaults whose victims were women dressed in western clothing, progressive elements, and cultural events. At this point in time the recruitment of young people for Afghanistan reaches its height. Representatives of the Pakistani fundamentalist organization, Tabligh Jamaât, remain in Algeria for this purpose. At the end of 1980, 3,000 to 4,000 Algerian volunteers were dispatched in Pakistan and in Afghanistan through the intervention of those who will become leaders of Islamic parties (who were prosperous and highly respected). Here, one can reflect on the passivity of the regime at that time or about its complicity with regard to this multitude of Algerian nationals sent to fight in a distant place, without considering the consequences of this action for the stability of Algeria upon their return.

Admittedly, the deterioration of the living conditions, unemployment, arbitrary actions and social injustice fed, to a certain extent, Islamic subversion, but they do not explain it nor justify it in any case. It is nevertheless the vehicle for an alternative derived from a regime which can be criticized, since, in some respects, it aims the destruction of the Nation State itself in order to replace it with an aberrant theocracy that runs counter to universal norms.

What really gave consistency to the Islamist campaign in Algeria was the massive contribution of the carefully trained and hardened elements in Pakistan and in Afghanistan, not to mention the camps financed by Bin Laden in Sudan or those of Hezbollah in Lebanon.

In 1989, the Soviets left Kabul. Shortly before, a congress of Tabligh had been held in Chicago, where 6,000 participants assembled from the four corners of the world. In 1990, the Arab-Afghans gathered in Peshawar, and it was, on the one hand, the setting-up of Al-Qaeda of bin Laden and, on the other, the creation of the GIA, under the impetus of Abdelkrim Gharzouli, alias Kari Saïd, son-in-law of bin Laden. This last organization would be known in Algeria starting in October 1992. Abdelhak Layada, aka Abou Adnan, would be the chief.

The post-Afghan Jihad took shape. It had footholds in Tajikistan, in Azerbaijan, in Chechnya, in Sykiang (China), in the Philippines (Abou Sayyaf formerly of Afghanistan), in Saudi Arabia (anti-American attacks in Khobar and Riyadh), in Africa (attacks in Nairobi and in Dar Es Salaam ), in Egypt (attack in Luxor) and, of course, in Algeria, with the massacres at Guemmar in November, 1991 and the horrific attacks of Bouzrina street and the Amiraute d'Alger in February, 1992, and the Houari-Boumediène airport attack in August of the same year.

The tremendous rise of FIS in 1991–92 coincided with the return of the Algerian Afghans. They constituted the spearhead of terrorist violence. They could be seen marching in the main streets of Algiers like they were in conquered country, wearing their Afghan dress. One would have to blind not to link the terrorism that struck Algeria throughout the decade with the Afghan jihad. But one would be equally blind not to realize that what gave the jihad its incredible virulence and its dominating self-confidence were the petrodollars from Saudi Arabia and the Gulf countries, the zealous Pakistani Inter Service Intelligence (ISI) and the technical support of the CIA.

The electoral process, stopped or not, the seed was planted and Pandora's box was opened: veterans of Afghanistan, in any event, were trained to instill Dawla *islamiyya*, whatever the circumstances and whatever the price. As the Special Envoy of President Boudiaf in February 1992, I remember drawing the attention of the White House national security adviser, Anthony Lake, witnessed by his assistant, Martin Indyk, on the subject of the Afghan Arabs, whose presence in Pakistan and Afghanistan no longer had a purpose since the Soviets had left Kabul "It is as if, having dined at a banquet, you leave the table without cleaning up," I declared, underlining the potential danger that these veterans could constitute for their respective countries. They responded that the question had indeed been raised, but that the Pakistani government was too weak to address it.

The virulence and the scope of the terrorist phenomenon in Algeria were by no means correlated to the logic of a resurgence of violence from the war of Independence. The Algerian patriots acted gripped by a necessity: to shake off the colonial yoke in the name of the universally recognized right to self-determination. Religious faith certainly played a great role in the struggle, but this fighting was to further the aim of national Independence. In this respect, the strategy of the FLN was unambiguous. The first issue of El Moudjahid—*The combatant*—, published in 1956, specified that this title did not have any connotation of holy war, and that its significance did not exceed that of self improvement and of moral abnegation.

Moreover, neither FIS nor other terrorist organizations that spawned from it possessed a clear strategy. And this deficit could be made up only by the systematic exercise of terror. Fetwas justified this in its character of barbaric cruelty, indistinctly targeting women, old men, and children. One wonders about the origin of these bloodbaths.

Meanwhile, Liamine Zeroual became president, and made various decisions. He announced that the FIS file was closed and that presidential elections would be held at the end of the year. They took place on November 16, 1995, under the banner of the antiterrorism struggle and witnessed record participation in spite of the boycott by the coalition of Sant' Egidio formed in Rome on January 12, 1995, by FIS, FLN, Nahda, FFS and PT.

How can Algerians commit such incredibly monstrous acts against other Algerians in cold blood? This reveals the total power of ideology, of brainwashing to which these young people were subjected in camps like that of Peshawar, "the key principle of this latest armed conflict of the cold war is based on the propagation of militant Islam in the world" (John Cooley). The terrorist action in Algeria developed on two levels: the individual murders and mass massacres that destroyed infrastructures, businesses and schools. The individual murders targeted, in addition to security agents—military, police, gendarmes—university professors, journalists, trade unionists, doctors. Victims range from two successive directors of the Institute of Global Strategy (ISG), Mohamed Boukhobza and Djilali Liabès, to the secretary-general of the Union General of the Algerian workers (UGTA), Abdelhak Benhamouda, from Rabah Asselah, Director of the National School of Fine Arts to Ali Mansouri, Director of Polytechnic of Architecture and Urban Plannine school (EPAU), and extended to the Rector of the Science and Technology University of Algiers, Salah Djebaïli, to professor Mahfoud Boussebsi to Doctor Djillali Benkhenchir, to the playwright Abdelkader Alloula to the poet Tahar Djaout, to the members of the National Advisory Council, Abdelhafid Sanhadri, El Hadi Flici, Miloud Bediar all the way to Mohamed Fathallah, president of the League of Humans Right. More than 100 journalists, and a considerable number of teachers, like the teacher killed in her school, at Birkhadem, before the eyes of her horrified students.

This relentless assault against the intelligentsia follows from the deliberate amalgamations cunningly diffused by the International fundamentalists, equating intellectuals to Communists. It was also the result of the local fundamentalist discourse which banned westernized people—Al *moutagharibine*—, considered a residue of colonization. Is there a need to mention that this discourse is long-lasting and it is always in style? These tragedies, which occurred in particular in 1993-1994, had sown astonishment and one could feel society wavering. It was essential to halt by all means necessary this deadly delirium that attacked the foundations of our society. This could be done by taking protective measures to shelter these foundations, by accentuating the antiterrorist fight through the strict application of the law and by endowing the political discourse with an unwavering rigor, interpreting the determination of the State, one of whose constitutional functions is to protect people's lives and property. It is in this context that the diplomatic relations with Iran broke down and that the Algerian Ambassador in Khartoum was recalled.

Always trying to shock, the terrorist groups turned to the countryside, attacking populations in the outskirts of Algiers: Beni Messous, Hai Raïs, Bentalha—where in a night 400 people had their throats slit—, in the region of Algiers, but also in the areas of Bel Abbès, Saïda, Tiaret, Aïn Defla, Médéa Parallèlement, the systematic massacre of young people of the national service youth in accordance with a fetwa of FIS - always in force!—deserves to be remembered. It is the same for the foreigners of various nationalities, among whom the first victims were two French nationals killed in 1994 in the Bel Abbès region. Strangely enough, this crime coincided with the promulgation of a new investment code. It is also important not to forget the tribute paid in blood by religious Muslims and Christians. The massacre of the seven monks of Tibhirine and the murder of Monseigneur Chaverie, bishop of Oran, underscore the degree of abominable hatred that unbridled intolerance can reach. Let us add finally the 2,000 to 3,000 moudjahidine fallen under the blows of fundamentalist barbarism. Terror had a theoretical construct. In addition to many fetwas for which the Palestinian Abu Qutada, spokesperson of the GIA in London, explicitly claimed responsibility, a letter from Jamal Zitouni, aka Abu Abderrahman Amine, chief of the GIA from November 1994 to July 1996, addressed in 1995 to Ayman Dhawahiri—collaborator of Bin Laden—, is very significant. The chief terrorist justifies the massacres of innocents as a principle and an end in and of itself, not as a tactic or a means of coercion as his Egyptian correspondent seemed to suggest. One will consequently include/understand the political position of the GIA, formulated hermetically by the slogan: "No dialogue, no truce, no peace"

In fact, all attempts at dialogue with the leaders of FIS dissolved into fruitless exercises. At the beginning of 1994, Liamine Zeroual, then Minister for Defense in my government, went to the military prison of Blida to meet Abassi Madani and Ali Benhadj. Three of their collaborators were released, benefiting from parole. In early September they were transferred, to a State residence where they could receive guests and communicate as they saw fit with the outside world. But the dialogue raised one question: would they be capable of publicly condemning terrorism and launching an appeal to those who practice it to renounce their activities? The response was clear: it's a matter of jihad and not of terrorism, and the Jihad does not stop. The two leaders had to return to prison. A new attempt at secret dialogue, made public in April 1995, did not have any more success.

The adventure of Islamic terrorism in Algeria reached such proportions as to threaten the stability of the entire region. The spillover to France, demonstrated in the high-jacking of the Air France's Airbus and the attack of the RER in Paris, is an example. However, Western States kept their distance, leaving Algeria to its fate. The nongovernmental organizations (NGO) were limited to addressing attacks on human rights, but took care not to accuse terrorism that killed. Amnesty International did not hesitate to qualify the latter as armed opposition.

This brings us to question the passivity of certain states whose territory was continuously crossed by Algerian terrorists and where the media, with some exceptions, went along with the Islamists.

Admittedly, the problem is sensitive, but it is our duty to try to clarify it. That Algeria was in the midst of a true national tragedy did not fail to delight certain nostalgic circles in France, driven by a desire for post-colonial revenge. The most progressive saw it as an internal conflict and an expression of sympathy for the idea of a sphere of influence to fight the antidemocratic junta.

In addition, realpolitik concerns were present. The possibility of an FIS victory was also present. At the end of 1994, many observers expected it and were vocal about it. Experts drafted analyses to prepare their governments for this eventuality. It seemed advisable to play a double game in order to prepare for the future. This wait-and-see policy translated into a policy of "laissez-faire, laissez-passer", which clearly benefited the terrorists and contribute to the prolonging of the crisis in Algeria.

There was thus a more basic reason for prudence. Denouncing terrorism would not remain without consequences. Attacks were likely to result from it in France and elsewhere in Europe. Thus the terrorist blackmail could carry as far as influencing the diplomacy of a great State. This short sighted policy forgot that Islamic terrorism, more particularly since the first Afghanistan war which indirectly drew in the United States and the Soviet Union, took an international dimension. September 11 was the shocking confirmation. Even if people's eyes were opened by this aggression which provoked world consternation, Algeria, where terrorism always prevails in spite of civil harmony, still did not concretely profit from this awakening. And the question remains: are there two terrorisms, one that strikes the powerful and that necessitates a global coalition and another that attacks the weak and does not garner indignation or regret? The relentlessness of terrorism in Algeria is also explained by its geo-strategic position. Those who perpetrate it in Algeria will bring it to all the states of the area.

But thanks to the resistance of its people and its security forces, Algeria will contribute to preserving its neighbors from a contamination which could have cataclysmic ramification similar to those that ravaged Afghanistan.

Islamist terrorism has already, by its own excesses, lost the battle of the population.

Its drastic backward flow must be made irreversible by choking the throat of the fundamentalist discourse and by draining the financial resources which were its engine.

But all the efforts will be in vain unless the rule of law is strengthened and as long as the education system continues to manufacture graduates rather than to train citizens. By mixing the word of God with the most atrocious acts, Islamic terrorism will reveal the at once tragic and grotesque side of an Islam transformed into totalitarian ideology, fascist style. Ibn Khaldoun, in 13th century, had already formulated a definitive judgment on the fundamentalists of his time. For him, those who aim to seize power by manipulating religion are either sick and should be helped, or fools and should be ridiculed, or troublemakers and should be punished. It is now obvious that, on a more general level, the global struggle against terrorism will not be successful unless four minimal conditions are satisfied:

- An urgent intellectual and moral reform revaluing critical reasoning and rational thought which Islamic cultural legacy has offered from Mouatazila in the tenth century — to Mohamed Abdou in the nineteenth century. This step falls to the intellectuals and on the fukaha, but also addresses the heads of state, in these difficult times when the destiny of Islam and more specifically the future of the Muslims are determined. It is time to distinguish between Islam and its deviations and to fight these deviations by providing a credible alternative;
- The setting up in Muslim countries of an education policy taking into account the necessity for a enlightened culture, with the stress on critical intelligence and autonomous judgment;
- The setting up of an outward looking policy, with regard to the destination of funds and the assistance coming from oil monarchies of the Middle East;
- The absolute necessity of the United States to protect itself against any amalgam between terrorism and national fight, as is the case in Palestine, and to refrain from all interventions in the Middle East that are likely to exacerbate international terrorism by providing it with new motives to continue its extortions. In any event, Algeria knew, by its own accord, to seize its independence. And it is under the terms of the same principle that it will overcome the bloody obscurantism and that it will open the way towards progress and light.

Rédha Malck, Former Chief of Government,
President Republican National Alliance (ANR).

M. BOUDJEMAA

# TERRORISM IN ALGERIA: TEN YEARS OF DAY-TO-DAY GENOCIDE

T HE TOLL EXACTED BY TERRORISM IN ALGERIA, estimated to be more than 100,000 dead and one million victims by the end of the year 2000, can on its own adequately indicate the extent of the drama that has affected the Algerian people. But mere statistics do not reveal the full horror of the reality: a terrorism in which the darkest and most barbaric compulsions of armed violence have been taken to their utmost limits. It is a movement that is genocidal in character, with no equivalent in Africa or the world, except perhaps the disastrous toll of the Khmer Rouge in Cambodia.

A religious political movement, whose roots go deep down into the contemporary history of Algeria since independence, embodies this terrorist violence. If endogenous and exogenous factors that gave birth to it are excluded, our attempts to gain a non-exhaustive comprehension of this phenomenon in Algeria leads us to a political and subversive movement that became the repository of this violence, which is the Islamic Salvation Front, known as the FIS (a political party dissolved on March 14, 1992).

Simplistic analyses place the onset of this terrorist violence at the interruption of the electoral process in January, 1992, but the beginning and development of terrorism in Algeria precede this date.

As early as November 1991, about ten soldiers of the Algerian army were savagely massacred in Guemmar (in southeast Algeria) by an Islamic terrorist group, practically all of whose members had received training in camps in Afghanistan. This attack, the first of its kind, launched the terrorist campaign in Algeria and revealed to national public opinion the existence of groups structured, armed, trained and organized with the aim of seizing power to install a theocratic state. These groups called themselves the Armed Islamic Movement (MIA), with reference to a terrorist movement that had appeared in 1981, led by Mustapha Bouyali. At the political and ideological level, this movement was based on and inspired by a document called "Jihad in Algeria," comprising 22 items of instruction to terrorist groups. It was written by the two principal leaders and founders of the FIS, Abassi Madani and Ali Benhadj.

The Armed Islamic Group (GIA) was created in the same period, with the aim of taking control of the organisational structure of the MIA and extending areas of terrorist activity to the whole of the national territory. The institution of a military command (*imarat*), a political structure (*madliss echourra*) and terrorists brigades and sections (*katiba* and *serya*) are the main forms adopted by the GIA groups that have planned to install an Islamic state (*khalifat*) in Algeria.

It was as a result of this organization that terrorism was able to develop so speedily and violently. Between 1992 and 1997, the GIA conducted a series of violent campaigns against an unarmed population and a security service that had never faced such a phenomenon. Their actions included bombings, purposeful criminal acts, the massacre of isolated citizens, sabotage, rape, mutilation, torture and the systematic liquidation of any Algerian citizen who refused to support the extremist fundamentalist solution.

A bomb exploded in a cemetery in November1994, killing four young scouts and seriously wounding seven others, who had to have limbs amputated. The violence would escalate to a state of total, absolute terror, with no discernment, as even children were regarded as legitimate targets.

Thus factories, bridges, railways, schools and cultural centres have been systematically destroyed and burned, causing losses of over $20 billion in ten years. All those with a different religious view—including administrative officials, artists, journalists, working women (who were asked to stop working), doctors, teachers, farmers and men of religion (*imans* have been systematically eliminated).

Through the assassination of foreigners, the terrorists have also targeted women and men of religions other than Islam, even those that preach tolerance and forgiveness. Catholics, Protestants, monks (seven of whom belonged to the Trappist order) and high dignitaries of the church, have been killed, such as Bishop Claverie, who was killed in a bomb attack in Oran in August, 1995.

The criminal logic of terrorism has also been directed against foreign interests in Algeria—more than 120 foreign citizens were killed in the early stages of the campaign. This wave of assassinations provoked the departure of many foreigners, as well as many airlines and foreign companies. This has to a certain extent achieved its aim: that of weakening the country economically and sustaining the mistrust of foreign partners.

In January, 1995, the GIA also launched a campaign of bomb attacks in main cities. That was when a suicide bomber drove a car containing explosives into the headquarters of the national police on Amirouche Boulevard, killing 42 Algerians and wounding 265. Thousands of other attacks would follow, with an ever-increasing list of victims.

The circumstances that led to the formation of the GIA are to be found in the availability of a large fringe of Algerian terrorists in Afghanistan. Experts estimate that the GIA was created in the house of the *Muhajirin* in 1989 in Peshawar. It was from this town, located on the borders of Pakistan and Afghanistan, that the first hard core of "Algerian Afghans" launched their terrorist campaign against Algeria.

This link is all the more important since it marks, with the conclusion of the Afghan-Soviet war and the end of the division caused by the cold war, the emergence of the decision of Islamic groups to reproduce, intra muros, the conditions of a second Afghan war. From that moment, all the efforts of the groups originating in Afghanistan were aimed at reinforcing the hard cores of the GIA and waging a total, determined and implacable war against all layers of Algerian society.

The logic of the terror being imposed was aimed at destroying all capacity of resistance to the inauguration of a theocratic state, even though it contradicts the values of Islam as experienced in Algeria and the Maghreb. These veterans of Afghanistan, trained in the Afghan militias, returned to Algeria with the help of international networks, via Bosnia, Albania, Italy, France, Morocco or Sudan.

Algeria, which has paid and continues to pay a heavy tribute to terrorism, has always called for the necessity of an international action to combat terrorism that would not just stop at the doors of Europe.

A terrorist, Mohamed Berrached, tried by an Algerian court, confessed in 1998 that Osama bin Laden, leader of Al-Qaeda, was at the origin of the creation of the GSPC (Combat and Prediction Salafist Group), a dissident group of the GIA. One year earlier, in 1997, Algeria had experienced its worst massacres in the villages of Bentalha, Rais, Sidi Mhamed, Sidi Youcef or Relizane that caused, in the space of two months, the death of more than 3,000 people.

Exceptional material means, including vast quantities of arms and money collected all over Europe, arrived from the principal European capitals. London, Paris, Berlin, Rome, Madrid, Geneva or Brussels were harboring more than 5,000 Islamic activists who constituted the backbone of the Algerian terrorist networks abroad, of which the investigations following the September 11 attacks have only revealed the tip of the iceberg.

During all these years, terrorist networks were being deeply rooted in Europe in order to support the armed groups, taking advantage of the liberal laws in democratic countries. Many terrorists have been able to settle legally in Europe, where they have organized the financing of terrorism and the despatch of arms.

Paradoxically, while Algeria was facing a destabilising movement that threatened the whole region, these terrorist groups enjoyed international support, active or passive, enabling the despatch of arms, men and financial means to the terrorist networks in Algeria.

Fortunately, the involvement of the population in reaction against the atrocities, carried out on a huge scale by the terrorist groups, has forced them to retreat towards the mountains, where they are isolated from the population. They have begun to split up and their struggle has degenerated into acts of banditry and the settling of scores between rival factions. But in the opinion of the Algerian people, still subject to the capacity for harm of these terrorist groups, the toll of 100 000 dead is far from over.

---

Published in *Monograph* No. 74, July 2002

# Terrorism—East, West, and South

# INTRODUCTORY NOTE

**M**OST OF THE TERRORISM IN THE CONTEMPORARY WORLD takes place in the Muslim world or is launched by Islamist groups against other Muslims (for instance in Central Asia) or against people of other creeds and nationalities. But, to repeat once again, this has not always been the case. Central and South America (and Europe, to a lesser extent) were the main battlefields during the 1970's. Relatively little attention has been paid to terrorist activities in these parts of the world (such as Central Asia, Kashmir, the Caucasus, or the Philippines) even though the number of victims even in a country such as Tadzhikistan—was infinitely larger than, for instance, in Palestine and Israel. The reason is quite obvious: there were few if any journalists and television cameras in Tadzhikistan. It was of no interest to the world media.

However, even at the present time terrorist groups continue to be active in other parts of the globe. While terrorism has died down in the major Latin American countries, it still continues in Colombia. It was until recently an important political factor in Peru, in Sri Lanka, and even in Europe where it has not ceased altogether, as the Spanish example (ETA) tends to show. And there is, unfortunately, no certainty that terrorism may not reappear in countries which are at present relatively quiet.

It was frequently believed during the 1970s that terrorism was a strategy of the extreme revolutionary left. It was not true then, and it is even less correct now. Terrorism of the far right was rampant then in many parts of the globe, even in the United States. Today the application of labels such as "left" and "right" with regard to terrorist groups has become altogether senseless and even misleading. To ask whether Osama bin Laden is a man of the left or the right is to invite ridicule. But this is true not only with regard to Islamic terrorism; ETA (to give but one example) shared the ideology of the far left but gradually shed the Marxist-Leninist ballast and adopted a populist-nationalist line. The same is true with regard to other terrorist groups.

At the same time right-wing, para-fascist groups aware that their ideological appeal was not sufficiently strong, put out feelers to the (former) extreme left—they were anticapitalist; so was the left. They were anti-American and this conviction, too, was shared by the extremists of right and left. Was it unthinkable to find a common platform for action on this common basis? This new ideology has become known as the "third position."

But the new developments are not always of a doctrinal character. The two major Colombian terrorist groups were initially aligned with the far left. But in the course of time they became heavily involved in the growing, manufacturing, and trading of drugs. The same is true with regard to several other terrorist movements in other parts of the world, notably in Southeast Asia. The drug trade was originally entered in order to acquire the funds to pay for terrorist activities, but involvement in the drug trade had a momentum of its own and gradually it acquired considerable importance, both as a motive for continuing the terrorist struggle, and with regards to the impact on its strategy.

Lastly there is the issue of weapons of mass destruction. It seems likely that it may take longer than popularly believed before such weapons will be put to use by terrorist. The technical difficulties are considerable and there are also political considerations that may induce terrorists to think twice before using weapons of this kind. But with all this, it seems only a question of time before such weapons will appear in the hands of a terrorist group, and, as the last entry in this volume shows, the matter is now openly discussed among the world's most active terrorists.

# AN INTERVIEW WITH COMMANDER PIRABAKARAN

"The chances of attaining Eelam are bright because the people's determination is firm. We are prepared for a long-drawn struggle [to attain Eelam]."

**FRONTLINE:** How were you attracted to the liberation movement? What were the factors that impelled you to take up this cause?

**Pirabakaran:** It is a long story. When I was young. my parents used to talk a lot at home against the 1958 racial riots directed against the Tamils in which many people were affected. This affected me. I used to read a lot of books which came from Madras, including magazines like *Ananda Vikatan, Kalki, Kumudam*, etc. All magazines used to run stories on India's freedom struggle, which used to fascinate me. Besides, books like *Mahabharata*, which says that good will vanquish evil, left a deep impression on me. When I was studying in school, I used to receive private tuition from a master called Home-Guard V. Navarathinam, who had left the Tamil Federal Party. The youth of the Federal Party also followed suit. He used to talk to us on the various world movements, how nothing can be accomplished by parliamentary means, etc. I was fifteen years old then and I got the feeling that we also should hit back and that we should have a separate country of our own.

**FRONTLINE:** What is the LTTE's ideology? Unlike other organizations, the LTTE began as a military outfit and later acquired Marxist-Leninist leanings. Some organizations like the EPRLF began as a "communist party" and later added a military wing.

**Pirabakaran:** We had an ideology from the beginning that was to form a socialistic state. If we did not give shape to that ideology, it was because we (LTTE) got straightway into the struggle.

**FRONTLINE:** What is your outlook on Eelam, towards the struggle, the experiences of your sufferings? Do you think you can achieve Eelam?

**Pirabakaran:** The chances of attaining Eelam are bright because the people's determination is firm. We are prepared for a long-drawn struggle [to attain Eelam].

**FRONTLINE:** The LTTE's general style of operation seems to be to indulge in hit-and-run tactics. But after a hit-and-run attack, the army turns on the Tamil civilians. For example, it is widely believed that your ambushing and killing the thirteen soldiers presaged the 1983 riots against the Tamils. Other liberation organisations like the PLO and the IRA do not indulge in hit-and-run tactics. Further, they have expanded their base among the people. Have you expanded your base?

**Pirabakaran:** For the PLO. there is no room for adopting hit-and-run tactics because they are fighting from a foreign soil. The IRA is fully in-dulging in hit-and-run operations. But the British Army does not attack the civilians. But, we work with a lot of hardship in terms of finance and the resistance from [Sri Lankan] military. Yet, in Jaffna and other places, we have controlled the army and we have made them into liberated zones. This was because there is no gap between the people and us in Jaffna, and in Nilaveli at Trincomalee. These areas are under our control. There is no government control. We are running the civil administration. This means, we have gone a step above the hit-and-run methods, even though we adopted hit-and-run methods in the beginning. Gradually, we have not allowed the troops to come in and as time goes on, it will become a mass struggle. Right now, in places like Jaffna, it has become a mass struggle.

Besides, we are running a guerrilla force. Out of several tactics in guer-rilla warfare, one is hit-and-run. In the initial development of the LTTE we did hit-and-run operations. But now, after an attack, we give protection to the people. The Sri Lankan government attacks the people because we are close to the people and also it does it to create a gap between the people and us. Without people's support we would have been betrayed and our movement would not have been there.

**FRONTLINE:** To go back, have you expanded your base among the people? Like, have you established trade unions, etc.?

**Pirabakaran:** Outwardly, we don't have trade unions. In all places, the LTTE's base has expanded.

**FRONTLINE:** What is your attitude towards the government of India, its efforts to bring about a solution to the crisis? Is it pressuring you to accept a solution?

**Pirabakaran:** Till now, we have not been pressured. At the same time, the government of India is trying to solve the problem through talks. But our history shows that nothing can be solved through talks. Yet, we have to support the government of India's efforts and so; we are taking part in the talks.

But at the same time, the Sri Lankan government has not, so far, arrived at any worthwhile solution. For example, it is violating the cease-fire and it has not properly implemented it. There should be peace as a prelude to talks [with the Sri Lankan government]. Everyday they are killing us.

**FRONTLINE:** Supposing, all the Tamil liberation organisations are asked to go out of India, what will you do?

**Pirabakaran:** All our important training bases are in Sri Lanka. We are here only to expose the political situation there. We are prepared to go back to our country any time. As the Sri Lankan government accuses us, we do not have any training bases or anything here. All our training bases, recruitment, are all done in our country. These problems can never affect us.

**FRONTLINE:** Recently, you went on a tour of Tamil areas of Sri Lanka and you also met your regional commanders. How is the morale of your cadres and what is the situation there?

**Pirabakaran:** There is only progress [increasing determination]. There is no retardation in the struggle. There is a feeling dominant among the people that instead of slowly dying in batches it is better to fight and die together. Our boys—comrades—are closer to the people. As a result, they are strong and firm. There cannot be any talk on morale because as long as there is one soldier [in the LTTE], they will fight for our ideal [to achieve Eelam]. Till there is a last comrade we will fight for our independence...liberation.

**FRONTLINE: Do you think anything will come out of the talks [with the Sri Lankan Government]?**

**Pirabakaran:** We don't have faith. We know the history of the last thirty years and Jayewardene's history also. Even common people do not have any faith that anything will come out of the talks. When the government of

India invites us for talks...it gives us political support... for its satisfaction, we are participating. But the results are in Jayewardene's hands. I don't have faith that he will put forward something viable proposals.

**FRONTLINE:** What do you think of Prime Minister Rajiv Gandhi's approach and also of Foreign Secretary Romesh Bhandari?

**Pirabakaran:** As far as Rajiv Gandhi's approach is concerned, he thinks he can solve this through peaceful means namely, talks. Destruction is certain through struggle. He wants to minimize the scale of destruction and is trying to solve the problem. When it is a struggle, it will be long-drawn. Even the refugee problem will be there for the government of India. So. Rajiv Gandhi wants to solve it through peaceful means. But Jayewardene is falsifying such efforts. Romesh Bhandari's approach...he is a representative of the government of India. On behalf of the Prime Minister, he is trying his level best to solve the problem through peaceful means. But till now, Jayewardene has not implemented even the terms and conditions of the cease-fire. So, Romesh Bhandari has not succeeded, even in cease-fire efforts.

**FRONTLINE:** What is your assessment of the Thimpu talks, the proposals offered by the Sri Lankan government?

**Pirabakaran:** There cannot be talks till... prevails. The Thimpu talks made the people hate us. If the Sri Lankan government is not keen on a peaceful atmosphere, how can you believe that it will implement the proposals offered?

**FRONTLINE:** There is a belief that there is not much democracy either in your organisation or other Tamil militant organizations. Is it true?

**Pirabakaran:** You should ask our organization's members that question. We have given them so much of freedom. There is no problem like that.

**FRONTLINE:** What is your attitude towards to TULF, the PLOT and other ENLF organizations?

**Pirabakaran:** They are also fighting for liberation like us.

---

*www.eelamonline.com*

SUMANTRA BOSE

# KASHMIR: ROOTS OF CONFLICT, PATHS TO PEACE

## THE FIDAYEEN PHASE (1999–2002)

The onset of the *fidayeen* phase of insurgency was presaged by a brief thaw in India-Pakistan relations. The year 1998 was south Asia's nuclear summer, when India tested five nuclear devices and Pakistan responded with six tests a few weeks later. Initially, it seemed that overt nuclearization of the subcontinent might produce some benign side effects. In February, 1999 India's prime minister Atal Behari Vajpayee traveled to Pakistan on the first run of a bus service connecting Delhi with Lahore, a major Pakistani Punjab city close to the border with Indian Punjab. Vajpayee and his Pakistani counterpart, Nawaz Sharif, "sharing a vision of peace and stability" and "recognizing that the nuclear dimension of the security environment of the two countries adds to their responsibility for avoidance of conflict," signed a "Lahore Declaration" during the visit. The declaration pledged a "composite and integrated dialogue process" on the basis of an "agreed bilateral agenda," and resolved to "intensify efforts to resolve all issues, including the issue of Jammu and Kashmir."

Vajpayee's decision to extend an olive branch to Pakistan was possibly encouraged by the Indian security establishment's upper hand over guerrilla militancy in IJK. But the promise of Lahore evaporated on the barren peaks and ranges of Kargil, in IJK's Ladakh, in the summer of 1999, as Pakistani regular units supported by jehadi volunteers infiltrated the Indian side of the LOC and the Indian military launched a massive land and air campaign to evict the infiltrators. Indian officials and commentators have claimed that the Pakistani operation was masterminded by General

458

Pervez Musharraf, then Pakistan's chief of army staff. Six weeks into the fighting, Nawaz Sharif agreed to withdraw Pakistani forces after a tense meeting with U.S. President Bill Clinton on July 4, 1999 in Washington. The humiliating climbdown sealed the fate of Sharif's civilian regime, already unpopular in Pakistan because of rampant corruption and perse-cution of critics and political opponents. In October, 1999 Sharif moved to dismiss Musharraf in a failed preemptive strike, and the armed forces deposed Sharif. The border conflict in Kargil aroused jingoistic national-ism throughout India, with the notable exception of Indian Jammu and Kashmir, where public opinion in most areas ranged from sullenly indif-ferent to bitterly hostile.

The first *fidayeen* (literally, "life-daring") raid occurred in July, 1999, shortly after the end of the Kargil hostilities, when two guerrillas simply barged into a BSF camp in Bandipore, a northern valley town, firing indiscriminately from automatic rifles and lobbing grenades. The Indian army's cantonment area in Srinagar's Badami Bagh locality was penetrated with the same simple but deadly tactic later in 1999. Between mid-1999 and the end of 2002, at least fifty-five *fidayeen* attacks, usually executed by two-man teams, were targeted against police, paramilitary and army camps, and government installations in IJK, mostly in the Kashmir Valley. Of these, twenty-nine took place in 2001, making that year the high point of the *fidayeen* campaign. According to Indian counterinsurgency authori-ties, 161 military, paramilitary, and police personnel died in these attacks (the Indian army alone lost eighty-two men), and ninety militants perished while executing them.

The bulk of the raids have been attributed by Indian security sources to one militant group, Lashkar-e-Taiba (LeT), which consists of religious radicals from Pakistan and was headquartered until early 2002 at Muridke, near Lahore in Pakistan's Punjab province. Most of the rest have been at-tributed to Jaish-e-Mohammad (JeM), another zealot group that is led by Pakistanis, has a predominantly Pakistani membership, and is the direct descendant of Harkat-ul Ansar, which was active in IJK in the mid-1990s. LeT denies that its raids are suicide missions—preferring to call them "daredevil" actions—since the group follows an ultra-orthodox version of Sunni Islam that strictly prohibits suicide, but the raids nonetheless have an undeniably suicidal character. The attackers almost never return from these penetrate-and-kill missions; their aim is not to save their own lives but to maximize the frightening psychological impact on the enemy by in-flicting death and destruction on their targets. The LeT's mouthpiece *Jihad Times* (published until 2001 from Islamabad, Pakistan's capital) and JeM's fortnightly Urdu journal (also published in Pakistan) have both discussed suicidal warfare in Kashmir. LeT refers to members who execute such operations as *fidayeen* ("those who dare their lives"), while JeM refers to its *khudkush shaheed dasta* ("self-sacrificing martyrs' unit").

In December 2001 a heavily armed five-man squad managed to enter the compound of India's parliament building in New Delhi and then attempted to enter the building itself, where hundreds of parliamentarians and government ministers were present at the time. The attackers were killed by security officers after a forty-five-minute battle with guns and grenades. Nine other people, including security staff, parliament stewards, and a gardener tending the grounds, also died. Indian authorities said the raiders were Pakistanis and had been helped and harbored by three men from the Kashmir Valley residing in Delhi. India began a massive military buildup on Pakistan's borders. Primarily in response to U.S. pressure, in January 2002, General Musharraf announced a crackdown on jehadi groups operating across the LOC from Pakistani territory. LeT and JeM were banned along with several other violent sectarian groups active within Pakistan.

But after a four-month lull, three gunmen struck again in *fidayeen* style in May 2002, targeting a camp near Jammu city housing families of Indian soldiers. They killed more than thirty people, mostly civilians, and war tensions escalated sharply in the subcontinent. In July, 2002 gunmen suspected by Indian authorities to be LeT members struck on the outskirts of Jammu city, massacring twenty-nine Hindus in a slum district before fleeing. Whether by design or accident, the date of the massacre was the seventy-first anniversary of the July 13, 1931 Srinagar massacre of twenty-one Muslim protesters by police, the incident that catalyzed mass political awareness in Kashmir. The Hurriyat Conference coalition and other groups favoring "self-determination" organized protests in Srinagar against the massacre. In an interview given to an Indian news agency by satellite phone from his mountain base, the top Hizb-ul Mujahideen commander for the Jammu region condemned the carnage as "inhuman and un-Islamic" and said he "suspect[ed] that the massacre was carried out by foreign militants." In early August, 2002 an annual Hindu pilgrimage in the southern part of the Kashmir Valley was attacked, and nine pilgrims and a gunman were killed. In November, 2002 two gunmen struck in the heart of the old bazaar in Jammu city, and one of them entered a popular Hindu shrine in the neighborhood, firing indiscriminately. A dozen people, mostly civilians, were killed in the incident, along with the two attackers. Indian authorities once again suspected the LeT of being behind the raid.

By the end of 2002, however, it was clear that the frequency of *fidayeen* raids had decreased significantly in IJK compared to 2001 or even 2000.

At the same time, the selection of targets had widened beyond the security forces, and targets appeared to be chosen, and attacks timed, to increase communal antagonisms in IJK and, most important, to keep India-Pakistan relations in a precarious limbo. The highly publicized attacks, especially those against "soft" targets, provided the Indian government's Hindu nationalist leadership with the main justification for its hard-line stance rejecting resumption of a dialogue on Kashmir with the Musharraf regime—branded in India as the "sponsor" of "cross-border terrorism"—overruling mild pressure on New Delhi by the United States and other western countries.

Peace efforts faltered in this atmosphere of violence. In July, 2000 HM, the only insurgent force composed predominantly of IJK residents (augmented by some from AJK), declared a temporary cease-fire, but withdrew it after two weeks amid a sharp escalation of guerrilla violence, including a carbomb explosion in the center of Srinagar claimed by HM and a series of massacres of Hindus in the Kashmir Valley and the Jammu region for which jehadi groups of Pakistani origin were generally considered responsible. The episode exposed a rift between moderate and hardline HM members, and pro-truce commanders were purged from the organization in 2001. In November, 2000 Prime Minister Vajpayee announced a one-month halt to offensive operations by Indian security forces in IJK to coincide with the Muslim holy month of Ramzan/Ramadan. This, too, petered out within months amid intensified guerrilla and state violence. In July, 2001 Musharraf visited India at Vajpayee's invitation for talks with the top members of India's government, which proved inconclusive. The Indians emphasized the destabilizing effect of "cross-border terrorism" originating in Pakistan, while the Pakistanis emphasized the need for Indian commitment to a serious political dialogue on the Kashmir question.

Three points can be made about the *fidayeen* phase of insurgency in Kashmir. First, the use of suicidal tactics as a weapon of war is neither novel nor the monopoly of militant Muslims. The Japanese kamikaze of World War II used the tactic extensively. Among contemporary political movements, Palestinian militants—especially but not exclusively their Islamist wing—have resorted to the tactic with increasing frequency and decreasing discrimination since the second intifada began in the autumn of 2000. But the most effective and most deadly practitioners of suicidal warfare in the south Asian subcontinent—and possibly in the world—since the 1980s have been the Tamil Tigers of Sri Lanka, whose fighters are Hindu, Christian, agnostic, or atheist.

Second, it is true that the main ideologues and practitioners of suicidal warfare in the Kashmir war are radical Islamist groups of Pakistani provenance. JeM, for example, claimed responsibility for an October 2001 raid by a *fidayeen* squad on the Indian legislative assembly complex in Srinagar in which thirty-eight people were killed—mostly local Muslim policemen on guard duty and Muslim civilian employees of the legislature secretariat—and even identified a member from Peshawar, Pakistan, by name as the driver of the jeep bomb that exploded at the heavily guarded entrance and enabled the other members of the suicide squad to enter the complex (the group retracted the claim two days later).

However, suicidal warfare in Kashmir is *not* exclusively a "cross-border" phenomenon, but rather is the product of the incendiary infusion of the ideology and tactics of transnational Islamist militancy into a brutalized, desperate local environment—that is, of a conjunction of internal and external factors. In May 2000 JeM carried out its first suicide attack in the Kashmir Valley when a JeM militant exploded a car bomb at the entrance to the Srinagar headquarters of the Indian army's 15th Corps, which is deployed in the valley. The militant was Afaq Ahmed Shah, aged seventeen, a high school student from Srinagar's Khanyar neighborhood. Born in 1983 into a religious family, Afaq had endured a childhood consumed by rebellion, oppression, and despair. Like Nadeem Khatib, he was internally tormented by what he saw around him and eventually decided that he could no longer be a passive witness.

If Ashfaq Wani and Yasin Malik personify the intifada generation of the *azaadi* movement, Afaq Shah and Nadeem Khatib represent its *fidayeen* generation. In December, 2000 another JeM car bomber attempted to breach the perimeter of the 15th Corps headquarters—this time it was twenty-four-year-old Mohammed Bilal from Manchester, England, a British citizen of Pakistani descent. In September, 2000, on a day I happened to be in the Kashmir Valley, a RR camp in the town of Beerwah in Badgam district—not far from the village of Soibugh—was attacked by two *fidayeen*. They killed an Indian major and thirteen soldiers before they were finally cornered and killed. One of them was a jehadi militant from Pakistan, the other a Kashmiri-speaking Muslim from a mountain village in the Jammu region's Udhampur district. Two years later, in November, 2002, a *fidayeen* duo armed with assault rifles and hand grenades penetrated a CRPF camp in the heart of Srinagar, killing six troopers and losing their own lives. An LeT spokesman named the attackers as Abu Younis, a Pakistani militant, and Reyaz Ahmad Khan, a local fighter from the southern Valley town of Qazigund.

The third point about *fidayeen* phase is that its most spectacular and most publicized attacks have been directed against such high-profile targets as the Indian army's cantonment and operational headquarters in Srinagar, the headquarters of the SOG in Srinagar, Srinagar's airport, and the legislature's premises in Srinagar, in addition to multiple attacks at various locations in Jammu city, including its railway station, its old bazaar, and at least one shantytown district. However, the crucial theaters of war in this phase lie away from urban centers, in the rural areas, dotted with small towns, of IJK's sprawling interior. These remote locales and frontiers of conflict in Rajouri-Poonch (Jammu region) and Kupwara (Kashmir Valley)—scenes of a deadly daily war of attrition—are key to an understanding of the complexity of the contemporary Kashmir problem.

YOGINDER SIKAND

# KASHMIR, FROM NATIONAL LIBERATION TO ISLAMIC JIHAD

## THE JIHAD IN KASHMIR AND INDIA

The Markaz sees the conflict in Kashmir not as a territorial dispute between India and Pakistan, nor even as a clash between cultures, but as nothing less than a war between two different and mutually opposed ideologies: Islam, on the one hand, and disbelief [*kufr*], on the other. This is portrayed as only one chapter in a long struggle between the two that is seen as having characterized the history of the last fourteen hundred years. The roots of the Kashmir problem are seen as its Muslim rulers having been replaced, first by the Sikhs and then by the Hindu Dogras, through British assistance. With India (the "Hindus") having taken over Kashmir in 1947, a long and protracted reign of bloody terror is seen to have been unleashed on Kashmiri Muslims. This is seen as a direct and logical consequence of the teachings of Hinduism itself, because, it is alleged, "the Hindus have no compassion in their religion." Hence, it is the duty of Muslims to wage jihad against the "Hindu oppressors." All Hindus are tarred with the same brush. Thus, Hafiz Muhammad Saleed declares, "In fact, the Hindu is a mean enemy and the proper way to deal with him is the one adopted by our forefathers...who crushed them by force. We need to do the same." This sort of anti-Hindu rhetoric is not a prominent feature in Gilani's writings, and thus represents a further radicalization of the Kashmiri jihadist discourse.

The armed struggle in Kashmir is depicted as only one stage of a wider, indeed global, jihad against the forces of disbelief. Here, the Markaz goes far beyond Gilani's limited jihadist project, which aims at simply freeing Kashmir from Indian control and merging it with Pakistan. The Markaz's jihad is far more ambitious: it aims at nothing less than the conquest of the entire world. As Qari 'Abdul Wahid, former emir of the LIT in Indian-controlled Kashmir put it, "We will uphold the flag of freedom and Islam through jihad not only in Kashmir but in the whole world." Likewise, Colonel Nazir Ahmed, head of public relations for the Markaz, declares that through the jihad the mujahidin have launched, "Islam will be dominant all over the world, Inshallah? [God willing]. This war is seen as a solution to all the ills and oppression afflicting all Muslims, and it is claimed that "if we want to live with honour and dignity, then we have to return back to jihad." Through jihad, it is believed, "Islam will be supreme throughout the world." "The mujahidin are promised that with the launching of the global jihad against all the unbelieving oppressors of the world, "the day is just round the corner when Islam will prevail in this earth." Insha,41lab?, Jihad has its more mundane benefits, too. Thus, it is also said to be "the way that solves financial and political problems."

India is a special target for the Markaz's mujahidin. According to the emir of the Markaz, Hafiz Muhammad Saleed, "The jihad is not about Kashmir only. It encompasses all of India." Thus, the Markaz sees the jihad as going far beyond the borders of Kashmir and spreading through all of India.

The final goal is to extend Muslim control over what is seen as having once been Muslim land, and, hence, to be brought back under Muslim domination. Thus, at a mammoth congregation of Markaz supporters in November 1999, shortly after the Kargil debacle, Hafiz Muhammad Saleed declared "Today I announce the break-up of India. We will not rest until the whole of India is dissolved into Pakistan." On the same occasion, Emir Hamza, senior Markaz official and editor of its Urdu organ, *ad-Da'awa*, thundered, "We ought to disintegrate India and even wipe India out." Those who take part in this anti-Indian jihad are promised that "Allah will save [them] from the pyre of hell," and "huge palaces in paradise" await those who are killed in fighting the disbelieving enemies.

This project for the disintegration of India, followed by its take over by Pakistan and then the establishing of an Islamic state, seeks justification by an elaborate set of arguments that use the rhetoric of liberation. Thus, instances of human sacrifice, untouchability, infanticide, the cruel oppression of the "low" castes by the Brahmins and the suppression of women in Hinduism are described in great detail, and on this basis it is shown that Hinduism should not "be allowed to flourish." This is a theme to which

Gilani refers in some of his writings, but he does not go beyond offering Islam as an alternative to Brahminical Hinduism. In Markaz literature, the mass slaughter of Muslims by Hindu chauvinist groups, often in league with the Indian state and its agencies, and the growing wave of attacks on other marginalized groups in India such as the "low" caste Dalits, Shudras and Christians, are presented in stark colors. The point is forcefully made that such a country "where non-Hindus are not allowed to exist" should break up. The Markaz presents itself as a champion of not just the oppressed Muslims of Kashmir or India but even of the "low" caste Shudras and Dalits. It sees itself as having a divinely appointed mission of saving the Shudras from Brahminical tyranny. Thus, it says, "It is incumbent upon us to save the Shudras of India...from the clutches of Brahmins." Although it claims that its jihad is aimed only against "the tyrannical government and the army" and that "nowhere do the mujahidin target non-Muslim or innocent people," there are reports that speak of LIT fighters being involved in the killing of several Hindu villagers in Jammu, Kashmir, and in neighboring Himachal Pradesh.

In this way, the Markaz attempts to go beyond even Gilani's relatively less radical project, by converting the Kashmir struggle into a full-blown war between Islam and disbelief. By doing so, it attempts to assert its own understanding of the nature of the Kashmir problem, replacing the Kashmiri nationalist framework with one that is constructed within the general discursive universe of Islamism.

As we have seen, there has been, especially since the early 1990s, a marked transformation in the terms of discourse with which the Kashmiri liberation struggle has sought to express itself. The nationalists, fighting for a secular, democratic Kashmir, have increasingly had to give way to Islamist voices, first principally to the JIJK and then to even more radical groups based in Pakistan, as the latter's influence and power grew. The success of the efforts of the Islamists in shifting the terms of debate has had to do with a host of internal as well as external factors. Internally, the growing strength of the Islamists can be traced back to the 1950s with the establishment of the JIJK in 1952. It cultivated an essentially lower-middle-class constituency, consisting of traders, students and lower-level government employees, many of whom were disillusioned with the politics of secular groups, such as the National Conference and the Congress as well as with the perceived other-worldliness, ritualism and limited personal piety associated with the cults of the Sufi shrines. Its network of schools that provided a mix of modern and Islamic disciplines, its social work programs, such as setting up village-level *bait-ul* mat? for the collection and distribution of *zakat*? funds, as well as its focus on publishing large amounts of literature, won it a growing support base. So did its consistent championing of the issue of plebiscite for the Kashmiri people for determining their own future.

On the other hand, the perceived failure of the National Conference, first under Sheikh 'Abdullah and then his son Farooq 'Abdullah, in articulating the genuine demands of the Kashmiris, the growing corruption within the party and its open collusion with the Indian establishment to subvert the democratic process in and the autonomy of Kashmir, as well as mounting economic problems and the growing unemployment of an increasing number of educated Muslim youth, generated a widespread disillusionment. This worked to the advantage of the Islamists.

The increasing salience of the Islamist element within the Kashmiri struggle can also been seen, in a crucial sense, as a response to the escalation in anti-Muslim violence in India, and the increasing threat to Muslim community identity at the hands of chauvinist Hindu groups in league with the Indian state.

This point is repeatedly referred to in the writings of ideologues of the JIJK as well as of Pakistan-based jihadist groups. The growing insecurity of Muslim life and identity in India had as a natural consequence the assertion of an Islamic identity in Kashmir. Making matters more complicated was the sheer brutality of the Indian army response to the Kashmiri struggle, which was seen by many, by both Kashmiri Muslims as well as Indian Hindus, in purely religious terms. On the other hand, the Pakistan factor has been of major significance in the rise of the Islamists. There is clear evidence to show the close links between the Pakistan-based Islamist groups such as the Markaz and the Pakistani establishment. The Islamist groups are seen as playing a central role in pursuing Pakistani strategic interests. Unlike the JKLF, all the Islamists advocate the accession of Kashmir to Pakistan. Within Pakistan itself, the rise of the Islamist groups active in the Kashmir war can be seen as a result of the crisis of the state and the economy, with Islamist parties riding on a crest of popular discontent. The Afghan factor is particularly crucial here, for many of the Pakistani Islamists now active in Kashmir received their military training in the Afghan jihad, and some of them, including the Markaz, are said to be linked with the Taliban and the Saudi dissident Osama bin Laden and his International Islamic Front for Jihad Against the United States and Israel.

It may, however, be and indeed does actually seem that the Islamist attempt at hegemonzing the terms of discourse in which the Kashmiri liberation struggle has sought to express itself has been only partially successful, at best. It may be argued that the apparent influence of the Islamists is deceptive, for while indeed they have marginalized the JKLF in military terms, owing, of course, to liberal patronage from Pakistan, they have received little support from the Kashmiri masses themselves, who seem to favor a considerably more liberal version of their faith. On the other hand, the relatively low-profile of the Kashmiri nationalists presently owes principally to three factors: the large-scale killing of JKLF activists and leaders by the Indian armed forces; killing of numerous activists in clashes with Islamists; and the cutting off of major arms and other supplies from Pakistan, with such assistance being diverted to Islamist groups instead. Despite the present lull in the Kashmiri nationalist camp, it still seems to reflect the aspirations of the vast majority of Kashmiri Muslims. It appears that the war-weary Kashmiris have not responded enthusiastically to jihadist appeals of groups like the Markaz. The simple fact that the LIT has only a very marginal Kashmiri component among its fighters is proof enough for this.

The experience of Afghanistan after the Soviet withdrawal, and the mounting economic problems, political instability, and sectarian and ethnic violence in Pakistan, in which the Islamists have had no small role to play, have convinced many Kashmiris of the futility of the jihadist rhetoric. Moreover, the stern Wahhabism of groups like the Markaz, based on an unremitting hostility towards religious liberalism and laxity and Sufism, is bound to be unpopular among most Kashmiris, for whom Sufism is the normative expression of their faith and Islamic commitment. As it is, one of the reasons for the inability of the JIJK to develop a mass base has been its perceived hostility to Sufism, although JIJK leaders, many of whom are actually from families with Sufi backgrounds, have tried to dispel this notion by presenting themselves as inheritors of the legacy of the Sufis. According to them, the Sufi mission was the establishment of the Islamic system as the JIJK conceives it. The openly condemnatory attitude of the Markaz and other such groups vis-a-vis Sufism is thus even more unlikely to win it many supporters in Kashmir. In other words, the radical Islamist rhetoric, to a considerable extent, represents an external agenda that is being sought to be imposed on Kashmir, and one that seems at odds, in several respects, with the internal conditions in Kashmir itself.

It would seem, then, that the Kashmiri nationalist forces, with their dream of a free, democratic, independent Kashmir, still do command the loyalties of most Kashmiris, the efforts the Islamists and of both the Indian as well as Pakistani establishments notwithstanding.

---

*Muslim World*, April 1, 2001

# THE RED BRIGADES

# A MANIFESTO

## CASERTA 24
## THE TEXT OF DEMANDS OF THE RED BRIGADES
### March 21, 2002

March 19, 2002, was the day when, in Bologna, an armed cell of our organization executed Marco Biagi, an adviser of the Minister of Labor Maroni, the originator and promoter of the general outline and legislative drafts of the plan to rework the regulations on using wage-earning labor and to redefine both the neo-corporative relations among the executive branch, the Italian Manufacturers' Association[1]? and the confederated labor union[2]?, and also the function of neo-corporative negotiation in relation to the new model of representative democracy. This provides for a "governing" democracy, which has already increased the powers of the executive over the last ten years and also those of the governing majority with the amendment of Article V of the (so-called "federal") constitution, where local political powers and functions will be divided up among centralized limits of direction and balance and linked to the European monetary centralization, for the purpose, of stabilizing the directed alternation between political coalitions focused on the interests of the neo-imperialist bourgeoisie, by taking advantage of the restriction of the national productive base not only as a comparative advantage in terms of taking advantage of the labor force with respect to other countries, but as a condition for readjusting

---

1 *Translator's note:* i.e. *Confindustria,* a shortened form of *Confederazione generale dell'Industria.* This Italian term will be used in the remainder of the text.
2 *Translator's note:* in Italian *Sindicato confederale.*

the domination of the imperialist bourgeoisie and strengthening it in the face of proletarian centers of influence and trends for their development in antistatutory and anticonstitutional political autonomy that arise from these structural conditions.

With this combative action, the Red Brigades are attacking the political agenda of the dominant fraction of the imperialist bourgeoisie of this country, whereby the concentration of powers in the executive branch, neo-corporatism, alternation between governing coalitions centered on the interests of the imperialist bourgeoisie and "federalism" constitute the conditions for managing the crisis and the class conflict at this historic phase marked by economic stagnation and imperialist wars.

The political collapse of the Warsaw Pact and of the Soviet Union itself and the general retreat of revolutionary processes and struggles for liberation have resulted in a change in international balances in favor of the imperialist chain and strengthen the dominance of the U.S. within it. However, what is happening now without any generalized and prolonged war like World Wars I and II, which destroyed huge masses of capital and productive forces that had been overproduced with to the levels of crisis that had been reached by capital itself, would launch an expansive cycle starting from the degree of current capitalistic concentration and centralization, but from a level of overall accumulation that is appropriately reduced. Instead, a process of capitalistic penetration and economic integration has been developed with respect to the areas with planned socialist economies, a process supported by the dominant states in the imperialist chain, in which a relationship of dependence of a particular type has been set up. These industrial economies cannot be assimilated to those in the south of the world, or even to the capitalistically advanced economies. [This process] has led to the altering of the structure of these economies and to their plundering, and also to a rapid collapse in the living conditions of the population far below the historically determined levels of subsistence. This very condition has pushed thousands of people to emigrate to the west and, within this space, even western European political intervention has found a space, intent on defining the lines for the reform of the labor market in those countries, more conducive to realizing profitable levels of exploitation.

The subsequent capitalistic concentration and centralization, the increase in the exploitation of wage-earning labor, the responses of restructuring and reformist economic policy—or anti-cyclical responses—that have been given to the crisis and the advantageous positions in the international balances of the chain have not cancelled out the crisis or its causes. Instead, the higher levels of accumulation and the subsequent internationalization of capital have made the crisis more potent, inasmuch as these [phenomena] are intrinsic to the mechanism of existence of capital, to the mechanism of accumulation and to their very nature; they are not external causes. This structural given, with the end of the 1990s, is what is causing the retreat of the economic into a new recessive cycle, in which the contradictions wherein monopolistic capital and bourgeoisie move, is laid bare. All the major capitalistic areas are in crisis, manifesting simultaneously various phenomena, which can feed upon one another. The U.S., which has acted as the world engine for the last ten years, is exposed to high levels of indebtedness and unused productive capacity. Japan, which is the second largest economy in the world, has been in a recession for years (in 2001 alone, it experienced a 4.5 percent drop in its gross domestic product), is undergoing galloping deflation and will have to prevent the collapse of its banking system. In Germany, the recession is going to exert downward pressure on industrial production, causing drastic drops, thus reducing its weight in the European Community? itself, while it should have had a pivotal role in the imminent expansion to the east. A country like Argentina, which observed the dictates imposed by the International Monetary Fund to the letter, has headed into an economic and financial crisis without any foreseeable way out. Even a country like Saudi Arabia, which has had a central role in supporting the war expenditures of the U.S., the sales of its military industries and the strategic needs of imperialism, has experienced a precipitous drop in its per capita income and is being shaken by political crisis on account of the presence of U.S. troops and the social transformations imposed by the economic reforms aimed at the privatization of the productive sectors and the internationalization of capital. To this can be added the levels of misery spread throughout the southern part of the world, which have also gripped the former socialist camp and are deepening in China with its entry into the World Trade Organization, accompanying their capitalistic "development."

This is a picture that reconfirms the current state and the deepening of the causes that are generating the historical necessity of moving beyond the capitalistic mode of production and the domination of the imperialist bourgeoisie. It also shows how the complete abandonment of the socialist transition in countries that were the first to make the revolutionary break, through opening up and setting up a capitalist system, is nothing more than a lull in the historical process of the Communist revolution, with respect to which the proletariat, having experienced it, can readjust the terms for carrying on the revolutionary process, inasmuch as imperialism is showing increasingly widespread points of vulnerability that are determined and can be determined. Around these [points of vulnerability], it is possible to draw up the [appropriate] revolutionary strategy and to direct the revolutionary confrontation.

The fact that the surplus profits of capital resulting from the deepening of unequal development have not been realized by leaving unchanged the wages and working conditions of the metropolitan proletariat in the imperialist states, but that all the relative and absolute terms of exploitation have been deepened, empirically demonstrates that the western metropolitan proletariat has not been joined to the imperialist bourgeoisie in taking advantage of these surplus profits, or else that the increase in the exploitation to which the proletariat is called upon in order to sustain the competitiveness of capital not only is neither a definitive nor a temporary solution to the crisis of capital on the market. This fact cannot help but to allow for the relative and transitory hold of capital alone on the market, and it converges in deepening the causes that reside in the mechanism of the accumulation of capital, which, precisely because capital increases, while the live labor exploited diminishes, periodically and to an ever increasing extent, and it is no longer possible to make good use of and to ensure the maintenance of the productive forces.

On the level of international balances, the imperialist chain formed starting from period after World War II centered around the dominant pole of the U.S. on levels of the internationalization of capital and the integration and interdependence of growing economies, brought to maturity progressive forward steps in the trend toward war along the East-West axis. However, these steps did not take on the features of a generalized war, but rather they involved limited conflicts that were highly destructive for the countries assaulted by imperialism, in the framework of the various alignments within the Western alliance and arrangements articulated in the military assigned tasks as related to the set of the political, military, and economic in each state. The 1990's were characterized by repeated wars of aggression, which were the expression of the imperialist chain and aimed at redrawing the international balances and to reorganize the division of labor. In this process, the imperialist states committed themselves to action in order to sustain their own monopolistic capital and, given the integrated and interdependent nature of the chain, in order to agree on common policies. This process of redefinition and expansion of areas of influence, however, did not resolve the causes of the capitalist crisis, as was empirically demonstrated by the stagnant conditions of the world economy and the ever increasing inability of capitalism to absorb growing productive capacities. A new expansive cycle would require a broad destruction of capital and means of production with an imperialist war on a grand scale, but as of yet, neither the political nor the military conditions for this had come together for such a war. Therefore, in the current phase, imperialism is a position to sustain levels of growth in the economy essentially in the dominant pole and is developing policies and initiatives aimed at equipping the States of the chain to advance subsequent fractures in international balances to their own favor, with an articulated strategy that contrasts the opposition of those countries that are seeking to get out from under the imperialist yoke and, using destabilizing measures, is seeking to subject countries that present economic and social models that cannot be integrated as such into the capitalist division of labor, or whose political position is dysfunctional with respect to the imperialist strategy. It is in this framework that it becomes possible to understand the nature of the process of European political integration, which has as its engine the development of monopolistic capital. It also accounts for the policies of the eastward expansion of NATO and the European Union? and the process of readapting the military and counterrevolutionary instruments in operation in all the imperialist States guided by the initiative of U.S. re-armament and aggression, and the lines of development and the qualitative steps of this can be identified.

The attack on the lines of constructing European integration, on the lines of deepening and on their anti-proletarian and counterrevolutionary function, is a program point on which the revolutionary forces in Europe can be built up and alliances can be planned in the framework of an anti-imperialist combat front, inasmuch the deepening of European integration and the implementation of its policies is an integral part of the strategy of the imperialist bourgeoisie to manage the polarization of the divergent interests from the levels of crisis that capital has attained and to bring together and mobilize the imperialist states in military projection, in order to redefine the capitalist division of labor and to consolidate imperialist domination.

The dynamics of the crisis that is pushing imperialism toward the integration of new economic areas for their exploitation, therefore, was generating a trend toward war that is moving and will continue to move along the East-West axis, because it is toward the areas of Eastern Europe and Asia that imperialism must direct its expansionism by opening up conflicts with antagonistic interests. This is a movement, impelled by the natural dynamics of capitalism, which is therefore not on its way, as in the first imperialist wars, toward a military clash between imperialist states. These states are today areas that are crisscrossed by the internationalization of capital, which has created the underlying conditions for the integration and interdependence of their economies, in which a dominant fraction of imperialist bourgeoisie has taken shape, as the expression of multinational monopolistic capital added to U.S. financial capital, around which rotate all the other fractions of the imperialist bourgeoisie.

In the 1990s, the war against Iraq, the destabilization and later the submission and occupation of the Balkans, and the Oslo Accords to achieve the normalization of the Middle East, in the strategy of the U.S. and the West, were supposed to be so many steps to advance and consolidate the positions of the imperialist chain that would advance its strategic objectives, inasmuch as the Middle East, precisely since it is pivotal to the strategic balances between east and west, and once the balances were altered, would move from being a field for exerting force aimed at eroding the positions of their adversaries to becoming a field for conquering more advanced positions for the imperialist chain as opposed to the east.

The contradictions triggered by these moves are the factors that indicate the dimension of the opposition that can be stirred up by the interests and the thrusts of imperialism, to which the causes of the conflicts set up on this line are being ascribed. These include, in particular, the resistance of Iraq to the continuing imperialist aggression that has forced the United States military siege of Saudi Arabia, the Afghan resistance to the pressures that the U.S. has been exerting for some time in order to achieve its submission and to guarantee its own strategic control over the country, which is a natural corridor in Central Asia, and finally the Palestinian resistance to be submitted to the Zionist entity. This latter is the real content of the Oslo accords, which, in the medium term, have fed the struggle for liberation. This is a struggle that the United States would like to contain today by pushing the Arab States to recognize "Israel" in order to legitimatize its military action; all the more so, given the high level the clash has reached, it would function as an authorization for genocide, this being a pre-condition for controlling the area in order to launch the offensive against Iraq.

In this framework, the September 11 attack represented a specific element of contrast to the imperialist strategy and represented its vulnerability, forcing it to modify plans and steps, obviously without being able to allow any failure of the strategic interests that are behind it. The entire imperialist chain had to measure the possible implications of the relationship of exploitation and oppression that it had instituted and perpetuated against the implications of its constant action of aggression, which was being geared up and was about to be intensified with the plans for an antimissile shield that had been launched again by Bush, along with the plans for re-armament and the construction of a European rapid intervention force, along with the propaganda put in place to justify the aggression against Afghanistan. Therefore, it was forced to accelerate its own mobilization, enlarging its scope of intervention and intensifying domestic counterrevolutionary measures within, while sustaining the economic and military costs of spreading out its forces on more fronts, exposing itself to the contradictions in the options it had to take as a reaction and not at the time and in manner intended. It had to limit itself to constructing a coalition to support the aggression against Afghanistan, which was not completely activated in the offensive action, on account of the internal political contradictions and the risks in the field. Since the elevated destructive power of the attack and its specific selectivity had struck a destabilizing systemic blow, it forced the imperialist counterrevolution into making a qualitative leap by compelling it to adopt uniform specific measures, and no longer common directions and structures, which constitute a strain on political mediation by forcing more rigid and delimitated responses that can be given to normalize class antagonisms and also the international balances for the imperialist peace, by deepening the break with certain bourgeois social components in the Middle East, which had constituted the natural point of support for the normalizing strategies in the region and by weakening the position of the political classes allied with imperialism. These factors of the specific weakness of imperialism were only partially offset by its political and ideological propaganda aimed at exploiting the civil casualties caused by the attack, in order to obtain popular support for the imperialist war and the counterrevolutionary measures. This propaganda is unable to mystify the obvious fact that the imperialist wars and counterrevolution, unlike the attacks on the Pentagon and on the twin towers of the World Trade Center in New York, are not causing civil casualties only as a "collateral effect" of a military objective, which is to achieve the destabilization of an enemy to force it to step back from its intentions of aggression and to withdraw from the countries it occupies militarily.

Imperialism causes civil casualties because it commits aggression in order to subject peoples to its domination and to be able to exploit them. These casualties are therefore a military objective that is an integral part of imperialist warfare; in other words, they are the terrorist objective of a counterrevolutionary policy aimed at forcing the proletariat to withdraw from its autonomous political objectives, as has been repeated demonstrated by the NATO stratagem in Italy with bombs at the Piazza Fontana in Milan, the Piazza della Loggia in Brescia, and the railroad station in Bologna...

The September 11 attack has opened a phase in which the imperialist chain, from its dominant pole, the U.S., has been compelled to accelerate its militaristic projection, to develop new acts of aggression and, above all, to prepare for a new campaign of war aimed at definitively resolving the challenge of bringing Iraq into submission. To let live a people and a government like the Iraqi one, which, though it has been fought against for ten years without ever surrendering, would be a manifestation of impotence on the part of the United States and thereby the entire chain, in a strategic context where it has been shown that it is possible to make a highly destructive attack against the heart of the enemy's territory with destabilizing systemic effects, even without using its advanced technologies. This is a new reality that has deprived the U.S. of the deterrent power constituted by the idea that its forces and national territory are immune from attack, thus compelling it to maintain a constant offensive capability either to root any guerrilla forces that oppose it, which, in order to make this "ongoing offensive" the new central factor of deterrence alongside nuclear missiles, the anti-missile shield, high-yield bombing and the whole complex of advanced technologies at its disposal, which signified its strategic superiority. The U.S. was thus rendered powerless by the sudden attack.

The politico-military action of the imperialist chain, led by the U.S., was developed following the end of the bipolar balance, thrown into crisis by the deterrent weight of its own strategic superiority, on which its capacity for political conditioning was also based. However, at the present time, it has been forced to react to recover this superiority, while demonstrating the inopportunity of carrying out nonconventional attacks against it, it is suffering the high price in terms of destruction that Western military power and its rapid and widespread capacity for intervention can make it pay, cannot construct the political conditions, which, in the framework of a linear advancement of its strategy, would have been basis on which the military victories and successes could have consolidated international balances more favorable to subsequent advances. This is demonstrated by the pressures and the forcing that have been exerted to impose the Israeli peace on the Palestinian people and to open the way for the intervention against Iraq.

The imperialist chain, led by the U.S., therefore, must expands the fronts of conflict and expose itself to the dispersion of its own armed forces, with which it will also have to establish its military occupation to preserve or even to conquer, as in Afghanistan, control over the territory, which is a condition that fosters resistance and the anti-imperialist counterattack.

The attack on imperialism is a programmatic axis of the strategy that the Red Brigades practice and propose to the [working] class, and with which they have historically substantiated the necessity and the possibility of anti-imperialist alliances among revolutionary forces in the area of Europe, the Mediterranean, and the Middle East to be tightened in the construction of an anti-imperialist fighting front, which has the purpose of weakening and destabilizing imperialism. This is a point of the revolutionary program that the Red Brigades are pursuing with the attack on the core policies of imperialism, which, today more than ever, are framed in the advancement and the spread of war and the imperialist counterrevolution. These do not constitute a linear strengthening of the enemy, but are even a factor that is deepening its vulnerability, and they underscore the function that an anti-imperialist attack in the heart of imperialism can fulfill, and also the necessity, for the overall and historic interests of the proletariat and for the revolutionary forces that take charge of these interests, to construct the force and the initiative capable of rising to the level of the clash, in order to have an impact on the political and military steps being taken in developing the strategy, war and the imperialist counterrevolution.

# "NEITHER LEFT NOR RIGHT"
## The Extreme Right and the Battle
## Against the New World Order

### THE SPREADING BATTLE AGAINST THE FORCES
### OF ECONOMIC GLOBALISM IS SHAPING THE EXTREMISM
### OF THE NEW MILLENNIUM

As the streets of Seattle exploded into 1960s-style violence [...], stunned Americans were told that "anarchists" and other left-wingers were leading a huge riot aimed at protesting capitalist globalism. Black-masked youths vandalized corporate property, squatters put up "Rent is Theft" signs and hundreds of protesters engaged in pitched street battles with rubber bullet-firing police as they contested the growing power of the pro-free trade World Trade Organization (WTO).

And these reports were true—but only to a point.

Right alongside the "progressive" groups that demonstrated in Seattle—mostly peaceful defenders of labor, the environment, animal rights and similar causes—were the hard-edged soldiers of neofascism. They carried signs decrying "The New World Order Agenda," bitterly denounced "Jewish media plus big capital," and, in at least one case, fought it out with black youths amidst the tear gas. The "Battle in Seattle" brought erstwhile antagonists together to face a common enemy in the streets.

What was behind this truly remarkable mix? How was it that members of the far "left" and "right" found themselves facing down police together? In the answers to these questions may lie the shape of future American extremism.

"The New American Patriot will be neither left nor right, just a freeman fighting for liberty," white supremacist ideologue Louis Beam wrote in the aftermath of Seattle. "New alliances will form between those who have in the past thought of themselves as right-wingers, conservatives and patriots, with those who have thought of themselves as left-wingers, progressives, or just liberal."

"The new politics of America is liberty from the NWO ["New World Order"] Police State and nothing more," Beam wrote. Whatever their political sympathies, the violent Seattle protesters were bravely fighting the "Police State goons" who were there "to protect the slimy corporate interest of 'free trade' at the expense of free people."

## THE COMMON ENEMY WAS, IN A WORD, GLOBALISM, A PRECURSOR TO THE FUTURE

More and more, people on both ends of the traditional political spectrum—particularly those who are young—are finding that their world views overlap. They are opposed to what are seen as the homogenizing forces of globalism. They despise capitalism, with its tendency to concentrate wealth and to make people and economies more and more alike—turning the planet into what is seen as a bland and materialistic "McWorld." They pine for nations of peasant-like folk tied closely to the land and to their neighbors. They fight for a pristine environment, a land unsullied by corporate agriculture and urbanization. They detest man-centered philosophies, seeing animals as no less important than humans. They reject rationalism in favor of a kind of mystical spirituality. Above all, these mainly young people—in some ways, the descendants of the "back-to-the-land" hippies of the 1960s—favor decentralization.

One neofascist group in Britain—which is experiencing a similar left/right convergence—puts it like this: "The [National Revolutionary Faction] is committed to fighting globalisation whenever and wherever it raises its ugly head ... There will definitely be a convergence between groups presently considered to be opposed to one another. ... [W]e are witnessing the gradual emergence of two distinct phenomena: the centralists and the decentralists. The time is approaching when activists from all antiCapitalist groupings will be forced to decide which 'side' they are on."

Just listen to Matt Hale, the leader of the neo-Nazi World Church of the Creator, who was in Seattle: "[T]he riots ... can be considered the first riots in recent memory by white people....What happened in Seattle is a precursor for the future, when white people in droves protest the actions of World Jewry ... by taking to the streets and throwing a monkey wrench into the gears of the enemy's machine.... "It is from the likes of the white people who protested the WTO and who, in some cases, went to jail for illegal actions, that the World Church of the Creator must look for our converts—not the stale right wing which has failed miserably to put even one dent in the armor of the Jewish monster," Hale said. "[W]e should concentrate on these zealots, not the meet, eat and retreat crowd of the right wing."

## AMERICAN FRONT AND THE THIRD POSITION

That the right and left share certain ideas is not an entirely new phenomenon. Since the 1980s, neo-Nazi Tom Metzger, leader of the California-based White Aryan Resistance, has rejected the left-right dichotomy and concentrated on labor issues he believes will draw in working-class whites. Concerns about ecology and animal rights also have been long shared by progressives and many neofascists. But in the aftermath of Seattle, it is clear that this left-right convergence on many issues is growing. Today, this phenomenon is most evident in the development of the so-called "Third Position"—neither capitalism nor communism, as its backers say, but a third way.

Already, these ideas have had a real impact on the American racist rock scene. They have influenced many of the U.S. "racialist" elements of neo-pagan religions like Odinism and Asatru. They are important to many members of the American-based Hammerskin Nation, the largest neo-Nazi skinhead coalition in the world. But they are most explicit in the Harrison, Arkansas-based group American Front (AF).

Started around 1990, the neo-Nazi AF was long based in Portland, Oregon, headed by a skinhead named Bob Heick, and composed mainly of other skinheads, many of whom had records of violence. But when it was taken over in the last couple of years by its current leader, James Porazzo, the group's mailing address was moved to Arkansas. At the same time, AF began to adopt explicitly Third Position ideas, using as its slogan, "National Freedom, Social Justice, Racial Identity."

What Porazzo says he is working for is "social revolution in a racialist context." "We propose a workable, realistic alternative, and that is separatism!" he says. "White autonomy, black autonomy, brown autonomy, and death to the current twisted system.... The only other obvious route would be an eventual winner take all race war: I don't think anyone with any sense would want that.... [L]et me make it clear that American Front would rather fight the REAL ENEMY—the system."

For Porazzo, that system is "the dictatorship of the dollar." Behind this tyranny, behind the capitalist and globalist forces Porazzo sees sweeping the world, lie "the Zionists and the Race that spawned them ... a filthy, evil people the world would be better without." Charging interest, "is a filthy Jewish practice."

## FIGHTING GLOBALISM WITH CMDR. DOOLITTLE

AF is not the only explicitly Third Positionist U.S. organization. The American Coalition of Third Positionists, a group based in Rockville, Maryland, publishes a newsletter called "Neither Left Nor Right." American skinhead publications like *Thule, Fenris Wolf* and *Hammerskin Press* have carried ads in recent months touting Third Position ideology. And in Canada, Affiliates of the Liaison Committee for Revolutionary Nationalism—a Europe-based Third Position coalition that counts the AF as a member—are located in Saskatoon and Hearst, Ontario.

Third Position ideas have also made themselves felt in such places as the American Nationalist Union (ANU), a group that opposes "Third World" immigration and calls for "voluntary racial separation." The January issue of ANU's Nationalist Times attacks other right-wing groups for not recognizing the contribution made by leftists in Seattle and being too focused on race and taxes. Seattle, it says, was "the first large-scale display of grassroots anti-globalist dissent in America in years."

Feeding into this anti-globalist vision shared by many on the left and right are very real economic dislocations. Martin Lee, author of *The Beast Reawakens*, a book on the rebirth of European fascism, says such pressures are important: "As economic globalization has accelerated, producing definite losers and winners, so too has the momentum of neofascist and right-wing extremist organizations."

The radical right has added other ideas into the mix. More and more, its ideologues applaud the actions of terrorist groups like the Animal Liberation Front and sometimes violent "deep ecologists" like those in Earth First! and the Earth Liberation Front, which claimed the $12 million arson of a Vail, Colorado, ski resort in 1998. They support the "national liberation" struggles of countries with terrorist histories like Iraq and Libya. They cheer black groups like the Nation of Islam.

This embrace of non-white battles against the "New World Order" is particularly remarkable. Most Third Positionists spring from a neofascist and anti-Semitic background. Yet, calling themselves "national revolutionaries," they say they must support anticapitalist, anticommunist struggles everywhere.

"Europe is our home," one British Third Positionist group leader wrote recently. "[B]ut... the struggle is one. So if we end up in the jungles of Paraguay fighting alongside the National Revolutionary Parrots League of

Commander Doolittle, it would mean that we would have to say: 'OK, it is a little warmer here. The people are a little more dusky than back home. But the struggle continues.' Why? Because the New World Order is seeking to establish itself everywhere."

## ECOLOGY FOR ARYANS

It isn't only the specter of globalism that attracts those on the "left." Concerns about the environment have also brought traditional "leftists" into bizarre coalitions with right-wing extremists—a fusion known as the "green-brown" alliance.

It is a fusion with a long history.

Since its beginnings in nineteenth-century Europe, ecological thought has been associated with the racist right, with key early thinkers calling for Teutonic racial purity and a "survival of the fittest" attitude to famines and similar disasters in the undeveloped world. Many war-time Nazi officials were distinctly ecologically minded. Forty years later in America, Tom Metzger's neo-Nazi war tabloid was declaring, "Ecology is for Aryans, too." Also in the 1980s, American Ben Klassen, founder of the neo-Nazi Church of the Creator, said in his book *Salubrious Living* that whites should "avail ourselves of a clean, wholesome environment; fresh, unpolluted air; clean water; and the beneficial therapy from the direct rays of the sun."

At around the same time, several heroes of the counterculture of the 1960s became embroiled in debates. After making allegedly racist remarks, Edward Abbey, author of the "deep ecology" classic *The Monkey Wrench Gang,* bemoaned the immigration into the United States of "culturally-morally-genetically impoverished people." David Foreman, the founder of Earth First!, was forced out after describing an ongoing Ethiopian famine as "nature's method of population control."

Then, in 1998, the Sierra Club was nearly destroyed by an internal debate over immigration. Members were asked to vote on a resolution declaring both legal and illegal immigration to be an environmental ill. After a public and embarrassing debate, the measure was defeated—but only after 40 percent of those polled backed it.

Today, the radical right's use of "green" issues is growing. In a December editorial, for instance, Tom Metzger says that in the past environmentalists and racists "damned" one another. "Not so in the twenty-first century," Metzger said in his WAR tabloid. "The best interests of the environment will meld into the best interests of race. The health of the race and the health of the environment will be one." As the German Nazis said: "Blood and Soil."

"Ecology is warped for mystical-nationalist ends by a whole series of neofascist groups and parties," Janet Biehl, a specialist on "eco-fascism," wrote recently. "Their programmatic literature often combines ecology and nationalism in ways that are designed to appeal to people who do not consider themselves fascists...." American Front, for instance, describes itself as "whole-heartedly a Green movement."

## "WAKE UP AND SMELL THE TEAR GAS"

Another fertile area for Third Position growth is among the followers of pre-Christian polytheistic theologies, notably the racist elements of Odinism and Asatru.

Racist adherents of these nature-based belief systems—mainly young Skinheads—long for a return to the genetically based tribe, or folk. They mythologize the misty past of white northern Europeans as a romantic tableau of boar-slaying warriors, dewy-eyed Aryan maidens and pristine Alpine scenery—precisely the kind of vision of nature-loving, fiercely independent peoples held up by most Third Positionists.

In Seattle, the left and right did not exactly march arm in arm. Militia members decrying international conspiracies were largely ignored. Members of the neo-Nazi National Alliance who were there reported back about "the most utterly disgusting street punks and campus Jews" they had met—and battled—in the streets.

Still, it seems clear that the hard right will draw increasingly from the ranks of its former enemies. "The radical Left has much more potential to produce true Revolutionaries than the Right," the AF's Porazzo says. "We're seeing more Leftists coming to the Revolution and American Front than I ever dreamed possible. These comrades have, generally, been able to grasp [our] ideas much, much quicker than the ex-Rightists ... "

Or, in the concluding words of Louis Beam's angry essay: "A new dawn is breaking upon the American political scene. The old words of divide and conquer will come to mean less and less to thinking people. There will be no meaningful differences between those who want freedom. But rather, just 'Americans' who want to be free and are fighting the police state to gain that freedom. Wake up and smell the tear gas, freedom is calling its sons and daughters."

Southern Poverty Law Center
*www.splcenter.org/imtelligenceproject/ip-4m3.html*

# THE SECOND CHECHEN WAR

## VARIANT II

### *Complete Annihilation*

Any guerrilla war will go on until supported by the local population. Here I have in mind both psychological readiness to help in defiance of the authorities and the demographic resource (number of civilians). During the first war both factors were considerable enough which made Russia's defeat inevitable.

Today, the level of guerrilla movement is as high as in the past. The Russian authorities are obviously not prepared to use the Soviet experience of deportation. This means that extermination is possible. This is a purely theoretical supposition: so far there were no signs of such intentions. What the Russian troops were doing can be described as "an inadequate use of force" but not as "genocide" or "ethnic purges."

The second variant can become possible if the federal powers transcend this dividing line: the zone of clashes with the guerrillas will be inevitably extended to include the areas to the south of Grozniy and the Chechen villages in Ingushetia and Daghestan where rebels can stay concealed. There might be "bombing by mistake" of Chechen villages in Georgia.

This variant will somewhat increase the number of forced migrants (as compared with February, 2000) and change its direction yet it will hardly reach the scale of December, 1999 when over two hundred thousand people, more than half of them from Grozniy, left their homes after massive bombings of the main Chechen cities. The cities' migration potential has exhausted itself: it will be rural dwellers much less mobile than urbanites who will set in motion.

This means that forced migration will be limited by the specific features of the migrants themselves: less chances of professional adaptation, hence a temporal nature of migration as close to the abandoned homes as possible so that to return on time for the agricultural season; strong religious feelings and traditional consciousness that demand burials in the native land; low level of material well-being; language skills limited to Chechen and Russian which calls for continued living in the habitual linguistic environment.

The main thing about migration is the fact that Chechens prefer to live where there is a Chechen diaspora: the migration pattern will correspond to the Chechen settlement pattern outside the republic.

Over 60 percent of all Chechens outside Chechnya are living in the neighboring southern regions of Russia, up to Volgograd region. At worst this area will receive a similar share of Chechen migrants; 30 percent of the Chechen diaspora are found in other regions. This means that at least a third of the migrants will settle there. Ukraine and Kazakhstan come next where the sizes of the Chechen diasporas are concerned. They also attract new migrants because there are more than fifty thousand Chechens living in both states; the frontier is open (through Astrakhan region to Kazakhstan and through Rostov region to Ukraine); Russian is spoken and the Soviet way of life to which Chechens are accustomed predominate there. Their proximity to Chechna is also important. Georgia and Azerbaijan may attract up to ten thousand each (including those already living there) some of them former fighters. In case of massive exodus two or three thousand may find home among the Chechens living in Kirghizia, Uzbekistan and other Central Asian republics. The number of Chechen migrating outside these areas will be small.

Turkey, for example, may attract not more than five or six thousand: fighters, except those several hundreds who need medical aid or are looking for sponsors to continue armed struggle; the rest will stay as close to Chechnya as possible to go on with the guerrilla warfare. The majority of the civilians have no money to move to Turkey which is unwilling to accept refugees from the zones of ethnic conflicts, the Turks from the Ferghana valley being no exception. After the pogroms of 1989 they mainly scattered across Russia and Azerbaijan, few reached Turkey.

In any case, a war waged to kill off more Chechens will decrease the demographic potential of guerrilla warfare and make the federal victory more possible, yet it may be short-lived: new generations will pay for the insults inflicted on their fathers and grandfathers. This explains why ethnopolitical conflicts extend for several generations.

A favorable development will be secured only by post-war economic upsurge in Chechnya and a higher living standards for its population. Unfortunately, while a military victory of the federal forces is probable, post-war restoration at the expense of the Russian taxpayers is improbable.

One cannot fail to see that while the three problems are hard to resolve individually, taken together they defy any solution. Indeed, how can Chechnya be restored if the budget has allocated 10 percent of the sum Vice Premier Nikolai Koshman asked for?

Even if the money is found who can guarantee it is not stolen? Where will new jobs be created? Normally, people worked at an oil refinery in Grozniy, which is now completely ruined. The federal powers are doing nothing to restore it. Will it be possible to find employment for people in Chechnya while there are no jobs in other north Caucasian republics that have experienced neither bombing nor guerrilla warfare?

To sum up: an annihilation war will create no positive results and Moscow is aware of this as well as of its other obviously negative sides.

The world community will become even more negative in its attitude to Russia which will affect the position of western governments. Under certain conditions these countries will be forced to introduce economic sanctions against Russia.

Besides, more cruel methods of warfare will invite a wider scope of terrorism which may involve not only trained saboteurs from Chechnya but also Chechens living outside the republic. This happened in Astrakhan region in autumn, 1999.

Expanding terrorism may affect public opinion at home: there will be more hatred and readiness to exterminate the Chechens among some groups yet the majority will be possibly willing to separate the obstinate republic from Russia.

---

*www.ca-c.org/online/2000/journal-eng/eng04-2000/16.pain.shtml*

IGOR DOBAEV

# ISLAMIC RADICALISM IN THE NORTHERN CAUCASUS

I T IS ONLY AT A STRETCH that the modern Islamic movement in the Northern Caucasus can be seen as a monolithic social force. It is effectively represented by diverse and heterogeneous sociopolitical elements. Each of them has their own special interests and objectives—oftentimes with a purely nominal religious/political coloring.

Meanwhile, the sphere of their actual interests is predetermined by competition of regional elites.

The first group of such elements is constituted by the administration and management *apparat* of religious organizations: Spiritual Administrations of Muslims. The official Islamic structure suffered tangible losses in the wake of the breakup of spiritual administrations that existed in the Soviet Union. As a result, there are seven territorial administrations in the Northern Caucasus alone: in Daghestan, Chechnya, Ingushetia, North Ossetia, Kabardino-Balkaria, Karachaevo-Cherkessia and Stavropol Territory, Adigey, and Krasnodar Territory. Moreover, whereas the organizations in Adigey and Krasnodar Territory, Daghestan and Karardino-Balkaria are affiliated with the Council of Muftis of Russia, which is headed by Ravil Gainutdin, mufti of the Spiritual Administration of Muslims of the Central European Region of Russia (DUMTSER), the administrations in Karachaevo-Cherkessia and Stavropol Territory, North Ossetia, Ingushetia, and Chechnya are autonomous.

Changes within the leadership undermined the unity of traditionalists' ranks, providing fertile soil for politicization of Islam and the emergence of fundamentalist trends, hitherto unknown in the region, e.g., Wahhabism.

The second group are institutionalized organizations as part of the existing spectrum of political and administrative structures. A case in point is the All-Russia Islamic Revival Party (IPV) and the Union of Muslims of Russia. They were represented in federal power structures, actively trading on their legal status to monopolize the position as sole representatives of the federal center in the regions. Meanwhile, this representation could have helped them bring all local Islamic organizations under their control and to restore the hierarchic structure ruled from the top.

Nonetheless, recently these organizations have virtually lost their positions both on the federal and on the regional level. Thus, the All-Russia Islamic Revival Party today exists, rather, in name only since as of 1993-4, its most active members began forming eponymous regional parties with a pronounced ethnic thrust while many adopted radical Islamic positions. The Union of Muslims of Russia, founded in 1995 and headed by Nadirshakh Khachilaev, despite considerable assistance from abroad, effectively lost its influence in the wake of the events in Daghestan and Chechnya in May 1998 and August-September, 1999, and the subsequent discrediting of its leader.

The third force are national movements and organizations: the United Congress of the Chechen People, the International Chechen Association, Birlik, Tenglik, Democratic Jamagat, and others. These organizations, amid the growing sociopolitical instability, have often exerted tangible pressure on republic governments while the vociferous Muslim rhetoric provided an ideological basis and substantiation for their openly separatist and corporate aspirations.

The fourth group is comprised of fundamentalist Islamic groups of a Wahhabi orientation. The Wahhabi movement in the region (as well as, incidentally, in other Islamic states) is not monolithic, but is divided into moderate and radical trends. Their ultimate aim is to spread Islam across the Northern Caucasus and to create an Islamic state ("from sea to sea"). While not differing in their strategic objectives, they use different tactics.

Moderate Islamists avoid an open confrontation with the authorities, declaring readiness for cooperation with official religious leaders and institutions. They believe that the movement's success is contingent on compromise with the ruling regime while open confrontation is counterproductive. The moderate wing includes young intellectuals who received a traditional religious education as well as the Muslim intelligentsia—as a rule, elderly people. Thus, in Daghestan, this wing was led (right until his death in March, 1998) by Akhmadkadi Akhtaev, one of the most prominent representatives of Russian politicized Islam (founder of the All-Union Islamic Revival Party). The wing was marked by relative tolerance of traditional Sufi brotherhoods in Daghestan and various religious/legal schools in Islam. It did not show particular public or political activism, placing a special emphasis on agitation and enlightening activity. Akhtaev repeatedly condemned radical Muslims who referred to all other Muslims as infidels. He and his allies did not seek to seize power, rather demonstrating an aspiration to participate in the work of power structures. After his death, the *Znamia islama* newspaper (published by the Kavkaz Islamic center) pointed out that the version of Wahhabism proposed by Akhtaev was far milder than one imposed by Bagautdin or Khattab, but their aims are basically the same: "Tactically, he was far ahead of the intransigent, blunt Bagautdin," whose positions are weakened by his association with Chechen bandits and Arab terrorists. The paper also stressed that "Akhtaev's demise is a big loss for Saudi Arabia" since he could have probably managed to achieve at least a temporary unification of Islamists in Daghestan "for the sake of the common goal of taking power."

Radicals are more decisively minded and are ready for open confrontation with the authorities. They do not want to wait while jihad for them is an open war not only with "infidels" but also with the "worst of Muslims"—those who refuse to take part in the "holy war" in the interests of establishing the power of "pure Islam." They are in effect dividing Islam from within for the sake of achieving their objectives, and if a respected religious figure is publicly critical of extremism tactics, he will either be removed or threatened with punishment.

Moderates talk about the need to enlighten the public and to build mosques, religious schools, and so forth. Although radicals also engage in missionary work, they believe that it is necessary to complete the preparation phase as soon as possible and to go ahead with building an Islamic state.

Whereas moderate Wahhabis prefer "civilized" or parliamentarian methods, radicals advocate tough methods based on the use of force and are intolerant of official religious structures, often teaming up with Nazis. Even so, there is no hard and fast line between moderate and radical Wahhabis; moreover, they seek to preserve their internal unity.

Islamic extremism in the form of the so-called North Caucasian Wahabism is the most active in the eastern part of the region: In the post-Soviet period, Daghestan and Chechnia ended up as zones of a highly acute socioeconomic, political, and ethnic crisis, one outcome of which was the 1994-6 war in Chechnya. Finally, of all other areas, Chechnya and Daghestan drew the attention of foreign forces seeking to use the Islamic factor in their own geopolitical and geo-economic interests. In Chechnya, foreign influence was facilitated above all by the situation that resulted from the war, while in Daghestan it was the great demand for religious education that the local clergy could not meet single-handedly.

In both republics, the events of the past few years have proceeded within an Islamic political paradigm with Wahhabis criticizing the ruling authorities, seeking to establish the Shari'a law, and rejecting secular laws "invented by man." Noteworthy in this context were the unmistakable signs of an internal Islamic conflict between the followers of the so-called "pure Islam" and of traditional Tariqat, which first manifested themselves in Daghestan and then in Chechnya.

Prior to the August-September, 1999 events, there were several thousand Islamic extremists in Daghestan. The most prominent, high-profile radical Wahhabi in Daghestan is admittedly Bagautdin Magomedov (Bagautdin Muhammad, Muhammed of Kizil-Iurt, or Mullah Bagautdin), former head of the Kizil-Iurt Wahhabi-Salafi Center.

In 1992, he headed up the Mudrost Muslim society in Kizil-Iurt, preaching Wahhabi ideology and constantly strengthening and consolidating the ranks of his followers. Bagautdin stressed the need for jihad against "infidels" as well as for an Islamic state to be formed in Daghestan, oriented, above all, toward Saudi Arabia. In the village of Pervomaiskoie, he established a publishing center, Santlada.

The leadership of this wing maintained close contacts with religious leaders in many countries in the Middle and Near East, making a substantial contribution to providing a theoretical religious base for Chechen resistance. After the end of the 1994–1996 war in Chechnya, M. Bagautdin began setting up, in Daghestan, Wahhabi cells—"Islamic societies" (*jamaats*)—leading, in mid-1997, to the formation of a public-political organization, the Islamic Community of Daghestan (Jamaat ul-Islamiyun, or IDD), which was officially registered by the republic's Ministry of Justice. The IDD's main political objective is Daghestan's secession from Russia and creation of an Islamic state. To this end, power structures are being set up, parallel to official bodies, which are proclaimed as the sole legitimate power vehicles that can stabilize the situation and overcome the crisis. Meanwhile, Islamic extremists are setting up paramilitary groups—in particular, the Central Front for Liberation of Daghestan with a network of special field camps and training centers on the territory of Chechnya and Daghestan, under the command of the main headquarters of the Islamic Community of Daghestan with "Amir" Bagautdin at the head.

Nonetheless, when, in the fall of 1997, the republic's state council approved a number of tough measures designed to check Wahhabi extremism (above all, amendments to the Law on Religion) while Islamic terrorists attacked a military unit in Buinaksk, M. Bagautdin and his close associates had to move to Chechnya. There, in Urus-Martan, the "jamaat" leadership engaged in active religious-ideological indoctrination and combat training of young Daghestani "Islamists" recruited into the so-called "insurgent army of the Imam," closely coordinating their actions with warlord Khattab and other foreign Islamic emissaries. B. Magomedov and his followers took a most active part in armed attacks on Daghestani territory in August–September, 1999 and then in combat operations against federal forces in Chechnia.

The Wahhabis' extremist leadership, tapping the resources of the Islamic Party of Daghestan, the Kavkaz Islamic center, the Union of Islamic Youth of Daghestan, and a number of other radical organizations, worked hard to recruit Daghestani youth into its movement.

It was hardly surprising that by 1996 the "Islamic world" set up, in Daghestan and Chechnya, regional bridgeheads with infrastructure ensuring its cultural, ideological and, in the future, also political expansion—the so-called Wahhabi enclaves. The best known among these is the Kadar zone, including the towns of Kadar, Karamakhi, and Chabanmakhi. They were funded with "sponsor money" coming in from abroad (mainly from Saudi Arabia) and were essentially a vehicle of geopolitical expansion on the part of the Muslim world. We believe that the Wahhabis sought to implement their doctrine in two stages: first, form "enclaves" in all republics of the Northern Caucasus, and second, begin political integration of these "enclaves" into a single fundamentalist state. Thus, back in 1998, the Wahhabis in Daghestan constituted a well-organized politico-religious and military structure.

In Chechnya, Wahhabism began to gain ground under Dudaev. In Grozniy, Wahhabis opened an information center disseminating religious literature, organizing collective praying, and spreading their ideas through the mass media. All of that was facilitated by the Dudaevites' statements to the effect that they were building an Islamic state that needed a uniform ideology. According to Dudayev ideologues (Z. Iandarbiev, M. Udugov, and others), the role of such ideology was to be played by Wahhabism. There were at least several reasons for that: counting on support of Chechen independence from rich Arab countries where this ideology is officially recognized; reliance on supporters of the movement who received sufficient military training, and the hope that the spread of "pure," "austere," "classical" Islam would help remove religious differences and contradictions not only within the republic but also between Muslims of the Northern Caucasus as a whole. Fundamentalism received a strong impetus from the 1994–96 events and the subsequent declaration of "sovereignty" in Chechnya.

The ideas of Muslim unity brought together the *teyp-* "clan"-based Chechen society, torn apart by contradictions in peacetime, in its military confrontation against the federal center. That idea also became a rallying point to hundreds of jihad warriors from Pakistan, Afghanistan, Turkey, and Arab countries taking part in the Chechen campaign.

Numerous Islamic parties, movements, nongovernmental organizations and sometimes Islamic states themselves (Saudi Arabia, Kuwait, Qatar, Syria, Pakistan, Turkey, Afghanistan, and others), according to Algerian *La Tribune*, have been providing, through their special services, financial, military, ideological, and other assistance to Chechnya in its struggle against "infidels." During the Chechen war, several large-scale terrorist acts organized by notorious warlords turned the situation around, leading the process of "enforcing law and order" to a deadlock. That applies above all to the 1995 raid on Budennovsk, led by Sh. Basaev, and the 1996 events in Kizliar and Pervomayskoie, masterminded by S. Raduev. Accompanied by Islamic rhetoric and other trappings, those unprecedented terrorist acts brought about, first, Khasaviurt and then Moscow agreements.

The war in Chechnya gave a new impetus to the spread of Wahhabism. In the spring of 1995, a group of foreign mercenaries, Jamaat Islami, was formed in the republic, under the command of Habib Abd al-Rahman Khattab, a Jordanian subject. When the military campaign was over, he set up, in the Shali District, a training center—the Islamic Institute of the Caucasus (IIK)—which in effect became an affiliate of the international extremist organization Muslim Brotherhood. Umar Ben Ismail, amir of the Wahhabi Jamaat of Urus-Martan, described the IIK as a "scholarly and educational center": "the Khattab group was formed well before [the war in] Afghanistan; it operated in Tajikistan; his *mujahideen* fought, in the name of Allah, in Bosnia, Abkhazia, Karabakh, Ingushetia, and Ichkeria. His center is extremely significant for the Muslims; the importance of such centers today in incontestable, as is borne out by Russia, Israel, and the United States." This "scholarly and educational" center provided training (in guerrilla warfare; combat, terrorist, and commando training, and ideological indoctrination) to hundreds of young people from the Northern Caucasus. All IIK graduates without fail had to take a practical test. The terrorist raid in Buinaksk (Daghestan) in December 1997 is a good example of how Khattab fighters translate the ideas of Wahhabi extremism into practice.

In April, 1998, A. Maskhadov, appearing on republic television, said that Chechnya would build an independent Islamic state where Shari'a norms would be the law (prior to that such "Islamic institutions" as the " Shari'a court," the " Shari'a Guard," and so forth, would be created). According to him, "jihad of the Chechen people begins with strengthening the state, enforcing law and order, and building an army." The Chechen state, "which will be called the Chechen Republic of Nokhchiyo, will live according to the norms of Islam and the Shari'a law. The Koran will be the basis of the Constitution."

It is quite clear, however, that Maskhadov's interpretation of jihad differs from that of the ideology of belligerent Wahhabism. Moreover, Muslim extremists have a different objective: to build an Islamic state in the Northern Caucasus—initially in Chechnya and Daghestan. Chechnya alone, even if "Islamic," is not part of their plans. So confrontation between traditionalists and fundamentalists within the republic has been growing. The former include President A. Maskhadov with his followers, espousing the ideology of traditional Islam (Sufism) and supporting the Spiritual Administration of the Republic's Muslims, at the time headed by Mufti Ahmad-Haji Kadyrov. At the other end of the spectrum are Sh. Basaev, M. Udugov, Z. Landarbiev, al-Khattab, and other advocates of "pure" Islam as well as foreign Islamic organizations, institutions, and foundations supporting them. After a brief anti-Wahhabi propaganda show, S. Raduev, the number two terrorist, joins the Wahhabis. In his address to graduates of a terrorist training school on March 14, 1997, he presented the plans of the Chechen extremist movement: "Your task is to strike terror into the hearts of those who betrayed Allah; they must feel the cold touch of death all the time... Your task is to penetrate Russia's power structures, administrative and fiscal agencies. Your task is to destabilize the situation, the economy, and the financial sphere. ... Set up bases, recruit people—you won't have to wait long... Spread national strife in ethnic republics, set nationalists against ethnic Russians... Blame Russians for everything...It is also important to take up leading positions within mafia structures."

Although there were fewer Wahhabis in Chechnia than in Daghestan at the time, they constituted a real combat force. In the wake of the bloodshed at the Grozniy television center and the massacre in Gudermes (in July 1998, the Islamic Special Purpose Regiment, under Khattab's command, engaged a Ministry of the Shari'a Security guard force), the republic's president issued an edict outlawing Wahhabism, ordering some Jordanian missionaries out of the country while Wahhabi armed units were to be disbanded. Yet they ignored the order and continued to build up their forces as though nothing had happened.

*www.ca-c.org.online2000/journal*

# UZBEKISTAN

## UZBEKISTAN—THE WEST'S MURDEROUS ALLY AGAINST ISLAM

In Uzbekistan, away from the spotlight of the world's attention, a bloody campaign of immeasurable brutality has been raging. A campaign is sweeping across the whole countryand terrorising an entire society in what can only be described as "mass intellectual cleansing." All this is happening as the political leaders of Western powers are queuing up to make friends with Uzbekistan, giving their blessing for the work done by their new ally Islam Karimov in 1992 when the Soviet Union broke up Uzbekistan gained its independence, though it still remained linked to Russia militarily, politically, economically and in terms of security, through "The Commonwealth of Independent States" (CIS) which was established as a substitute for the former Soviet Union.

No sooner did the godless communism collapse its inhabitants felt that they had become freed from the slavery of communism and the dictatorship of the Russians that suppressed their love for Islam which was forbidden to them for three-quarters of a century.

It was a time to rejoice Islam could now finally become a major part of their lives they could now live their rich heritage which contributed so much to the Muslim Ummah and gave birth to some of the great scholars, like Bukhari, Tirmidhi, Nasafi and Zamakhshari.

They began to return to the fold of Islam. They went back to cleaning their Mosques, most of which the Russians had turned into alcohol storehouses and pig-pens.

They proceeded to give money and accept donations from their Muslim brothers outside the country in order to restore old mosques and to build new ones.

And when it seemed to Uzbekistan's Muslims that they where turning a new leaf, that the future was looking bright, darkness descended upon them when the ruling party, under the presidency of Islam Karimov, began to forbid the acceptance of any donations coming from outside if it was for building mosques, establishing Islamic schools or any type of Islamic activity. And as rapidly as it left, the legacy of the communist era had returned to Uzbekistan.

They began again to close down mosques and imprison Imams and Khatibs who did not sing the praises of the ruling party. They forbade the use of loudspeakers for the Adhan in the mosques and shut down a majority of them.

For example, in the city of Namangan there were ninety-eight Jami'a mosques. The authorities closed all of them down except nine and began to plot the assassination of certain daw'ah carriers, causing the rest to disappear and arresting countless others.

It was repression all over again for Uzbekistan's Muslims, for a war of oppression began to be waged against them that still continues today.

## KARIMOV THE TYRANT

For over the past decade the government of Islam Karimov has waged a relentless war on the Muslims of Uzbekistan to make the people to reject Islam all together, for the call for Khilafah in Uzbekistan began to win favour among the majority of Muslims, the young and the old, the poor and the rich to the point that it spilled through Uzbek borders and has now become a driving force in the whole of the central Asian region. As a result he began to target all mosques and Imams ensuring that the only Islam that they preached was his version a secular Islam devoid of any substance.

Any discussion on political Islam was officially banned and considered a crime, Muslims who prayed regularly were arrested, bearded Muslims were arrested, Muslims who attended group discussions on Islam were arrested.

Sisters who wore hijab were forbidden, even from walking the streets and banished completely, and any one who criticized his war on Islam was arrested.

And when it seemed to him that he was on top of things that no one would dare to challenge his fascist fist, the strength of Islam began to display itself in the Uzbek society.

From amongst the people men were lining up to account his every move, to challenge his every step, to criticize him openly and shame him to the world for the criminal that he is, without any fear seeking only Allah's pleasure adopting only non-violent political means.

And as his brutality increased the call for Khilafah strengthened and its success reached such an extent in Uzbekistan that the state mufti went on television a number of times to attack the concept of Khilafah, saying that there is no Khilafah system in Islam. He said "expunge the word Khilafah from your hearts and get it out of your minds." And the head of the committee of religion stated on television: "there is no state, Khilafah or jihad in Islam."

And when the people ignored the words of these hypocrites and no government imam was able to counter this call the countries top thinkers, philosophers and clergy where called in to develop an new ideology to appeal to the people instead of Islam and the call for Khilafah. "To fight an objective with an objective, a thought with a thought, and ignorance with knowledge" became a slogan of Karimov new propaganda.

And when he failed to develop an ideology better than that of Allah's, he began to fight an objective with killing, a thought with imprisonment, and combat the light carried by the carriers of the dawah with the darkness of his torture chambers hoping to break the spirit of these men and women.

Tens of thousands of Uzbek Muslims have been unlawfully arrested, thousands have been tortured and dozens have been killed in extrajudicial executions.

Uzbek Muslim women have been threatened with gang rape during interrogation, elderly women in their seventies have been stripped naked and exposed to rapists and murderers in an attempt to make their sons confess to fictitious terrorism charges.

Muslims in prison report that they have been subjected to continuous and cruel battery, repeated anal rape and the insertion of metal bars in the private parts, incarceration in basement cells in conditions intolerable for any human being.

Some have been injected with HIV infected blood for adhering to their Islamic prayer rituals and refusing to seek clemency from President Karimov.

---

www.khilafa.com

# *KHILAFA*: TADJIKISTAN

## "YOU ARE THE BEST OF PEOPLES, BROUGHT FORTH FROM MANKIND..."

It has been almost eighty years that Muslims have been experiencing the life of instability and darkness. The major reason for this state of affairs is the agent rulers imposed over Muslims in Islamic countries. They occupy their seats not to please Allah, but to satisfy the greedy thirst of colonialist crusaders. The president of Tajikistan and his surrounding clique are of the same type. Their tyranny and humiliation of Islam and Muslims, particularly the callers to Islam is not a secret to anyone anymore. Even though Rakhmonov himself is a son of the Islamic *Ummah*, he labels the members of *Hizb ut-Tahrir* as terrorists, separatists and extremists, and arrests them simply for conveying the call to Islam in order to unite all Muslims under the flag and *Sharee'ah* of Islam as well as to make *"La ilaha ilallah Muhammadur Rasulullah"* prevalent over all other things. The main reason for such enmity to Islam and Muslims is based on his desire to please his masters. It is this exact desire that drives him against Allah and His orders.

To commit these crimes he gets the support of imperialist states such as America, Britain, Israel, and Russia. Additionally, they present themselves as assistants to the people, trying to accustom Muslims to the presence of different missionaries guised under the mask of funds and non-profit organizations. These missionaries build churches and distribute books and leaflets aimed at diverting Muslims from their faith. The infidel America and her allies have become dominant over us and teach us what is right and what is wrong, what is *halal* and what is *haram*. Moreover, they establish ties with schools and higher education institutions, set up exchange programs, under which they send children of the Islamic *Ummah* to their countries, poisoning their minds with nationalism and patriotism as well as with outdated faulty relationships, which fully contradict Islam, thus fulfilling their malicious plots. History has proved a thousand times that the Jews and Christians are the worst enemies of Islam and Muslims. Their enmity had sprung from the very first day of the revelation of Islam. Therefore, this enmity shall never cease to exist until they exterminate Islam and force Muslims into their own religion.

[...]

Truly, their enmity to Islam is overwhelming. That is why they impose over us the laws of capitalism, democracy, and others, stating: "They are based on Islam and do not contradict it in any sphere." However, the reality of them is that they are systems and laws of *kufr* ("unbelief"), whereas believing in them and solving problems in accordance with them is prohibited for Muslims. The Creator of all things forbade accepting any religion or laws except Islam. Allah the Exalted says:

[...]

O Muslims! You are the best of people, brought forth from mankind. To survive under the rule of infidels, to occupy such a humiliated position against them, applying their thoughts, solutions and laws is not appropriate for you. What is appropriate for you is to unite all Islamic lands under the flag of a single khaleefah, apply the rules of the Islamic shari'ah, spread it to the whole world as the guidance and light by means of jihad, face America and her allies as one entity and fight them under the flag of Islam.

O Muslims of Tajikistan! You, as an inseparable part of this great Ummah, should act to establish an Islamic Khilafah in order to resume the Islamic way of living. To fulfill this great task join the members of Hizb ut-Tahrir, who are carrying out this activity amongst you. It is definite, that—even though the infidels are trying to stop it—the Khilafah shall return back to life. Its return, in addition to being the peak of obligations for Muslims as ordered by Allah Almighty and being prophesized by the Messenger of Allah: [...]is a necessity to relieve the world from the tyranny and corruption it has sunk into, due to the absence of the leader and protector of the Muslims and their own state."

*www.khilafa.com*

# TERROR IN SPAIN

B ASQUE REVOLUTIONARY ORGANIZATION that supports the use of violence to achieve its goal: the creation of an independent state comprised of the Basque territories, Navarre and the Basque region of France. Since 1967 its definition includes the term "socialist." Nevertheless, the two factors that have defined the uniqueness of ETA within Basque nationalism, under both the dictatorship and the democracy, are: the emphasis on independence as an unwaivable goal; and the acceptance of violence on a theoretical level as well as a practical policy. In accordance with the first factor, ETA rejected the concession of autonomy as soon as democracy was restored in Spain; in accordance with the second, while democratic and autonomous consolidation eliminated the final pretexts for its actions, the organization evolved into a terrorism progressively more stark and devoid of objectives. The acceptance of the legitimacy of violence was soon converted, at least by the early 1980s, as the principle requirement for self-identification (and differentiation from others) of the radical nationalism that had risen within ETA.

ETA made its first appearance under this name in 1959, though its founders always insisted that a continuity existed between the founding group and that which, under the name of *Ekin* ("to do") began its activities six or seven years earlier. Ekin brought together a number of young people who met, according to the account of one of them, to study "vanguard European intellectual movements and Basque history." The initial group was formed by eight individuals: in Bilbao, Julen Madariaga, José María Benito del Valle, Iñaki Gainzarain, José Manuel Aguirre and Alfonso Irigoyen; and in San Sebastián, Rafael Albisu, Iñaki Larramendi, and José Luis Álvarez Enparantza (the writer Txillardegi). Other sources add a few additional names. All were students and members of middle class nationalist families.

The transition to external political activity took place after Ekin members initiated contact with the Partido Nacional Vasco (PNV). Following complicated negotiations, Ekin agreed to absorption within Eusko Gaztedi ("Basque Youth"), the youth wing of the PNV. This integration took place between 1956 and 1957, first in Guipúzcoa and later in Vizcaya. Despite mediation attempts by *lehendakari* Aguirre and other exiled nationalist leaders, organizational differences, coupled with personal conflicts, precipitated a separation after less than two years of coexistence. Among other motives for the dissolution, some role was evidently played by mutual suspicions of being manipulated by the CIA via the organization "Servicios," the PNV wing created during the Second World War to facilitate collaboration with the United States, and which continued to maintain contact with the CIA into the 1950s.

Following the schism, Ekin's core founders elected to create a fully independent organization, thus giving birth to ETA on an undetermined date in 1959. The founders disagree with respect to both the precise day and month, but it has become customary to cite the date as July 31, the festival of San Ignacio de Loyola, doubtlessly to permit synchronism with the founding of the PNV, in 1895. Until 1961, discussions over formation and recruitment continued to be the group's principal activities. This same year marked the appearance of the journal *Zutik,* whose production and distribution consumed a large part of the group's militant energy from that point forward. In its first issues, this broadsheet did not betray major political or ideological differences with the PNV, though its greater emphasis on the Basque language and on the goal of independence revealed a definite connection to the most radical tradition of the party, represented in the 1920s by the *Aberri* section and in the 1930s by splinter group *Jagi-Jagi.*

Nor were there significant differences with respect to initial activism: the pamphlet drops carried out in disguise, and the destruction of Franquista symbols were also activities pursued by PNV youths. However, on July 18, 1961 ETA attempted to derail a train carrying hundreds of former Franquista soldiers to a commemoration [of the rebel uprising of 1936]. The action failed but had it not been discovered it might well have caused injuries or even deaths. The multiple arrests that followed the attempt provoked a hardening of organizational guidelines (including the establishment of a sector in exile) and an ideological radicalization that precipitated the already irreversible differentiation with traditional nationalism.

This differentiation was expressed in the resolutions of successive conferences. The first of these, which took place in 1962 in a Benedictine monastery in southern France, approved the principles that were to define the objectives of the movement. In conference III (1964), the principle of revolutionary war was accepted, a decision that sought to adapt for the Basque country the guerrilla strategy that had been central to the liberation movements in the colonies. This strategy was clarified in conference IV (1965) and conference V (1966-67) in a plan of provocation christened with the name "spiral of action-repression-action." This theory posits that to enlist the populace in a revolutionary struggle, the enemy—the Spanish state—must be defied through a series of increasingly violent actions that will succeed in provoking blind acts of repression against the general population.

From this point forward, seeds of internal division would evolve around the contradictions between the original nationalist principles and the increasing adoption of socialist and leftist ideas. These suppositions involved a position of solidarity with immigrant workers and their struggles: but ETA had been born for the most part as a reaction against the danger of denationalization that the nationalists had attributed to the massive influx of foreign workers following the civil war. Although these ideas would be justified with other arguments, the contradiction became the fundamental cause of the schisms produced during the V and VI conferences (1966 and 1970, respectively). The breakaway sectors would gravitate towards leftist, Maoist or Trotskyist positions in the 1970s.

Between these two conferences, the strategy of action-repression saw its first deadly consequences in 1968. The *guardia civil* José Pardines, who had stopped a car carrying two members of ETA, became the first of more than seven hundred victims attributed to the organization in course of the following twenty-five years (seven hundred fifty-nine as of January 1, 1996). The trial in Burgos, which took place in December, 1970 against the principal leaders of ETA (in the period after the V conference), led to major demonstrations throughout Spain, as well as in many other countries, and forced the Franco regime to commute the sentences of death handed out to six of those tried. Three years later, an ETA group succeeded in assassinating the admiral Carrero Blanco, the successor *in pectore* to Franco. Two months after his death, the dictator approved five death sentences, two of which were against ETA gunmen; both were executed. At this point the organization was responsible for the deaths of forty-one people.

One year prior to the death of Franco, ETA was broken into military and political-military groups. On this occasion the split was the result of organizational rather than political disputes, and was the indirect consequence of divergent reactions to ETA's first deadly indiscriminate attack: the detonation of a bomb in a bar near the Madrid police headquarters, on

September 13, 1974, which caused eleven deaths. Both wings continued to practice violence, even intensifying their actions during the initial period of democratic reform. Between 1978 and 1980, the three decisive years of this process—that of the constitutional debate, approval of Basque and Catalan statutes and first autonomous elections—ETA assassinated two hundred thrity-nine people, one third of the total number produced between 1968 and 1993. This took place despite the announcement of a policy of amnesty which placed on the streets all ETA prisoners and permitted the return of its exiles.

Following the failed coup d'etat in 1981 and the subsequent stabilization of the democracy, ETA continued to carry out increasingly indiscriminate attacks, though now rationalized as a way of pressuring institutions to agree to conditions of a cease-fire. These conditions were variously expressed, though in general they adhered to the points contained in the so-called Alternativa KAS—amnesty, legalization of independent parties, the expulsion from the Basque territories of the armed forces of the state, better living conditions for workers, an autonomy statute that would include Navarre and consider (among other things) the recognition of the right to self-determination, the control of the military by the Basque government, etc. The socialist government agreed in 1989, following a truce with ETA, to initiate a dialogue with representatives of the organization in Algeria, warning, nevertheless, in accord with the pact of 1988 with the democratic Basque parties, that no political objectives would enter into negotiation (although the personal predicaments of the activists were up for discussion, including the possibility of pardons for those condemned by the courts). ETA's desire to break up this process led to the conclusive disruption of communication in March 1989. Since then, ETA's primary motive has been to reestablish a process of negotiation.

*Encyclopedia del Nacionalismo*
Andres del Blas (ed.) Madrid, 1997

# THE COMBATANT FORCES

T HERE ARE THREE SETS OF ACTORS in Colombia's longstanding conflict: guerrilla groups, paramilitary groups, and government security forces. While guerrillas and paramilitaries do not appear to have a significant support base, but most are well-funded and control vast amounts of territory. All combatants commit serious abuses of human rights and international humanitarian law.

## GUERRILLA GROUPS

### *Revolutionary Armed Forces of Colombia (FARC)*

What today is the hemisphere's largest guerrilla group began after a U.S.-supported attack on a Communist Party-inspired peasant cooperative in southern Tolima department calling itself the "independent republic of Marquetalia." According to the guerrilla group's version of events, the May, 1964 raid pitted sixteen thousand military personnel against a community of one thousand, of which forty-eight were armed.

Survivors of the Marquetalia raid founded the FARC shortly afterward, led by Manuel Marulanda, a peasant guerrilla who had fought since 1948 in a period of partisan bloodletting known as *La Violencia.*

Still headed by the septuagenarian Marulanda, the FARC now has about eighteen thousand members in almost seventy fronts plus mobile columns and urban militias. The group controls or operates freely in 40 to 60 percent of country, much of it sparsely populated jungles and plains east and south of the Andes. Its leadership has declared that it expects to grow to thirty thousand within the next few years. The FARC regularly recruits minors, at times by force.

While it received limited assistance from the Soviet bloc during the cold war, today the FARC finances itself through kidnapping for ransom, extortion, and involvement in Colombia's drug trade. Together with the ELN (described below), the FARC is responsible for the majority of kidnappings committed in Colombia today. The group's extortion has reached such an extent that in 2000 it promulgated a "law" demanding contributions from any Colombian whose assets exceed U.S. $1 million. The FARC and ELN are responsible for about 15 percent of killings associated with Colombia's conflict, many of them civilian non-combatants. The FARC regularly carries out massacres, and has claimed many innocent lives through indiscriminate use of inaccurate gas-cylinder bombs.

Much of Colombia's coca is grown in FARC-controlled areas, and the guerrillas' link to the drug trade is the source of much controversy. While this link is chiefly "taxation" of coca-growers in the areas it controls, U.S. Drug Enforcement Administration director Donnie Marshall testified to Congress in March that it goes further.

Some FARC units in southern Colombia are indeed involved in drug trafficking activities, such as controlling local cocaine base markets. Some insurgent units have assisted drug trafficking groups, transporting and storing cocaine and marijuana within Colombia. In particular, some insurgent units protect clandestine airstrips in southern Colombia.

The Colombian Armed Forces estimate that the FARC gets about half its income from involvement in narcotics trafficking, an amount that is probably between $200 million and $400 million per year (estimates range from $100 million to $1 billion).

Aided in part by this income source, the FARC grew rapidly during the 1990s, and dealt the Colombian military several humiliating defeats in 1996-8. It has since lost some momentum, losing key battles to the army and some territory to paramilitaries.

The FARC was involved in unsuccesful attempts to negotiate peace in 1984-7, 1991, and 1992. During the first peace process—which even brought a cease-fire—the FARC set up a political party, the Patriotic Union, which the group had hoped to use as a vehicle for an eventual entry into non-violent political participation. Between the Patriotic Union's founding in 1985 and the early 1990s, at least two thousand of the party's congress members, mayors, candidates and activists were killed by paramilitaries, security forces, and drug cartels. The slaughter of the Patriotic Union left the FARC's military structure intact, but left the group with few articulate political spokespeople.

On January 7, 1999, the FARC and Colombian government launched a new peace process. Since that date, sporadic talks have taken place in five municipalities in Meta and Caquetá departments in southern Colombia. Security forces pulled out of this area as a precondition for talks, making the FARC the only armed presence in a 16,200 square-mile area. This "clearance zone" is at least theoretically temporary and is due to expire in November, 2001.

Many observers question the FARC's level of commitment to the negotiations, and several speculate that it is a subject of some disagreement among the group's leadership.

## National Liberation Army (ELN)

The ELN was founded in 1964 by a group of Colombian students who underwent training in Cuba. The group launched its first military operations in Colombia's northcentral Magdalena Medio region the following year. Attempting to follow the Cuban model of rural rebellion, the ELN grew slowly but attracted many radical students and priests. Among the priests were Camilo Torres, a radical firebrand who died during his first combat in 1966, and two Spaniards, Domingo Laín and Manuel Pérez. Pérez served as the group's supreme leader from the 1970s until his death of natural causes in 1998.

Today, ELN membership is estimated at about 3,500 members, down from a late-1990s high of about five thousand. The group, which does not profit significantly from the drug trade, has lost ground to paramilitary groups.

The ELN relies more heavily on kidnapping and extortion to support itself. It frequently targets Colombia's oil sector, which it regards as dominated by foreign interests. Bombings of pipelines and energy infrastructure (such as power lines) are frequent. The group has also carried out several high-profile mass kidnappings since 1999.

The ELN was involved in brief peace talks with the government in 1991 and 1992, participating together with the FARC in a now-defunct structure called the "Simón Bolívar Guerrilla Coordination." Beginning with a 1998 meeting in Mainz, Germany, its leaders have talked with Colombian civil society representatives about starting another peace process with the government. "Talks about talks" with government peace officials have proceeded sporadically since 1999.

For years, the ELN has declared its intention to negotiate its peace agenda through a several-month "convention" with Colombia's civil-society and popular groups. In 1999, ELN negotiators insisted that this event must take place in a "clearance zone" similar to that granted to the FARC. Since early 2000, the government and ELN have agreed in principle to establish a temporary zone in two municipalities in southern Bolívar department. The zone has yet to be established, however, due to the active and at times violent resistance of paramilitary groups who control much of the area to be "demilitarized."

## SMALLER GUERRILLA GROUPS

Colombia has at least three other, much smaller insurgent groups. The Popular Liberation Army (EPL) is a remnant that refused to go along when the original EPL, a Maoist-inspired group, negotiated a peace accord with the government in 1991. Perhaps a few hundred members remain; the group's leader, Francisco Caraballo, is in prison. The ERG (Guevarist Revolutionary Army) and ERP (Popular Revolutionary Army), with perhaps a few dozen members, carry out occasional kidnappings and terrorist attacks.

## PARAMILITARY GROUPS

### United Self-Defense Groups of Colombia (AUC)

Colombia has a long history of privately-financed peasant self-defense groups, usually suffused with their wealthy patrons' right-wing beliefs. These groups' numbers began to grow rapidly in the 1980s.

The growth coincided with the advent of Colombia's drug trade. Newly wealthy drug traffickers laundered their profits by buying up as much as 2.5 million acres of land in northern Colombia during the 1980s. These new landholders put together private armies to deal with the guerrillas who kidnapped and extorted wealthy ranchers in the area. One of the first, and most feared, was a group calling itself "Death to Kidnappers" (*Muerte a Secuestradores*, or MAS), active in the Magdalena Medio region of north-central Colombia.

With funding from drug traffickers and other large landholders, and close and open collaboration with Colombia's armed forces, the paramilitaries gained strength throughout the 1980s. Their tactics—selective assassinations and forced disappearances, massacres, forced displacement of entire populations—quickly made them one of the country's main human rights abusers. They also played a strong role in the decimation of the Patriotic Union political party (see FARC section above).

The abuses of groups like MAS caused paramilitaries to be declared illegal in 1989. Little was done to disband them, though. Human rights groups have documented widespread post-1989 collaboration between Colombia's armed forces and paramilitary groups.

In the early 1990s the United Self-Defense Forces of Córdoba and Urabá, a group headed by brothers Carlos and Fidel Castaño, emerged in northwestern Colombia. (Fidel is now assumed to be dead.) Using extreme brutality toward civilian populations, the group has weakened guerrillas and established a permanent presence throughout northern Colombia. The ACCU forms the nucleus of the United Self-Defense Forces of Colombia (AUC), an umbrella group headed by Castaño and formed around 1997. The AUC began making inroads into FARC-controlled coca-growing areas in southern Colombia in the late 1990s.

The paramilitaries support themselves with donations from landowners and drug lords, and are increasingly involved in the drug trade itself. DEA Administrator Donnie Marshall explained the extent of paramilitary involvement to a congressional committee in March 2001.

Carlos Castaño "has recently admitted in open press that his group receives payments—similar to the taxes levied by the FARC—from coca growers in southern Colombia in exchange for protection from guerrillas. Several paramilitary groups also raise funds through extortion, or by protecting laboratory operations in northern and central Colombia. The Carlos Castaño organization, and possibly other paramilitary groups, appears to be directly involved in processing cocaine. At least one of these paramilitary groups appears to be involved in exporting cocaine from Colombia.

Fueled in large part by drug money, the paramilitaries have have expanded ninefold since 1992 and have more than doubled in size since 1998, now counting with more than eight thousand members. The groups are growing about five times as fast as the FARC. They also currently commit about 80 percent of killings associated with Colombia's conflict.

Official Colombian government policy regards the paramilitaries as a threat to be confronted. General Fernando Tapias, commander of the Colombian Armed Forces, said in 2001 that the AUC would be the greatest threat the government faces within two or three years. Yet allegations of military-paramilitary collaboration at the local level remain widespread and very well documented by human rights groups, the United Nations, the U.S. State Department, and Colombian government investigators.

The Colombian government has refused to grant the paramilitaries the "political status" given to guerrillas, meaning that it will not negotiate anything with the right-wing groups beyond their terms of disarmament.

## GOVERNMENT SECURITY FORCES

Though Colombia has avoided most Latin American countries' histories of chronic military coups, its armed forces operate with considerable autonomy and often challenge civilian leaders. Over the years, Colombia's security forces, especially its Army, have developed a reputation for corruption, human rights abuse, and poor performance on the battlefield.

The military has nonetheless maintained very close relations with the United States since at least since the early cold war (Colombia even sent a battalion to Korea in 1950). This collaboration has intensified since 1999, when the bulk of US counter-drug aid shifted from the National Police to the army.

Colombia's Defense Ministry, headed by a civilian since the 1991 Constitution was ratified, includes the army (about one hundred forty-six thousand members), police (about one hundred twenty thousand), air force (about ten thousand) and navy (about five thousand).

Colombian law exempts anyone with a high school education from serving in combat units. With a large contingent of these *"bachilleres"* and many soldiers guarding oil installations and infrastructure, perhaps half of the Army—maybe less—is available to fight illegal armed groups. The Colombian government has announced its intention to reduce the number of *"bachilleres"* and add ten thousand professional volunteer soldiers per year from 2001 to 2004.

The 2000-1 U.S. aid package funds the creation of three new counternarcotics battalions, adding another twenty-four hundred troops and giving the Army its largest-ever counter—drug role. However, the police—particularly its counter-narcotics unit (DIRAN)—remain the lead agency for counterdrug activities, carrying out aerial fumigation of drug crops and most other antidrug operations.

The armed forces have improved their battlefield performance since suffering embarrasing defeats at the hands of the FARC in 1996-8. In 2000 and 2001 the Army won decisive battles in Sumapaz, a zone fifty miles south of Bogotá, in Santander department ("Operation Berlín"), and in Vichada and Guanía departments ("Operation Black Cat").

Though their share of direct involvement in killings and disappearances has fallen sharply in recent years, the armed forces nonetheless continue to face serious allegations of indirect human rights abuse through collaboration with paramilitary groups. Except for a few high-profile cases, past abusers continue to enjoy near-complete impunity.

---

Center for International Policy Washington. Colombia
Project, August, 2002

# DAMAGED BUT STILL DANGEROUS

## INTRODUCTION

Jemaah Islamiyah (JI) remains active and dangerous from its Indonesian base despite the recent arrests of some of its top operatives. On August 5, 2003, members of the South East Asian terrorist organization bombed the Marriott hotel in Jakarta, clear evidence that JI is still capable of planning and executing a major operation in the heart of the capital.

Just a week later, one of JI's most senior leaders and the most wanted man in Southeast Asia, Riduan Isamuddin alias Hambali, was arrested in Thailand, joining some two hundred men linked or suspected of links to JI who are now in custody. Hambali's arrest was unquestionably a major blow. He was JI's top link to Al-Qaeda and one of its major strategists and fund-raisers. But he was not indispensable, and JI is far from destroyed. Indications from the interrogation of JI suspects suggest JI is larger than first believed, with a depth of leaders that allows it to make up losses and regenerate itself. The significance of the arrest will thus depend in part on the information that Hambali discloses and how that information is acted on, but JI does not depend on one man.

If some early accounts painted JI as an Al-Qaeda affiliate, tightly integrated with the bin Laden network, the reality is more complex. JI has elements in common with Al-Qaeda, particularly its jihadist ideology and a long period of shared experience in Afghanistan. Its leaders revere bin Laden and seek to emulate him, and they have almost certainly received direct financial support from Al-Qaeda. But JI is not operating simply as an Al-Qaeda subordinate. Virtually all of its decision-making and much of

509

its fund-raising has been conducted locally, and its focus, for all the claims about its wanting to establish a Southeast Asian caliphate, continues to be on establishing an Islamic state in Indonesia. If, since September 11, 2001, and particularly since the Bali bombings, the aim has seemed more destructive than constructive, especially in terms of attacking the U.S. and its allies as the biggest enemies of Islam, the emphasis on jihad in Indonesia remains strong.

Documentary evidence from the mid-1990s and more recent interrogation of JI suspects suggest that JI has a rigidly hierarchical structure headed by an emir. In practice, however, members of the central command, the *markaziyah*, appear to be more important in setting policy and deciding on operations and are not constrained by the formal hierarchy. JI also maintains alliances with a loose network of like-minded regional organizations all committed in different ways to jihad. The Makassar bombings of December 5, 2002 were not the work of JI, for example, but they were carried out by men who had been trained by JI in Mindanao and who had the motivation, manpower, and skills to undertake a JI-like attack. JI has also made very pragmatic use of thugs (*preman*) as necessary, particularly in Ambon.

## BOTH THE CORE ORGANIZATION
## AND THIS LOOSER NETWORK

I, Wan Min bin Wan Mat, a JI suspect detained in Malaysia, told interrogators that once an Islamic state in Indonesia was achieved, members would work toward a larger *daulah islamiyah nusantara* encompassing Malaysia, Indonesia, Thailand, Singapore and the Philippines, and then move on to restoring the Islamic caliphate.
*Wan Min interrogation deposition, March 11, 2003.*

They share a commitment to implementing *salafi* teachings—a return to the "pure" Islam practiced by the Prophet—and to jihad. More than two hundred members trained in Afghanistan from 1985 to 1995 and even more than that in Mindanao from 1996 to 2001. These bonds are likely to enable the network to survive police efforts to dismantle it.

It is sobering in particular to note that several leaders in the central command have not been identified, let alone apprehended. Senior figures with proven capacity to do serious damage, such as Zulkarnaen, the head of JI military operations, and the Malaysian national, Zulkifli bin Hir alias Musa alias Marwan, remain at large in the region, and the cell structure is probably more extensive than originally believed.

This report examines the ties that bind members of JI and its associate networks together, particularly the Afghanistan and Mindanao experiences, and assesses JI's potential for conducting operations. It is based on examination of interrogation depositions of many of the suspects arrested in connection with the Bali bombings as well as confidential interviews with people close to the network. The former are valuable documents but ICG does not take the information within them at face value; several Bali suspects, in particular, have given misleading information to interrogators. But through cross-checking different accounts of the same incident, it is possible to get a reasonably reliable description of events.

[…]

## CONNECTIONS TO AL-QAEDA

While many Indonesians still question whether JI exists as a formal organization, most appear to have accepted that the men on trial for the Bali bombings were likely responsible for the crime and that Indonesia does indeed have some home-grown terrorists. What is much more difficult for many to accept is that those terrorists have links to Al-Qaeda.

The arrest of Hambali could change this, but only if U.S. authorities quickly transfer him to Indonesian custody or at least give credible Indonesian authorities access to him. It is clear that an Indonesian connection with bin Laden was established in the mid-1980s through Abdul Rasul Sayyaf and the Afghanistan training.

Hambali provided the most important ongoing contact with the Al-Qaeda leadership but he was not the only person with direct connections. Zulkarnaen, Syawal Yasin, and Fathur Rahman al-Ghozi have similar ties.

Few details have come out of the Bali trials that add to what is already known about reported Al-Qaeda financing of JI activities, Wan Min asserted that Mukhlas told him that Al-Qaeda provided funding for some JI operations. He testified that the Bali bombing realised a fatwa from Osama bin Laden as conveyed by Hambali, but he claimed not to know what the origins were of the U.S.$35,500 that he helped transfer to the bombers. The way in which Al-Qaeda systematically began to establish operations in Southeast Asia, beginning in the Philippines in 1991 through bin Laden's brother-in-law, Mohammed Khalifa, has been well documented.

By 1994, a Malaysian named Wali Khan Amin Shah was a key member of the cell established in Manila by Khalifa and Ramzi Youssef, the man responsible for the December, 1993 bombing of the World Trade Center in New York. Shah and Hambali were partners in a Malaysian business, Konsojaya SDN BHD,

In January, 2000, Hambali and Yazid Sufaat, now detained in Malaysia and suspected of involvement in the Medan Christmas Eve bombings, are reported to have hosted two of the September 11 hijackers in Kuala Lumpur, Khalid al-Midhar and Nawaq Alhazmi. JI also consulted with Al-Qaeda about a proposed plan to blow up U.S. installations and other foreign targets in Singapore in 2000, a plan that was discovered through videos and other documents found in Afghanistan after the Taliban fled.

In addition to Omar al-Faruq, Reda Seyam (often miswritten as Seyam Reda), a German citizen of Egyptian origin who was arrested in Jakarta on September 16, 2002 and had previously lived in Bosnia and Saudi Arabia, is suspected of being an Al-Qaeda operative. He had visited Jakarta twice before trying to establish permanent residency in August 2002, using journalism as a cover.

Seyam was apparently al-Faruq's boss. He also was reportedly a financier of JI and the Al-Qaeda conduit for channelling funds to it for the Bali bombing. That information reportedly came through interrogation of Khalid Sheikh Mohamed, the al-Qaeda leader arrested in Pakistan on March 1, 2003.

The involvement of Al-Qaeda operatives in the Ambon and Poso operations has been noted above. Their commander, and the leader of Al-Qaeda operations in South East Asia more generally, appears to have been Sheikh Hussein al-Munawar, who reportedly left his Indonesia base shortly after September 11, 2001.

Despite these clear ties, JI's relationship with bin Laden's organization may be less one of subservience, as is sometimes portrayed, than of mutual advantage and reciprocal assistance, combined with the respect successful students have for their former teachers.

One source familiar with JI described its relationship to Al-Qaeda as similar to that of an NGO with a funding agency. The NGO exists as a completely independent organization, but submits proposals to the donor and gets a grant when the proposal is accepted. The donor only funds projects that are in line with its own programs. In this case, Al-Qaeda may help fund specific JI programs but it neither directs nor controls it.

---

International Crisi Group (ICG)
Crisis Watch Report 2003/4

JEFFREY M. BALE

# ABU SAYYAF
# IN THE PHILIPPINES

## THE IDEOLOGY OF THE ASG

It is hard to describe the underlying ideology of the ASG in any detail given the paucity of doctrinal tracts, treatises, and communiqués published by the group. The most that one can do is extrapolate on the basis of possibly unrepresentative snippets of information gleaned from media interviews with some of the group's spokesmen. In the beginning, at least, the ASG espoused an Islamist agenda that was far more radical than that associated with the MILF. Janjalani's primary objective was to unify "all sectors of the predominantly Muslim provinces in the South" and establish an Islamic state governed by the *shari'a* in that region, a state where "Muslims can follow Islam in its purest and strictest form as the only path to Allah." Moreover, he intended to accomplish this objective by means of armed struggle rather than through the gradual and peaceful process of proselytization (*da'wa*) embraced by Muslim evangelical groups like the Tabligh. As he further argued, the *Qur'an* says nothing about the "revolution" that secularized Moro leaders like Misuari had once advocated, but rather repeatedly urges the faithful to wage jihad in the defense of Islam and specifically authorizes it in cases—like in the GRP—where Muslims are presently ruled by unbelievers (*kuffar*). In this connection the following Janjalani quotes are particularly illustrative:

"The first difference is that revolution is not mentioned in the Holy Koran. But jihad is mentioned so many times. Second, the command of Allah is to wage jihad, not revolution. Third, and as a consequence, if you wage jihad, you must follow the law of Allah. You are not allowed to deviate to the right or to the left. If the Koran commands that negotiating is not allowed, there should be no negotiation. In a revolution, you are free to follow the thoughts of Mao Tse-tung, Lenin, Stalin, Karl Marx, Che Guevara, Ho Chi Minh, and Fidel Castro. It's up to you, since you are simply staging a revolution.... Another difference is, in a revolution, you are free to select whatever law you want to establish...In jihad, this is not allowed. Upon winning, what you should establish should only be the Koran and the Hadith. These are the only ones to be followed. Nothing else. The objective of the *jihad* is not the implementation of the Tripoli Agreement. It is not the attainment of autonomy. It is not just independence. The objective of *jihad* is the attainment of independence as a means of establishing the supremacy of the Koran and the Hadith ... In jihad, if you win, it should be the laws of the Koran from the beginning, to the middle, to the end ... There are no ideas of men to be followed here."

It would be hard to find a clearer statement differentiating the fundamentalist and Islamist conceptions of Janjalani from the secularized and nationalist views of Misuari.

Apart from promoting the use of violence to achieve these rather vague and grandiose goals, Janjalani provided very few specifics about the precise nature of the Islamic state that he eventually intended to create. However, there is no doubt that his views were influenced both by his earlier religious studies in Mecca and his later sojourn in Afghanistan as a *mujahid*, where he was probably exposed on a daily basis to the radical jihadist doctrines peddled by Afghan hardliners such as Abdul Sayyaf and their foreign "Afghan Arab" allies like bin Laden. Given Janjalani's own apparent adoption, first of Wahhabi and then of jihadist Salafi currents of thought, it is not surprising to learn that he and his associates were disgusted by the "impure" Muslim governments of Libya, Indonesia, and Saudi Arabia, or that they later viewed the Taliban regime in Afghanistan as a model which Muslims in the Philippine archipelago might do well to emulate. According to hostage Gracia Burnham, a devout Christian, the ASG felt it necessary to establish harsh rules governing the conduct of believers in order to prevent them from being tempted by western-inspired immorality.

There is nothing particularly distinctive about this, since efforts by Islamists to establish their own state and restore what they regard as pristine Islamic values are common, but within its own milieu the ASG was noticeably uncompromising by comparison with normal Moro rebel standards. Unlike the MNLF and the MILF, both of which had advocated more inclusive conceptions of the future Bangsamoro state, one of the ASG's specific goals was to rid Sulu and parts of Mindanao of all Christians and non-Muslims, by force if necessary, since according to Janjalani Islam permitted the killing of "our enemies" and "depriving them of their wealth." Indeed, anti-Christian animus seems to have been the principal motive underlying the group's initial wave of terrorist attacks, all of which specifically targeted "crusaders," and such sentiments were thereafter consistently used as a rationale to justify its violent actions. Furthermore, there are indications that these extreme objectives were not confined exclusively to the borders of present-day Moroland. In the wake of the 9/11 attacks on the United States, one of Gracia Burnham's rapturous captors confided that the ASG would not be satisfied even if the GRP decided to return Tawi-Tawi, Sulu, Jolo, Basilan, and southern Mindanao to the Muslims: "That would be only a beginning. Then we would be obligated to take all of Mindanao." He added that afterwards they would seize control of the Visayas and Luzon, then move on to Thailand and other countries where Muslims were oppressed, since "Islam is for the whole world." This internationalist perspective may help to explain why ASG spokesmen sometimes included the freeing of captured Al-Qaeda-linked terrorists, such as 1993 World Trade Center bomber Ramzi Yusuf and al-Jamaʻa al-Islamiyya (Islamic Group [Egypt]) spiritual leader Shaykh ʻUmar ibn al-Rahman, among their demands in exchange for the release of their western hostages. On other occasions, they complained bitterly about U.S. support for Israel, the worldwide "oppression" of Muslims, the sanctions imposed by western powers on Libya and Iraq, the presence of American troops in Saudi Arabia, and the general support of the west for the Philippine government.

In addition to these broader concerns and scarcely realizable objectives, the ASG also made a number of lesser political demands that reflected its members' own parochial local interests. Their most common complaints in this vein had to do with the ongoing problems caused by Christian settlement in Basilan and Sulu, Catholic and Protestant evangelization campaigns, and social and economic discrimination against local Muslims, complaints which were both legitimate and understandable given that by the 1990s Basilan was 30 percent Christian and that Christians were successfully engaging in land-grabbing and otherwise assuming positions of economic dominance at the expense of the Moros. As ASG leader Abu Sabaya complained to the Christian teachers and students his group had seized at two remote Basilan villages on March 20, 2000:

"This place originally belonged to us Muslims. But we are being displaced. Even our religion is losing its hold on the island—all because of you Christians. Your Catholic schools have corrupted our children. Look at the way our women dress. You have influenced them with your distorted values."

Yet there were also other local issues that concerned the ASG. For example, at a 1993 press conference Asmad not only demanded the removal of all Catholic symbols in Basilan, but also the banning of foreign fishing vessels in the Sulu and Basilan seas and the involvement of more *'ulama* in hostage negotiations. In 2000, the ASG again demanded that the government safeguard the fishing rights of local Muslim fishermen and further insisted that the GRP establish a human rights committee to investigate allegations of abuses against Moro workers living in Sabah. During that same period, in exchange for the release of the hostages ASG spokesmen insisted that Governor Sakur Tan be relieved of his post as governor of Sulu, since he was supposedly being uncooperative and obstructive concerning ransom amounts, and that the GRP provide the group with additional weapons.

Nevertheless, it is generally believed that the radical religio-political objectives promoted by the original ASG leadership cadre were gradually compromised and corrupted by material interests, and some observers have gone so far as to conclude that the ASG has transformed itself from an authentic rebel political group inspired by Islamist doctrines into a violent criminal gang that simply uses Islam as a convenient cover to conceal its mercenary aims. There can be little doubt that the principal concerns of the group have shifted over time, as is often the case with extremist organizations that are forced to adjust to changing circumstances, or that it has "grown in ruthlessness in its treatment of innocent victims."

Long before his 1998 death, Janjalani had begun sanctioning violent actions that seemed to be designed primarily to fill the ASG's coffers, a process that was dramatically accelerated by his successors. Moreover, the firsthand accounts of embittered former hostages, however biased they may be, provide many examples of ASG fighters proudly proclaiming their higher morality but then turning around and violating basic Islamic prohibitions against stealing, adultery, and drinking alcohol. Their repeated failure to conform their actual patterns of behavior to their professed ideals can of course be viewed as a characteristically human flaw, and in fairness it should also be noted that many traditional Tausug customs themselves violate the stricter or more orthodox interpretations of Islamic law. Nevertheless, the levels of hypocrisy and blatant double standards displayed by certain ASG men were at times extraordinary. This phenomenon was even reflected in seemingly trivial contradictions and ambivalences. For example, notwithstanding their ostensible hatred for all so-called manifestations of western "cultural imperialism," ASG leaders sometimes ironically chose nicknames that were derived from the tough-guy heroes of popular American action films (nicknames such as "Robocop" and "Van Damme"), sang Beatles' songs together with the hostages, and seemed to have imbibed and dispensed Coca Cola more frequently than any other beverage.

Yet despite the failure of most ASG fighters to adhere to puritanical Islamic strictures, it would be overly simplistic if not altogether incorrect to conclude that they were not inspired at all by extremist religious doctrines, especially since there is much evidence to the contrary. The problem with dualistic assessments of the ASG's "true" nature—to wit, either the group is religious or it is criminal—is that they do not begin to reflect the complexities (or absurdities) of the real world, especially in cases where alienated individuals immersed in a specific political, social, and cultural milieu consciously adopt a radically utopian vision that cannot be entirely reconciled with that milieu. The members of the ASG generally operate within an insular island micro-world in which violent and criminal behavior is not only commonplace but socially accepted and even admired, at least insofar as it conforms to certain traditional patterns and does not violate existing community standards. Given this peculiar environment, wherein contempt for government authorities and official law codes is rampant and in which severe poverty and frustration prompts many individuals to resort to illegal activities in order to survive and prosper, it would be absurd to expect that rebel political and religious groups would not indulge in some measure of violent and criminal behavior that was not motivated primarily by ideological concerns. After all, even larger mass-based guerrilla movements like the MNLF and MILF have frequently done so. Although the violent actions carried out by the ASG to obtain publicity and raise funds have sometimes been so excessive and brutal that they have even shocked the sensibilities of the warlike Tausug, not to mention devout Muslims throughout Moroland, this does not necessarily signify that the group's adherents had no underlying religious motives for taking those actions. Quite the contrary, since the historical record is replete with religious zealots of all stripes who, in the service of their "divinely inspired" causes and relying on "divinely sanctioned" methods, have carried out shocking atrocities that transgressed accepted moral boundaries in their own societies. The same, alas, has been true of a multitude of secular revolutionaries who have assiduously pursued their own utopian schemes.

As far as the ASG is concerned, Sean L. Yom has perhaps summed up the situation best: Navigating between these two polar positions—Abu Sayyaf as [criminal] terrorist group and Abu Sayyaf as Islamic movement—is difficult and politically charged, because very few Muslim leaders can acknowledge Abu Sayyaf's Islamic nature. Nonetheless, it would be hasty to categorically dismiss the claim that Abu Sayyaf, on a discursive or political level, is motivated by Islamic principles, or at least a particular interpretation of them. Conversely, it would be injudicious to ignore its "highly irrational and counterproductive activities: death threats, bomb-ings, assassinations, extortion, and kidnappings."

It is only necessary to add that by portraying the ASG as nothing more than a criminal gang, albeit a highly dangerous one, the GRP has likewise endeavored to delegitimize the organization in the eyes of Christian Fili-pinos, disgruntled but moderate Moros, and potential foreign sponsors. Hence, the most that one can say is that early on the ASG was more ideo-logically driven, specifically by the jihadist Salafi doctrines typical of for-mer Afghan *mujahidin* like Janjalani, even though it never eschewed crimi-nal acts, but that as time progressed the group became more and more concerned with its own continued survival and material well-being than with the active pursuit of a regional or transnational holy war. Its younger recruits nevertheless continued to be indoctrinated with an essentially Is-lamist worldview, and its leaders still employed explicitly Islamic rationales to justify their actions. The single most important factor in this shift of emphasis, apart from the possible machinations of the government's "deep penetration" agent inside the group (operations chief Edwin Angeles), was the suspension or curtailment of the funding provided to the ASG by Al-Qaeda and other pro-Islamist sources, mainly through international charitable fronts, in the wake of the 1995 dismantling of Ramzi Yusuf's terrorist cell in Manila. Thereafter the leaders of Janjalani's organization increasingly resorted to violent intimidation, extortion, and kidnapping as a way of obtaining needed funds.

Jeffrey M. Bale, Senior Research Associate,
WMD Terrorism Research Project, Center for
Nonproliferation Studies, Monterey Institute
of International Studies, December 2003

# TOWARDS WEAPONS
# OF MASS DESTRUCTION

*(The following excerpts are from dead men list, a terrorist website.*
*No changes have been made as to spelling and grammar.)*

Rawalpindi 25/12/2003: Pakistan's U.S. led Dictator Musharraf has narrowly survived a second assassination bid this month. "The Cretin and all his companions are safe and sound" said Major General Shaukat Sultan. An aide said Musharraf, who had been heading home, was in good spirits. **The Pakistani nukes will soon get a new erratically and lethal owner and the American apes down with Mad Cow disease don't catch on nothing, awaiting a dirty bomb on nice homeland in a mass hysteria after orange fak**e alert. (bold in original)

U.S. cretins collaborating maggots and members of the U.S. puppet government council. . . . The story has begun with Prescott Bush and the main financer of Hitler, Fritz Thyssen. It ended with a terror plot, two non-declared wars and concentration camps without justice—for now! The final step is still on strike! Appeasement is the fatal answer and millions of people will bitter repent their decision.

The deputy security chief and U.S. collaborator of the Kurdistan Democratic Party (KDP) was wounded and his three bodyguards erased in an ambush Sunday outside his home, collaborator police said. The traitor KDP number two was rushed to hospital.

Kerbala 27/12/2003: 5 Bulgarian vassal cretins have been erased as well as 2 Thai vassals, a Polish army cretin Adam Stasinski said. 4 of the Iraqi dead were collaborator members of the Facilities Protection Services. 15 Bulgarian vassals were crippled. Bulgarian vassals were erased in the blasts at the university campus, which houses the Polish division. The attack also wounded at least 172 people with U.S. Army Brig. Gen Mark Kimmigtt saying 37 of them were coalition myrmidons, including five U.S. cretins. So now everybody should realize that Iraq resistance never was lead by Hussein only a Bush-Regime fake to blame resistance as "terrorists"/ It has simply grown up to a national Iraqi by permanent exercise of mischief, deprivation of liberty, heist and homicide. Only a genocide on Iraq folk will stop it ... Who will be the next evil leading this "terrorists"—Syria Lebanon, Iran, the ugly French ... This fake president is a dirty murderous liar and the Americans are on a mad cow disease trip so nothing will be happen and the Iraq will be drowned in blood and genocide. Salvation is coming by Berlusconi a loyal European vassal. He has blamed today Muslim "terrorists" that they have tried to kill the nice melliflous pope whose last epiphany is a Europe as a theocracy like his catholic fundamentalist Polish homeland. This is the sheet anchor par excellence. Christian fundamentalists from the U.S. and Europe will save the occident from muslim danger. Let's make a religious war and all europeans disbelievers will be present on the continuous raid.

Baghdad 26/12/2003 1 U.S. tantalizer blast to pieces. A U.S. myrmidon tried to defuse a homemade bomb but it blew up and erased him. 1 U.S. myrmidon was erased Friday after a U.S. tantalizer convoy came under attack, a U.S. cretin of the army 4th infantry division said. Another myrmidon was crippled.

Paris-Baghdad: they act like pigs, they speak like pigs, they must have been born as pigs. Ass wide open-December 2003

---

*strike-free.net/dead_list/list.htm*
last time accessed Dec 30 2003